ŚRĪ MANAḤ-ŚIKṢĀ

Splendid Instructions to the Mind

by Raghunātha Dāsa Gosvāmī

Volume Two

With the commentaries
Bhajana-darpaṇa and *Manaḥ-śikṣā Bhāṣā*
by Śrīla Bhaktivinoda Ṭhākura

Translated by Hari Pārṣada Dāsa,
Kṛṣṇa-abhiṣeka Dāsa, and Prāṇa Govinda Dāsa

Including commentaries
of contemporary Vaiṣṇavas

Illumination Education
Padma Inc.

Volume Two
Version 1.2 (February 2017)

Published by Padma Inc., 2016
Hillsborough, NC, USA.

Printed by CreateSpace, an Amazon.com company.
Available from Amazon.com and other retail outlets.

Designed by Michael Best.
Set in Adobe Arno Pro.

DEDICATION

This edition of *Manaḥ-śikṣā* is dedicated to the pleasure of the residents of Vṛndāvana (*goṣṭhālayiṣu sujane*), as well as to those persons who aspire for their company.

CONTENTS

Part Three – Commentaries by contemporary Vaiṣṇavas

Part Four – Appendices

NOTES FOR THIS EDITION

The reader may wonder why a new edition of Raghunātha Dāsa's Gosvāmī's *Manaḥ-śikṣā* is needed. Over the years, many devotees of Kṛṣṇa expressed a longing for a trustworthy, literal translation of both the verses of *Manaḥ-śikṣā* and Bhaktivinoda Ṭhākura's commentary. We have tried our best to produce such a translation. Additionally, this edition contains Bhaktivinoda's song meditations on the original verses – the first time these songs are being published. This edition is also the first to be illustrated, a response to Raghunātha Dāsa Gosvāmī's use of metaphors and similes – tigress, ropes of wicked deeds, jewel of love, and so forth – that practically beg for paintings. Bhaktivinoda's commentary is also filled with descriptions which inspire illustrations.

The color illustrations are designed for deep meditation on each verse. In many cases, the details of those paintings are based on related descriptions from various *śāstras* and works of the *ācāryas*. The black-and-white drawings are based on the twelve verses as well as Bhaktivinoda's commentary, both prose and song.

We have produced this work as two printed volumes – one in color for meditation and the other in black-and-white for more in-depth study. The second volume adds significantly to our understanding of the original text by including the commentary of contemporary Vaiṣṇavas. We hope and trust that our expansion of the ocean of nectar in this way is pleasing to the predecessor *ācāryas*. *Manaḥ-śikṣā* was written as a guide for serious practitioners of *bhakti-yoga*, and it is helpful for such practitioners to have commentary which relates the eternal principles in this centuries-old work to current applications.

When reading the commentaries by Jayādvaita Swami, Śivarāma Swami, Śacīnandana Swami, and Bhaktivijnana Goswami, the reader should keep in mind that they were originally spoken seminars. Additionally, Bhaktivijnana Goswami's seminars were translated from Russian.

Readers familiar with BBT publications will likely notice that this edition uses lowercase for pronouns connected with the divine, as well as lowercase for descriptions of the divine that are not proper nouns (such as "divine couple"). Our reason is that Śrīla Prabhupāda wanted books to be in line with current scholarly standards. Such was his rationale for insisting on the use of diacritics rather than phonetic spellings for Sanskrit. Scholarly standards change with time and circumstance, and it is desirable, therefore, that our publications reflect current usage in order to follow Prabhupāda's desire.

Discerning readers will also note that the word-for-word translations of Raghunātha Dāsa Gosvāmī's verses follows the order of words in the translations rather than in the Sanskrit. We have adopted this method as both Bhaktivinoda Ṭhākura and his son, Bhaktisiddhānta Sarasvatī, favored it in their own publications. Because to a large extent this book is Bhaktivinoda's book, we felt it appropriate to follow his preference.

In Bhaktivinoda's commentary, there were six instances where we were able to use Śrīla Prabhupāda's translations for verses the Ṭhākura quoted. Those are noted in the text as being from the *Bhagavad-gītā*, *Śrīmad-Bhāgavatam*, or *Caitanya-caritāmṛta*.

Prints of the twelve color pictures and some of the black-and-white drawings are available at www.radharani.com.

The publishers

PART ONE

Summaries and background

INTRODUCTION TO *MANAḤ-ŚIKṢĀ*

by Śacīnandana Swami

I read *Manaḥ-śikṣā* many years ago with various learned commentaries, but it struck me only recently how essential this book is. At that time, I had removed myself a little bit from my normal busy preaching pace, doing extensive studies into our philosophy and into the question of how to present Kṛṣṇa consciousness to a post-modern audience. I asked myself, "Do we have in our tradition a guidebook to *bhakti* in its different stages, a book which will bring a person from the beginning to perfection?"

As I was asking and looking around, essentially to find a book which would save me the tremendous work of writing something myself, I again and again came upon *Manaḥ-śikṣā*. Then Ravīndra-svarūpa Prabhu told me that *Manaḥ-śikṣā* is the guidebook which takes us to full Kṛṣṇa consciousness.

But I was still a little doubtful whether or not this is really *the* book, *the* guidebook to Kṛṣṇa consciousness, until I received a letter by our Śrīmatī Devī Dāsī. Śrīmatī presented to me a statement from Bhaktivinoda Ṭhākura in *Jaiva-dharma* where he says that *Manaḥ-śikṣā* is the *paddhati* for Gauḍīya Vaiṣṇavism. When we call something a *paddhati*, it means a step-by-step guide to progress; *pada* (foot), and *hati* (progress). So Bhaktivinoda Ṭhākura says in his commentary to *Manaḥ-śikṣā*, called *bhajana-darpaṇa*, or the mirror of *bhajana**, that when a living entity has understood that it is his prime duty in life to develop his Kṛṣṇa consciousness, when he has awakened his faith in this understanding, then he will ask how to do it. *Manaḥ-śikṣā* will answer this question. If we, the readers and I, have this question, and have awakened some faith that we should develop our Kṛṣṇa consciousness, then we are qualified to hear the secrets of this guidebook.

When I was a young boy there was a rumor amongst my friends

* In this case, *bhajana* indicates systematic worship, and the mirror indicates that his commentary reflects or indicates his mood in such worship.

that you could learn to make gold by an alchemical process. I remember the moment I heard about it. I said to my friends, "Teach me all about it. How can I make gold?" Then we went into the cellar. My friend Lawrence brought all sorts of things with him, and we little boys were there in the cellar trying to make gold, but it didn't work. What we were doing only exploded in our face, and we couldn't go to school for two weeks. In general, I remember that from childhood on I was extremely curious to get any guidebook for getting something valuable. When I stumbled upon this *Manaḥ-śikṣā*, I thought, "See, Śacīnandana Swami, you have now found what you were looking for as a child. You have really found something to get the highest value." I practice according to these guidelines.

Once, I was finishing a month's time in a kind of private alchemical laboratory where I tried to do something with this *Manaḥ-śikṣā*, and I found miracles developing just by instructing my mind with these verses. Raghunātha Dāsa Gosvāmī promises after the eleven verses, "Becoming a follower of Śrī Rūpa and his companions, one who with a sweet voice loudly recites these eleven supreme verses, which give instructions to the mind, and strives to understand all of their meanings completely, obtains the incomparable jewel of worshiping Śrī Śrī Rādhā-Kṛṣṇa in the forests of Gokula."

Now, at the very outset, I will be extremely blunt. As we follow Raghunātha Dāsa Gosvāmī, you will see some open wounds in your heart and mind, into which the words of Raghunātha Dāsa Gosvāmī will go. It will not be easy. You will have to be very honest, because he presents a deep psychological analysis of the obstacles we face on our path, and it will be embarrassing. However, I can encourage you, because at the end of going through *Manaḥ-śikṣā*, you will have love of Godhead in your heart.

Manaḥ-śiksā means "instructions to the mind." He is using a technique of Vaiṣṇava writers to address all of their readers by addressing their own minds. In the *Nectar of Instruction* Śrīla Prabhupāda describes Kṛṣṇa consciousness as a culture of the mind. This means we should gradually train our minds so that throughout the twenty-four hours of the day we can't think of anything other than Kṛṣṇa. Now, we know it is very difficult to train the stubborn mind to always think of Kṛṣṇa twenty-four hours a day. Arjuna, the celebrated hero of the *Bhagavad-gītā*, has expressed himself very candidly on this point. He says, "The mind is so restless, so turbulent, so obstinate, so strong, O Kṛṣṇa, that I think it is more difficult to control it than to control the wind. Don't ask for too much, Kṛṣṇa, when you tell me I should control my mind. How will I control a raging storm?" But Kṛṣṇa is a good teacher. He answers the arguments of his disciple, and he defeats them step by step. In the end, he encourages Arjuna to start a *sādhana*, a practice of mind control, when he says, "It is undoubtedly very difficult to curb the restless mind, but it is possible with suitable practice and by detachment." So *Manaḥ-śikṣā* does exactly these two things which Kṛṣṇa talks about in the *Gītā*. It tells us a suitable practice we can do every day, and it also helps us to detach ourselves from material things.

To get the greatest benefit from this book, we need to keep in mind that there are two very powerful forces in this world. The first is *kāma* (lust). *Kāma* means not just the desire of man and woman to meet each other for sensual stimulation, but it means all desires separate from giving pleasure to Kṛṣṇa. The other force is *prema* (love), which is not self-centered or pleasure-seeking but is the desire to *give* pleasure or love to Kṛṣṇa.

I think all *sādhakas* (spiritual aspirants) have to deal with *kāma*. The *Ṛg* Veda says, "*Kāma* is the basis of this world." And this desire for enjoyment, as Kṛṣṇa tells us, becomes many-branched (*bahu-śākhā hy anantāś ca*). *Kāma* is concentrated on many sense objects for selfish enjoyment. *Prema* is concentrating only on Kṛṣṇa. To some extent, these two forces sometimes struggle. There's a voice in our heart which tells us, "Follow the scriptures, chant Hare Kṛṣṇa, concentrate on Kṛṣṇa," and so on, and there's the other voice that says, "Yeah, yeah, yeah, yeah, yeah, how theoretical, how impractical."

It's very interesting that these two drives, *kāma* and *prema*, have something in common. Let's look at their verbal roots. *Kam* and *prem* both mean *to desire*. So when we want to develop love for Kṛṣṇa, we have to learn to do the practices which the *Manaḥ-śikṣā* will tell us about, practices which will help us look up in the direction of the spiritual reality. If we want to develop *kāma,* the desire to enjoy, we will look down to the body and the mind. *Manaḥ-śikṣā,* or the training of the mind, will teach us to look to spiritual things. This will activate *bhakti* first and the *hlādinī-śakti* next. Then we enter into the realm of the pre-stage of *prema* – *bhāva* – and finally *prema* itself.

I can direct my attention down to selfish enjoyment, *kāma.* I can desire sense objects, such as women, gold, ice cream, and pizza, and then I will see how my consciousness degrades. I can also choose to follow *Manaḥ-śikṣā* and look upwards, learning where to focus my mind. This is how the first verse starts. We will read about guru, the land of Vraja, the *brāhmaṇas,* and the devotees. As I look upwards, I will feel in contact with these spiritual objects and persons. I will feel some *bhakti* and be pulled upwards in a very nice way. These are the secrets of *bhakti.*

Under which energy do we want to work in our lives? We can look down toward our ordinary material consciousness, the materialistic mind which talks like a monkey, and we will see a degrading influence. Or we can train our mind to truly think of those agents and elements which will fill the heart with *bhakti-śakti* and *karuṇā-śakti.* We will be pulled upwards, not degraded, and it will be very good for us.

Śrīla Prabhupāda writes in the *Nectar of Instruction* in this connection, "In the *Bhagavad-gītā* it is stated, *saṅgāt sañjāyate kāmaḥ.* One's desires and ambitions develop according to the company one keeps. It is often said that a man is known by his company, and if an ordinary man associates with devotees, he will certainly develop his dormant Kṛṣṇa consciousness."

I want to take this statement a little bit further. If you allow your mind to associate with the beautiful instructions of Raghunātha Dāsa Gosvāmī your whole existence will be transformed. It really works. Association accompanied by mental practice is so important. If you don't have this mental practice and you always associate with material sense objects and material thoughts, then your Kṛṣṇa consciousness is only a hallucination.

MANAḤ-ŚIKṢĀ AT A GLANCE

Verses 1-3: Qualification for the inner path of spontaneous attraction to Kṛṣṇa in Vṛndāvana

Verses 4-7: The process of eliminating obstacles, going subtler and closer to the root with each step by the mercy of, and love for, Kṛṣṇa and his devotees

Verses 8-11: Engaging in our eternal spiritual position through taking shelter, meditating, and serving Kṛṣṇa's internal, pleasure potency

Verse 12: Glories of these verses

MANAḤ-ŚIKṢĀ AT A GLANCE, EXPANDED

Verses 1-3: Qualification for the inner path of spontaneous attraction to Kṛṣṇa in Vṛndāvana

- Basic humility and lack of pride: a mentality conducive to face and eliminate one's inner contaminations, to serve others, and to beg for mercy
- Loving affection for everyone and anything connected with Kṛṣṇa in Vṛndāvana
- Detachment from materialistic activities on the path of karma
- Desire for loving service
- Engagement in chanting the Hare Kṛṣṇa mantra, Gāyatrī mantras, and worshiping Vraja Kṛṣṇa as taught by guru(s) in the path of Lord Caitanya through Svarūpa Dāmodara Gosvāmī and Rūpa Gosvāmī

Verses 4-7: The process of eliminating obstacles, going subtler and closer to the root with each step by the mercy of, and love for, Kṛṣṇa and his devotees

- Verse 4 – Problems: Absorption in mundane topics, desires for liberation, and desires for the opulences of Nārāyaṇa; Solution: Serve Rādhā and Kṛṣṇa in Vṛndāvana to receive a jewel of love of God.

- Verse 5 – Problem: Wicked deeds fueled by lust, anger, greed, and so forth; Solution: Cry for help from the devotees of the killer of Baka (Deceit).
- Verse 6 – Problem: Deceit and pretense; Solution: Immersion in a bath of love for Rādhā and Kṛṣṇa (the artistic singer and the lifter of Govardhana Hill).
- Verse 7 – Problem: Desires for fame and honor; Solution: Service to a very exalted devotee of Kṛṣṇa.

Verses 8-11: Engaging in our eternal spiritual position through taking shelter, meditating, and serving Kṛṣṇa's internal, pleasure potency

- Kṛṣṇa, the lifter of Govardhana eliminates our wickedness, gives us glowing love of God to drink, and engages us in worshiping his *hlādinī-śakti*, Rādhā, the artistic singer.
- We drink and taste varieties of flavors of love of God by hearing about, mediating on, worshiping, and serving in various ways – Kṛṣṇa, Rādhā, Lalitā, Viśākhā, Rādhā-kuṇḍa, and Govardhana.

Verse 12: Glories of these verses

- Singing or trying to understand these verses gives one the jewel of service to Rādhā and Kṛṣṇa in Vṛndāvana as a follower of Śrī Rūpa Gosvāmī.

METER OF *MANAḤ-ŚIKṢĀ* FOR SINGING AND CHANTING

The meter for the verses of *Manaḥ-śikṣā* is *śikhariṇī,* the same meter that is used in the *Jagannāthāṣṭakam*. Each verse is divided into four *pādas,* which each consist of 17 syllables. The *pādas* are further divided into two parts of six and eleven syllables. The metrical scheme is as follows (⏑: a light syllable, –: a heavy syllable):

⏑ – – – – – | ⏑ ⏑ ⏑ ⏑ ⏑ – – ⏑ ⏑ ⏑ – |

OVERVIEW OF *ŚRĪ MANAḤ-ŚIKṢĀ*

by Śivarāma Swami

The first verse of *Śrī Manaḥ-śikṣā* explains what conditioned living entities should do when faith in Kṛṣṇa manifests within them. In *Manaḥ-śikṣā*, Kṛṣṇa means Śyāmasundara Kṛṣṇa. It doesn't mean Kṛṣṇa in Dvārakā, Kṛṣṇa in Mathurā, or any incarnation of Kṛṣṇa. It simply means Kṛṣṇa, the son of Nanda Mahārāja.

So by good fortune, *bhāgyavān jīva guru-kṛṣṇa-prasāde pāya bhakti-latā-bīja*, by the mercy of both Kṛṣṇa and the spiritual master, one receives the seed of the creeper of devotional service. This is *śraddhā*, a very difficult commodity to achieve. When someone acquires faith in *kṛṣṇa-kathā* (hearing the topics about Kṛṣṇa) then one should accept *dīkṣā*, initiation from a spiritual master, taking the mantra from guru. One then worships Rādhā and Kṛṣṇa, Vaiṣṇavas, and gurus – *dīkṣā-guru* and *śikṣā-gurus*. This first verse moves us from *adhau śraddhā* (the preliminary stage), to *sādhu-saṅga* (the association of Vaiṣṇavas and the spiritual master). Then, the process of *dīkṣā* takes the practitioner to *bhajana kriyā*.

Some questions may arise just by reading the first verse. We are advised to worship Rādhā-Kṛṣṇa, the Vaiṣṇavas, and gurus. So, first, if we're supposed to just take *dīkṣā* and chant Hare Kṛṣṇa all day long, then how are we meant to maintain our body as well as perform our religious duties? How are we supposed to work and live in this world while being totally dedicated to spiritual life? This is a familiar question for spiritual practioners. It's also Arjuna's question when he hears about work and renunciation. He considers it a contradiction, that renunciation means to go to the forest, which is irreconcilable with working.

The first verse says just to worship Rādhā-Kṛṣṇa, Vaiṣṇavas, and gurus; Lord Caitanya is not mentioned. So, second, one may ask what the relationship is between Lord Caitanya Mahāprabhu's worship and the worship of Rādhā and Kṛṣṇa.

And the third question concerns the statement that one should also worship Vaiṣṇavas and the gurus. We may ask about the mood of worshiping gurus or the spiritual master. We need to know how, when, and at what point we worship our gurus.

In verse two, we find the answers to these three questions. To the first question, the answer is that there are two levels at which someone chants Hare Kṛṣṇa after receiving *dīkṣā*. One is as a practitioner (a *sādhaka*). The second is when someone has become a *siddha*. As long as one is a *sādhaka* still struggling to purify *anarthas* and come to the perfectional stage, one should perform one's religious duties, such as householder duties. But one should do them in a mood of detachment and as a service to Lord Kṛṣṇa.

When, through the process of offenceless chanting, one purifies one's *anarthas* and comes to the perfected platform, then he or she is considered to be *siddha*. At that point one can give up one's obligations, *sarva-dharmān parityajya*, and one can renounce and go to Vṛndāvana.

Verse two also answers the second and third questions that arise from verse one. Guru and Gaurāṅga should also be worshiped. Bhaktivinoda Ṭhākura says in his commentary that worship must be done in that order—first guru and then Gaurāṅga, before one worships Rādhā and Kṛṣṇa. In other words, worshiping Rādhā and Kṛṣṇa means one first must worship one's spiritual master and Caitanya Mahāprabhu *ajasram* (unceasingly). Raghunātha Dāsa Gosvāmī uses *ajasraṁ* to indicate that we will always worship. There is never any time when we are not worshiping, and in that particular order.

Verse three answers an often-asked question: can a person achieve the perfection of achieving *vṛndāvana-dhāma*, where Kṛṣṇa is engaging in loving pastimes, technically known as *rāgātmikā-bhakti*, outside of the Gauḍīya *sampradāya*? In the third mantra, Raghunātha Dāsa Gosvāmī says, in effect, that it is possible, but it is difficult and very rare. Of course anything is possible, but in the Gauḍīya *sampradāya*, if one follows in the footsteps of Caitanya Mahāprabhu then this goal becomes very easy.

Verses four through seven deal with obstacles in this practice of devotional service, *rāga-bhajana*. These four verses are an extension of a phrase which Raghunātha Dāsa Gosvāmī gives in the first verse, *dambhaṁ hitvā*. *Dambha* means pride. He says in verse one, "You should throw out pride." And then he goes on to answer, in verses two and three, questions as discussed above. Now in verse four he begins the explanation of this point about getting rid of pride.

In verse four, he discusses external obstacles. First is mundane talk, or what we call *prajalpa*. The second is the desire for impersonal liberation as an impediment to *rāga-bhajana*. And the third, one may be surprised, is not particularly considered to be an *anartha* but is rather an obstacle to going back to *vṛndāvana-dhāma*; and that is becoming attached to Lord Nārāyaṇa and Lakṣmī, or other incarnations or forms of Kṛṣṇa. *Lakṣmī-pati-ratim ito vyoma-nayanīṁ*. *Lakṣmī-pati-rati* — to become attached to Lakṣmī-pati, or the husband of Lakṣmī.

The fourth verse also shows how these things can be removed. Raghunātha Dāsa Gosvāmī instructs that one should worship Rādhā and Kṛṣṇa in Vṛndāvana. Thus it is a codified answer. Without Bhaktivinoda Ṭhākura's commentary it would be impossible to actually understand these brief instructions.

In the fifth verse, Raghunātha Dāsa Gosvāmī indicates that there are six internal obstacles starting with lust. Bhaktivinoda lists them as lust, anger, greed, delusion, pride, and envy. Raghunātha Dāsa Gosvāmī says that in order to be free of them, a person has to know how to cry out for the help of the devotees. We can't get their help unless we know how to actually ask for it. A little child who slams a finger in a door immediately starts to call out for mother. Children don't have any qualms about crying if there's a problem. So similarly we also have to cry. And what obstructs us from that crying is often our pride: pride that we are something other than what we actually are.

In the sixth and seventh verses, Raghunātha Dāsa Gosvāmī considers the results of being free from lust, anger, greed, etc., which are in one sense the gross manifestations of internal obstacles. But still this is not freedom from deceit and false prestige (*pratiṣṭhā*). Deceit means duplicity. To be free of internal obstacles, aside from calling out for help from Vaiṣṇavas, we must worship the pure devotees of the Lord.

Verse eight answers the question, "What if there are no pure devotees available?" Raghunātha Dāsa Gosvāmī answers that one should pray to Kṛṣṇa with great humility and become Rādhārāṇī's servant. In other words, one should simply pray and Kṛṣṇa will do what is needed.

Verse eight of *Manaḥ-śikṣā* is the turning point. If a spiritual practitioner has come this far, then by applying this particular instruction, one will become absorbed and realize that the end, or the goal, is sufficient to satisfy us and free us from all obstacles.

Happily one comes to the ninth verse where Raghunātha Dāsa Gosvāmī no longer speaks about *anarthas,* or absorbing ourselves in our own deficiencies. In verse eight he gave the general instruction to pray to Kṛṣṇa with humility. In verse nine we learn specifically what to pray for. We pray to Kṛṣṇa for his mercy and to Śrīmatī Rādhārāṇī for her service. We pray to Lalitā to be accepted as Rādhārāṇī's servant, and to Viśākhā to develop spontaneous devotional service. We worship Rādhā-kuṇḍa to be able to get *darśana* of Rādhā and Kṛṣṇa and we worship Girirāja, Govardhana Hill, as a place of residence.

In verse ten there is a hint of the glories and aspects of service to Śrīmatī Rādhārāṇī, as well as the requirements to understand her service. These are humility, spiritual greed, and determination.

The eleventh verse is the last instruction. Here we learn the specific details of this service to Rādhārāṇī to which we aspire. The twelfth verse is what is called a *phala-stuti,* an explanation of the fruit, or the benefit, of hearing and regularly reading this *Manaḥ-śikṣā.*

One should practice *Manaḥ-śikṣā* and memorize the verses, not just hear them. This book is certainly something we need: instructions to the mind. We are always getting instructions *from* our mind, so this is an opportunity to give some instructions *to* our mind.

THE IMPORTANCE OF *MANAḤ-ŚIKṢĀ*

Bhaktisiddhānta Sarasvatī Ṭhākura and *rāgānuga-bhakti*

by Ūrmilā Devī Dāsī

Without any doubt, one of the key purposes for the appearance of Śrī Caitanya Mahāprabhu was to teach the path of spontaneous love, *rāgānuga-bhakti*. As Mahāprabhu said (*Caitanya-caritāmṛta, Ādi* 4.33):

vrajera nirmala rāga śuni' bhakta-gaṇa
rāga-mārge bhaje yena chāḍi' dharma-karma

> Then, by hearing about the pure love of the residents of Vraja, devotees will worship me on the path of spontaneous love, abandoning all rituals of religiosity and fruitive activity.
>
> *Purport by Śrīla Prabhupāda:* Many realized souls, such as Raghunātha Dāsa Gosvāmī and King Kulaśekhara, have recommended with great emphasis that one develop this spontaneous love of Godhead, even at the risk of transgressing all the traditional codes of morality and religiosity. Śrī Raghunātha Dāsa Gosvāmī, one of the Six Gosvāmīs of Vṛndāvana, has written in his prayers called the *Manaḥ-śikṣā* that one should simply worship Rādhā and Kṛṣṇa with all attention. *Na dharmaṁ nādharmaṁ śruti-gaṇa-niruktaṁ kila kuru,* "One should not be much interested in performing Vedic rituals or simply following rules and regulations."

Certainly Bhaktisiddhānta Sarasvatī, his disciples, grand-disciples, and followers are dedicated to this mission of Śrī Caitanya Mahāprabhu. Yet, historically until the present day there has been a controversy regarding whether or not Bhaktisiddhānta made the *rāga-mārga* a core part of his teaching and practice. A study of *Manaḥ-śikṣā* is pivotal to resolve this doubt. To understand the importance of *Manaḥ-śikṣā* in this regard, we turn to Bhaktivinoda Ṭhākura's *Jaiva-dharma*. Here is the relevant section from chapter 39:

> Gosvāmī: The *Śrī Manaḥ-śikṣā* has laid down a systematic procedure for one to enter into and become absorbed in the pastimes

of Śrī Śrī Rādhā-Kṛṣṇa; one should follow it without guile. One should practice one's *bhajana* according to the *bhāva* of ecstatic love expressed in the *Śrī Svaniyama-daśaka-stotram*. These five books have all been composed by Śrīla Raghunātha Dāsa Gosvāmī. Śrīla Rūpa Gosvāmī has exhaustively elaborated upon the details of *rasa-tattva*. Śrī Caitanya Mahāprabhu personally gave him this service and specially blessed him to fulfil the responsibility. However, the methods by which an aspiring soul may develop such *rasa* in the intimate service of Rādhā Kṛṣṇa have been compiled by Śrīla Raghunātha Dāsa Gosvāmī from the famous diaries of Śrīla Svarūpa Dāmodara Gosvāmī. All followers received their particular missions on the order of Śrī Caitanya and were empowered by the Lord for the successful fulfilment of their particular order.

Vijaya: Gurudeva, I am very curious to know what further responsibilities were given to whom by the Lord.

Gosvāmī: Śrī Caitanya instructed Śrīla Svarūpa Dāmodara to disseminate *rasa-upāsanā*, the process of *bhajana* inculcated with *rasa*. Accordingly, he composed his diaries on *rasa-upāsanā* comprising two sections: *antaḥ-panthā*, the esoteric, internal means of attainment; and *bahiḥ-panthā*, the exoteric, external means of attainment. The esoteric process was entrusted to Śrīla Raghunātha Dāsa Gosvāmī, as amply exhibited in his books, and the exoteric *rasa-upāsanā* was allocated to Śrīla Vakreśvara Paṇḍita, which is the treasure of our spiritual lineage. This exoteric *rasa-upāsanā* was passed on to me by Śrīla Vakreśvara Paṇḍita and from me to Śrī Dhyānacandra who has compiled it in a book of which you are now the fortunate recipient.

Bhaktivinoda Ṭhākura accepted as bona fide both the exoteric and esoteric paths. He refers to each in his books and seems to combine the two to some extent. Such a combination can be observed when reading his commentary to *Manaḥ-śikṣā*, in the many prayers and verses he quoted for meditation, especially in the later verses. Such meditative prayers remind us of one of the main practices Dhyānacandra favors on his path. The fact that Bhaktivinoda brought such prayers into his *Manaḥ-śikṣā* commentary should refute the sometimes-heard claim that the esoteric and exoteric paths are mutually exclusive. Rather, we find in Bhaktisiddhānta Sarasvatī's writing and lectures, as well as his personal practices and the general practices among his disciples, the manifestation of both Raghunātha Dāsa Gosvāmī's verses and Bhaktivinoda's commentary.

Apparently, the controversy about whether or not Bhaktisiddhānta taught the *rāga-mārga* arose because he and his disciples, among them A.C. Bhaktivedanta Swami Prabhupāda, mostly taught Raghunātha Dāsa Gosvāmī's inner path as outlined here in *Manaḥ-śikṣā,* rather than the (equally bona fide) outer system of Vakreśvara Paṇḍita as described in Dhyānacandra's *Śrī Gaura-govindārcana-smaraṇa-paddhati.* Those who focus entirely on the exoteric path, without proper understanding of the esoteric path, then wrongly conclude that practical instruction in *rāgānuga-bhakti* is virtually absent from the Gauḍīya Maṭha and ISKCON.

First we will examine the overall nature of each path, along with the differences and similarities between them. Then we will consider the reasons why Śrīla Bhaktisiddhānta did not at all favor the exoteric path, although he did bring in some of its elements. Finally, we will discuss the specific ways in which the esoteric path is an integral part of the process Bhaktisiddhānta taught, and which A.C. Bhaktivedanta Swami Prabhupāda has so faithfully followed.

The nature of the external or exoteric path is a series of mantras with corresponding meditations on various personalities. There are some instructions about when to say which mantras, particularly in relation to waking in the morning, taking a bath, and doing formal external Deity worship. Indeed, the name of the manual includes the word *arcana,* meaning Deity worship. The book is lengthy, and it would take quite some time each day to follow all the procedures, which are mostly in addition to what a practitioner would be doing already in terms of the *aṅgas* of *bhakti.*

Dhyānacandra Gosvāmī prescribes meditations on Lord Caitanya, the Pañca-tattva, one's guru, oneself as a pure *sādhaka,* oneself in a *siddha-rūpa* of a young *gopī,* Śrī Kṛṣṇa, Śrīmatī Rādhārāṇī, Rādhā's eight chief friends (*sakhīs*) and eight chief maidservants (*mañjarīs*). There are also meditations on the holy places of Navadvīpa and Vṛndāvana, as well as the daily eight-fold activities of Lord Caitanya and of

Rādhā-Kṛṣṇa, each very briefly. The meditations are progressive and to be done in a particular order. The book concludes with blessing anyone who follows the process with the attainment of service to Rādhā and Kṛṣṇa in Vṛndāvana.

The inner or esoteric path of *Manaḥ-śikṣā* describes a practitioner's internal states of desire, motivation, and emotion progressing from spiritual inclination and orientation, through increasingly deep and subtle purification, to fully realized spiritual service. Raghunātha Dāsa Gosvāmī, in many cases, describes corresponding external behaviors only using metaphor. He also describes external behavior using general words such as: meditating, serving, glorifying, offering of obeisances, and worshiping. However, he does not give any details of how to do those activities. His *paddhati* is very short and does not in any way prescribe a particular daily or regular routine of activities or mantras. The book concludes by blessing anyone who sings the verses and applies them with the attainment of service to Rādhā and Kṛṣṇa in Vṛndāvana.

Both the exoteric and esoteric paths as given in *Śrī Gaura-govindārcana-smaraṇa-paddhati* and *Manaḥ-śikṣā* have similar implicit parameters of qualification for following their instruction. In both cases, the qualified practitioner would have a guru or gurus, have received the holy name and mantras from a guru, be aiming toward Rādhā and Kṛṣṇa in Vṛndāvana, and be in the line of Lord Caitanya. Meditation on Lalita, Visakha, and Śrī Rūpa are in both. The esoteric path has a strongly implied template of the practitioner being a *mañjarī-gopī* (or possibly a *sakhī-gopī*) in Rādhā's group. The exoteric path has the same template, but very explicitly so.

The main difference is that the outer, exoteric path is all about the details of what a practitioner should do, say, and think about. The inner, esoteric path has brief and general prescriptions for what to do, say, and think about, being mostly about the deep inner changes of motive, drive and desire that occur within as the path is traversed. The inner path has the additional explicit qualifications – in the beginning – of giving up pride, having *rati*, and already having spontaneous attraction (*rāga*) for Kṛṣṇa in Vṛndāvana, all of which are notably absent in *Śrī*

Gaura-govindārcana-smaraṇa-paddhati. Certainly the two paths could be combined, with the exoteric path supplying the details for outer practice, and the inner path supplying the transformations which happen while engaged in that practice. There is no doubt that the outer path is dependent on the inner path for success. However, the inner path is not so dependent on the outer path. For example, as stated previously, we find that Bhaktivinoda's commentary on *Manaḥ-śikṣā* often gives extensive prayers for meditation when discussing a verse that simply prescribes meditation. However, those prayers are generally different from what Dhyānacandra Gosvāmī writes. Nor does Bhaktivinoda ever stipulate that a practitioner must learn or recite the specific prayers he cites. Rather, he cites them as examples.

The outer path is very open to misuse and cheap imitative travesty. A person could become expert at the rituals and prayers, even expert at the meditations in a superficial way, without either initial qualification or on-going purification. This path is thus highly dependent on the personal presence and guidance of a guru who is both highly perceptive and scrupulously honest. Also, as it involves lengthy procedures, the outer path is most suitable for persons who have retired from the world. It cannot easily be followed in many different circumstances.

The inner path, by its very nature, cannot be either imitated or ritualized. Also, as the external behaviors prescribed for this path are very general, there is broad scope for application to time, place, and circumstances. Of great importance is the fact that the superficial behaviors of those on the inner path can be almost indistinguishable from persons who are practitioners of *vaidhī-bhakti.* Therefore, those who are attached to the outer path, or do not know of the inner path, may then think that those who follow the inner path are not on the *rāga-mārga* at all!

From the above analysis, it is readily apparent why Śrīla Bhaktisiddhānta Sarasvatī did not teach the outer path to his followers, but in many places and in many ways, gave instructions that parallel the inner path. Let us examine the specific ways in which the outer path was misused in Bhaktisiddhānta's time (and still is today), prompting his emphasis on the inner path. The first misuse is an exclusive, or nearly exclusive, emphasis on attainment of the mood of Rādhā's *mañjarī-gopīs*. Even the mood of Rādhā's *sakhī-gopīs* is usually excluded, often with some disdain, what to speak of the mood of parental, friendly, or servant love. Instead of a guru aiding a practitioner to unfold and nurture an individual's own spontaneously awakened mood, a pseudo guru prescribes the same generic *mañjarī-gopī* mood to everyone.

A second misuse is defining *rāgānuga-sādhana* exclusively as solitary *bhajana* with specific prayers and meditation in a specific order. Even a preacher or teacher of Kṛṣṇa consciousness would be disqualified from being a practitioner of *rāgānuga-bhakti* in this concept, what to speak of a householder with a job or business.

There are even many persons in the line of Bhaktisiddhānta who misunderstand *rāgānuga-sādhana bhakti* according to those two ways in which the external path has been misinterpreted and applied, as explained above. However, it is in this next, third, area of misunderstanding and misapplication where confusion has been compounded. The third area where the external path has been misapplied is in how a person starts the *rāga* path, and the relationship among the path itself, the guru (or gurus), and the practitioner. We recall that in both the external and internal paths, a relationship with a guru or gurus is required. Instructions from, and meditation on, *sādhus*, whether physically present on the earth or departed, is also required in both paths. However, neither in *Gaura-govindārcana smaraṇa paddhati* nor in *Manaḥ-śikṣā* do we find clear or explicit instructions about what role, specifically, one's guru might or must play in the development of an individual's *rāga-mārga*, beyond the giving of the holy name and mantras. We do find general statements, for example in the *Śrī-muktā-caritram* of Raghunātha Dāsa Gosvāmī:

> *nāma-śreṣṭhaṁ manum api śacī-putram atra svarūpaṁ*
> *śrī-rūpaṁ tasyāgrajam uru-purīṁ māthurīṁ goṣṭhavāṭīm*
> *rādhā-kuṇḍaṁ girivaram aho rādhikā-mādhavāśāṁ*
> *prāpto yasya prathita-kṛpayā śrī-guruṁ taṁ nato 'smi*

I bow down to the beautiful lotus feet of my spiritual master, by whose causeless mercy I have obtained the supreme holy name, the

> divine mantra, the service of the son of Sacī-mātā, the association of Srīla Svarūpa Dāmodara, Rūpa Gosvāmī, and his older brother Sanātana Gosvāmī, the supreme abode of Mathurā, the blissful abode of Vṛndāvana, the divine Rādhā-kuṇḍa and Govardhana Hill, and the desire within my heart for the loving service of Srī Rādhikā and Mādhava in Vṛndāvana.

From the word *prāptaḥ* a reader could infer that the guru gives a *siddha-praṇālī* initiation, when the disciple is told his or her eternal name, form, dress, and so forth – the eleven items of identity. However, one could just as easily infer that the awakening and realization of the eleven items of our eternal identity happen from following our guru's general or specific instructions. There are statements in various places that a *rāgānuga-sādhaka* should consult with guru or *sādhus* as revelations unfold, and such could also be a reasonable meaning of *prāptaḥ*.

Unfortunately, deviant persons and groups, some perhaps well-intentioned, turned *siddha-praṇālī* into a farce by giving unqualified persons a generic list of the aspects of their so-called spiritual identity. However, meditation on a pseudo spiritual identity not only has no value, but also impedes the awakening of one's real identity. The parody of *siddha-praṇālī* has had ill effects for the Gauḍīya-Vaiṣṇava community in general. Equating *rāgānuga-sādhana* with *siddha-praṇālī* and rejecting the latter leads misinformed persons to reject the former also. Additionally, such equating prevents Vaiṣṇavas from recognizing a non-*siddha-praṇālī* path as bona fide. Therefore, they do not adopt the inner path even when they are qualified to do so.

In Bhaktisiddhānta Sarasvatī's time, Gauḍīya Vaiṣṇavas in general identified *rāgānuga-sādhana* primarily with the above three perversions of the external path. Bhaktisiddhānta, therefore, taught the inner path of Raghunātha Dāsa Gosvāmī. He denounced the false practices that imitated the external path, resulting in much confusion as to whether he taught *rāgānuga-sādhana* at all. Most certainly, he did so. Bhaktisiddhānta writes:

> You should not mistakenly consider *anartha-nivrtti* as *prayojana*, for one thus surmising can never enter into *artha-pravrtti*. Therefore,

> I will begin speaking about *aṣṭa-kālīya-līlā*... Let those who have chanted *harināma* for fifteen or twenty years hear such topics.... Do not think that *aṣṭa-kālīya-līlā* is the property of *prakṛta-sahajiyas*; it is actually our affair. It has to be retrieved from the hands of those cheaters. (*Gauḍīya* 13.214)

Let us very briefly examine some of the strongest evidence that Bhaktisiddhānta Sarasvatī was teaching the inner path of *rāgānuga-bhakti*. First, we can study the Gauḍīya Maṭha logo which Bhaktisiddhānta designed himself and which was on every issue of his official magazine. Lord Caitanya is at the top, and the words guru and Gauḍīya (the latter indicating the *saṅga*, or group of devotees) at the bottom. In the middle is the holy name, *oṁ nāma*, as truly the center

of everything. Counterclockwise from the top, on the left half of the circle, is the word *viddhi* (devotional practice impelled by scripture and logic). Clockwise from the top, on the whole right half of the circle, is the word *rāga*. The *viddhi* half contains a book of *pañcarātra*, the rules of Deity worship. The Lord and his consort are pictured on this left side as Laksmi-Nārāyaṇa, followed by a bell, incense, and the word *arcana* (Deity worship). The *rāga* half contains a book of *Bhāgavatam*, the stories and philosophy of Kṛṣṇa, his devotees, and his incarnations. Then there is a drawing of Rādhā-Kṛṣṇa, followed by a *mṛdaṅga* drum and printing press alongside the word: *kīrtana* (chanting the holy name). The inner points of the star have the words *yaśaḥ* (fame), *śrī* (beauty), *jñāna* (knowledge), *vairāgya* (detachment), *aiśvarya* (wealth, opulence) and *vīrya* (strength, power, or potency).

From the logo, it is clear Bhaktisiddhānta's process of *rāgānuga-sādhana bhakti* is based on the holy name and on *śāstra* such as the *Śrīmad-Bhāgavatam*, with the aim of pleasing Rādhā-Kṛṣṇa and obtaining their shelter. A.C. Bhaktivedanta Swami Prabhupāda used the same Gauḍīya Maṭha logo on the gate of the ISKCON property in Māyāpura, West Bengal. Here he writes about the principle behind the logo and then speaks about the logo itself:

> Neophyte devotees worship the Lord according to *pāñcarātrika-vidhi*, or the regulative principles enjoined in the *Nārada-pañcarātra*. Rādhā-Kṛṣṇa cannot be approached by the neophyte devotees; therefore, temple worship according to regulative principles is offered to Lakṣmī-Nārāyaṇa. Although there may be a Rādhā-Kṛṣṇa *vigraha*, or form, the worship of the neophyte devotees is acceptable as Lakṣmī-Nārāyaṇa worship. Worship according to the *pāñcarātrika-vidhi* is called *vidhi-mārga*, and worship according to the *bhāgavata-vidhi* principles is called *rāga-mārga*. The principles of *rāga-mārga* are especially meant for devotees who are elevated to the Vṛndāvana platform. The inhabitants of Vṛndāvana ... are actually on the *rāga-mārga* or *bhāgavata-mārga* platform. They participate in five basic *rasas: dāsya, sakhya, vātsalya, mādhurya,* and *śānta*. (*Śrīmad-Bhāgavatam* 4.24.45–46, purport)

My Guru Mahārāja introduced... You have seen the, what is called?

> That signia? One side, *pañcarātriki-vidhi,* one side *bhāgavata-viddhi.* That is... I have seen that Gauḍīya Maṭha emblem. Yes. And, so actually, *bhāgavata-mārga* is very strong. That is sufficient. But without *pañcarātrika-vidhi* this polluted body, polluted mind of the devotee, cannot be purified. (lecture *Śrīmad-Bhāgavatam* 6.2.24–25, February 13, 1971, Gorakhpur)

From Bhaktisiddhānta Sarasvatī's logo, we find both his emphasis on *rāgānuga* and the means to follow it. Let us examine his own personal practices and what he taught his disciples. Regarding his own practices, he was the disciple of Gaura Kiśora Dāsa Bābājī, who taught him the worship of Rādhā-Kṛṣṇa in *vipralambha,* the mood of separation. Bhaktisiddhānta especially liked one song of Raghunātha Dāsa Gosvāmī expressing separation from Śrīmatī Rādhārāṇī. He copied those songs of separation and made them the basis of his personal meditations. He revealed that Nayanamaṇī Mañjarī is his ultimate spiritual identity. It is well-known that Śrī Vrajapattana was the place of his intense *bhajana* where he had performed the vow of chanting a billion names. Therefore, rather than receiving formal *siddha-praṇālī,* we find evidence that Bhaktisiddhānta himself, under the guidance of his guru, accepted at least some of the major practices of the outer path. However, the bulk of his life was as an active preacher, establishing temples, distributing the holy name, and printing books.

Bhaktisiddhānta's critics claim that printing and preaching is merely preparation for private meditation. Yet, Bhaktisiddhānta's equating of book publishing with *kīrtana,* and both with *rāga-bhakti,* is firmly based on the esoteric path of spontaneous love. Let us consider these verses from *Caitanya-caritāmṛta, Madhya-līlā* 8.211–214 (verse 211 is quoted from *Govinda-līlāmṛta* 10.16):

sakhyaḥ śrī-rādhikāyā vraja-kumuda-vidhor hlādinī-nāma-śakteḥ
sārāṁśa-prema-vallyāḥ kisalaya-dala-puṣpādi-tulyāḥ sva-tulyāḥ
siktāyāṁ kṛṣṇa-līlāmṛta-rasa-nicayair ullasantyām amuṣyāṁ
jātollāsāḥ sva-sekāc chata-guṇam adhikaṁ santi yat tan na citram

yadyapi sakhīra kṛṣṇa-saṅgame nāhi mana
tathāpi rādhikā yatne karāna saṅgama

nānā-cchale kṛṣṇe preri' saṅgama karāya
ātma-kṛṣṇa-saṅga haite koṭi-sukha pāya

anyonye viśuddha preme kare rasa puṣṭa
tāṅ-sabāra prema dekhi' kṛṣṇa haya tuṣṭa

Rāmānanda Raya explains here how the *gopīs*, including Śrīmatī Rādhārāṇī, feel more happiness when bringing others to enjoy with Kṛṣṇa than when enjoying directly with Kṛṣṇa themselves. This attitude of feeling more happiness at the happiness of others brings Kṛṣṇa great satisfaction. Lord Caitanya himself, Kṛṣṇa in Rādhā's mood, spent a large portion of his manifest time on earth as a public preacher and teacher, bringing many persons to Kṛṣṇa consciousness. Many of his disciples who were the chief examples of *rāga-bhakti* spent much of their time both studying and writing books. It is entirely fitting that a person who follows Śrī Rūpa (*rūpānuga*) and who is aspiring for, or already on, the *rāga-mārga* would use a *mṛdaṅga* and printing press to nurture their attachment to the divine couple.

Bhaktisiddhānta consistently gave emphasis, as does Raghnunatha Dāsa Gosvāmī in *Manaḥ-śikṣā*, on an internal change of motive and consciousness that must occur when traversing the path of *rāga*. It is on this point more than any other where we find firm evidence for Bhaktisiddhānta teaching the inner path of *rāgānuga-sādhana*. He does not deny the role of guru and *sādhus* in understanding one's spiritual identity. Rather, the following letter encapsulates Bhaktisiddhānta's teachings and view:

> The *aṣṭa-kālīya-līlā* and related topics that you have heard about from Vaiṣṇavas in Vṛndāvana is undoubtedly worshipable. Yet how these pastimes are conceived in the state of infestation by *anarthas* is not at all worshipable. By repeated chanting, a special individual is capable of knowing these matters, which is the identity of the *svarūpa*. By attaining *anartha-nivṛtti*, one's *svarūpa* is automatically awakened, and the eternal mode of thinking that is innate to it manifests. Those who profess to teach or reveal this identity are deceitful, for it cannot be done.
>
> On the other hand, if a devotee receives some inspiration after

sincerely chanting for a long time, he should go to the *sad-guru* or an advanced devotee and ask that it be confirmed and purified by him. The *svarūpa* has eleven (*ekādaśa*) aspects. There are many cases of unscrupulous gurus who artificially force-feed these topics to unqualified practitioners, yet that cannot be called a symptom of spiritual perfection. Those who have achieved *svarūpa-siddhi* gain such realization through internal revelation; the guru's only involvement is to assist his disciples' ongoing advancement. As a *sādhaka* progresses toward *siddhi*, all these things are naturally revealed within the *sevan-mukha* heart. (Bhaktisiddhānta's letter, 17 November 1930 *Patravali* 2.89-90)

So, by the grace of guru and advanced devotees all is revealed, but a formal *siddha-praṇālī* is not necessary. As Bhaktivinoda Ṭhākura wrote:

pūrna vikaśita haiyā, braje more jāya laiyā,
dekhāya more svarūpa-vilāsa
more siddha-deha diyā, kṛṣṇa-pāśe rākhe giyā,
e dehera kare sarva-nāśa

Blossoming fully, the flower of the holy name takes me to Vraja and reveals to me his own love-dalliance. This name gives to me my own eternal spiritual body, keeps me right by Kṛṣṇa's side, and completely destroys everything related to this mortal frame of mine. (*Śaraṇāgati: Śrī Nāma-Māhātmya*: The Glories of the Holy Name, verse 7)

In a letter on 18 December, 1932, Bhaktisiddhānta similarly wrote: "Only the holy name can reveal the spiritual form of the living being and cause him to be attracted to Kṛṣṇa's form, qualities, and pastimes." Indeed, the potency of the holy name is one of the key teachings of Lord Caitanya himself, as we see in *Caitanya-caritāmṛta* (*Antya-līlā* 4.71): *tāra madhye sarva-śreṣṭha nāma saṅkīrtana, niraparādhe nāma laile pāya prema-dhana.*

The ultimate conclusion is that Bhaktisiddhānta taught purification of *anarthas* through chanting the holy name, Deity worship, study of the *śāstras*, visiting the holy places, serving the devotees, and helping others to take up Kṛṣṇa consciousness, all under the direction of guru. Let's look, very briefly, at the inner path of *Manaḥ-śikṣā* and compare Bhaktisiddhānta's teachings on *rāga-bhakti* with it.

Raghunātha Dāsa Gosvāmī says that a practitioner must have *ratim apūrvām atitarām* (unprecedented, excessive attachment for Kṛṣṇa and all related to him) at the very beginning of the path. Similarly, Bhaktisiddhānta writes: "When you are sincerely eager to serve Kṛṣṇa, your eternal connection to him in one of five rasas will be opened to you." (*Śrīla Prabhupādera Vaktṛtāvalī* 1.134) Throughout *Manaḥ-śikṣā,* especially in verses 8–11, there is an emphasis on serving the *svarūpa-śakti,* Rādhārāṇī. Similarly, Bhaktisiddhānta writes: "Without serving Rādhā, no one can ever be eligible to serve Kṛṣṇa. May you be overwhelmed with desire to be situated in your eternal individual serving position in *mādhurya-rasa* as an eternal maidservant of Rādhā's *pālya-dāsīs.*" (ibid)

One of the prime methods of purification given in *Manaḥ-śikṣā* is to cry out for help from the Lord and his devotees. Bhaktisiddhānta writes: "By sincerely calling out to Bhagavān the *jīva* may attain *anartha-nivritti*; there is no other means." (*Śrīla Prabhupādera Boktṛtābalī* 2.176)

> If we want to show ... the real glory of *rāgānuga-bhakti,* we ourselves must become expert in the art of *bhajana.... Bhajana* is not an external activity.... Loudly call out *nāma*; then the spirit of enjoyment in the form of laziness will not be able to devour us. (Letter 13 December, 1928)

Following *Manaḥ-śikṣā,* the practitioner must give up pride, interest in mundane talks, sinful behavior, deceitfully using Kṛṣṇa for one's own sense gratification, and the desire for honor. Only then does Giridhārī allow the *jīva* to fully worship Gāndharvā, and only then does a *jīva* fully enter into realized spiritual service. Bhaktisiddhānta writes, in *Prākṛta-rasa Śata-dūṣiṇī*:

> *nā uṭhiyā vṛkṣopari phala dhari' ṭāne nā*
> *rūpānugā krama-patha vilopa ta' kare nā*

One should never climb into a tree, grasp the unripe fruits and forcibly pull them off. Similarly, the followers of Śrīla Rūpa Gosvāmī never abolish the initial systematic process of devotional service. (57)

sevāya unmūkha ha'le jaḍa-kathā haya nā
natuvā cin-maya kathā kabhu śruta haya nā

When one is enthusiastic for constantly rendering unalloyed devotional service, there is never any possibility for becoming distracted by idle talks related to the mundane world. Otherwise, if one is not enthusiastic, then confidential topics about the all-conscious spiritual world should never be heard. (78)

The essence of the inner path involves getting rid of even the finest traces of *anarthas,* like the second cleaning out of fine (*sūkṣma*) dust and sand in the Guṇḍicā temple as described in *Caitanya-caritāmṛta, Madhya-līlā* 12.93–94:

sūkṣma dhūli, tṛṇa, kāṅkara, saba karaha dūra
bhāla-mate śodhana karaha prabhura antaḥpura

saba vaiṣṇava lañā yabe dui-bāra śodhila
dekhi' mahāprabhura mane santoṣa ha-ila

Bhaktisiddhānta also describes the awakening of *rāga* as a gradual process of internal purity:

Nāmāparādha-kīrtana is not *nāma-kīrtana.* As the bud of the holy name begins to sprout just a little, the supramundane forms of Kṛṣṇa and his associates become manifest, and when it reaches the flowering stage, the fragrance of Kṛṣṇa's sixty-four qualities is experienced. When the lotus of the holy name fully expands, Kṛṣṇa's *aṣṭa-kālīya-nitya-līlā,* although beyond material nature, manifests within this world. (*Gauḍīya* 13.213)

As is evidenced in this chapter, Bhaktisiddhānta Sarasvatī taught the path of spontaneous love for Kṛṣṇa in Vraja, *rāga-bhakti.* He accepted as bonafide both the external and internal paths which Svarūpa Dāmodara had imparted to Vakreśvara Paṇḍita and Raghunātha Dāsa, respectively. However, in Bhaktisiddhānta's time the external path had, generally, become a mockery due to unqualified persons' imitative methods. Bhaktisiddhānta and his faithful followers, therefore, emphasized the internal path of *Manaḥ-śikṣā,* which is almost impossible to counterfeit.

PART TWO

Śrī Manaḥ-śikṣā by Raghunātha Dāsa Gosvāmī with Śrīla Bhaktivinoda Ṭhākura's commentary, *Bhajana-darpaṇa,* and his poetic commentary, *Manaḥ-śikṣā Bhāṣā*

INVOCATION BY ŚRĪLA BHAKTIVINODA ṬHĀKURA

BHAJANA-DARPAṆA

śrī-śrī-guru-caraṇebhyaḥ namaḥ
śrī-śrī-kṛṣṇa-caitanya-candrāya namaḥ
śrī-śrī-rādhā-kṛṣṇābhyāṁ namaḥ

To compose this commentary on *Manaḥ-śikṣā,* I fall at the lotus feet of Śrīla Raghunātha Dāsa Gosvāmī. He is worshipable by the whole world because he displayed how to cut all worldly ties by taking full shelter of Śrī Caitanya Mahāprabhu.

By the instruction of Śrī Caitanya Mahāprabhu, Śrī Svarūpa Dāmodara Gosvāmī taught Raghunātha Dāsa Gosvāmī all the secrets and mystery of the worship of the name of the Lord, *hari-nāma-bhajana.* These twelve *ślokas* of *Manaḥ-śikṣā* are the wealth and life of all Gauḍīya Vaiṣṇavas because Śrīla Raghunātha Dāsa Gosvāmī, by addressing and instructing his own mind, is teaching everyone these same secrets. He reveals what people should or shouldn't do when, after the accumulation of devotional good fortune, they gain faith (*śraddhā*) in devotional service for Śrī Kṛṣṇa.

MANAḤ-ŚIKṢĀ BHĀṢĀ

śrī-śrī-guru-caraṇebhyo namaḥ
śrī-kṛṣṇa-caitanya-candrāya namaḥ
śrī-raghunātha-dāsa-gosvāmī-caraṇebhyo namaḥ

I offer my respects to the lotus feet of śrī-guru, the moon-like Śrī Kṛṣṇa Caitanya, and Śrī Raghunātha Dāsa Gosvāmī.

vraja-dhāma nitya-dhana, rādhā-kṛṣṇa dui jana,
līlā-āveśe eka-tanu haiyā
dhāma-saha gauḍa-deśe, prakaṭa hailā ese,
nija nitya-pāriṣada laiyā

The eternal treasure of Vraja, Śrī Śrī Rādhā and Kṛṣṇa, absorbed in their play, melded into one body and manifested in Bengal, along with their timeless abode and their entourage of eternal associates.

mana! tumi satya bali' jāna
navadvīpe gaurahari, nāma-saṅkīrtana kari',
premāmṛta gauḍe kaila dāna

O heart, know it to be true! By performing congregational chanting of the holy name (*nāma-saṅkīrtana*) in Navadvīpa, Gaurahari gave the immortal ambrosia of sacred love to Bengal.

sannyāsera chala kari', nīlācale sei hari,
śrī-kṛṣṇa-caitanya yatīśvara
dāmodara, rāmananda, la'ye kari parānanda,
gūḍha-tattva jānāya vistara

The same Hari became the best among wandering ascetics, Śrī Kṛṣṇa Caitanya, who lived in Nīlācala in the pretext of being a *sannyāsī*, enjoying unsurpassed bliss with Svarūpa Dāmodara and Rāmānanda Rāya, exploring deep and intimate mysteries [of Kṛṣṇa's love].

raghunāthe sei tattva, śikhāiyā paramārtha,
pāṭhāila śrī-rūpera kāche
śrī-dāsa-gosvāmī braje, rūpa-saha kṛṣṇa bhaje,
manaḥ-śikṣā-śloka likhiyāche

Teaching these spiritual truths, Caitanya Mahāprabhu sent Raghunātha Dāsa Gosvāmī to Rūpa in Vraja. It was there that Raghunātha Dāsa Gosvāmī adored and worshiped Kṛṣṇa alongside Śrī Rūpa, and wrote this *Manaḥ-śikṣā*.

tāhṅāra dāsera dāsa, haite yā'ra baḍa āśa,
e bhaktivinoda akiñcana
manaḥ-śikṣā-bhāṣā gāya, yathā śuddha-bhakta pāya,
dayā kari' karena śravaṇa

I, poor Bhaktivinoda, cherishing the intense desire to become the servant of their servants, sing these commentaries on *Manaḥ-śikṣā* wherever I find pure devotees. Please be merciful and listen!

VERSE ONE

गुरौ गोष्ठे गोष्ठालयिषु सुजने भूसुरगणे
स्वमन्त्रे श्रीनाम्नि व्रजनवयुवद्वन्द्वशरणे ।
सदा दम्भं हित्वा कुरु रतिमपूर्वामतितरां
अये स्वान्तर्भ्रातश्चटुभिरभियाचे धृतपदः ॥

gurau goṣṭhe goṣṭhālayiṣu sujane bhū-sura-gaṇe
sva-mantre śrī-nāmni vraja-nava-yuva-dvandva-śaraṇe
sadā dambhaṁ hitvā kuru ratim apūrvām atitarāṁ
aye svāntar bhrātaś caṭubhir abhiyāce dhṛta-padaḥ

aye—O; *bhrātaḥ*—brother; *svāntaḥ*—my inner self, my mind; *hitvā*—having given up; *dambham*—pride; *sadā*—always; *kuru*—please do; *apūrvām*—unprecedented; *atitarām*—excessive; *ratim*—attachment; *gurau*—to Śrī Guru; *goṣṭhe*—to the *goṣṭha* (the abode of cows), Vṛndāvana; *goṣṭha-ālayiṣu su-jane*—to the devotee residents of the *goṣṭha* Vṛndāvana; *bhū-sura-gaṇe*—to the earthly devotees (Vaiṣṇavas and *brāhmaṇas*); *sva-mantre*—to one's confidential mantra; *śrī-nāmni*—to *śrī-nāma*, the holy names of the Vṛndāvana couple; *vraja-nava-yuva-dvandva-śaraṇe*—in the shelter of the fresh youthful couple of Vraja, Śrī Śrī Rādhā-Kṛṣṇa; *dhṛta-padaḥ*—holding your feet; *abhiyāce*—I beg you; *caṭubhiḥ*—using pleasing words.

O dear brother! O mind! Having given up all pride, please develop unprecedented and excessive attachment to Śrī Guru; to Śrī Vṛndāvana, the abode of cows; to the devotee residents of Vṛndāvana; to all the devotees on this planet; to the confidential mantra [given by Śrī Guru]; to the holy names of Śrī Śrī Rādhā-Kṛṣṇa; and to the process of surrendering to the fresh youthful couple of Vraja. Holding your feet, I beseech you with sweet words.

Have exclusive and one-pointed devotion to Rādhā-Kṛṣṇa's feet as dear as life.

Elvira Lukman

Cultivate loving attachment to one's *dīkṣā-guru* and *śikṣā-gurus* as friends, not just saints.

ŚRĪLA BHAKTIVINODA ṬHĀKURA'S *BHAJANA-DARPAṆA* COMMENTARY

ŚLOKĀRTHA: MEANING OF THE VERSE

1 **Śrī Guru** Guru includes both *dīkṣā-guru* and *śikṣā-gurus* (initiating guru and instructing gurus). The types of attachment one should develop towards the gurus while serving them is clearly explained in the next verse (*Manaḥ-śikṣā* 2).

2 **Goṣṭha: Śrī Vraja-dhāma** This includes Gokula, Nandīśvara, Govardhana, Śyāma-kuṇḍa, Yāvat and all other places of Kṛṣṇa's pastimes in *vraja-maṇḍala*.

3 **Goṣṭhālayin: The residents of Vraja** Those who reside in *vraja-dhāma* for the purpose of pleasing the Lord through devotional service are called *vraja-vāsī-gaṇa*. Vrajavāsī indicates a pure devotee, an elevated *uttama-bhāgavata*. Such a person resides in *vraja-dhāma*, both physically and in mediation, or just in meditation.

4 **Sujana: The Vaiṣṇavas*, devotees of the Lord** Vaiṣṇavas may belong to any Vaiṣṇava *sampradāya* (school). Perhaps they may not reside in *vraja-dhāma* even in meditation, but still they are bona-fide and are devotees of the Supreme Lord, Bhagavān. These are the intermediate, *madhyama-bhāgavata*, devotees.

5 **Bhū-sura-gaṇa: The brāhmaṇas** These are persons who are teachers, priests, intellectuals, scholars, counselors, or healers, and who are firmly fixed in the scriptural duties for their occupation and life stages, *varṇāśrama-dharma*. Such persons also teach the worship of the Lord, *vaiṣṇava-dharma*, to all pious persons, *varṇāśrama* followers. They are known as juniors, or *kaniṣṭha-bhāgavata*.

* Some people say that Śrīla Raghunātha Dāsa Gosvāmī has placed *sujana* (Vaiṣṇavas) and *bhū-sura-gaṇa* (*brāhmaṇas*) in two separate categories to show that a Vaiṣṇava is not automatically a *brāhmaṇa*. However, if the term *bhū-sura-gaṇe* is taken as an adjective of the term *sujane*, then it will translate as "to all the Vaiṣṇavas, who are also *brāhmaṇas*."

Cultivate loving attachment to all the places in Vraja.

Elvira and Dinara Lukman

Nourish attachment to the *uttama-bhāgavata*, those whose body and mind live in *vraja-dhāma* for the purpose of pleasing the Lord.

Elvira Lukman

Have attachment to intermediate (*madhyama*) devotees of any genuine tradition whether or not they reside in Vraja in body or mind.

Elvira Lukman

Have attachment to beginners in devotion, such as *brāhmaṇas* who follow and teach dedication of life and occupation to God (*varṇāśrama*).

6 **Sva-mantra: One's dīkṣā-mantra** This is the spiritual mantra, or *bhagavan-mantra,* that a bonafide guru gives as part of initiation (e.g. *kāma-gāyatrī*).

7 **Śrī Hari-nāma** Primary names of the Supreme Personality of Godhead in relation to the spiritual world and the spiritual eternal function are names like Śrī Hari, Śrī Rādhā-Kānta, Śrī Kṛṣṇa, Śrī Govinda, and so forth. Secondary names, such as Patita-pāvana (the deliverer of all fallen souls), and Paramātmā (Supersoul), are related only to the material world. One should always take shelter of the Lord's primary names.

8 **Vraja-nava-yuva-dvandva-śaraṇa: Surrender to the youthful, divine couple of Vraja** One should take shelter exclusively and one-pointedly of *vraja-yuvā,* the divine couple Śrī Śrī Rādhā-Kṛṣṇa.

9 **Dambhaṁ hitvā: Give up pride** The varieties of *dambha* include *māyā* (illusion and trickery), *avidyā* (ignorance), *kapaṭatā* (cheating), *asaralatā* (lack of direct simplicity) and *śāṭhya* (deceit and duplicity). While cultivating pure devotional service, if there is any other motive besides progression in *bhakti,* then one is engaged in a kind of cheating or duplicity. If philosophical detachment (*jñāna*) or good works for material enjoyment (*karma*) is prominent in the devotional process, then ignorance (*avidyā*) will be seen as more powerful than *bhakti.* If any unfavorable mood is present in the development of *bhakti,* it is a disguised form of *māyā.* One must give up all such things. When one engages in the cultivation of pure devotional service, illusions about duties of occupation and stage of life (*varṇāśrama-dharma*), material desires, the self, God, material energy, life's goal, and the process of success will all disappear.

10 **Apūrvā-rati** The love inherent in the soul is pure love for the Lord (*ātma-rati* is *śuddha-rati*). When that pure love in the conditioned soul comes into contact with the dull matter of *māyā,* it transforms into material attachment. In pure *kṛṣṇa-bhakti,* the original, eternal, deeply emotional attachment remains fixed and visible at all times because Śrī Kṛṣṇa is the soul of all souls. During conditioned life, while performing

ॐ भूर्भुवः स्वः तत्सवितुर्वरेण्यं भर्गो देवस्य धीमहि
धियो यो नः प्रचोदयात्॥

Dinara Lukman

Have attachment to one's *dīkṣā* mantras.

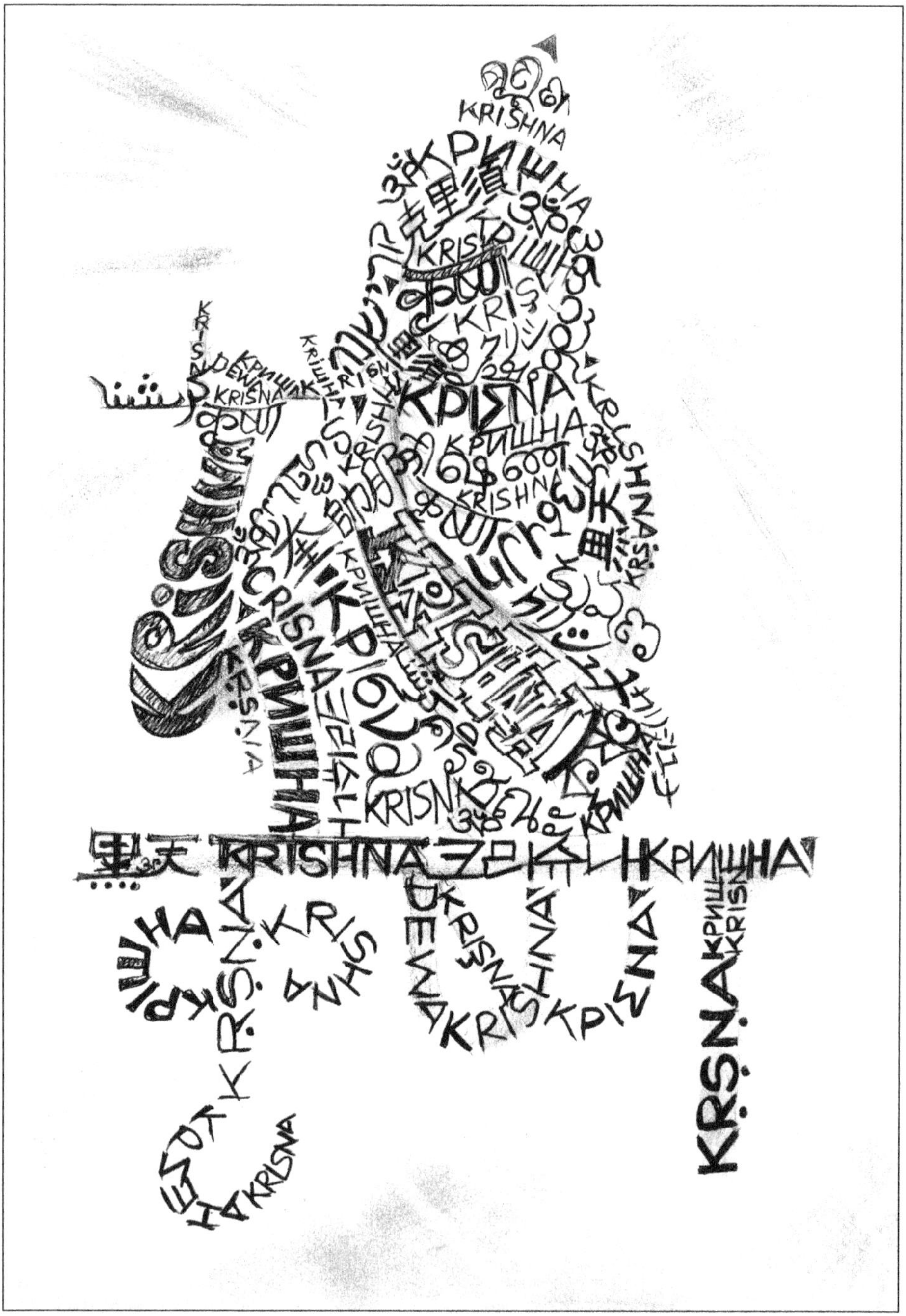

Elvira Lukman

Have attachment to taking shelter of primary names of God.

devotional service, a soul becomes filled with *apūrvā-rati,* love that has no material precedent, in proportion to the expression of the soul's inherent emotional attachment.

11 **Atitarāṁ kuru: Make intensive endeavor (atiśaya-vidhāna)** Enthusiastically feel encouraged to progress and take full shelter in the devotional path. Do not become complacent, thinking, "If I am lucky I will get spiritual success, or, if it is not in my fortune, then I may not achieve it." As much as the mercy of guru and Kṛṣṇa combine with one's own endeavors, one gets spiritual potency. As much as that spiritual potency manifests, one's desires to enjoy the fruits of one's own actions will be diminished.

INSTRUCTIVE COMMENTARY

To be eligibile to receive the pure instructions in this verse, a person should already have achieved faith, *śraddhā,* in the path of loving devotion to Kṛṣṇa. Such faith comes from the potency of the association of saintly persons, *sādhu-saṅga,* manifesting within the heart. That potency diminishes the tendency to perform *karma,* actions for material gain. When *śraddhā* develops, the first action is to accept and take shelter of an initiating spiritual master, *dīkṣā-guru,* as well as the *dīkṣā-mantra* to worship *yugala-kiśora,* the divine couple Śrī Śrī Rādhā-Kṛṣṇa. After receiving the mantra one should worship one's *śikṣā-* and *dīkṣā-gurus* with pure devotion and attachment to their lotus feet (*ātma-rati*). One should not only respect gurus as saints, using rational intelligence, but one should also deal with one's gurus as well-wishing friends. Always respect and serve the three types of Vaiṣṇavas [junior, intermediate, and advanced] accordingly to their eligibility, with love and in a friendly manner. One should also develop deep attachment to chanting the mantras and serving the holy name. One should come to the point of complete surrender to the lotus feet of the divine couple, knowing them to be one's life and soul. This surrender is called *śaraṇāgati.*

ŚRĪLA BHAKTIVINODA ṬHĀKURA'S *MANAḤ-ŚIKṢĀ BHĀṢĀ* – SONG ONE

gurudeve, vraja-vane, vraja-bhūmi-vāsī jane,
śuddha-bhakte, āra vipra-gaṇe
iṣṭa-mantre, harināme, yugala-bhajana-kāme,
kara rati apūrva yatane

[Oh mind,] desire to serve the young couple of Vraja with uncommon, wonderful attachment. Gurudeva, the forest of Vraja, the residents of Vraja, the pure devotees and the *brāhmaṇas,* your *iṣṭa-mantra* and the holy name –

dhari, mana, caraṇe tomāra
jāniyāchi ebe sāra, kṛṣṇa-bhakti vinā āra,
nāhi ghuce jīvera saṁsāra

O heart! I beg you, falling at your feet, to please love all of them. I know the essence – without devotion for all these, along with devotion for Kṛṣṇa, the soul will not escape the cycle of birth and death (*saṁsāra*).

karma, jñāna, tapaḥ yoga, sakali ta' karma-bhoga,
karma chāḍāite keha nāre
sakala chāḍiyā bhāi, śraddhā-devīra guṇa gāi,
yāṅ'ra kṛpā bhakti dite pāre

Consider that action, knowledge, asceticism, and yoga only further bind one to karma and certainly are unable to free one from it. Renounce all these, O brother, and sing the praise of the goddess of faith, whose grace can bestow devotion.

chāḍi' dambha anukṣaṇa, smara aṣṭa-tattva mana,
kara tāhe niṣkapaṭa rati
sei rati-prārthanāya, śrī-dāsa-gosvāmī pāya,
e bhaktivinoda kare nati

Give up all pretenses and meditate on the eightfold truths (guru, Vṛndāvana, Vṛndāvana's residents, Vaiṣṇavas, *brāhmaṇas,* one's mantra, the holy name, and the process of surrendering) at every moment. Love them all without ulterior motives. With prayers for attaining such love, Bhaktivinoda bows at the lotus feet of Śrī Raghunātha Dāsa Gosvāmī.

Elvira Lukman

Devotees of Kṛṣṇa rise above worldly duties, speculative knowledge, and mystic yoga.

VERSE TWO

न धर्मं नाधर्मं श्रुतिगणनिरुक्तं किल कुरु
व्रजे राधाकृष्णप्रचुरपरिचर्यामिह तनु ।
शचीसूनुं नन्दीश्वरपतिसुतत्वे गुरुवरं
मुकुन्दप्रेष्ठत्वे स्मर परमजस्रं ननु मनः ॥

na dharmaṁ nādharmaṁ śruti-gaṇa-niruktaṁ kila kuru
vraje rādhā-kṛṣṇa-pracura-paricaryām iha tanu
śacī-sūnuṁ nandīśvara-pati-sutatve guru-varaṁ
mukunda-preṣṭhatve smara param ajasraṁ nanu manaḥ

nanu—indeed; *kila*—certainly; *na*—do not; *kuru*—do; *dharmam*—pious acts; *na-adharmam*—nor sinful acts; *śruti-gaṇa-niruktam*—which is spoken of in the Vedas and supporting literature; *iha*—here; *vraje*—[residing] in Vraja; *tanu*—please expand upon; *rādhā-kṛṣṇa-pracura-paricaryām*—the profuse service of Śrī Śrī Rādhā-Kṛṣṇa; *manaḥ*—O mind; *ajasram*—unceasingly; *smara*—remember; *śacī-sūnum*—the son of Śacī; *nandīśvara-pati-sutatve*—[as being] the son of Nanda Mahārāja; *guru-varam*—[and] Śrī Guru; *mukunda-preṣṭhatve*—[as being] one who is dear to the Lord; *param*—topmost.

Indeed, do not perform any pious acts prescribed in the Vedas and supporting literature, or sinful acts forbidden in them. Staying here in Vraja, please perform profuse service to Śrī Śrī Rādhā-Kṛṣṇa. O mind, unceasingly remember the son of Śacī as the son of Nanda Mahārāja, and Śrī Guru as the dearest servant of Lord Mukunda.

Aṣṭasakhī-līlā Devī Dāsī

Give up ordinary *dharma* and *adharma*, offering everything to Kṛṣṇa.

ŚRĪLA BHAKTIVINODA ṬHĀKURA'S *BHAJANA-DARPAṆA* COMMENTARY

PŪRVA-PAKṢA*

This verse deals with three doubts. The first doubt concerns how an individual *jīva* who gives up false pride and takes shelter of *kṛṣṇa-bhakti* will earn a living. It might appear that no one who gives up *dharma* and *adharma*, as prescribed in this verse, could maintain a livelihood. The second doubt concerns accepting the worship of Śrī Śrī Rādhā-Kṛṣṇa, the divine couple, as the ultimate and only object. Such a person needs to understand how to know and regard Śrī Kṛṣṇa-Caitanya Mahāprabhu without disturbing one-pointed worship. The third doubt concerns needing to know the method in which one should meditate on Śrī Guru. Answers to all of these are provided below with proper analysis.

ŚLOKĀRTHA: MEANING OF THE VERSE

1 **Na dharmaṁ nādharmaṁ śruti-gaṇa-niruktaṁ kila kuru: Do not perform the pious or sinful activities mentioned in the śrutīs.** The *śrutīs'* essence is the esoteric conclusion that one should serve the divine couple Śrī Śrī Rādhā-Kṛṣṇa uninterruptedly. Externally, whatever a human being does falls in one of these two categories of *dharma* and *adharma*. If we reject both, life cannot be sustained even for a moment. Therefore, Śrīla Raghunātha Dāsa Gosvāmī did not actually prohibit all activities in relation to engaging the senses in the world. Nor did

* In traditional Indian dialectics, scriptural commentary is performed according to the following process: *viṣayaḥ saṁśayaś caiva pūrva-pakṣas tathottaraḥ/ nirṇayaś ceti pañcāṅgaṁ śāstre 'dhikaraṇaṁ smṛtam*, "It should be known that scriptural exegesis (*adhikaraṇa*) is dependent on the following five-fold dialectic process: 1 *viṣaya*, introducing a subject matter to be studied; 2 *saṁśaya*, raising a doubt about it; 3 *pūrva-pakṣa*, specifying the prima-facie view about the doubt; 4 *uttara-pakṣa*, specifying the opposing view about the same; and 5 *nirṇaya/siddhānta*, specifying the conclusion by an unbiased judge." (*Bhāṭṭa-cintāmaṇī, tarka-pāda* of Paṇḍita Gāgā-bhaṭṭa) The subject matter, *Manaḥ-śikṣā*, is already in front of us. Śrīla Bhaktivinoda Ṭhākura takes up the doubts and gives the *pūrva-pakṣa, uttara-pakṣa* and conclusions.

he prohibit all prescribed duties in relation to awakening a soul to the ultimate goal of life.

In this world there are two categories of living beings, the spiritually ignorant and the spiritually intelligent. For spiritually ignorant living beings, the Vedas as *śruti* and *smṛti* list many rules and prohibitions to promote piety and discourage sin. Fear of punishment motivates spiritually ignorant *jīvas* to follow such rules. Whenever they do anything independently of such scriptural guidelines, their actions have an inauspicious result.

Those who have attained self-realization are spiritually intelligent, conscious of their spiritual identity as servant of God. They do not need, and shouldn't do, actions motivated by fear. Śrīla Raghunātha Dāsa Gosvāmī has instructed such persons who have realized their spiritual identity to pursue the worship of the divine couple without much regard to *dharma* or *adharma*. Even while performing whatever required duties are needed in their life, spiritual practitioners (*sādhakas*) should infuse those activities with service to the divine couple, Śrī Śrī Rādhā-Kṛṣṇa.

Those persons who live according to *varṇāśrama-dharma* (scriptural rules of occupation and life stages) should do those actions in a mood related to pure devotional service. For example, those who are married (*gṛhastha*) should establish the Deity form of the Lord (*śrī-vigraha*) at home. Then all activities such as earning money, farming, supporting one's family, protecting wealth and assets, building houses, and so forth, should be done in the mood of identifying oneself as a servant of the Deity who is the enjoyer of all those activities. One should never think, "I am the enjoyer and master. I can exploit the fruits of my work for my own enjoyment." According to *Hari-bhakti-vilāsa*, even rituals such as the *śrāddha* (oblation) offering to ancestors should be performed in the mood of the service to the Deity.

When a person has no more attachment and dependency upon the principles of *varṇāśrama-dharma*, the pure intrinsic nature of devotional service for the pleasure to the divine couple is easily available. Then one can live in *vraja-dhāma* at least mentally, if not both physically and mentally.

Meditate on Lord Caitanya, Śacī's son, as being the same as Kṛṣṇa, Nanda's son.

2 **Śacī-sūnuṁ nandīśvara-pati-sutatve: Meditate on Lord Caitanya, the son of Śacī, as non-different from Lord Kṛṣṇa, the son of Nanda.** The very beginning of worshiping the divine couple starts with worship of one's gurus (*śrī-guru-pūjā*) and pleasing the gurus. Then one remembers Lord Gaurāṅga, meditating upon him to appear in the form of Kṛṣṇa. If worship is done otherwise, the ultimate perfection will not come. However, if someone worships Śrī Caitanya separately from the divine couple, one will be unable to understand how he is non-different from Śrī Kṛṣṇa. Having established that Śrī Kṛṣṇa, Śrī Nanda-nandana, is non-different from Lord Caitanya, Śrī Śacī-nandana, one is then able to remember Śrī Caitanya even while worshiping Śrī Kṛṣṇa.

3 **Guru-varaṁ mukunda-preṣṭhatve smara: Meditate on Śrī Guru as being the dearest to Mukunda, Kṛṣṇa.** The term *mukunda-preṣṭha* means someone who is very dear to Lord Mukunda, the Lord who gives *mukti*, freedom from the material world. The worshiper should think, "Śrī Kṛṣṇa, who is like an ocean of mercy, has sent his intimate associate in order to take me home, back to Godhead." It is also most appropriate to respect and regard Śrī Gurudeva as an intimate friend (*priyā-sakhī*) of Śrīmatī Rādhārāṇī.

ŚRĪLA BHAKTIVINODA ṬHĀKURA'S *MANAḤ-ŚIKṢĀ BHĀṢĀ* – SONG TWO

'dharma' bali' vede yā're, eteka praśaṁsā kare,
'adharma' baliyā ninde yā're
tāhā kichu nāhi kara, dharma-adharma parihara,
hao rata nigūḍha vyāpāre

Engage neither in anything that the Vedas proclaim to be *dharma*, nor in anything that it censures. Rather, leaving all *dharma* and *adharma* aside, enrapture yourself in the supreme mystery.

yāci mana, dhari' tava pāya
se-sakala parihari', vraja-bhūme vāsa kari',
rata hao yugala-sevāya

O heart! I beg you, holding on to your feet. Abandoning everything, live in Vraja and be always absorbed in the loving service of the divine couple, Śrī Śrī Rādhā-Kṛṣṇa.

śrī-śacīnandana-dhane, śrī-nandanandana-sane,
eka kari' karaha bhajana
śrī-mukunda-priya-jana, gurudeve jāna', mana,
tomā' lāgi' patita-pāvana

Worship our treasure Śrī Śacīnandana (the son of Śacī, Gaurahari) and Śrī Nandanandana (the son of Nanda, Kṛṣṇa) as one. Know that Gurudeva is Śrī Kṛṣṇa's beloved, who manifested in this world, dear mind, as a savior of the fallen, for you!

jagate prakaṭa bhāi, tāṅhā vinā gati nāi,
yadi cāha āpana kuśala
tāṅhāra caraṇe dhari', tad ādeśa sadā smari',
e bhaktivinode deha' bala

You cannot progress without guru. If you want your own welfare, hold tight onto the guru's lotus feet, always keeping the guru's instructions in mind. Bhaktivinoda, begs, "Please grant me strength [that I may do this myself]."

Aṣṭasakhī-līlā Devī Dāsī

Meditate on the guru as being very dear to Kṛṣṇa.

VERSE THREE

यदीच्छेरावासं व्रजभुवि सरागं प्रतिजनुर्
युवद्वन्द्वं तच्चेत्परिचरितुमारादभिलषेः ।
स्वरूपं श्रीरूपं सगणमिह तस्याग्रजमपि
स्फुटं प्रेम्णा नित्यं स्मर नम तदा त्वं शृणु मनः ॥

yadīccher āvāsaṁ vraja-bhuvi sa-rāgaṁ pratijanur
yuva-dvandvaṁ tac cet paricaritum ārād abhilaṣeḥ
svarūpaṁ śrī-rūpaṁ sa-gaṇam iha tasyāgrajam api
sphuṭaṁ premṇā nityaṁ smara nama tadā tvaṁ śṛṇu manaḥ

śṛṇu—listen; *manaḥ*—O mind; *yadi*—if; *iccheḥ*—you desire; *āvāsam*—residence; *sa-rāgam*—with loving attachment; *vraja-bhuvi*—in the land of Vraja; *pratijanuḥ*—in every birth; *cet*—if [you desire]; *paricaritum*—to serve; *yuva-dvandvaṁ tat*—that youthful couple, Śrī Śrī Rādhā-Kṛṣṇa; *ārāt*—while staying nearby; *abhilaṣeḥ*—you desire; *tadā*—then; *tvam*—you; *nityam*—always; *sphuṭam*—clearly; *smara*—remember; *nama*—offer obeisances; *premṇā*—with love to; *svarūpam*—to Śrī Svarūpa; *śrī-rūpam*—to Śrī Rūpa; *sa-gaṇam iha*—with all associates staying here in Vṛndāvana; *tasya-agrajam api*—and also Śrī Rūpa's elder brother Śrī Sanātana.

Listen, O mind. If you desire, in every birth, to reside in the land of Vraja with loving attachment and to serve the youthful couple Śrī Śrī Rādhā-Kṛṣṇa in close proximity, then clearly remember and offer obeisances to Śrī Svarūpa, to Śrī Rūpa and his associates in Vṛndāvana, and to Śrī Rūpa's elder brother, Śrī Sanātana.

Dinara Lukman

The books of Svarūpa Dāmodara, Raghunātha Dāsa Gosvāmī, Rūpa Gosvāmī, and Sanātana Gosvāmī shower jewels of service to Rādhā-Kṛṣṇa upon their readers.

ŚRĪLA BHAKTIVINODA ṬHĀKURA'S *BHAJANA-DARPAṆA* COMMENTARY

PŪRVA-PAKṢA

This verse addresses whether or not it is possible for someone to attain residence in Vṛndāvana with spontaneous love (*rāgātmikā-bhakti*) if one accepts initiation (*dīkṣā*) and instruction (*śikṣā*) from any of the Vaiṣṇava schools (*sampradāya*).

ŚLOKĀRTHA: MEANING OF THE VERSE

1 **Rāgātmikā-bhakti** We will first consider the words in this verse, *sa-rāgaṁ,* which refer to *rāgātmikā-bhakti.* The practice and perfection of pure *bhakti* is categorized into three states – *sādhana-bhakti, bhāva-bhakti,* and *prema-bhakti.*

Śrīla Rūpa Gosvāmī's conclusions in this matter is explained in the following verses:

ādau śraddhā tataḥ sādhu-
saṅgo 'tha bhajana-kriyā
tato 'nartha-nivṛttiḥ syāt
tato niṣṭhā rucis tataḥ

athāsaktis tato bhāvas
tataḥ premābhyudañcati
sādhakānām ayaṁ premṇaḥ
prādurbhāve bhavet kramaḥ

Sādhana-bhakti begins with faith (*śraddhā*), followed by association with pure devotees (*sādhu-saṅga*), engagement in devotional service (*bhajana-kriyā*), removal of unwanted desires in the heart (*anartha-nivṛtti*), firm faith in the process of *bhakti* (*niṣṭhā*), experience of taste in performing activities of *bhakti* (*ruci*), feelings of affection towards the Lord (*āsakti*), attainment of deep attachment to the Lord (*bhāva*), and attainment of spontaneous love for the Lord (*prema*). These are the stages of attaining pure love of Kṛṣṇa for the *sādhakas.* (*Bhakti-rasāmṛta-sindhuḥ* 1.4.15–16)

Sādhana-bhakti, which is performed during the devotee's stage of practice, is divided into two categories. These are *vaidhī-bhakti,* or regulative devotional service, and *rāgānugā-bhakti,* or spontaneous devotional service. There is a subtle distinction that is maintained between these two categories of practice and a different result at maturation.

Śrīla Rūpa Gosvāmī gives his definition of regulative devotional service, *vaidhī-bhakti,* as follows:

yatra rāgānavāptatvāt
pravṛttir upajāyate
śāsanenaiva śāstrasya
sā vaidhī bhaktir ucyate

śāstroktayā prabalayā
tat-tan-maryādayānvitā
vaidhi bhaktir iyaṁ kaiścan
maryādā-mārga ucyate

When engagement in *bhakti* occurs solely by the discipline given in scriptures, and not due to spontaneous attachment, such practice is known as *vaidhī-bhakti.* Due to being restricted (*maryādā*) by the strong statements of the scriptures, some people call *vaidhī-bhakti* the path of scriptural restriction (*maryādā-mārga*). (*Bhakti-rasāmṛta-sindhuḥ* 1.2.6, 269)

Śrīla Rūpa Gosvāmī describes spontaneous devotional service, or *rāgānugā-bhakti,* as follows:

virājantīm abhivyaktāṁ
vraja-vāsī janādiṣu
rāgātmikām anusṛtā
yā sā rāgānugocyate

rāgānugā-vivekārtham
ādau rāgātmikocyate

iṣṭe svārasikī rāgaḥ
paramāviṣṭatā bhavet
tan-mayī yā bhaved bhaktiḥ
sātra rāgātmikoditā

sā kāmarūpā sambandha-
rūpā ceti bhaved dvidhā

The eternal residents of Vraja possess and vividly express *rāgātmikā-bhakti,* or devotional service fully in spontaneous love. Engagement in *bhakti* as a follower of the eternal residents of Vraja is known as *rāgānugā-bhakti.* To better understand *rāgānugā-bhakti,* we must define *rāgātmikā-bhakti* first. *Bhakti* composed of spontaneous attraction to Lord Kṛṣṇa according to one's natural inclination to love is known as *rāgātmikā-bhakti.* It can be based either on amorous attraction or on other relationships [parents, friends, etc.]. (*Bhakti-rasāmṛta-sindhuḥ* 1.2.270–3)

Who is qualified for *rāgānugā-bhakti,* or spontaneous *vraja-bhakti*? In this regards, Śrīla Rūpa Gosvāmī has given his conclusion:

rāgātmikāika-niṣṭhā ye
vraja-vāsi-janādayaḥ
teṣāṁ bhāvāptaye lubdho
bhaved atrādhikāravān

tat-tad-bhāvādi-mādhurye
śrute dhīr yad apekṣate
nātra śāstraṁ na yuktiṁ ca
tal-lobhotpatti-lakṣaṇaṁ

vaidha-bhakty-adhikārī
tu bhāvāvirbhavanāvadhi
atra śāstraṁ tathā tarkam
anukūlam apekṣate

kṛṣṇaṁ smaran janaṁ cāsya
preṣṭhaṁ nija-samīhitam
tat-tat-kathā-rataś cāsau
kuryād vāsaṁ vraje sadā

sevā sādhaka-rūpeṇa
siddha-rūpeṇa cātra hi
tad-bhāva-lipsunā kāryā
vraja-lokānusārataḥ

Dinara Lukman

Kṛṣṇa's servants are headed by Raktaka and Patraka.

Dinara Lukman

Kṛṣṇa's friends are headed by Ujjvala and Subala.

Elvira Lukman

Yaśodā, Nanda, Rohiṇī feel parental love for Kṛṣṇa and Balarāma.

Dinara Lukman

On Rādhā's order, Candravālī has put dye on Madhumaṅgala, Kṛṣṇa's friend, during the Holi festival (from *Ānanda-vṛndāvana-campū* of Kavi-karṇapūra).

śravaṇotkīrtanādīni
vaidha-bhakty-uditāni tu
yāny aṅgāni ca tāny atra
vijñeyāni manīṣibhiḥ

The *rāgātmikā* variety of one-pointed devotion is found solely in the residents of Vraja. Those *sādhakas* who are eager to obtain a similar mood are eligible candidates for *rāgānugā-bhakti*. A symptom of the emergence of this spiritual greed is that one's intelligence immediately becomes attracted to the mood of the residents of Vraja on hearing about its sweetness, without caring for scriptural instructions or logical arguments. [In contrast], a person eligible for *vaidhī-bhakti* depends on scripture and logic until *bhāva* or *prema* has arisen.

One who is eligible for *rāgānugā-bhakti*, always meditating on Śrī Kṛṣṇa and his devoteees, should choose a dear associate of Kṛṣṇa [favorable to one's mood] and, residing in Vraja, become absorbed in hearing the pastimes of that devotee and Kṛṣṇa. One who desires to obtain the specific mood of a particular resident of Vraja should perform service externally in the form of a *sādhaka* and internally in the form of a *siddha* according to the mood of that eternally liberated devotee. An intelligent devotee should consider the limbs of *vaidhī-bhakti*, such as hearing and chanting, as limbs of *rāgānugā-bhakti* also. (*Bhakti-rasāmṛta-sindhuḥ* 1.2.291–6)

When devotional service in practice matures, one is endowed with the stage of *bhāva-daśā*, also known as *rati*, or strong attachment. Śrīla Rūpa Gosvāmī describes *rati* as follows:

iyam eva ratiḥ prauḍhā
mahābhāva-daśāṁ vrajet
yā mṛgyā syād vimuktānāṁ
bhaktānāṁ ca varīyasām

syād dṛḍheyaṁ ratiḥ premā
prodyan snehaḥ kramād ayam
syān mānaḥ praṇayo rāgo
anurāgo bhāva ity api

bījam ikṣuḥ sa ca rasaḥ
sa guḍaḥ khaṇḍa eva saḥ

Dinara Lukman

Devotees follow the various processes of *bhakti*.

sa śarkarā sitā sā ca
sā yathā syāt sitopalā

ataḥ prema-vilāsāḥ syur
bhāvāḥ snehādayas tu ṣaṭ
prāyo vyavahriyante'mī
prema-śabdena sūribhiḥ

yasyā yādṛśa-jātīyaḥ
kṛṣṇe premābhyudañcati
tasyāṁ tādṛśa-jātīyaḥ
sa kṛṣṇasyāpy udīyate

When this *rati* [*samarthā*, in which the desire for enjoyment attains oneness with *rati*] attains maturity, it becomes *mahā-bhāva*. It is a difficult state to obtain for devotees in general and even for the liberated souls. When *samarthā-rati* becomes intense, it is called *prema*. On becoming more intense, *prema* turns successively into *sneha* (affection), *māna* (indignation), *praṇaya* (love), *rāga* (attachment), *anurāga* (higher attachment), *bhāva* (ecstasy), etc.

This intensifying is just like sugarcane, which progressively turns to juice, jaggery, candy-sugar, ordinary sugar, white sugar and refined white sugar. The root of all these transformations is the sugarcane. Similarly, *prema* is the root of all the transformations such as *sneha* and *māna*. Thus, devotees sometimes use the general term *prema* for all of these transformations. There are unlimited varieties and details in such *prema* due to the unlimited variety in the living entities. Whatever variety of *prema* arises in those devotees [who are in amorous love with him] Kṛṣṇa reciprocates with them in the same way. (*Ujjvala-nīlamaṇiḥ* 14.57, 59–62)

To answer the original question, with deeper analysis of the love which is connected to the *śṛṅgāra-rasa* of Vraja, we can understand that this *prema* is not generally available from other *sampradāyas*, and then only to a small degree. For this reason, Śrīla Raghunātha Dāsa Gosvāmī instructs all practitioners who desire to attain the mood of the *vrajavāsīs* to accept Śrī Svarūpa Dāmodara, Śrī Sanātana Gosvāmī, Śrī Rūpa Gosvāmī, and all the other recipients of Śrī Kṛṣṇa Caitanya's mercy as their instructing spiritual masters.

2 **Pratijanuḥ: Life after life** Generally, it takes many lives to perfect spontaneous devotional service with symptoms of pure love. However, with mercy perfection can happen very quickly.

ŚRĪLA BHAKTIVINODA ṬHĀKURA'S *MANAḤ-ŚIKṢĀ BHĀṢĀ* – SONG THREE

rāgāveśe vraja-dhāma-vāse yadi tīvra kāma,
thāke tava hṛdaya-bhitare
rādhā-kṛṣṇa-līlā-rasa-paricaryā-sulālasa,
haya yadi nitānta antare

If there is a spontaneous desire and an extreme craving in your heart to live in Vraja in intense blissful passion, and if you have the longing to understand the divine sweetness of Rādhā and Kṛṣṇa's divine play –

bali tabe, śuna, mama mana
bhajana-catura-vara, śrī-svarūpa-dāmodara
prabhu-sevā yāṅhāra jīvana

Then, O heart, listen to me. Svarūpa Dāmodara is the best among experts in *bhajan*, and his very soul is the service of his lord (Caitanya Mahāprabhu).

sa-gaṇa śrī-rūpa-yini, rasa-tattva-jñāna-maṇi,
līlā-tattva ye kaila prakāśa
tāṅhāra agraja bhāi, yāṅhāra samāna nāi,
varṇila ye yugala-vilāsa

Śrī Rūpa and his associates revealed sweet pastimes [of Kṛṣṇa] as the crest jewel of the entire knowledge of *rasa* theory. Rūpa's elder brother [Sanātana], who has no equal, has described the divine couple's eternal, all-blissful love affair.

sei saba mahājane, spaṣṭa prema-vijñāpane,
smara, nama tumi nirantara
bhaktivinodera nati, mahājana-gaṇa prati,
vijñāpita karaha satvara

Offer your respects and constantly remember all such great souls who revealed this love so clearly. Bhaktivinoda respectfully asks all these great souls to quickly grant him attainment of all they have described.

Dinara Lukman

Love of Kṛṣṇa gradually unfolds and blossoms in the heart of a devotee.

VERSE FOUR

असद्वार्तावेश्या विसृज मतिसर्वस्वहरणीः
कथा मुक्तिव्याघ्र्या न शृणु किल सर्वात्मगिलनीः ।
अपि त्यक्त्वा लक्ष्मीपतिरतिमितो व्योमनयनीं
व्रजे राधाकृष्णौ स्वरतिमणिदौ त्वं भज मनः ॥

asad-vārtā-veśyā visṛja mati-sarvasva-haraṇīḥ
kathā mukti-vyāghryā na śṛṇu kila sarvātma-gilanīḥ
api tyaktvā lakṣmī-pati-ratim ito vyoma-nayanīṁ
vraje rādhā-kṛṣṇau sva-rati-maṇi-dau tvaṁ bhaja manaḥ

manaḥ—O mind; *visṛja*—abandon; *asat-vārtā-veśyā*—the prostitute named mundane talk; *mati-sarvasva-haraṇīḥ*—the plunderer of all intelligence; *na śṛṇu kila*—do not listen at all to; *kathāḥ*—talks; *mukti-vyāghryāḥ*—the tigress named liberation; *sarva-ātma-gilanīḥ*—the devourer of all souls; *api tyaktvā*—also give up; *lakṣmī-pati-ratim*—attachment to the husband of Lakṣmī, Śrī Nārāyaṇa; *vyoma-nayanīm*—leading to Vaikuṇṭha; *itaḥ*—here; *vraje*—in Vraja; *tvam*—you; *bhaja*—serve; *rādhā-kṛṣṇau*—Śrī Śrī Rādha-Kṛṣṇa; *sva-rati-maṇi-dau*—the givers of the jewel of their own love.

O mind, abandon the prostitute of mundane talks, who plunders all intelligence. Do not listen at all to the stories of the tigress named *mukti* (liberation), who devours all souls. Moreover, also give up attachment to the husband of Lakṣmī, Śrī Nārāyaṇa, who only leads one to Vaikuṇṭha. Instead, here in Vraja, serve Śrī Śrī Rādha-Kṛṣṇa, who give one the jewel of their own love.

Fadma-gopī Devī Dāsī

The prostitute of mundane talk steals the desire for love of God from the heart.

ŚRĪLA BHAKTIVINODA ṬHĀKURA'S *BHAJANA-DARPAṆA* COMMENTARY

ŚLOKĀRTHA: MEANING OF THE VERSE

1 **Mati-sarvasva-haraṇī asad-vārtā-rūpā-veśyā: Mundane gossip is like a prostitute who plunders the treasure of the heart.** Just as a prostitute takes away wealth and everything else from an immoral person, material gossip plunders one's intelligence. The only wealth of a living being is discriminating intelligence that has spiritual attainment as the goal of life. In contrast, any material gossip in relation to sense enjoyment, or any kind of connection to sense enjoyment, is all temporary and useless.

Even lessons in *śāstra* which promote greed for more wealth, sexual pleasure, or connection with people who are attached to sex are all *asat* – temporary, material, and useless. Any process that increases one's association with and attachment for temporary useless objects is called *asat-vārtā*.

Regarding Kṛṣṇa conscious intelligence (*mati*), Śrī Rāmānanda Rāya has said the following:

kṛṣṇa-bhakti-rasa-bhāvitā matiḥ
krīyatāṁ yadi kuto 'pi labhyate
tatra laulyam api mūlyam ekalaṁ
janma-koṭi-sukṛtair na labhyate

If it is possible to obtain intelligence absorbed in the *rasa* of pure devotional service to Kṛṣṇa, then one must acquire it without delay. Intense greed for that *rasa* is the only price. It cannot be obtained even by pious activity in millions of births. (*Padyāvalī* 14)

2 **Sarvātma-gilanī mukti-vyāghryā kathā: Discussions of mukti, or merging into impersonal Brahman, are like a ferocious tigress which devours everyone's soul.** Here the word *mukti*, or liberation, refers to *brahmā-nirvāṇa*, also called *sāyujya-mukti*. This type of liberation involves merging into either the impersonal Brahman effulgence of God or the body of God directly. *Sāyujya-mukti* negates the eternal

Talk of impersonal liberation is a tigress ready to eat the soul.

individuality of the self. The establishment of this merging as ultimate liberation is based on word manipulation. It is not the ultimate truth, any more than there are flowers growing in the sky. In reality, the only ultimate truth (*parama-tattva*) is the Supreme Personality of Godhead, who is the possessor of all inconceivable potencies.

Those supreme potencies of the Lord are eternal. The divine potency (*cit-śakti*) manifests the Lord's transcendental pastimes. In the form of *māyā* she creates endless material universes, as well as the physical and subtle material bodies of conditioned souls. In her aspect as the marginal potency (*taṭasthā-śakti*) she manifests countless, miniscule living beings (*jīvas*).

Some people are envious of Bhagavān (the Supreme Personal form of God) and his devotees. There are also some who are apathetic to Bhagavān's name, form, qualities, and pastimes, considering them to be imaginary. Although such envious or apathetic persons continue to suffer the reactions of their karma, they experience some sort of pleasure by discussing impersonal liberation. But that happiness is like the happiness of a criminal who commits suicide in order to escape punishment. Therefore, we must very carefully abandon all topics and all contemplation of the process of worship for attaining impersonal liberation. Also, one must give up the association of those who are eager for impersonal liberation. Such liberation is like a tigress who devours the soul.

Śrīla Rūpa Gosvāmī explains this topic as follows:

bhukti-mukti-spṛhā yāvat
piśācī hṛdi vartate
tāvad bhakti-sukhasyātra
katham abhyudayo bhavet

śrī kṛṣṇa-caraṇāmbhoja-
sevā-nirvṛta-cetasām
eṣāṁ mokṣāya bhaktānāṁ
na kadācit spṛhā bhavet

The desire to enjoy the material world and the desire to become liberated from material bondage are considered to be two witches, who

Padma-gopī Devī Dāsī

Impersonal liberation is like a prisoner who contemplates suicide.

Padma-gopī Devī Dāsī

Desires for material enjoyment and liberation are like two witches.

haunt one like ghosts. As long as these witches remain within the heart, how can one feel transcendental bliss? Those dedicated devotees whose minds are always absorbed in the loving service to the lotus feet of Śrī Kṛṣṇa never have the slightest desire for impersonal liberation. (*Bhakti-rasāmṛta-sindhuḥ* 1.2.22, 25)

3 **Vyoma-nayanī lakṣmīpati-rati: The attachment for Lakṣmī-pati Nārāyaṇa takes one to Vaikuṇṭha.** The abode of Nārāyaṇa is known as *para-vyoma* or Vaikuṇṭha, the spiritual world. There, the Supreme Personality of Godhead, the possessor of all opulences in full, resides eternally. In this abode, one can achieve four kinds of liberation by serving the husband of Lakṣmī, Nārāyaṇa: 1 *sārūpya*, achieving the same features and form as Nārāyaṇa; 2 *sāmīpya*, living in Nārāyana's close association; 3 *sālokya*, residing on the same planet with Nārāyana; and 4 *sārṣṭi*, obtaining the same opulences as Nārāyana.

Śrīla Rūpa Gosvāmī very clearly described this as follows:

atra tyājyatayaivoktā
muktiḥ pañca-vidhāpi cet
sālokyādis tathāpy atra
bhaktyā nātivirudhyate

sukhaiśvaryottarā seyaṁ
prema-sevottarety api
sālokyādir dvidhā tatra
nādyā sevā-juṣāṁ matā

kintu premaika-mādhurya-
bhuja ekāntino harau
naivāṅgīkurvate jātu
muktiṁ pañca-vidhām api

tatrāpy ekāntināṁ śreṣṭhā
govinda-hṛta-mānasāḥ
yeṣāṁ śrīśa-prasādo'pi
mano hartuṁ na śaknuyāt

siddhāntatas tv abhede'pi
śrīśa-kṛṣṇa-svarūpayoḥ

Padma-gopī Devī Dāsī

Give up affection for Nārāyaṇa and focus on Kṛṣṇa in Vṛndāvana. The gopīs ask Nārāyaṇa where Kṛṣṇa is.

rasenotkṛṣyate kṛṣṇa-
rūpam eṣā rasa-sthitiḥ

Although this book (*Bhakti-rasāmṛta-sindhuḥ*) has suggested that a devotee give up all five types of liberation, still four out of them [*sārūpya, sāmīpya, sālokya,* and *sārṣṭi*] are not very much against *bhakti*. These four types of liberation may be motivated either by the desire for personal opulence and happiness or by the desire for *prema* in service to Kṛṣṇa. Of these, the first motivation is not suitable for those who only desire loving service.

However, one-pointed devotees of the Lord, who desire to experience only the sweetness of *prema*, do not accept any type of liberation to Vaikuṇṭha. Among all these devotees, those whose minds have been stolen by Govinda are the best. Even the favor of the lord of Lakṣmī, Nārāyaṇa, cannot capture their minds. Although in principle there is no difference between the forms of Nārāyaṇa and Kṛṣṇa, Kṛṣṇa is superior due to principles of *rasa* [divine aesthetics]. Such is the conclusion of the *rasa* point of view. (*Bhakti-rasāmṛta-sindhuḥ* 1.2.55–59)

In this regard Śrīla Haridāsa Ṭhākura has expressed transcendental sentiment:

alaṁ tri-diva-vārtayā kim iti sārva-bhauma-śrīyā
vidūratara-vārtinī bhavatu mokṣa-lakṣmīr api
kalinda-giri-nandinī-taṭa-nikuñja-puñjodare
mano harati kevalaṁ nava-tamāla-nīlaṁ mahaḥ

I've had enough with talk of celestial planets and have no use for a great kingdom on earth! Even the opulence of liberation should go far away from me! My heart is stolen by that person in the groves by the Yamunā whose shining dark-bluish complexion is like a young *tamāla* tree. (*Padyāvalī* 103)

4 **Sva-rati-maṇi-dau: Giving the jewels of their own love** *Sva-rati-dau* also means *ātma-rati-dau.** The soul of all souls is Śrī Śrī Rādhā-Kṛṣṇa, and the love that each individual has towards them is called

* The commentary on verse one gives an explanation of *ātma-rati*.

ātmā-rati. That love is covered by various desires born of ignorance when souls are enchanted by *māyā,* although such love is the *jīvas'* eternal *dharma* in the perfected state. Śrī Īśvara Puri exemplifies this love:

dhanyānāṁ hṛdi bhāsatāṁ girivara-praty-agra-kuñjaukasāṁ
satyānanda-rasaṁ vikāra-vibhava-vyāvṛttam antar-mahaḥ
asmākaṁ kila vallavī-rati-raso vṛndāṭavī-lālaso
gopaḥ ko 'pi mahendra-nīla-ruciraś citte muhuḥ krīḍatu

May the cowherd boy who is a festival of ecstatic bliss for the hearts of the fortunate creatures residing in the groves of Govardhana, who eagerly enjoys loving pastimes in the forests of Vṛndāvana with the *gopīs,* and whose complexion is as splendid as a great sapphire, eternally enjoy transcendental pastimes in our hearts. (*Padyāvalī* 75)

Śrī Mādhavendra Purī has beautifully expressed his enduring attachment for Lord Kṛṣṇa:

rasaṁ praśaṁsantu kavitva-niṣṭhā
brahmāmṛtaṁ veda-śiro-niviṣṭāḥ
vayaṁ tu guñjā-kalitāvataṁsaṁ
gṛhīta-vaṁśaṁ kam api śrayāmaḥ

Those devoted to poetry may praise its sweetness, and those devoted to Vedic study may praise the nectar of impersonal Brahman. We praise neither. We simply take shelter of that person who plays a flute and wears a necklace of *guñjā* berries. (*Padyāvalī* 76)

Śrī Kaviratna also states:

jātu prārthayate na pārthiva-padaṁ naindre pade modate
sandhatte na ca yoga-siddhiṣu dhiyaṁ mokṣaṁ ca nākāṅkṣati
kālindī-vana-sīmāni sthira-taḍin-megha-dyutau kevalam
śuddhe brahmaṇi ballavī-bhuja-latā-baddhe mano dhāvati

My mind never prays for the post of an earthly king nor desires the post of Indra. It does not like the yogic perfections nor yearn for liberation. It only runs after the pure supreme Brahman, who, in the forests by the Yamunā, is bound by the vine of a *gopī's* arm, and so appears like a dark raincloud surrounded by lightning. (*Padyāvalī* 78)

Padma-gopī Devī Dāsī

Rūpa Gosvāmī and Raghunātha Dāsa Gosvāmī talk about Rādhā and Kṛṣṇa near Rādhā-kuṇḍa.

Śrī Mādhavendra Puri also expresses such spiritual sentiments:

anaṅga-rasa-cāturī-capala-cāru-netrāñcalaś
calan-makara-kuṇḍala-sphurita-kānti-gaṇḍa-sthalaḥ
vrajollasita-nāgarī-nikara-rāsa-lāsyotsukaḥ
sa me sapadi mānase sphuratu ko 'pi gopālakaḥ

I pray that a certain cowherd boy, who expertly casts amorous glances from the corners of his beautiful restless eyes, whose splendid cheeks are decorated with glistening, swinging shark-shaped earrings, and who is very eager to enjoy the *rāsa* dance with the radiant girls of Vraja, may at once appear within my heart. (*Padyāvalī* 97)

Only through worshiping Śrī Śrī Rādhā-Kṛṣṇa, the divine couple in Vṛndāvana, will these jewels of attachment awaken within the practitioner's heart, elevating the *sādhaka* to a higher state of ecstasy of love of Godhead called *mahābhāva*.

ŚRĪLA BHAKTIVINODA ṬHĀKURA'S *MANAḤ-ŚIKṢĀ BHĀṢĀ* – SONG FOUR

kṛṣṇa-vārtā vinā āna, asad-vārtā bali' jāna,
sei veśyā ati bhayaṅkarī
śrī-kṛṣṇa-viṣayā mati, jīvera durlabha ati,
sei veśyā mati laya hari'

Discussions about useless things without speaking of Kṛṣṇa are like a frightening prostitute. Such talk takes away thoughts about Kṛṣṇa, which are extremely rare for living beings.

śuna, mana, bali he tomāya
'mukti' nāme śārdūlinī, tā'ra kathā yadi śuni,
sarvātma-sampatti gili' khāya

Listen, O mind, let me tell you. If you listen to the crouching tigress called liberation, *mukti*, it devours all the opulence of the soul.

tad-ubhaya tyāga kara, mukti-kathā parihara,
lakṣmī-pati-rati rākha dūre

se rati prabala ha'le, para-vyome deya phele',
nāhi deya vāsa vraja-pure

Renounce both liberation and useless discussions, and even give up attachment for the Lord's form as Lakṣmī's husband (Nārāyaṇa). If your love for Nārāyaṇa is too strong, it will send you to Vaikuṇṭha (*paravyoma*) and you will not find shelter in Vraja.

braje rādhā-kṛṣṇa-rati, amūlya dhanada ati,
tāi tumi bhaja cira-dina
rūpa-raghunātha-pāya, sei rati-prārthanāya,
e bhaktivinoda dīna-hīna

But love for Rādhā and Kṛṣṇa in Vraja grants a unique and incomparable treasure, so pray for that every day. This lowly and poor Bhaktivinoda prays for such love at the feet of Rūpa and Raghunātha.

VERSE FIVE

असच्चेष्टाकष्टप्रदविकटपाशालिभिरिह
प्रकामं कामादिप्रकटपथपातिव्यतिकरैः ।
गले बद्ध्वा हन्येऽहमिति बकभिद्वर्त्मपगणे
कुरु त्वं फुत्कारानवति स यथा त्वां मन इतः ॥

asac-ceṣṭā-kaṣṭa-prada-vikaṭa-pāśālibhir iha
prakāmaṁ kāmādi-prakaṭa-patha-pāti-vyatikaraiḥ
gale baddhvā hanye 'ham iti bakabhid-vartmapa-gaṇe
kuru tvaṁ phutkārān avati sa yathā tvāṁ mana itaḥ

iha—here [in this world]; *prakaṭa-patha-pāti*—attackers of the sparkling path [of devotion]; *vyatikaraiḥ*—the mob; *prakāmam*—by my own desire; *kāma-ādi*—[who are] lust, etc.; *gale baddhvā*—binding the neck; *vikaṭa-pāśālibhiḥ*—with dreadful nooses; *kaṣṭa-prada*—troublesome; *asat-ceṣṭā*—of wicked endeavors; *hanye aham iti*—I am being killed; *kuru tvam*—you cry out; *phutkārān*—pitieously; *iti baka-bhid-vartmapa-gaṇe*—like this to devotees of Kṛṣṇa, the killer of Baka; *manaḥ*—O mind; *avati sa yathā*—so that they will save; *tvām*—you; *itaḥ*—from these enemies.

"While here on the revealed path of devotion, I have been attacked by the gang of my own lust, etc., who have bound my neck with the troublesome dreadful ropes of wicked deeds. I am being killed!" Cry out piteously like this to the devotees of Śrī Kṛṣṇa, the destroyer of Baka. O mind, they will save you from these enemies.

Six highway robbers wait to attack people who travel on the shining path of *bhakti*.

Anger

Envy

Greed

Elvira Lukman

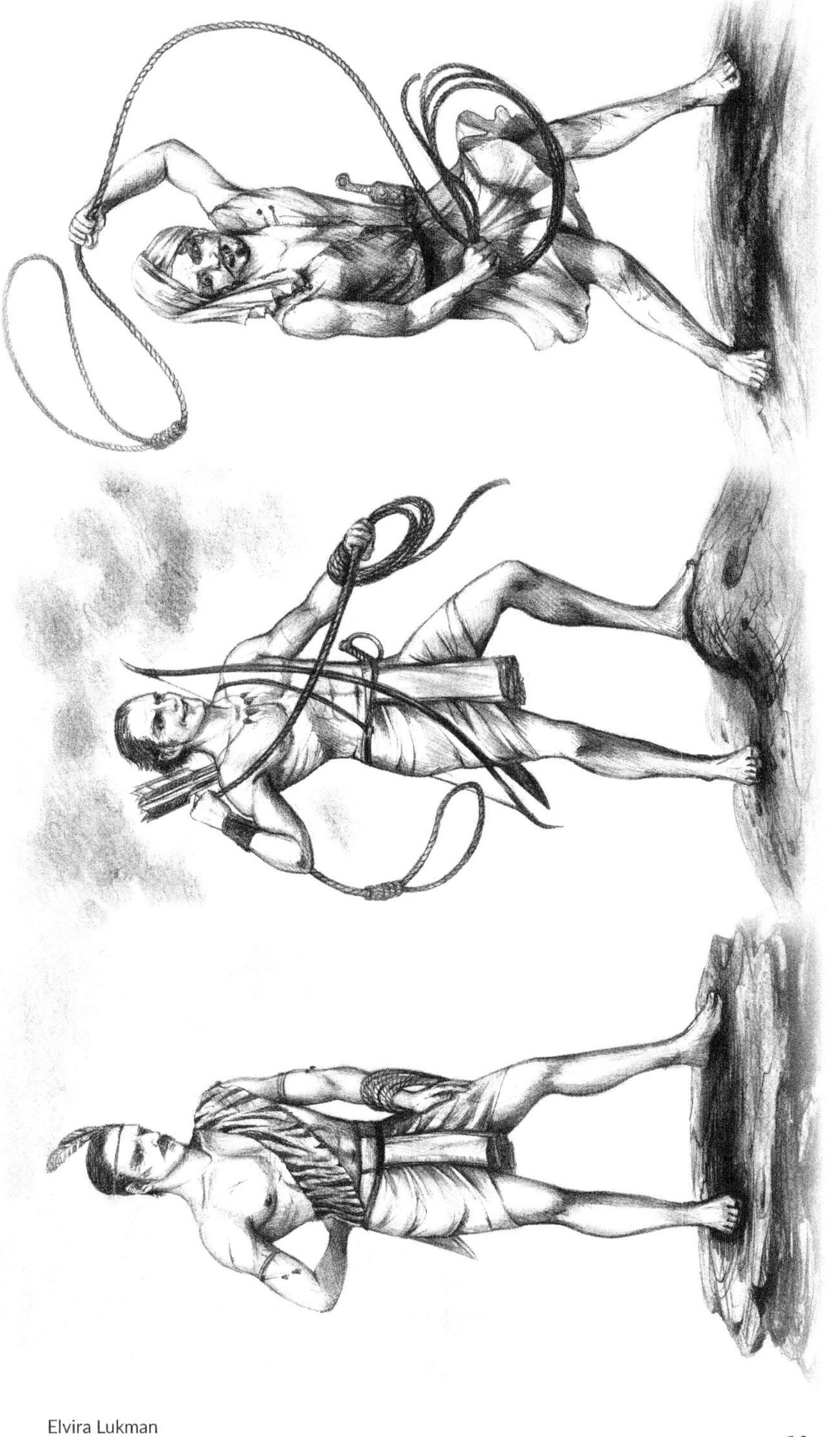

Illusion

Lust

Madness

The six enemies capture devotees by putting nooses around their necks.

Elvira Lukman

Call for the help of the servants of Kṛṣṇa, killer of Baka.

The servants of Baka's killer, Kṛṣṇa, can free us from the ropes of wicked deeds.

Dinera and Elvira Lukman

The teachings of the great devotees can free us from the ropes of wicked deeds.

ŚRĪLA BHAKTIVINODA ṬHĀKURA'S *BHAJANA-DARPAṆA* COMMENTARY

ŚLOKĀRTHA: MEANING OF THE VERSE

1 **Kāmādi-prakaṭa-patha-pāti-vyatikaraiḥ: Lust, etc. – the gang of plunderers on the open road** Lust, anger, greed, illusion, false pride, and envy are plunderers on the open road of one's spiritual life. These six muggers attack their victims forcefully upon meeting together.

In *Śrīmad Bhagavad-gītā* (2.62–3), a clear explanation is given on this subject matter.

dhyāyato viṣayān puṁsaḥ
saṅgas teṣūpajayate
saṅgāt saṣjāyate kāmaḥ
kāmāt krodho 'bhijāyate

krodhād bhavati saṁmohaḥ
sammohāt smṛti-vibhramaḥ
smṛti-bhraṁśād buddhi-nāśo
buddhi-nāśāt praṇaśyati

While contemplating the objects of the senses, a person develops attachment for them, and from such attachment lust develops, and from lust anger arises. From anger, complete delusion arises, and from delusion bewilderment of memory. When memory is bewildered, intelligence is lost, and when intelligence is lost one falls down again into the material pool.

Śrīla Baladeva Vidyābhūṣaṇa has explained the meaning of these two verses:

vijitendriyasyāpi mayy aniveśita-manasaḥ punar anartho durvāra ity āha dhyāyata iti dvyābhyām. viṣayān śabdādīn sukha-hetutva-buddhyā dhyāyataḥ punaḥ punaś cintayato yoginas teṣu saṅga āsaktir bhavati. saṅgād dhetos teṣu kāma-tṛṣṇā jāyate. kāmāc ca kenacit pratihatāt krodhaś citta-jvālas tat-pratighātako bhavati. krodhāt saṁmohaḥ kāryākārya-viveka-vijṣāna-vilopaḥ. saṁmohāt smṛter indriya-vijayādi-prayatnānusandher vibhramo vibhraṁśaḥ.

Elvira Lukman

Contemplation of sense enjoyment leads to attachment, lust, anger, bewilderment of memory, loss of intelligence, and material bondage.

Elvira Lukman

The ropes are made of wicked deeds.

smṛti-bhraṁśād buddher ātma-jṣānārthakasyādhyavasāyasya nāśaḥ. buddhi-nāśāt praṇaśyati punar viṣaya-bhoga-nimagno bhavati saṁsaratīty arthaḥ. madanāśrayaṇād durbalaṁ manas tāni sva-viṣayair yojayantīti bhāvaḥ. tathā ca mano-vijigīṣuṇā mad-upāsanaṁ vidheyam.

"Even for those persons who have conquered their senses; if their mind is not fixed on me (Kṛṣṇa), then the mind again becomes unfavorable and irrepressible," the Lord says in these two verses (2.62–63). The Lord continues to say, "When the sense-objects such as sound, touch etc. are meditated upon in order to attain gratification, then the *yogi* who thinks repeatedly about them develops a strong attachment to such sense objects. Due to such association with sense objects, a strong desire for those objects is born [in the *yogi's* mind]. If somehow the *yogi* is able to check the fulfillment of such strong desires, then the result is the generation of anger due to dissatisfaction, which burns the heart, thereby disturbing the *yogi*.

"From such disturbing anger comes bewilderment, which is nothing but a loss of discrimination about what should be done and what should be avoided. Due to loss of discriminatory power of the intelligence, the efforts of conquering over the senses start faltering, and by such forgetfulness the enthusiasm of the intelligence to gain knowledge of the self is lost. By such loss of intelligence, the *yogi* falls down. In other words, such a *yogi* again becomes absorbed in sense-enjoyment and wanders in such enjoyment. The gist is that the weak mind, having taken shelter of the lust god, engages such *yogis* in the service of its own objects. Therefore, my worship is prescribed for those who wish to fully conquer the mind." (*Gītā-bhūṣaṇa-bhāṣya*)

2 **Asac-ceṣṭā-kaṣṭa-prada-vikaṭa-pāśa: The troublesome dreadful ropes of wicked deeds** The six enemies – lust, anger, greed, illusion, madness, and envy – have been previously explained. They create wicked deeds that are like a rope that ties up the neck of the living being, and which causes pain and fear.

3 **Baka-bhid-vartmapa-gaṇe: Protectors of the path leading to the killer of the Baka demon** *Baka-bhid* refers to Śrī Kṛṣṇa, the killer of the Baka demon. The demon Baka (crane) is the embodiment of

Elvira Lukman

Kṛṣṇa is the killer of the personification of hypocrisy, Bakāsura.

duplicitous hypocrisy. Śrī Kṛṣṇa killed Baka by splitting his beak into two pieces. *Vartma* indicates following the devotional path, which brings about cultivation of love for Kṛṣṇa. The suffix *pa* refers to the Vaiṣṇavas, the devotees of Kṛṣṇa, who are the protectors and guardians of that devotional path. The conclusion is that one should cry desperately to the Vaiṣṇavas for protection from all unwanted enemies such as lust, anger, greed, and all other *anarthas*. The merciful Vaiṣṇavas will definitely provide protection upon hearing a living being's cries.

For example, one great devotee from southern India prays:

prahlāda-nārada-parāśara-puṇḍarīka-
vyāsāmbarīṣa-śuka-śaunaka-bhīṣma-dalbhyān
rukmāṅgadoddhava-vibhīṣaṇa-phālgunādīn
puṇyān imān parama-bhāgavatān namāmi

To the saintly devotees of the Lord, headed by Prahlāda, Nārada, Parāśara, Puṇḍarīka, Vyāsa, Ambarīṣa, Śuka, Śaunaka, Bhīṣma, Dalbhya, Rukmāṅgada, Uddhava, Vibhīṣaṇa, and Arjuna, I offer my respectful obeisances. (*Padyāvalī* 52)

Śrī Sarvajña prays:

tvad-bhaktaḥ saritāṁ patiṁ culukavat khadyotavad bhāskaraṁ
merum paśyati loṣṭravat kim aparaṁ bhūmeḥ patiṁ bhṛtyāvat
cintāratna-cayaṁ śilā-sakala vat kalpa-drumaṁ kaṣṭavat
saṁsāraṁ tṛṇa-rāśivat kim aparaṁ dehaṁ nijaṁ bhāravat

O Lord, your devotee sees the king of rivers as a handful of water, the sun a firefly, Mount Meru a clump of earth, the emperor of the world a servant, a multitude of *cintāmaṇi* jewels simply pebbles, a valuable *kalpa-vṛkṣa* tree a mere stick, the entire world a bunch of straw, and his own body a burden only. (*Padyāvalī* 56)

Śrī Mādhava Sarasvatī describes further:

mīmāṁsā-rajasā malīmasa-dṛśāṁ tāvan na dhīr īsvare
garvodarka-ku-karkaṣa-dhiyāṁ dūre 'pi vartā hareḥ
jānanto 'pi na jānate śruti-mukhaṁ śrī-raṅgi-saṅgād ṛte
su-svāduṁ pariveśayanty api rasam gurvī na darvī spṛśet

Elvira Lukman

Non-devotee scholars who study the scriptures are like ornate serving spoons that distribute the sweetest nectar but cannot taste it themselves.

> Those whose eyes are blinded by the dust of the *karma-mīmāṁsā* philosophy cannot fix their hearts on the Supreme Personality of Godhead. Those whose intelligence is atrophied by illogical conclusions dictated by pride stay far away from the topics of Lord Hari. Those who seem to understand the Vedas but cannot become devotees of Lord Kṛṣṇa do not actually understand the Vedas. They are like large ladles that distribute the sweetest nectar but cannot taste it themselves. (*Padyāvalī* 57)

The glories of the devotees' association are explained when Hiraṇyakaśipu speaks to Prahlāda about the importance of association in general.

yasya yat-saṅgatiḥ puṁso
maṇivat syāt sa tad-guṇaḥ
sva-kula-rddhyai tato dhīmān
sva-yūthān eva saṁśrayet

> Just as a transparent crystal takes on the colors of nearby objects, the association of a person determines one's qualities. Therefore, the intelligent take shelter in like-minded, similarly practicing groups for the sake of bringing auspiciousness and prosperity to their group. (*Hari-bhakti-sudhodaya*, quoted in *Bhakti-rasāmṛta-sindhuḥ* 1.2.229)

The essence is that the impurities of the heart cannot be obliterated with yoga or fire sacrifices. Through the association of a Vaiṣṇava who is free from envy, gradually those impurities will be removed.

ŚRĪLA BHAKTIVINODA ṬHĀKURA'S *MANAḤ-ŚIKṢĀ BHĀṢĀ* – SONG FIVE

kāma-krodha-lobha-moha-mada, matsaratā-saha,
jīvera jīvana-pathe basi'
asat-ceṣṭā-rajju-phāṅse, pathikera dharma-nāśe,
prāṇa la'ye kare kaṣākaṣi

Desire, anger, greed, bewilderment, intoxication, and pride are six enemies that wait on the path of a soul's journey of life. They have lassoes which pull that soul so he slips from righteousness (*dharma*)

Dinara Lukman

Association with great devotees makes our heart,
like a crystal gem, reflect their qualities.

and performs unscrupulous activities (*asat-ceṣṭā**). These enemies pull tightly to drag away one's life.

mana, tumi dhara vākya mora
ei saba bāṭapāḍa, atiśaya durnivāra,
yakhana gheriyā kare jora

O heart! Please seriously consider my words. These highway robbers are incredibly difficult to resist. Thus, whenever they surround and attack you, –

āra kichu nā kariyā, vaiṣṇavera nāma lai'yā
phukāriyā ḍāka uccarāya
baka-śatru-senā-gaṇe, kṛpā kari' nija-jane
yā'te kare uddhāra tomāya

Do nothing else but utter the name of Vaiṣṇavas at the top of your voice. Then the soldiers of Kṛṣṇa, the slayer of Bakāsura, will come to save you out of their mercy. The devotees of Lord Kṛṣṇa will come and save you from these enemies!

bāṭapāḍa chaya-jana, asate-ceṣṭā rajju-gaṇa,
diyā gale karila bandhana
prāṇa-vāyu gata-prāya, rūpa-raghunātha hāya,
kara bhaktivinode rakṣaṇa

Bhaktivinoda says, "These six horrible enemies have tied me up and tightened the noose of unscrupulous activities around my neck. My life-breath has almost left me, O Rūpa-Raghunātha! Please protect me!"

* In Sanskrit, *asat* means impermanent (*sat* is existence), but can also mean untruth. In Bengali, *asat* means unscrupulous, and *ceṣṭā* means efforts or activities.

VERSE SIX

अरे चेतः प्रोद्यत्कपटकुटिनाटीभरखर
क्षरन्मूत्रे स्नात्वा दहसि कथमात्मानमपि माम् ।
सदा त्वं गान्धर्वागिरिधरपदप्रेमविलसत्
सुधाम्भोधौ स्नात्वा त्वमपि नितरां मां च सुखय ॥

are cetaḥ prodyat-kapaṭa-kuṭināṭī-bhara-khara-
kṣaran-mūtre snātvā dahasi katham ātmānam api mām
sadā tvaṁ gāndharvā-giridhara-pada-prema-vilasat-
sudhāmbhodhau snātvā tvam api nitarāṁ māṁ ca sukhaya

are—O ruffian; *cetaḥ*—mind; *katham*—why; *dahasi*—do you burn; *ātmānam*—yourself; *api mām*—and me [the soul]; *snātvā*—by bathing; *kṣaran-mūtre*—in the trickling urine of; *bhara-khara*—the great donkey named; *prodyat-kapaṭa-kuṭināṭī*—full-blown hypocrisy and duplicity; *sadā tvam*—[instead] you should always; *snātvā*—by bathing; *nitarām*—always; *sudhā-ambhodhau*—in the nectarean ocean of; *gāndharvā-giridhara-pada-prema-vilasat*—the love emanating from the lotus feet of Śrī Śrī Gāndharvikā-Giridhārī; *sukhaya*—delight; *tvam*—yourself; *api māṁ ca*—and me too.

O ruffian mind! Why do you burn yourself and me [the soul] by bathing in the trickling urine of the great donkey of full-blown hypocrisy and duplicity? Instead, you should always bathe in the ocean of love emanating from the lotus feet of Śrī Śrī Gāndharvikā-Giridhārī, thereby delighting yourself and me.

Elvira Lukman

Those devotees who have defeated the six enemies headed by lust
may still be burned by the donkey urine of hypocrisy and deceit.

ŚRĪLA BHAKTIVINODA ṬHĀKURA'S *BHAJANA-DARPAṆA* COMMENTARY

This verse gives advice to those practitioners who may be able to subdue the six enemies of lust, anger, greed, illusion, madness and envy, but have failed to vanquish the great enemies of deceit and hypocrisy.

ŚLOKĀRTHA: MEANING OF THE VERSE

1 **Prodyat-kapaṭa-kuṭināṭī-bhara-khara-kṣaran-mūtre snātvā** This verse describes bathing in the trickling urine of the donkey of complete, ostentatious duplicity and hypocrisy.

There are three categories of spiritual practitioners, or *sādhakas*. The *sva-niṣṭha-sādhaka* only endeavors to please Śrī Bhagavān, Lord Hari, and completely rejects all the regulations and injunctions of *varṇāśrama-dharma*.* *Pariniṣṭha-sādhakas* engage themselves in all prescribed activities, taking shelter of all the rites and rituals used to worship the Supreme Lord. These two types are *gṛhasthas*, householders. The third type of *sādhaka* is *nirapekṣa*, a devotee who is renounced. Such persons are of a detached nature and not in the *gṛhastha-āśrama*. All three types are benefited only when they become thoroughly honest and give up deceit, pretense, and hypocrisy; otherwise, they are surely vanquished.

Each type of *sādhaka* has distinct ways of exhibiting a deceitful nature. The deceitful nature of the *sva-niṣṭha-sādhaka* can be exhibited in six ways: 1 indulging in sense gratification on the pretext of satisfying the supreme God, 2 serving rich influential materialists instead of serving simple *nirapekṣa* servants of Kṛṣṇa, 3 accumulating more wealth than would ever be needed, 4 enthusiasm for meaning-

* The original Bengali commentary reads, *sva-niṣṭha sādhaka-gaṇa varṇāśrama-vihita vidhi-samūhera pālana o niṣedha-samūhera sampūrṇa parihāra karata bhagavān harike santuṣṭa karite ceṣṭā karena*. Based on how a reader applies grammatical rules, the meanings may vary. The words *sampūrṇa parihāra*, or complete rejection, apply to *varṇāśrama vidhi-samuhera pālana*, or observing the rules of *varṇāśrama*, coupled with *niṣedha-samūha*, or collective prohibitions. More literally, *pālana* (observing) and *parihāra* (rejecting) can be taken to apply to *varṇaśrama-vihita vidhi* and *niṣedha* respectively. These two variant readings offer quite different meanings.

Sva-niṣṭha householder devotees only try to please Kṛṣṇa without the need for *varṇāśrama-dharma*.

A *sva-niṣṭha* devotee may exhibit hypocrisy by seeking sense enjoyment instead of pleasing the Lord, serving rich materialists instead of Vaiṣṇavas, desiring to accumulate wealth and opulence, or engaging in twisted logic instead of spiritual knowledge.

Dinara and Elvira Lukman

Parinișṭha householder devotees worship the Lord by engaging in prescribed activities and rituals.

Dinara and Elvira Lukman

Elvira Lukman

A *parinișțha* devotee may exhibit hypocrisy by pretending to be strict but privately being attached to mundane things, or by preferring the company of non-devotees.

less temporary gains, even at the cost of envying and harming others, 5 teaching twisted logic and self-motivated speculation in the name of giving education, instead of cultivating spiritual knowledge, and 6 wearing the dress of a materially disinterested renunciate in order to gain material prestige.

The decitful nature of the *pariniṣṭha-sādhaka* can be exhibited in two ways: 1 making an external show of strictly following rules and prohibitions while inwardly being very attached to material subjects unrelated to Kṛṣṇa, and 2 preferring the association of non-devotees rather than Kṛṣṇa conscious devotees.

The deceitful nature of the *nirapekṣa-sādhaka* can be exhibited in eight ways: 1 thinking of oneself as an advanced Vaiṣṇava, 2 thinking of oneself as superior to others simply by wearing the dress of a renounced person, 3 collecting material wealth for food and clothing

Nirapekṣa devotees are detached and live as renunciates.

Elvira Lukman

Dinara and Elvira Lukman

Elvira Lukman

Elvira Lukman

A *nirapekṣa* devotee may exhibit hypocrisy by thinking, "I am an advanced Vaiṣṇava," acting superior to others, collecting more than required, associating improperly with the opposite sex in the name of spiritual practices, ...

Dinara and Elvira Lukman

Dinara and Elvira Lukman

Dinara and Elvira Lukman

Dinara and Elvira Lukman

… befriending materialistic people with the hope for wealth, being concerned with external dress and rules, or neglecting the main purpose of spiritual life – keeping one's heart locked in a box while externally engaging in *bhakti*.

more than required, 4 improperly associating with the opposite sex in the name of spiritual practices, 5 staying with materialistic people with the expectation of receiving wealth rather than visiting Kṛṣṇa's temple, 6 being inwardly anxious and worried about collecting more wealth while making a pretense of performing devotional service or chanting, 7 being more concerned with external dress and rules and regulations than devotion for Kṛṣṇa, and 8 overlooking or neglecting the main purpose of spiritual life (developing love for Kṛṣṇa).

Various cheating propensities (*kapaṭatā*), such as bad arguments (*ku-tarka*), false philosophical conclusions (*ku-siddhānta*), and maintaining impediments to devotional service (*anarthas*), arise from a deceitful nature. All of these propensities are very detrimental to true Kṛṣṇa consciousness and are compared to the urine of a donkey. Many practitioners may think they are getting cleansed by bathing in the unholy urine of the donkey of deceit. Factually they are just burning and destroying their own lives.

2 **Gāndharvā-giridhara-pada-prema-vilasat-sudhā-ambhodhau snātvā** Instead, one should bathe in the ocean of nectarean love that emanates from the lotus feet of Śrī Śrī Gāndharvā-Giridhārī.

Gāndharvā refers to Śrīmatī Rādhikā, who is the internal energy (*svarūpa-śakti*) of the Supreme Personality of Godhead. Giridhārī refers to Śrī Kṛṣṇa, the Supreme Personality of Godhead, who possesses all unlimited inconceivable potencies, and is thus known as *śaktimān-puruṣa*. Here one is advised to bathe in the *viśuddha-cid-vilāsa*, the ocean of nectar of transcendental spiritual transformation. This nectar arises from love of the shelter of Gāndhārva-Giridhārī's lotus feet.

To elaborate this subject, Śrīla Rūpa Gosvāmī prays in the *Śrī Prārthanā-paddhatiḥ* of his *Stava-mālā* as follows:

śuddha-gāṅgeya-gaurāṅgīṁ
kuraṅgī-laṅgimekṣaṇām
jita-koṭīndu-bimbāsyām
ambudāmbara-saṁvṛtām

navīna-vallavī-vṛnda-
dhammillotphulla-mallikām

divya-ratnādy-alaṅkāra-
sevyamāna-tanu-śriyam

vidagdha-maṇḍala-guruṁ
gaṇa-gaurava-maṇḍitām
atipreṣṭha-vayasyābhir
aṣṭābhir abhiveṣṭitām

cañcalāpāṅga-bhaṅgena
vyākulīkṛta-keśavām
goṣṭhendra-suta-jīvātu-
ramya-bimbādharāmṛtām

tvām asau yācate natvā
viluṭhan yamunā-taṭe
kākubhir vyākula-svānto
jano vṛndāvaneśvari

kṛtāgaske 'py ayogye 'pi
jane 'smin kumatāv api
dāsya-dāna-pradānasya
lavam apy upapādaya

yuktas tvayā jano naiva
duḥkhito 'yam upekṣitum
kṛpād-dyota-dravac-citta-
navanītāsi yat sadā

O Śrī Rādhā, I offer obeisance to you. You have a complexion of pure golden hue, possess of a pair of doe-like restless eyes, have a face that conquers the beauty of millions of full moons, and dress in dark cloud-like garments. Your hair is decorated by the *gopīs* using *mallikā* (jasmine) flowers, and your body is decorated with divine gems and ornaments. You are the guru of all the expert *gopīs,* the receiver of the admiration of your followers, extremely dear to your confidantes, and surrounded by your eight primary *sakhīs* (female friends). By a mere movement of the corners of your eyes, you make Lord Keśava restless, and the nectar of your delightful lips is the only source of life for the son of Nanda Mahārāja.

Having offered obeisances in these ways, I, a distressed soul belonging to you, beg you with sweet words while rolling on the banks

Dinara Lukman

"O Śrī Rādhā, please bestow on me a fragment of the gift of service to you."

of the Yamunā! Although I am unfit, an offender with a crooked mind, please bestow on me a fragment of the gift of service to you. This unhappy soul is not fit to be neglected by you, for you have a butter-soft heart that melts constantly by the warmth of your compassion.

Śrīla Rūpa Gosvāmī further elaborates on this subject matter in his *Śrī Śrī Rādhā-Mādhavayor Nāma-yugāṣṭakam* of his *Stava-mālā*:

rādhā-mādhavayor etad
vakṣye nāma-yugāṣṭkam
rādhā-dāmodarau pūrvaṁ
rādhikā-mādhavau tataḥ

vṛṣabhānu-kumārī ca
tathā gopendra-nandanaḥ
govindasya priya-sakhī
gāndharvā-bāndhavas tathā

nikuñja-nāgarau goṣṭha-
kiśora-jana-śekharau
vṛndāvanādhipau kṛṣṇa-
vallabhārādhikā-priyau

I now recite the following eight names of Śrī Śrī Rādhā-Mādhava: 1 She is Rādhā and he is Dāmodara, whom she bound during the month of Kārttika. 2 She is Rādhikā and he is Mādhava, the husband of the goddess of fortune. 3 She is *vṛṣabhānu-kumārī,* the daughter of Vṛṣabhānu, and he is *gopendra-nandana,* the son of Nanda Mahārāja, the king of cowherds. 4 She is *govinda-priya-sakhī,* the dear female friend of Govinda, and he is *gāndharvā-bāndhava,* the dear male friend of Gāndharvā. 5 They are *nikunja-nāgarau,* the couple enjoying amorous moods in the forest bowers of Vṛndāvana; 6 *goṣṭha-kiśora-jana-śekharau,* the leaders of the young *gopīs* and *gopas* of Vṛndāvana; and 7 *vṛndāvanadhipau,* the two presiding rulers of Vṛndāvana. 8 She is *kṛṣṇa-vallabhā,* the dear darling of Kṛṣṇa, and he is *rādhikā-priya,* the beloved of Śrī Rādhikā.

One's deceitful nature is removed when the heart is completely pure with humility. Taking shelter of such names and soaking one's mind in the spiritual *rasas,* please ceaselessly wander around in the land of Vṛndāvana, meditating on Śrī Śrī Rādhā-Govinda's pastimes throughout the periods of the day (*aṣṭa-kālīya-līlā*). Then the mind, purified by humility, will not give any space to deceit. Otherwise, the moment any other thought is given an opening, deceit again attacks.

ŚRĪLA BHAKTIVINODA ṬHĀKURA'S *MANAḤ-ŚIKṢĀ BHĀṢĀ* – SONG SIX

kāma-krodha-ādi kari', bāhire se saba ari,
āche eka gūḍha śatru tava
'kapaṭatā'- nāma tā'ra, tāre kuṭi-nāṭi bhāra
khara-mūrti parama kitava

Aside from desire, anger and the other thieves, there is one subtler enemy of yours. His name is Deceit, and is also known as Insincerity. That enemy is a tricky entity, and is in the form of a donkey.

ore mana, gūḍha kathā dhara
sei khara-mūtre bhule, snāna kari' kutūhale,
'pavitra' baliyā mane kara

My dear mind, please try to understand the deeper essence. You are joyfully bathing in this donkey's urine by mistake, thinking it to be something pure.

vane vā gṛhe thāka, sei khare dūre rākha,
yā'ra mūtre tumi āmi jvali
chāḍiyā kāpaṭya-vaśa, yugala-vilāsa-rasa-
sāgare karaha snāna-keli

Whether you live in a forest or at home, keep away from that donkey whose urine burns both you and me. Let's escape the charm of our own duplicity, and sportingly bathe in the beautiful ocean of the divine couple's sweet love.

rūpa-raghunātha-pāya, e bhaktivinoda cāya,
dekhite yugala-rasa-sindhu
jīvana sārthaka kare, sarva-jīva-citta hare,
sei sāgarera eka bindu

At the lotus feet of Rūpa and Raghunātha, Bhaktivinoda begs to see that beautiful ocean of the divine couple's love. A single drop from that ocean makes life worth living, and steals away the hearts and minds of all living beings.

Dinara Lukman

There is an ocean of love in the service of Kṛṣṇa, the son of King Nanda and his queen, Yaśodā.

VERSE SEVEN

प्रतिष्ठाशा धृष्टा श्वपचरमणी मे हृदि नटेत्
कथं साधुप्रेमा स्पृशति शुचिरेतन् ननु मनः ।
सदा त्वं सेवस्व प्रभुदयितसामन्तमतुलं
यथा तां निष्काश्य त्वरितमिह तं वेशयति सः ॥

pratiṣṭhāśā dhṛṣṭā śvapaca-ramaṇī me hṛdi naṭet
kathaṁ sādhu-premā spṛśati śucir etan nanu manaḥ
sadā tvaṁ sevasva prabhu-dayita-sāmantam atulaṁ
yathā tāṁ niṣkāśya tvaritam iha taṁ veśayati saḥ

dhṛṣṭā—unchaste; *śva-paca-ramaṇī*—dog-eating woman; *pratiṣṭhā-āśā*—desire for prestige; *naṭet*—dances; *me hṛdi*—in my heart; *katham*—how can; *śuciḥ*—pure; *sādhu-premā*—chaste lady of love for Kṛṣṇa*; *spṛśati*—touch; *etan*—this heart; *nanu manaḥ*—O mind; *sadā tvam*—you should always; *sevasva*—serve; *atulam*—incomparable; *prabhu-dayita-sāmantam*—beloved devotee commander of the Lord's army; *yathā*—so that; *saḥ*—he [the devotee commander]; *tāṁ niṣkāśya*—throw her [the prostitute] out; *tvaritam*—immediately; *taṁ veśayati*—establish her [*premā*]; *iha*—here [in the heart].

As long as the unchaste, dog-eating woman of desire for prestige dances in my heart, how can the chaste and pure lady of love for Kṛṣṇa touch it? Therefore, O mind, you should always serve the incomparable, beloved devotee commander of Kṛṣṇa's army, who will immediately throw out the unchaste woman and establish the pure lady of love in the heart.

* *Sādhu-premā* can mean: 1 love for *sādhus,* 2 the love that *sādhus* give to you, or 3 the love of Kṛṣṇa that *sādhus* help manifest in your heart. By using *premā,* a feminine form of *prema,* Raghunātha Dāsa Gosvāmī emphasizes the feminine nature of this love to contrast with the unchaste, dog-eating woman of desire for prestige.

Elvira Lukman

"As long as the unchaste, dog-eating woman of desire for prestige dances in my heart, how can the chaste and pure lady of love for Kṛṣṇa touch it?"

Elvira Lukman

The promiscuous woman dances with her illicit lover, deceit.

ŚRĪLA BHAKTIVINODA ṬHĀKURA'S *BHAJANA-DARPAṆA* COMMENTARY

This verse answers any doubts about why a person who has given up material enjoyment may still have deceit in the heart.

ŚLOKĀRTHA: MEANING OF THE VERSE

1 **Dhṛṣṭā śvapaca-ramaṇī pratiṣṭhāśa: The desire for prestige is an unchaste, dog-eating woman.** *Pratiṣṭhāśā* is the desire or hope for honor. Even though one may have dispelled the other *anarthas* (unwanted things), it is not easy to uproot *pratiṣṭhāśā*. It nourishes and generates the other forms of deceit. This desire for honor is the root of all other *anarthas,* but since it is never able to recognize its own fault, it is shameless. Fame is like dog-flesh, and one eager for such fame is called *dhṛṣṭā śvapaca-ramaṇī,* a dog-eating promiscuous woman.

In the previous verse the three types of *sādhakas* were explained. Each type demonstrates the desire for *pratiṣṭhā* in a different way. A *sva-niṣṭha-sādhaka* wants to become renowned as religious, benevolent, and sinless. A *pariniṣṭha-sādhakas* hopes to be known as a devotee of Viṣṇu, as a knower of spiritual subject matters, and as detached. And a *nirapekṣa-sādhaka* wants to be known as spotless and renounced, as a master of the conclusions of *śāstra,* and as having a perfect understanding of devotion. As long as one maintains a desire for honor (*pratiṣṭhā*), deceit (*kapaṭatā*) will also remain. And until one is free from deceit, one cannot obtain the saintly people's pure love.

2 **Śucir sādhu-premā: Pure love of God** Śrīla Rūpa Gosvāmī states:

samyaṅ-masṛṇita-svānto
mamatvātiśayāṅkitaḥ
bhāvaḥ sa eva sāndrātmā
budhaiḥ premā nigadyate

When *bhāva* condenses and intensifies, it softens the heart completely, and one becomes filled with great attachment and possessiveness towards Kṛṣṇa. That intense love is called *premā* [love for Kṛṣṇa of a feminine nature] by learned scholars. (*Bhakti-rasāmṛta-sindhuḥ* 1.4.1)

The generals of the devotee army cast out the woman and her lover from the heart.

Dinara and Elvira Lukman

Kṛṣṇa himself sends the woman and her lover out of the heart.

Elvira Lukman

The desire for honor is the root of the plant of deceit and pretentiousness.

Elvira Lukman

All three categories of *sādhakas* should avoid the desire to enjoy being honored and glorified.

Elvira Lukman

The chaste lady of spiritual love enters a clean heart.

Only when the desire for *pratiṣṭhā* is cast away does one's whole heart become softened. Otherwise it is not possible.

3 **Prabhu-dayita-atula-sāmanta: Powerful incomparable commanders of Śrī Kṛṣṇa** The meaning of *prabhu-dayita* is a pure servant of Kṛṣṇa. The word *atula* indicates that there is no comparison to such a servant who is a *sāmanta,* a special commander of the Lord. The rays of the Lord's internal pleasure potency are always reflected in the heart of such a devotee. This potency can very easily flow and accumulate in the heart of another individual, which will cast away any misgivings and help pure love to grow there. This flow of spiritual potency can happen through the pure devotees' embrace, the dust from their lotus feet, their leftover food, and their beautiful instructions. Thus, Lord Śiva says in the *Padma-purāṇa*:

ārādhanānāṁ sarveṣāṁ
viṣṇor ārādhanaṁ param
tasmāt parataraṁ devī
tadīyānāṁ samarcanam

Of all kinds of worship, worship of Lord Viṣṇu is the best. Recommended more than worship of Viṣṇu is worship of the Vaiṣṇava.

In *Śrīmad-Bhāgavatam* (3.7.19–20) it is further stated:

yat-sevayā bhagavataḥ
kūṭa-sthasya madhu-dviṣaḥ
rati-rāso bhavet tīvraḥ
pādayor vyasanārdanaḥ

durāpā hy alpa-tapasaḥ
sevā vaikuṇṭha-vartmasu
yatropagīyate nityaṁ
deva-devo janārdanaḥ

By serving the feet of the spiritual master, one is enabled to develop transcendental ecstasy in the service of the Personality of Godhead, who is the unchangeable enemy of the Madhu demon and whose service vanquishes one's material distresses. Persons whose austerity is meager can hardly obtain the service of the pure devotees who

Dinara Lukman

The Pāṇḍavas, generals in the devotee army.

are progressing on the path back to the kingdom of Godhead, the Vaikuṇṭhas. Pure devotees engage one hundred percent in glorifying the Supreme Lord, who is the lord of the demigods and the controller of all living entities.

In the *Caitanya-caritāmṛta* (*Antya-līlā* 16.60–61) it is said:

bhakta-pada-dhūli āra bhakta-pada-jala
bhakta-bhukta-avaśeṣa, – tina mahābala
ei tina-sevā haite kṛṣṇa-prema haya
punaḥ punaḥ sarva-śāstre phukāriyā kaya

The dust of the feet of a devotee, the water that has washed the feet of a devotee, and the remnants of food left by a devotee are three very powerful substances. By rendering service to these three, one attains the supreme goal of ecstatic love for Kṛṣṇa. In all the revealed scriptures this is loudly declared again and again.

Śrīla Rūpa Gosvāmī says in the *Bhakti-rasāmṛta-sindhuḥ* (1.2.219):

yāvanti bhagavad-bhakter
aṅgāni kathitānīha
prāyas tāvanti tad-bhakta-
bhakter api budhā viduḥ

Of all the limbs of *bhakti* that have been described here in this book (*Bhakti-rasāmṛta-sindhuḥ*) in relation to Lord Kṛṣṇa, the intelligent consider most of them to also be applicable to the Lord's devotees.

Śrīla Rūpa Gosvāmī describes how *bhāva-bhakti* manifests by association with pure devotees in the *Bhakti-rasāmṛta-sindhuḥ* (1.2.241):

dṛg-ambhobhir dhautaḥ pulaka-patalī maṇḍita-tanuḥ
skhalann antaḥ-phullo dadhad atipṛthuṁ vepathum api
dṛśoḥ kakṣāṁ yāvan mama sa puruṣaḥ ko'py upayayau
na jāne kiṁ tāvan matir iha gṛhe nābhiramate

Ever since I saw that person whose heart was filled with spiritual ecstasy exhibited through flowing tears, erect bodily hair, stumbling, and shivering, I do not know what has happened. My mind simply refuses to take interest anymore in household affairs.

Dinara Lukman

The embrace of a devotee is purifying.

Dinara Lukman

The foot dust of the devotee is purifying.

Dinara Lukman

The child Nārada eats the food remnants of devotees and becomes purified.

Kṛṣṇa takes the water from washing his devotee's feet to put on his head.

Spiritual potency flows from the heart of a great devotee into one's heart.

ŚRĪLA BHAKTIVINODA ṬHĀKURA'S *MANAḤ-ŚIKṢĀ BHĀṢĀ* – SONG SEVEN

kapaṭatā haile dūra, praveṣe premera pūra,
jīvera hṛdaya dhanya kare
ataeva bahu-yatne, ānibāre prema-ratne,
kāpaṭya rākhaha ati dūre

Once deceit is cast away, a living being's heart becomes blessed, and one enters the city of sacred love. Therefore, take great care to keep pretense far away from you when try to acquire the jewels of love.

śuna, mana, nigūḍha vacana
pratiṣṭhā-āśā dhṛṣṭa-adhama, caṇḍālinī hṛde mama
yata-kāla karibe nartana

Listen, O mind, to these secret words. As long as my audacious desire for fame in the form of a fallen, low-class, dog eating woman shall remain within my heart –

kāpaṭya tad-upapati, nā chāḍibe mama mati,
śvapacinī yāhe haya dūra
tad-arthe yatana kari', prabhu-preṣṭha-pada dhari'
sevā tumi karaha pracura

Her paramour, deceit, will not stop holding sway over my mind. To cast away that dog eater, hold on to the feet of the beloved devotees of the Lord very carefully and render a lot of service.

teṅha prabhu-senāpati, vikrama kariyā ati,
śvapacinī-saṅga chāḍāiyā
rādhā-kṛṣṇa-prema-dhane, dibe kabe akiñcane,
bole bhaktivinoda kāṅdiyā

Bhaktivinoda weeps, asking, "When will the commander-in-chief of the Lord take me away chivalrously from the company of the dog eater and give me the treasure of the love of Rādhā and Kṛṣṇa?

VERSE EIGHT

यथा दुष्टत्वं मे दवयति शठस्यापि कृपया
यथा मह्यं प्रेमामृतमपि ददात्युज्ज्वलमसौ ।
यथा श्रीगान्धर्वाभजनविधये प्रेरयति मां
तथा गोष्ठे काक्वा गिरिधरमिह त्वं भज मनः ॥

yathā duṣṭatvaṁ me davayati śaṭhasyāpi kṛpayā
yathā mahyaṁ premāmṛtam api dadāty ujjvalam asau
yathā śrī-gāndharvā-bhajana-vidhaye prerayati māṁ
tathā goṣṭhe kākvā giridharam iha tvaṁ bhaja manaḥ

śaṭhasya-api—even though [I am] a cheater; *yathā*—so that; *kṛpayā*—by [his] mercy; *duṣṭatvaṁ me*—my inherent wickedness; *davayati*—is driven away; *yathā*—so that; *ujjvalam*—the glowing; *prema-amṛtam*—nectar of *prema*; *api*—is also; *dadāti*—bestowed completely; *mahyam*—on me; *yathā*—so that; *asau*—these; *śrī-gāndharvā-bhajana-vidhaye*—injunctions regarding worship of Śrī Gāndharvikā; *prerayati*—are inspired; *mām*—in my heart; *tathā*—for that purpose; *manaḥ*—O mind; *kākvā*—with pleading words; *tvaṁ bhaja*—you should worship; *giridharam*—Śrī Giridhārī, the lifter of Govardhana Hill; *iha*—here; *goṣṭhe*—in the land of cows, Vṛndāvana.

Even though I am a cheater, the Lord's mercy can drive away my inherent wicked nature, give me the glowing nectar of divine love, and inspire my heart with the process to worship Śrī Gāndharvikā. Therefore, O mind, with pleading words, you should worship Śrī Giridhārī here in Vṛndāvana.

Rādhe Devī Dāsī

Worship Śrī Giridhārī to completely receive the glowing nectar of divine love.

Rādhe Devī Dāsī

"O Devī! Falling on the ground like a rod, I, an extremely distressed soul, beg you to please count me as one of your near and dear ones."

ŚRĪLA BHAKTIVINODA ṬHĀKURA'S *BHAJANA-DARPAṆA* COMMENTARY

With the association of *sādhus* and the gradual transfusion of spiritual energy, wickedness in the heart of a devotee disappears and all success is achieved. But such association of sages cannot be obtained so easily. Therefore, Raghunātha Dāsa Gosvāmī gives us the instruction in this verse.

ŚLOKĀRTHA: MEANING OF THE VERSE

1 **Kākvā: The helpless, destitute practitioner's expression that is a humble plea** Devotion that is free of deception is always combined with the attitude that I am extremely destitute and wretched. Śrī Rūpa Gosvāmī's *Śrī Gāndharvā-samprārthanāṣṭakam* (*Stava-mālā*) expresses such feelings:

1 *vṛndāvane viharator iha keli-kuñje*
matta-dvipa-pravara-kautuka-vibhrameṇa
sandarśayasva yuvayor vadanāravinda-
dvandvaṁ vidhehi mayi devi kṛpāṁ prasīda

You are roaming freely in this pleasure-grove in Śrī Vṛndāvana, enjoying love like the greatest of intoxicated elephants. O Devī [Rādhārāṇī], please show me your face and the face of your beloved and kindly bestow your mercy on me.

2 *hā devi kāku-bhara-gadgadayādya vācā*
yāce nipatya bhuvi daṇḍavad udbhaṭārtiḥ
asya prasādam abudhasya janasya kṛtvā
gāndharvike nija-gaṇe gaṇanāṁ vidhehi

O Devī, falling on the ground like a rod, I, an extremely distressed soul, beg you in a stuttering voice filled with a piteous mood. Having bestowed your mercy on this unintelligent soul, O Gāndharvikā, please count me as one of your near and dear ones.

3 *śyāme ramā-ramaṇa-sundaratā-variṣṭha-*
saundarya-mohita-samasta-jagaj-janasya

Rādhe Devī Dāsī

"O Devī! When will I dress you in a cloud-colored *sārī*?"

śyāmasya vāma-bhuja-baddha-tanuṁ kadāhaṁ
tvām indirā-virala-rūpa-bharāṁ bhajāmi

O Śyāmā [Rādhārāṇī], Śyāma's [Kṛṣṇa's] beauty surpasses the beauty of Lord Nārāyaṇa and enchants the entire world. When will I be able to worship you in a form embraced by the left arm of Śyāma? Indeed, even Lakṣmī Devī rarely sees this form.

4 *tvāṁ pracchadena mudira-cchavinā pidhāya*
mañjīra-mukta-caraṇāṁ ca vidhāya devi
kuñje vrajendra-tanayena virājamāne
naktaṁ kadā pramuditām abhisārayiṣye

O Devī, when will I dress you in a cloud-colored *sārī*, remove your ankle-bells, and help you excitingly attain the forest grove where the son of Nanda resides at night [waiting for you]?

5 *kuñje prasūna-kula-kalpita-keli-talpe*
saṁviṣṭayor madhura-narma-vilāsa-bhājoḥ
loka-trayābharaṇayoś caraṇāmbujāni
saṁvāhayiṣyati kadā yuvayor jano'yam

The lotus feet of the two of you are resting in a forest grove, on a bed that is ornamented with hosts of flowers. Those feet have enjoyed delightful love sports and are the ornaments of the entire world. O Devī, when will this servant of yours be able to massage those feet?

6 *tvat-kuṇḍa-rodhasi vilāsa-pariśrameṇa*
svedāmbu-cumbi-vadanāmbu-ruha-śriyo vām
vṛndāvaneśvari kadā taru-mūla-bhājo
saṁvījayāmi camarī-caya-cāmareṇa

You two are seated under a tree on the banks of your *kuṇḍa* [the lake named Rādhā-kuṇḍa], O Vṛndāvaneśvarī. When will I use a yak-tail whisk to fan both of your faces which are kissed by moistening perspiration formed due to the effort of love-making?

7 *līnāṁ nikuñja-kuhare bhavatīṁ mukunde*
citraiva sūcitavatīṁ rucirākṣi nāham
bhugnāṁ bhruvaṁ na racayeti mṛṣāruṣāṁ tvām
agre vrajendra-tanayasya kadā nu neṣye

"When will this servant be able to massage the feet of Rādhā and Kṛṣṇa?"

O splendid-eyed beauty, when you, who are hiding in a secret spot in the forest grove, will be discovered by Mukunda, you'll then accuse me by saying, "You told him where I'm hiding." At that time, I will say in front of Kṛṣṇa, "It was not me but Citrā Sakhī who told him about you. Kindly do not be falsely angry with me like this." When will such a day come?

8 *vāg-yuddha-keli-kutuke vraja-rāja-sūnuṁ*
jitvonmadām adhika-darpa-vikāsi-jalpām
phullābhir ālibhir analpam udīryamāṇa-
stotrāṁ kadā nu bhavatīm avalokayiṣye

When you, having defeated the son of Vraja-rāja in a playful war of words, will express pride by speaking even more clever words [to celebrate your victory], your jubilant friends (*sakhīs*) will shout out heaps of praiseful words such as "Jaya Rādhe!" When will I witness this occasion?

9 *yaḥ ko'pi suṣṭhu vṛṣabhānu-kumārikāyāḥ*
samprārthanāṣṭakam idaṁ paṭhati prapannaḥ
sā preyasā saha sametya dhṛta-pramodā
tatra prasāda-laharīm urarīkaroti

The surrendered soul who beautifully recites this *Gāndharvā-samprārthanāṣṭakam* dedicated to the daughter of Vṛṣabhānu, will be able to approach her in a mood full of joy along with her lover, Śrī Kṛṣṇa, and will experience and spread their mercy.

2 **Śaṭhatā me duṣṭatvam: Cheating and deception are my wickedness** Deceit or pretense is the wickedness of the conditioned soul, whereas a pure soul is by nature simple and thoroughly honest. When souls take shelter of ignorance and illusion, they at once become deceitful, falsely proud, and obsessed with the desire for honor, worship, adoration, and prestige. They become hypocritical and consumed by dishonest activities. Such souls seek distance from everything related to the Lord.

When those unfortunate conditioned souls realize their true position as servants of the Lord, they feel more humble than the straw in the street and gain the intelligence to respect others according to their respective positions. If they also take complete shelter of the holy name of the Supreme Personality of Godhead, they receive the mercy of Śrī Kṛṣṇa and his beloved devotees.

3 **Ujjvala-premāmṛta: The supremely radiant nectar of love for Kṛṣṇa** Here *ujjvala* refers to *śṛṅgāra-rasa,* which is also known as *mādhurya-rasa,* the transcendental emotion of amorous love of God. Śrīla Rūpa Gosvāmī describes this as follows:

mukhya-raseṣu purā yaḥ
saṁkṣepeṇodito rahasyatvāt
pṛthag eva bhakti-rasa-rāṭ sa
vistareṇocyate madhuraḥ

vakṣyamāṇair vibhāvādyaiḥ
svādyatāṁ madhurā ratiḥ
nītā bhakti-rasaḥ prokto
madhurākhyo manīṣibhiḥ

> In the *Bhakti-rasāmṛta-sindhuḥ,* the king among all *rasas, mādhurya,* was described only briefly due to its confidentiality. Now here (in *Ujjvala-nīlamaṇiḥ),* I am separately elaborating on it. When *madhura-rati* becomes tasty with the presence of *vibhāva, anubhāva, sāttvika-bhāva* and *sañcāri-bhāva,* the experts call it *madhura-bhakti-rasa.* (*Ujjvala-nīlamaṇiḥ nāyaka-bheda-prakaraṇa* 1.2–3)

Śrīla Rūpa Gosvāmī describes in *Śrī Bhakti-rasāmṛta-sindhuḥ* that pure devotional service is cultivated in five different transcendental types of attachment, namely *śānta* (neutrality), *dāsya* (servitorship), *sakhya* (friendship), *vātsalya* (parenthood), and *mādhurya* (amorous love). These five primary relationships are also known as continual loving attraction, *sthāyī-bhāva.*

The support in *mādhurya-rasa* is Kṛṣṇa and his pleasure potency, and their qualities are the stimulants. During their amorous pastimes, the *gopīs,* including Śrīmatī Rādhārāṇī, and even Kṛṣṇa himself, display the eight symptoms of love (*sāttvika-bhāva*) and the thirty-three emotional waves (*vyabhicārī-bhāva*). These *bhāvas* rise up like tides causing the ocean of *bhakti-rasa* to swell.

Rādhe Devī Dāsī

The rays of *hlādinī-śakti*, the internal pleasure potency of the Lord, enter devotees' hearts, thus making visible those devotees' transcendental relationship with Kṛṣṇa.

When devotional service in practice is transformed into devotional service in ecstasy, one develops steady attraction (*sthāyī-bhāva*). That steady attractive attachment combined with *vibhāva, anubhāva, sāttvika-bhāva,* and *vyabhicārī-bhāva* attains the state of *rasa*. This state signifies the visible appearance of pure love (*prema*) and is known as *bhakti-rasa*. Śrī Kṛṣṇa's *vraja-līlā* and the *līlā* that he enacted with his dear *gopīs* all over *vraja-maṇḍala* are the best examples of this *rasa*.

Those who are fortunate and awaken a strong greed to obtain this transcendental amorous *rasa* should follow in the wake of the *gopīs*. They should pray continually with intense longing and anguish, and with voices choked with emotion. In such a state of intense prayer, the *sādhaka* obtains Śrīmatī Rādhārāṇī's mercy. The rays of *hlādinī-śakti,* the internal pleasure potency of the Lord, enter such a practitioner's heart, thus making this transcendental *rasa* visible. There is no other method or circumstance by which one can achieve this transcendental *mādhurya-rasa*.

4 **Śrī-Gāndharvā bhajana: Worship of Śrī Gāndharvikā** The infinitesimal living being in its limited capacity to experience bliss may sometimes experience *brahmānanda* (the bliss of realizing Brahman) or *ātmānanda* (the bliss of knowing oneself to be a spiritual soul). However, without the mercy of the internal pleasure potency (*hlādinī-śakti*) one can never experience the transcendental ecstasy of *paramānanda* (the supreme bliss of loving service).

One gets that mercy when, after hearing about the eternal loving emotions of the eternal residents of *vraja-dhāma,* a greed may awaken in the heart of the practitioner to achieve that very same devotional sentiment. In this way the sincerity to beg and pray for that sentiment will begin. Once that sincere desire has awakened, the devotee should take shelter of and serve one of Śrīmatī Rādhārāṇī's girl friends (*sakhīs* or *mañjarīs*). Only by the mercy of the *sakhīs* can one be eligible to serve the divine couple. By getting the mercy of a *sakhī,* one will gradually obtain the mercy of Śrī Rādhā. With the increase of such mercy, *hlādinī-śakti* proportionally manifests in the heart, which makes the spiritual bliss of service to the divine couple eternally available to the soul.

One takes the shelter of one of the girlfriends or assistants of Śrīmatī Rādhārāṇī and serves her, from which one gets the eligibility to serve the divine couple.

As long as a practitioner maintains mental masculinity, he remains ineligible to serve in this way. There is no connection of one's worldly male and female body to this mood and service. In its original form, the *jīva* has a spiritually feminine nature. If a person superimposes concepts of material gender everything is destroyed.

ŚRĪLA BHAKTIVINODA ṬHĀKURA'S *MANAḤ-ŚIKṢĀ BHĀṢĀ* – SONG EIGHT

vraja-bhūmi cintāmaṇi, cidānanda-ratna-khani,
yathā nitya rasera vilāsa
jīve diba gūḍha dhana, ciniti' kṛṣṇa vṛndāvana,
jaḍe āni karila prakāśa

The land of Vraja is a wish-fulfilling gem; indeed, it's a jewel mine of consciousness and bliss, where Śrī Kṛṣṇa's eternal sweet playful pastimes manifest. Kṛṣṇa thought, "If I bring Vṛndāvana and make it manifest on earth, then I can give the greatest, most secret treasure to the souls there."

kṛṣṇa mora dayāra sāgara
tumi mana, vraja-dhāma, bhrami' bhrami' avirāma,
ḍāka kṛṣṇe haiyā kātara

My Kṛṣṇa is an ocean of mercy! O heart! Keep wandering in Vraja ceaselessly and cry out for Kṛṣṇa in despair!

avidyā-vilāsa-vaśe, chile tumi jaḍa-rase,
duṣṭatā hṛdaye pāila sthāna
haile tumi śaṭha-rāja, bhulile āpana kāja,
hṛdaye varile abhimāna

You were in the grip of illusory delights reveling in mundane romance, and evil found a place in your heart. You became a master cheater, forgetting your own duties, and began to foster ego in your heart.

ebe upadeśa śuna, gāiyā yugala-guṇa,
goṣṭhe goṣṭhe karaha rodana

dayā kari' giridhara, śuniyā kākuti svara,
tabe doṣa karibe śodhana

Now listen to this instruction: sing the glories of the divine couple and cry, right here in the pastures of Vraja. When Giridhārī listens to such pitiful weeping, he will cleanse me of all my faults.

ujjvala rasera prīti, śrī-rādhā-bhajana-nīti,
anāyāse dibena āmāya
rūpa-raghnātha more, kṛpā kari ataḥpare,
ei tattva gopane śikhāya

He will give me that bright and shining sweetness of love, easily showing me the ways of worshiping Śrī Rādhā. When Rūpa and Raghunātha have mercy on me, they will teach me all these mysteries in secret.

VERSE NINE

मदीशानाथत्वे व्रजविपिनचन्द्रं व्रजवने
श्वरीं तन्नाथत्वे तदतुलसखीत्वे तु ललिताम् ।
विशाखां शिक्षालीवितरणगुरुत्वे प्रियसरो
गिरीन्द्रौ तत्प्रेक्षाललितरतिदत्वे स्मर मनः ॥

mad-īśā-nāthatve vraja-vipina-candraṁ vraja-vane-
śvarīṁ tan-nāthatve tad-atula-sakhītve tu lalitām
viśākhāṁ śikṣālī-vitaraṇa-gurutve priyasaro-
girīndrau tat-prekṣā-lalita-rati-datve smara manaḥ

smara manaḥ—O mind, meditate on; *vraja-vipina-candram*—Kṛṣṇa, the moon of the Vṛndāvana forest; *mad-īśā-nāthatve*—as the lord of my controller or leader [Śrī Rādhikā]; *vraja-vana-īśvarīm*—Śrī Rādhā, the queen of the Vraja forest; *tan-nāthatve*—as his dearest object of love; *tu lalitām*—and Lalitā; *tad-atula-sakhītve*—as the incomparable friend; *viśākhām*—Viśākhā; *śikṣālī-vitaraṇa-gurutve*—as the foremost guru distributing the teachings of love; *priya-saraḥ-giri-indrau*—Rādhā-kuṇḍa and Govardhana; *tat-prekṣā-lalita-rati-datve*—as givers of the sight and love of Śrī Śrī Rādhā-Kṛṣṇa.

O mind, meditate on Kṛṣṇa, the moon of the Vṛndāvana forest, as the lord of my leader, Śrī Rādhikā. Meditate on Śrī Rādhikā as his most dear object of love. Meditate on Śrī Lalitā as her incomparable friend. Meditate on Śrī Viśākhā as the foremost guru distributing the teachings of love. And meditate on Rādhā-kuṇḍa and Govardhana as givers of the sight and love of Śrī Śrī Rādhā-Kṛṣṇa.

Śyāmapriyā Devī Dāsī

Śrī Rādhikā offers flowers to Kṛṣṇa, the moon of the Vṛndāvana forest.

ŚRĪLA BHAKTIVINODA ṬHĀKURA'S *BHAJANA-DARPAṆA* COMMENTARY

In this verse, Śrīla Raghunātha Dāsa Gosvāmī guides the practitioner (*sādhaka*) on what the mutual relationship should be between spontaneous devotional service (*rāgānugā-bhajana*) and amorous transcendental love of God (*mādhurya-rasa*).

ŚLOKĀRTHA: MEANING OF THE VERSE

1 **Vraja-vipina-candram (smara): Meditate on Śrī Kṛṣṇa, the glowing moon of the forest of Vraja, Vṛndāvana** The following verses from Śrīla Rūpa Gosvāmī's *Mukunda-muktāvalī-stava,* in his *Stava-mālā,* exemplify this instruction:

nava-jaladhara-varṇaṁ campakodbhāsi-karṇaṁ
vikasita-nalināsyaṁ visphuran-manda-hāsyam
kanaka-ruci-dukūlaṁ cāru-barhāva-cūlaṁ
kam api nikhila-sāraṁ naumi gopa-kumāram

His complexion is like a new monsoon cloud. His ears are effulgent like *campaka* flowers. The smile on his face is like a blooming lotus in a lake. His effulgence is like the color of gold. His head is decorated with a host of peacock feathers. Truly, I offer my obeisances to that young cowherd [Kṛṣṇa] who is the essence of everything in the world.

mukha-jita-śarad-induḥ keli-lāvaṇya-sindhuḥ
kara-vinihita-kandur vallavī-prāṇa-bandhuḥ
vapur upasṛta-reṇuḥ kakṣa-nikṣipta-veṇur
vacana-vaśaga-dhenuḥ pātu māṁ nanda-sūnuḥ

His face defeats the excellence of the autumn moon. He is the great ocean of joy of sportive pastimes. He holds a ball in his hands. He is the *gopīs'* life support. His body is covered in the dust raised by cows' hooves. His flute is tucked in the belt around his waist. He captivates the cows with his voice. May he, who is the son of Nanda, protect me.

Śrīla Rūpa Gosvāmī prays to Kṛṣṇa in this mood in the following two verses from a supplementary section to the *Tri-bhaṅgī-pañcakam* in *Stava-mālā*:

Śyāmapriyā Devī Dāsī

Śrī Rādhikā is Kṛṣṇa's most dear object of love.

viracaya mayi daṇḍaṁ dīna-bandho dayāṁ vā
gatir iha na bhavattaḥ kācid anyā mamāsti
nipatatu śatakoṭir nirbharaṁ vā navāmbhas
tad api kila payodaḥ stūyate cātakena

O lord of the distressed, whether you inflict on me a strong punishment or your mercy, I have no other shelter but you. Indeed, the *cātaka* bird glorifies the cloud whether the cloud punishes it with a strong thunderbolt or [mercifully] showers rainfall on it.

prācīnānāṁ bhajanam atulaṁ duṣkaraṁ śṛṇvato me
nairāśyena jvalati hṛdayaṁ bhakti-leśālasasya
viśvadrīcīm aghahara tavākarṇya kāruṇya-vīcīm
āśā-bindūkṣitam idam upaity antare hanta śaityam

O killer of Agha, when I hear about how great souls in the past performed unparalleled devotional service even in most unfavorable conditions, the heart of a devotionally void person like me burns in disappointment. Then again when I hear of your omnipresent mercy on all living entities, my burning heart experiences a cooling sensation due to being moistened by a drop of hope.

2 **Vraja-vaneśvarīṁ tan-nāthatve (smara): Meditate on Śrīmatī Rādhikā as one's dearest queen of Vraja** Śrīla Raghunātha Dāsa Gosvāmī in his *Vilāpa-kusumāñjalī* (7–8) clearly acknowledges Śrīmatī Rādhārāṇī as his *svāminī* (female master). With intensity and great care, he prays with one-pointed devotion in order to attain Śrīmatī Rādhārāṇī's service, as follows:

aty utkaṭena nitarāṁ virahānalena
dandahyamāna-hṛdayā kila kāpi dāsī
hā svāmini kṣaṇam iha praṇayena gāḍham
ākrandanena vidhurā vilapāmi padyaiḥ

O Svāminī [Rādhikā], I, a certain maidservant belonging to you, cry here every moment in deep love. I am expressing my feelings in the form of poetry, as my heart burns with the excessive and constant fire of separation from you.

devi duḥkha-kula-sāgarodare
dūyamānam atidurgataṁ janam

VERSE NINE

tvaṁ kṛpā-prabala-naukayādbhutaṁ
prāpaya sva-pada-paṅkajālayam

O Devi [Rādhikā], this [maid-servant of yours] has fallen immensely into the depths of various oceans of distresses. Through the amazing boat of your strong mercy, kindly rescue this servant and make her attain the liberating shore of your lotus feet.

Śyāmapriyā Devī Dāsī

"O Devi Rādhikā! This servant of yours has fallen into the depths of various oceans of distresses. Through the amazing boat of your strong mercy, kindly rescue this servant and make her attain the liberating shore of your lotus feet."

3 **Lalitām tad-atula-sakhītve (smara): Meditate on Śrī Lalitā as the matchless bosom friend of Śrīmatī Rādhārāṇī, the queen of Vraja**

Śrīla Rūpa Gosvāmī elaborately expresses this mood in his *Śrī Lalitāṣṭaka* prayers from the *Stava-mālā*:

1 *rādhā-mukunda pada-sambhava-gharma-bindu-*
nirmañchanopakaraṇī-kṛta deha-lakṣām
uttuṅga-sauhṛda-viśeṣa-vaśāt pragalbhāṁ
devīṁ guṇaiḥ sulalitāṁ lalitāṁ namāmi

I offer obeisances to Lalitā-devī who is extremely expert due to her excellent qualities. Out of her elevated and intimate feelings of love, she wipes away glistening drops of perspiration from the lotus feet of Rādhā-Mukunda.

2 *rākā-sudhā-kiraṇa-maṇḍala-kānti-daṇḍi*
vaktra-śriyaṁ cakita-cāru-camūru-netrām
rādhā-prasādhana-vidhāna-kalā-prasiddhāṁ
devīṁ guṇaiḥ sulalitāṁ lalitāṁ namāmi

I offer obeisances to Lalitā-devī who is extremely expert due to her excellent qualities. Her beautiful face defeats the brilliance of the rays of the full moon and her eyes are ever-restless like those of a startled doe. She is famous for her extraordinary proficiency in the art of dressing Rādhā, of whom she is an expert servant.

3 *lāsyollasad-bhujaga-śatru-patatra-citra-*
paṭṭāṁśukābharaṇa-kañculikāñcitāṅgīm
gorocanā-ruci-vigarhaṇa gaurimāṇaṁ
devīṁ guṇaiḥ sulalitāṁ lalitāṁ namāmi

I offer obeisances to Lalitā-devī who is extremely expert due to her excellent qualities. Her body is decorated with an attractive blouse and [equally attractive] cloth whose design resembles the tail of an ecstatically dancing peacock. Her golden complexion defeats the brilliance of *gorocana*, a bright yellow pigment.

4 *dhūrte vrajendra-tanaye tanu suṣṭhu-vāmyaṁ*
mā dakṣiṇā bhāva kalaṅkini lāghavāya
rādhe giraṁ śṛṇu hitām iti śikṣayantīṁ
devīṁ guṇaiḥ sulalitāṁ lalitāṁ namāmi

Śyāmapriyā Devī Dāsī

Śrī Lalitā is Rādhā's incomparable friend and confidant.

I offer obeisances to Lalitā-devī who is extremely expert due to her excellent qualities. She teaches Rādhā by saying, "Listen to words of wisdom, O Rādhe-Kalaṅkinī (girl who has spoilt her reputation)! Never take a subordinate position and show a liberal heart to that great cheater Kṛṣṇa. Always dominate him in all ways."

5 *rādhām abhi-vraja-pateḥ kṛtam ātmajena*
kūṭaṁ manāg api vilokya vilohitākṣīm
vāg-bhaṅgibhis tam acireṇa vilajjayantīṁ
devīṁ guṇaiḥ sulalitāṁ lalitāṁ namāmi

I offer obeisances to Lalitā-devī who is extremely expert due to her excellent qualities. When she hears even a few crafty flirtatious words from Kṛṣṇa to Rādhā, she becomes furious, and, with reddish eyes, speaks clever words that immediately embarrass Kṛṣṇa.

6 *vātsalya-vṛnda-vasatiṁ paśupāla-rājñyāḥ*
sakhyānuśikṣaṇa-kalāsu guruṁ sakhīnām
rādhā-balāvaraja jīvita-nirviśeṣāṁ
devīṁ guṇaiḥ sulalitāṁ lalitāṁ namāmi

I offer obeisances to Lalitā-devī who is extremely expert due to her excellent qualities. Various parental affections of the queen of cowherds (Yaśodā) reside in her. She is the guru of all her friends (*sakhīs*) in the arts of friendship. She considers Rādhā and Balarāma's younger brother, Kṛṣṇa, as non-different from her own life.

7 *yāṁ kām api vraja-kule vṛṣabhānujāyāḥ*
prekṣya sva-pakṣa-padavīm anuruddhyamānām
sadyas tad iṣṭa-ghaṭanena kṛtārthayantīṁ
devīṁ guṇaiḥ sulalitāṁ lalitāṁ namāmi

I offer obeisances to Lalitā-devī who is extremely expert due to her excellent qualities. When she sees any young maiden anywhere in Vraja, she immediately considers whether that maiden is favorable to Vṛṣabhānu's daughter [Rādhā]. If so, Lalitā fulfils all of that maiden's desires and thus fills her with gratitude.

8 *rādhā-vrajendra-suta-saṅgama-raṅga-caryāṁ*
varyāṁ viniścitavatīm akhilotsavebhyaḥ

Śyāmapriyā Devī Dāsī

Yaśodā lovingly gazes at Lalitā, Rādhā's dear friend, making Rādhā and Viśākhā smile.

Śyāmapriyā Devī Dāsī

Śrī Lalitā-devī is extremely expert due to her excellent qualities such as her dancing for Rādhā, Kṛṣṇa, and their friends. (from a description in Kavi-karṇapūra's *Ānanda-vṛndāvana-campū*)

tāṁ gokula-priya-sakhī-nikuramba-mukhyāṁ
devīṁ guṇaiḥ sulalitāṁ lalitāṁ namāmi

I offer obeisances to Lalitā-devī who is extremely expert due to her excellent qualities. She gives priority to the great and colorful love-sports of Śrī Rādhā and the prince of Vraja [Kṛṣṇa] over all other festivals. She is the leader of the most prominent loving and friendly young girls of Gokula.

9 *nandann amūni lalitā-guṇa-lālitāni*
padyāni yaḥ paṭhati nirmala-dṛṣṭir aṣṭau
prītyā vikarṣati janaṁ nija-vṛnda-madhye
taṁ kīrtidā-pati-kulojjvala-kalpa-vallī

The person who, in a joyous mood and with clarified vision, recites these eight verses decorated with the qualities of Śrī Lalitā, receives the gift of being attracted to, and counted among, the near and dear associates of the desire-fulfilling creeper in the lineage of the husband of Kīrtidā [Śrīmatī Rādhikā].

4 **Viśākhāṁ śikṣālī-vitaraṇa-gurutve (smara): Meditate on Śrī Viśākhā as one's instructing teacher** Vidyabhūṣaṇa cited the following verse (commentary on *Yamunāṣṭakam* verse 1) to confirm that the Yamunā River is a non-different manifestation of Śrī Viśākhā*:

viśākhorasi yā viṣṇor
yasyāṁ viṣṇur jalātmani
nityaṁ nimajjati prītyā
tāṁ saurīṁ yamunāṁ stumaḥ

We offer prayers to the daughter of Sūrya (the sun god), the Yamunā River, where Lord Viṣṇu [Kṛṣṇa] sports with delight in her waters, and whose spiritual body is Viśākhā.

* Other references for this point: The *Lalita-mādhava* (6.1.39) states that Yamunā River is another form that Viśākhā takes to serve Rādhā and Kṛṣṇa. Also, Jīva Gosvāmī states in the *Mādhava-mahotsava*: "See friend! Lalitā is standing on the right side of Rādhā, holding a peacock feather fan. Rādhā is looking at her with distress and a crooked glance. Viśākhā is walking on her left side. In another form she is known as Yamunā. In her hand she is holding a picture of Hari."

Śyāmapriyā Devī Dāsī

Śrī Viśākhā shows the damsels of Vraja
how to decorate with flowers.

Śyāmapriyā Devī Dāsī

Rāmānanda Rāya, an incarnation of Viśākhā,
teaches Lord Caitanya, who is in Rādhā's mood.

Vidyābhūṣaṇa further remarks on the above verse as follows:

viśākhā yamunā-vapur iti vicāreṇa
yamunā-stutyā tat-stutir, iti vidyābhūṣaṇaḥ

Śrī Viśākhā is considered to be the spiritual body of the Yamunā River. Thus by humbly offering prayers to the Yamunā, one automatically offers prayers and worship to Śrī Viśākhā.

Śrīla Rūpa Gosvāmī has compiled these eight verses that glorify Śrī Yamunā as *Śrī Yamunāṣṭaka* in the *Stava-mālā*:

1 *bhrātur antakasya pattane 'bhipatti-hāriṇī*
prekṣayāti-pāpino 'pi pāpa-sindhu-tāriṇī
nīra-mādhurībhir apy aśeṣa-citta-bandhinī
māṁ punātu sarvadāravinda-bandhu-nandinī

May [Śrī Yamunā] the daughter of the lotus-friendly sun god always purify me. She saves one from entering the abode of her brother (Yamarāja, who punishes the sinful after death). She allows sinners who merely see her to cross over the ocean of sin. Through the sweetness of her waters, she binds the hearts of unlimited souls to herself.

2 *hāri-vāri-dhārayābhimaṇḍitoru-khāṇḍavā*
puṇḍarīka-maṇḍalodyad-aṇḍajāli-tāṇḍavā
snāna-kāma-pāmarogra-pāpa-sampad-andhinī
māṁ punātu sarvadāravinda-bandhu-nandinī

May the daughter of the lotus-friendly sun god always purify me. Her pleasing streams decorate the Khāṇḍava forest. Her lake is filled with hosts of lotuses, around which various birds dance and sing uproariously. She neutralizes the terrible sins of those lowly souls who even just want to bathe in her waters.

3 *śīkarābhimṛṣṭa-jantu-durvipāka-mardinī*
nanda-nandanāntaraṅga-bhakti-pūra-vardhinī
tīra-saṅgamābhilāṣi-maṅgalānubandhinī
māṁ punātu sarvadāravinda-bandhu-nandinī

May the daughter of the lotus-friendly sun god always purify me. She crushes the sins of those living entities who immerse themselves in

Śyāmapriyā Devī Dāsī

"May Śrī Yamunā-devī, the daughter of the lotus-friendly sun god, always purify me. She saves one from entering the abode of her brother Yamarāja, who punishes the sinful after death." [Sūrya-deva sits with his children, Yama and Yamunā.]

her waters. She greatly enhances the flood of internal loving devotion to Kṛṣṇa, the son of Nanda, and repeatedly bestows auspiciousness on those who come in contact with her riverbanks.

4 *dvīpa-cakravāla-juṣṭa-sapta-sindhu-bhedinī*
śrī-mukunda-nirmitoru-divya-keli-vedinī
kānti-kandalībhir indranīla-vṛnda-nindinī
māṁ punātu sarvadāravinda-bandhu-nandinī

May the daughter of the lotus-friendly sun god always purify me. She penetrates the seven rivers of the Ṛg Veda (Sindhu, Sarasvatī, Vitastā, Śutudri, Vipāśā, Paruṣiṇī and Askinī) which are served by those who live near them. She knows all of Śrī Mukunda's wonderfully divine pastimes, and with her abundant effulgence she surpasses the beauty of a host of blue sapphires.

5 *māthureṇa maṇḍalena cāruṇābhimaṇḍitā*
prema-naddha-vaiṣṇavādhva-vardhanāya paṇḍitā
ūrmi-dor-vilāsa-padmanābha-pāda-vandinī
māṁ punātu sarvadāravinda-bandhu-nandinī

May the daughter of the lotus-friendly sun god always purify me. She is beautifully decorated with the jewel of the circle of Mathurā around her. She increases the beauty of the path of *rāga-bhakti* for the Vaiṣṇavas devoted to divine love (*prema*). Śrī Yamunā's multitude of waves grab and serve the feet of he who has a lotus navel, Kṛṣṇa.

6 *ramya-tīra-rambhamāṇa-go-kadamba-bhūṣitā*
divya-gandha-bhāk-kadamba-puṣpa-rāji-rūṣitā
nanda-sūnu-bhakta-saṅgha-saṅgamābhinandinī
māṁ punātu sarvadāravinda-bandhu-nandinī

May the daughter of the lotus-friendly sun god always purify me. She is decorated with beautiful riverbanks around which herds of cows moo happily. The Yamunā is adorned with many divine and fragrant rows of *kadamba* flowers. She is very delighted by the association of the devotees of Nanda's son, Kṛṣṇa.

7 *phulla-pakṣa-mallikākṣa-haṁsa-lakṣa-kūjitā*
bhakti-viddha-deva-siddha-kinnarāli-pūjitā

Śyāmapriyā Devī Dāsī

The Yamunā River has swans and lotuses in her waters, cows and *kadamba* trees on her banks, and demigods in the sky praising her.

tīra-gandhavāha-gandha-janma-bandha-randhinī
māṁ punātu sarvadāravinda-bandhu-nandinī

May the daughter of the lotus-friendly sun god always purify me. She resounds with the joyous cries of *mallikākṣa* swans. Those who are regulated by devotion (Vaiṣṇavas), demigods, *siddhas* and *kinnaras* (classes of living beings belonging to higher planets) worship her. Even a trace of the fragrance from the mud on her riverbank decimates the bonds of material birth and death.

8 *cid-vilāsa-vāri-pūra-bhūr-bhuvaḥ-svar-āpinī*
kīrtitāpi durmadoru-pāpa-marma-tāpinī
ballavendra-nandanāṅgarāga-bhaṅga-gandhinī
māṁ punātu sarvadāravinda-bandhu-nandinī

May the daughter of the lotus-friendly sun god always purify me. Her waters, spiritualized by love-pastimes [of Kṛṣṇa], flow through the lower, middle and higher planetary systems. Her fame itself is sufficient to burn away the core of the toughest of sins, and she remains aromatically scented with the soap extract used by the son of Nanda, the cowherd leader.

9 *tuṣṭa-buddhir aṣṭakena nirmalormi-ceṣṭitāṁ*
tvām anena bhānu-putri! sarva-deva-veṣṭitām
yaḥstavīti vardhayasva sarva-pāpa-mocane
bhakti-pūram asya devi! puṇḍarīka-locane

O daughter of the sun god! O you with beautiful waves! O rescuer from all sins! May you increase the flood of *kṛṣṇa-bhakti* of the person who, with a self-satisfied mind, glorifies you with these eight prayers.

5 **Priyasaraḥ (smara): Meditate on Śrī Rādhā-kuṇḍa, the famous pond of Śrīmatī Rādhārāṇī** Rādhā-kuṇḍa bestows loving sublime attachment to and affection for serving the lotus feet of the divine couple. Śrīla Raghunātha Dāsa Gosvāmī expands the same instruction his wonderful prayer in the *Vilāpa-Kusumanjali* (98):

he śrī-sarovara sadā tvayi sā mad-īśā
preṣṭhena sārdham iha khelati kāma-raṅgaiḥ

Śyāmapriyā Devī Dāsī

Rādhā-kuṇḍa is a giver of the sight and love of Śrī Śrī Rādhā-Kṛṣṇa.

tvaṁ cet priyāt priyam atīva tayor itīmāṁ
hā darśayādya kṛpayā mama jīvitaṁ tām

O Rādhā-kuṇḍa, in your waters, my worshipable divine goddess Śrī Rādhā always sports in various pastimes with her beloved Kṛṣṇa. You therefore are extremely dearer to both of them than all their dear objects. Therefore, O divine lake, kindly reveal to me the spiritual form of Śrī Rādhā, who is the source of my life.

In the same song Śrīla Raghunāth Dāsa Gosvāmī prays sweetly to Śrī Viśākhā, making a similar request:

kṣaṇam api tava saṅgaṁ na tyajed eva devī
tvam asi samavayas tvān narma-bhūmir yad asyāḥ
iti sumukhi viśākhe darśayitvā mad-īśāṁ
mama viraha-hatāyāḥ prāṇa-rakṣāṁ kuruṣva

O beautiful Viśākhā, I shall not leave your association for even a moment. You are the same age as Śrī Rādhā and, for this reason, you are the abode of her confidential secrets. O goddess, showing me the form of my divine goddess Rādhā, please save the life of a person like me, who is dying in separation.

6 **Girīndra (smara): Meditate on Govardhana, who bestows sublime love to the lotus feet of the divine couple** Śrīla Raghunātha Dāsa Gosvāmī prays to Govardhana Hill in his *Śrī Govardhanavāsa-prārthanā-daśakam*:

giri-nṛpa-hari-dāsa-śreṇi-varyeti-nāmā-
mṛtam idam uditaṁ śrī-rādhikā-vaktra-candrāt
vraja-nava-tilakatve klpta-vedaiḥ sphuṭaṁ me
nija-nikaṭa-nivāsaṁ dehi govardhana tvam

O king of mountains [Govardhana], the moon-faced Śrī Rādhikā spoke a beautiful verse proclaiming you to be the best of all devotees. The confidential Vedas clearly glorify you as the *tilaka* decorating the land of Vraja. Kindly grant me residence near you!

The essence of the above composition is that Śrīla Raghunāth Dāsa Gosvāmī desires residence at the feet of Girirāja Govardhana, and

Śyāmapriyā Devī Dāsī

Govardhana is a giver of the sight and love of Śrī Śrī Rādhā-Kṛṣṇa.

prays that Śrī Girirāja will cause ecstatic love in his heart to awaken for the lotus feet of the divine couple Śrī Śrī Rādhā-Kṛṣṇa.

Seeing, or taking *darśaṇa* of, Rādhā-kuṇḍa and Govardhana invokes exclusive devotion in one's heart. Indeed, all of the locations of Kṛṣṇa's transcendental playing and pastimes bestow pleasure, and one should therefore always meditate on them.

The spiritual practitioner should always remember the above six subject matters with great affection.

ŚRĪLA BHAKTIVINODA ṬHĀKURA'S *MANAḤ-ŚIKṢĀ BHĀṢĀ* – SONG NINE

vraja-vana-sudhākara, vraja-vanera īśvara,
vrajeśvarī āmāra īśvarī
lalitā tāṅhāra sakhī, tulya tāra nāhi likhi,
viśākhā śikṣikā-pada dhari

My goddess [Śrī Rādhā] is the moon in the forests of Vraja, the ruler and the master of Vṛndāvana. I cherish and hold the feet of Śrī Lalitā, the divine couple's intimate friend beyond compare, as well as the feet of Śrī Viśākhā, the beloved teacher.

ei bhāve bhāva, ore mana
rādhākuṇḍa-sarovara, govardhana-girīśvara,
rati-prada tattva tadīkṣaṇa

O heart! Meditate on them like this! The lake, Rādhākuṇḍa! Govardhana, king of mountains! The sight of these places gives love, (*rati*) to the viewer.

braje gopī-deha dhari', mañjarī āśraya kari',
prāpta sevā kara sampādana
mañjarīra kṛpā ha'be, sakhīra caraṇa pā'be,
sakhī dekhāibe nitya-dhana

Dear mind, taking the body of a cowherd maiden in Vraja and taking shelter of a maidservant (*mañjarī*) do whatever service you have received according to her guidance. If you get the mercy of the *mañjarīs*, you will attain the *sakhīs'* lotus feet; then the *sakhīs* will show me their eternal treasure.

prahare prahare āra, daṇḍe daṇḍe sevā-sāra,
kariyā yugala-dhane ḍāka
sakala anartha yā'be, cid-vilāsa-rasa pā'be,
bhaktivinodera kathā rākha

Serve constantly according to the eight times of the day [*aṣṭa-kālīya-līlā*], completing your service every *daṇḍa**, and keep calling out the names of the divine couple, most beloved by you. In this way, all your *anarthas* will be gone and you will attain divine *rasa*. Please honor Bhaktivinoda's words [dear mind]!

* Every twenty-four hours is divided into eight *praharas,* which is further divided into six *daṇḍas*. Each *daṇḍa* is about half an hour.

VERSE TEN

रतिं गौरीलीले अपि तपति सौन्दर्यकिरणैः
शचीलक्ष्मीसत्याः परिभवति सौभाग्यवलनैः ।
वशीकारैश्चन्द्रावलिमुखनवीनव्रजसतीः
क्षिपत्याराद्या तां हरिदयितराधां भज मनः ॥

ratiṁ gaurī-līle api tapati saundarya-kiraṇaiḥ
śacī-lakṣmī-satyāḥ paribhavati saubhāgya-valanaiḥ
vaśīkārais candrāvali-mukha-navīna-vraja-satīḥ
kṣipaty ārād yā tāṁ hari-dayita-rādhāṁ bhaja manaḥ

bhaja manaḥ—offer worship, O mind; *tām*—unto her; *hari-dayita-rādhām*—Śrī Rādhā, the beloved of Lord Hari; *tapati*—[who] blazes; *ratim*—Rati [the wife of Kāmadeva]; *gaurī-līle api*—as well as Gaurī [the wife of Lord Śiva] and Līlā [the potency of Lord Viṣṇu]; *saundarya-kiraṇaiḥ*—by the effulgence of her beauty; *paribhavati*—[who] defeats; *śacī-lakṣmī-satyāḥ*—Śacī [the wife of Indra], Lakṣmī, and Satyā [Kṛṣṇa's wife]; *saubhāgya-valanaiḥ*—by the waves of her good fortune; *yā*—she who; *ārāt*—immediately; *kṣipati*—defeats; *navīna-vraja-satīḥ*—the newly married *gopīs* of Vraja; *candrāvali-mukha*—headed by Candrāvalī; *vaśīkāraiḥ*—through her power to control [Kṛṣṇa].

O mind, offer your worship unto Śrī Rādhikā, the beloved of Lord Hari. She outshines Rati [the wife of Kāmadeva], Gaurī [the wife of Lord Śiva], and Līlā [the potency of Lord Viṣṇu] by the effulgence of her beauty. She defeats Śacī [the wife of Indra], Lakṣmī, and Satyā [Kṛṣṇa's wife] by the waves of her good fortune. She defeats the pride of the newly married *gopīs* of Vraja, headed by Candrāvalī, through her power to control Kṛṣṇa.

Aṣṭasakhī-līlā Devī Dāsī

Rādhārāṇī outshines the wives of Indra, Śiva, and Viṣṇu.

Aṣṭasakhī-līlā Devī Dāsī

Rādhārāṇī defeats the pride of the newly married *gopīs* of Vraja.

ŚRĪLA BHAKTIVINODA ṬHĀKURA'S *BHAJANA-DARPAṆA* COMMENTARY

What is the foundation of this *śloka*? No one can ever obtain the lotus feet of Śrī Kṛṣṇa, the source and form of all powers, without first approaching and taking shelter of the Lord's internal potency called *svarūpa-śakti*. Therefore, Śrīla Raghunātha Dāsa Gosvāmī says to his mind to offer worship to the beloved of Lord Hari.

ŚLOKĀRTHA: MEANING OF THE VERSE

1 **Śrīmatī Rādhārāṇī's special, extraordinary qualities** Śrīla Rūpa Gosvāmī nicely elaborates Rādhā's twenty-five main qualities in *Śrī-rādhā-prakaraṇa* in the *Ujjvala-nīlamaṇiḥ* (4.11–15):

atha vṛndāvaneśvaryāḥ kīrtyante pravarā guṇāḥ
madhureyaṁ nava-vayāś calāpāṅgojjvala-smitā

cāru-saubhāgya-rekhāḍhyā gandhonmādita-mādhavā
saṅgīta-prasarābhijñā ramya-vāṅ narma-paṇḍitā

vinītā karuṇā-pūrṇā vidagdhā pāṭavānvitā
lajjā-śīlā su-maryādā dhairya-gāmbhīrya-śālinī

su-vilāsā mahābhāva-paramotkarṣa-tarṣiṇī
gokula-prema-vasatir jagac-chreṇī-lasad-yaśāḥ

gurv-arpita-guru-snehā sakhī-praṇayitā-vaśā
kṛṣṇa-priyāvalī-mukhyā santatāśrava-keśavā
bahunā kiṁ guṇās tasyāḥ saṅkhyātītā harer iva

Śrīmatī Rādhārāṇī's twenty-five chief transcendental qualities are: 1 She is very sweet. 2 She is always freshly youthful. 3 Her eyes are restless. 4 She smiles brightly. 5 She has beautiful, auspicious lines. 6 She makes Kṛṣṇa happy with her bodily aroma. 7 She is very expert in singing. 8 Her speech is charming. 9 She is very expert in joking and speaking pleasantly. 10 She is very humble and meek. 11 She is always full of mercy. 12 She is cunning. 13 She is expert in executing her duties. 14 She is shy. 15 She is always respectful. 16 She is always calm. 17 She is always grave. 18 She is expert in enjoying life. 19 She is situated at the topmost level of ecstatic love. 20 She is the reservoir of loving affairs in Gokula. 21 She is the most famous of submissive devotees. 22 She is very affectionate to elderly people. 23 She is very submissive to the love of her friends. 24 She is the chief *gopī*. 25 She always keeps Kṛṣṇa under her control. In short, she possesses unlimited transcendental qualities, just as Lord Kṛṣṇa does. (quoted from *Caitanya-caritāmṛta, Madhya-līlā* 23.87–91)

Śrīmatī Rādhārāṇī's glory is again elaborately described by Śrīla Rūpa Gosvāmī in the *Ujjvala-nīlamaṇiḥ* (4.3–6):

tayor apy ubhayor madhye
rādhikā sarvathādhikā
mahā-bhāva-svarūpeyaṁ
guṇair ativarīyasī

Of these two *gopīs* [Rādhārāṇī and Candrāvalī], Śrīmatī Rādhārāṇī is superior in all respects. She is the embodiment of *mahā-bhāva*, and she surpasses all in good qualities. (quoted from *Caitanya-caritāmṛta, Ādi-līlā* 4.70)

gopālottara-tāpanyāṁ
yad gāndharveti viśrutā
rādhety ṛk-pariśiṣṭe ca
mādhavena sahoditā
atas tadīya-māhātmyaṁ
pādme devarṣiṇoditam

Śrīmatī Rādhārāṇī is called Gāndharvā in the *Gopāla-uttara-tāpanī Upaniṣat*. In the *Ṛk-pariśiṣṭa* she is called Rādhā and described as being always with Mādhava. Therefore, her glories are explained in the *Padma-purāṇa* by Devarṣi Nārada.

yathā rādhā priyā viṣṇos
tasyāḥ kuṇḍaṁ priyaṁ tathā
sarva-gopīṣu saivaikā
viṣṇor atyanta-vallabhā

Just as Rādhā is dear to Lord Kṛṣṇa, so her bathing place [Rādhā-kuṇḍa] is dear to him. She alone is his most beloved of all the *gopīs*. (quoted from *Caitanya-caritāmṛta, Ādi-līlā* 4.215)

hlādinī ya mahā-śaktiḥ
sarva-śakti-varīyasi
tat-sāra-bhāva-rūpeyam
iti tantre pratiṣṭhitā

The great potency named *hlādinī* is the topmost among all potencies of the Lord. Her essential personified form is renowned by the name Rādhikā. This is established very well in the *tantras.* (*Sanat-kumāra-saṁhitā* 298)

Śrīla Rūpa Gosvāmī vividly glorifies Śrīmatī Rādhārāṇī in the *Cāṭu-puṣpāñjaliḥ* in the *Stava-mālā* as follows:

1 *nava-gorocanā-gaurīṁ pravarendrīvarāmbarām*
maṇi-stavaka-vidyoti-veṇī-vyālāṅgaṇā-phaṇām

O [Rādhikā], you are as fair as fresh *gorocana* (a bright yellow color) and have garments as splendid as a blue lotus. Your braids, being decorated with jewels and flowers, give the appearance of a serpent's hood.

2 *upamāna-ghaṭāmāna-prahāri-mukha-maṇḍalām*
navendu-nindi-bhālodyat-kasturī-tilaka-śriyam

Your incomparable face defeats any object of comparison. You have a beautiful forehead, decorated with an elegant musk *tilaka* which defies the beauty of the new moon.

3 *bhrū-jitānaṅga-kodaṇḍāṁ lola-nīlālakāvalim*
kajjalojjvalatā rājac-cakorī-cāru-locanām

Your eyebrows conquer the beauty of the love god's bow. You have dark bluish curly locks of hair, and your eyes, decorated with *kājala*, reign supreme, appearing as two splendid *cakorī* birds.

4 *tila-puṣpābha-nāsāgra-virājad-vara-maulikām*
adharodbhūta-bandhūkāṁ kundālī-bandhura-dvijām

The tip of your nose resembles a sesame flower and is decorated with a splendid pearl ring. Your lips defeat the beauty of the flowers that redden at noon, and your teeth are like a row of jasmines.

Aṣṭasakhī-līlā Devī Dāsī

Rādhārāṇī is the beloved of her father, Vṛṣabhānu.

5 *sa-ratna-svarṇa-rājīva-karṇikā-kṛta-karṇikām*
kastūrī-bindu-cibukāṁ ratna-graiveyakojjvalām

You have earrings which resemble a golden whorl of a lotus, embedded with jewels. Your chin is decorated with a dot of musk, and you wear a shining gem studded necklace.

6 *divyāṅgada-pariṣvaṅga-lasad-bhuja-mṛṇālikām*
balāri-ratna-valaya-kalālambi-kalāvikām

Your divine, lotus-stem-like arms are decorated with shining armlets and with tinkling bracelets made out of jewels and blue-sapphires.

7 *ratnāṅgurīyakollāsi-varāṅguli-karāmbujām*
manohara-mahā-hāra-vihāri-kuca-kuṭmalām

Your lotus hand has attractive fingers that shine with gem-studded rings. Your beautiful breasts have an attractive necklace that playfully moves around them.

8 *romāli-bhujagī-mūrdha-ratnābha-taralāñcitām*
vali-trayī-latā-baddha-kṣīṇa-bhaṅgura-madhyamām

The necklace on your heart is made of small-dark beads, in the center of which is a shining jewel, appearing like a scaly dark serpent having a gem on top of its head. Your graceful stomach has three folds of skin appearing as if they are three tender vines like a belt around your slender waist.

9 *maṇi-sārasanādhāra-visphāra-śroṇi-rodhasam*
hema-rambhā-madārambha-stambhanoru-yugākṛtim

Your broad hips are decorated with a belt composed of golden beads. Your two beautiful thighs defeat the pride of golden plantain trees.

10 *jānu-dyuti-jita-kṣulla-pīta-ratna-samudrakām*
śaran-nīraja-nīrājya-mañjīra-viraṇat-padām

Your knees defeat the beauty of a topaz-studded chest of jewels. The autumn lotus flowers worship your feet, along with their tinkling anklets.

11 *rākendu-koṭi-saundarya-jaitra-pāda-nakha-dyutim*
aṣṭābhiḥ sāttvikair bhāvair ākulī-kṛta-vigrahām

The splendor of your toenails defeats the beauty of millions of full moons. Your body is always agitated by the eight ecstatic symptoms.

12 *mukundāṅga-kṛpāpāṅgām anaṅgormi-taraṅgitām*
tvām ārabdha-śriyānandāṁ vande vṛndāvaneśvari

When you cast a sidelong glance at the transcendental body of Lord Mukunda, the waves of amorous desire toss you about. You then enjoy various pastimes with Kṛṣṇa. O queen of Vṛndāvana, I bow down and offer my respectful obeisances to you.

13 *ayi prodyan-mahā-bhāva-mādhurī-vihvalāntare*
aśeṣa-nāyikāvasthā-prākaṭyādbhuta-ceṣṭite

Your heart overflows with the sweetness of *mahā-bhāva*. Through your actions you exhibit the characteristics of all kinds of heroines.

14 *sarva-mādhurya-viñjolī-nirmāñchita-padāmbuje*
indirā-mṛgya-saundarya-sphurad-aṅghri-nakhāñcale

Your lotus feet are equipped with all varieties of sweetness, and even the goddess of fortune, Lakṣmī, seeks the beauty of your toenails.

15 *gokulendu-mukhī-vṛnda-sīmantottaṁsa-mañjari*
lalitādi-sakhī-yūtha-jīvātu-smita-korake

You are the flower worn in the parted hair of the moon-faced girls of Gokula. Your budding smile is the life of Lalitā and your other friends.

16 *caṭulāpāṅga-mādhurya-bindūnmādita-mādhave*
tāta-pāda-yaśaḥ-stoma-kairavānanda-candrike

A drop of the sweetness of your restless sidelong glance maddens Lord Mādhava. You are the moonlight of bliss for the white lotuses of your father Vṛṣabhānu's fame.

17 *apāra-karuṇā-pūra-pūritāntar-mano-hrade*
prasīdāsmin jane devi nija-dāsya-spṛhā-juṣi

The lake of your heart is filled with a limitless flood of mercy. O Devī, please be kind to this person who yearns to attain your service.

18 *kaccit tvaṁ cāṭu-paṭunā tena goṣṭhendra-sūnunā*
prārthyamāna-capālāṅga-prasādā drakṣyase mayā

Aṣṭasakhī-līlā Devī Dāsī

"O Rādhikā, you are the moonlight of bliss for the white lotuses."

When will I see the sweetly speaking prince of Vraja beg for the mercy of your restless sidelong glance?

> 19 *tvāṁ sādhu mādhavī-puṣpair mādhavena kalāvidā*
> *prasādhyamānāṁ svidyantīṁ bījayiṣyāmy ahaṁ kadā*

When will I fan you as you begin to perspire a little at the time when Śrī Mādhava artistically and carefully decorates you with *madhavī* flowers?

> 20 *keli-visraṁsino baka-keśa-vṛndasya sundari*
> *saṁskārāya kadā devi janam etaṁ nidekṣyasi*

O beautiful one, when will you order this person to fix your curly locks of hair now disarrayed due to your amorous pastimes?

> 21 *kadā bimboṣṭhi tāmbūlaṁ mayā tava mukhāmbuje*
> *arpyamāṇaṁ vrajādhīśa-sūnur ācchidya bhokṣyate*

O [Rādhikā], whose lips are like *bimba* fruits, when will the prince of Vraja snatch away and enjoy the betel nuts as I place them in your lotus mouth?

> 22 *vraja-rāja-kumāra-vallabhā-kula-sīmanta-maṇi prasīda me*
> *parivāra-gaṇasya te yathā padavī me na davīyasī bhavet*

O jewel in the parted hair of the *gopī* lovers of the prince of Vraja, kindly be pleased with me and keep me on the path of your intimate friends.

> 23 *karuṇāṁ muhur arthaye paraṁ tava vṛndāvana-cakravartini*
> *api keśaripor yathā bhavet sa caṭu-prārthana-bhājanaṁ janaḥ*

O queen of Vṛndāvana, at every moment I beg only for your kindness, by which this person may be able to offer proper prayers to Lord Kṛṣṇa, the enemy of Keśi.

> 24 *imaṁ vṛndāvaneśvaryā jano yaḥ paṭhati stavam*
> *cāṭu-puṣpāñjaliṁ nāma sa syād asyāḥ kṛpāspadam*

May whoever reads this prayer to the queen of Vṛndāvana, which bears the name *Cāṭu-puṣpāñjaliḥ* (a flower offering of sweet words), become the object of her mercy.

One should worship Śrīmatī Rādhārāṇī by always reciting these kinds of devotional prayers. Śrīla Raghunātha Dāsa Gosvāmī vividly reveals this mood in the *Vilāpa-kusumāñjali* (101–2).

lakṣmīr yad-aṅghri-kamalasya nakhāñcalasya
saundarya-bindum api nārhati labdhum īśe
sā tvaṁ vidhāsyasi na cen mama netra-dānaṁ
kīm jīvitena mama duḥkha-davāgnidena

āśā-bharair amṛta-sindhu-mayaiḥ kathañcit
kālo mayāti-gamitaḥ kila sāmpratam hi
tvaṁ cet kṛpāṁ mayi vidhāsyasi naiva kiṁ me
prāṇair vrajena ca varoru bakāriṇāpi

My queen, Lakṣmī is not able to attain even a drop of the beauty of the tip of your lotus toenails. If you do not give charity to my eyes, then what is the use of my life, ablaze with a great forest fire of sufferings? O Rādhā with the most beautiful thighs, now this servant of yours is somehow passing time in the material world, full of a nectarean flow of hopes [for your mercy]. If you do not bestow your mercy on me, then what is the use of maintaining my life, staying in Vṛndāvana, or having the association of Kṛṣṇa, the enemy of Baka?

Fortunate spiritual practitioners will develop deep spiritual attachment called *rati* towards *vraja-bhāva*, or devotional practice which is aligned with the eternal sentiment and devotional service that is displayed by the eternal associates of Kṛṣṇa. Then such persons must approach a guru to know their eternal identity. In that relationship they should execute spiritual practices (*bhajana* and *sādhana*), taking shelter of the *mañjarī* who manifests in the form of the guru.

Through continued service to that *mañjarī* [in the form of the guru: *gururupā*], the practitioner receives her grace to obtain the service of the *sakhīs* of Śrīmatī Rādhikā. Only by her* mercy can the practitioner be able to serve the divine couple in their eternal pastimes. All this becomes possible only when the practitioner possesses humility, eagerness, and focused resolve.

* The Bengali pronoun could refer either to the *mañjarī-guru* or to Śrī Rādhā.

Aṣṭasakhī-līlā Devī Dāsī

"Climb in the boat of the *sakhīs*' mercy and sail to Rādhā through the ocean of love."

ŚRĪLA BHAKTIVINODA ṬHĀKURA'S *MANAḤ-ŚIKṢĀ BHĀṢĀ* – SONG TEN

saundarya-kiraṇa-mālā, jine rati, gaurī, līlā,
anāyāse svarupa-vaibhave
śacī, lakṣmī, satyabhāmā, yata bhāgyavatī rāmā,
saubhāghya-balane parābhave

Her [Rādhā's] splendorous beauty overpowers that of the goddesses Rati, Gaurī, and Līlā. Her good fortune is far greater than the lucky divine women, Śacī, Lakṣmī and Satyabhāmā.

bhaja, mana, caraṇa tāṅhāra
candrāvalī-mukha yata, navīnā nāgarī śata,
vaśīkāre kare tiraskāra

Worship, O heart, her feet. She controls her beloved and wins his allegiance over Candrāvalī as well as thousands of other lovely young women.

se ye kṛṣṇa-prāṇeśvarī, kṛṣṇa-prāṇāhlāda-karī,
hlādinī svarūpa-śakti satī
tāṅhāra caraṇa tyaji', yadi kṛṣṇa-candra bhaji'
koṭi-yuge kṛṣṇa-gehe gati

She is the goddess of Kṛṣṇa's life-breath, the delighter of his soul. In fact, she is the embodiment of the power to give bliss, and the most chaste of all. If people neglect her lotus feet and only worship the moon-like Kṛṣṇa, though such persons may worship for a thousand years, they will not attain him.

sakhī-kṛpā-bhelā dhari', prema-sindhu-mājhe chari',
vṛṣabhānu-nandinī-caraṇe
kabe bā paḍiyā ra'ba, īśvarīra kṛpa pa'ba,
gaṇita haiba nija-jane

Climb in the boat of the *sakhīs*' mercy and sail into the ocean of love, where you will find the lotus feet of the daughter of Vṛṣabhānu, Rādhā. When will I fall at her feet and stay there? When will I get her mercy? When will she count me as one of her own?

VERSE ELEVEN

समं श्रीरूपेण स्मरविवशराधागिरिभृतोर्
व्रजे साक्षात्सेवालभनविधये तद्गणयुजोः ।
तदिज्याख्याध्यानश्रवणनतिपञ्चामृतमिदं
धयन् नीत्या गोवर्धनमनुदिनं त्वं भज मनः ॥

samaṁ śrī-rūpeṇa smara-vivaśa-rādhā-giri-bhṛtor
vraje sākṣāt-sevā-labhana-vidhaye tad-gaṇa-yujoḥ
tad-ijyākhyā-dhyāna-śravaṇa-nati-pañcāmṛtam idaṁ
dhayan nītyā govardhanam anudinaṁ tvaṁ bhaja manaḥ

manaḥ—O mind; *anu-dinam*—every day; *dhayan*—drink; *idam*—this; *pañca-amṛtam*—five nectars; *tad-ijyākhyā-dhyāna-śravaṇa-nati*—the worship (*ijyā*), glories (*ākhyā*), meditation (*dhyāna*), listening of pastimes (*śravaṇa*) and offering obeisances (*nati*); *tvaṁ bhaja*—you should worship; *govardhanam*—Govardhana; *nītyā*—following the rules; *samam*—same as; *śrī-rūpeṇa*—Śrī Rūpa; *sākṣāt-sevā-labhana-vidhaye*—to obtain the means of direct service; *smara-vivaśa-rādhā-giri-bhṛtoḥ*—[of] Śrī Śrī Rādhā-Giridhārī, who are captivated by god of love; *tad-gaṇa-yujoḥ*—and associates; *vraje*—in Vraja.

O mind, you should every day drink the five nectars—worship, glories, meditation, listening to divine pastimes, and offering obeisances—and worship Govardhana according to the rules. In this way, follow the instructions of Śrī Rūpa and obtain the direct service of Śrī Śrī Rādhā-Giridhārī, who are captivated by the god of amourous love, in the company of their associates in Vraja.

Aṣṭasakhī-līlā Devī Dāsī

Bathe Śrī Govardhana with five nectars (*pañcāmṛta*).

ŚRĪLA BHAKTIVINODA ṬHĀKURA'S *BHAJANA-DARPAṆA* COMMENTARY

What is the most confidential, deeply esoteric and exalted science of devotional service a *sādhaka*, practitioner, can perform to the divine couple? Raghunātha Dāsa Gosvāmī gives the answer within this text.

ŚLOKĀRTHA: MEANING OF THE VERSE

1 **Tad-gaṇa-yujoḥ: With confidential and eternal associates** Lord Śrī Kṛṣṇa is always surrounded by his friends such as Śrīdāma and Subala, and Śrīmatī Rādhārāṇī is surrounded by friends such as Śrī Lalitā Devī and Śrī Viśākhā Devī.

2 **Smara-vilāsa-parāyaṇa: Absorbed in attractive amorous pastimes** Become deeply absorbed in and attached to Rādhā-Kṛṣṇa's amorous *śṛṅgāra-rasa* after finding it more attractive than the other *rasas*, such as servitorship (*dāsya*), friendship (*sakhya*), and parental relationships (*vātsalya*).

3 **Vraje sākṣāt sevā lābha: Achieving direct service in Vraja-dhāma** Whatever service is rendered in the stage of *sādhana-bhakti* (devotional service according to scripture in practice) is a simulation of direct service. In the stage of perfection (*siddhi*) one first attains service to the Lord from a distance. After gradually serving under the guidance of a *mañjarī* from a distance, one gets service that brings one closer to the *sakhīs*. After that, the practitioner gradually achieves the direct service of the divine couple Śrī Śrī Rādhā-Govinda.

There are unlimited varieties of direct services such as cleaning the forest groves, making the bed of the divine couple, fetching water, preparing *tāmbūla* (betel nut and leaf), stringing garlands, and offering camphor. The services are endless, and unlimited maidservants are each engaged in their specific respective service.

The direct service of Rādhā and Kṛṣṇa is possible only when the living entity achieves an eternal, perfected, original spiritual form. In the direct service of amorous love, one experiences the highest, purest bliss at every moment in one's heart from the deepest emotions

Lord Śrī Kṛṣṇa is always surrounded by his friends such as Śrīdāma and Subala, and Śrīmatī Rādhārāṇī is surrounded by friends such as Lalitā and Viśākhā.

In the stage of perfection (*siddhi*) one first attains service to the Lord from a distance.

Aṣṭasakhī-līlā Devī Dāsī

Gradually one gets service that brings one closer to the *sakhīs*.

Aṣṭasakhī-līlā Devī Dāsī

The practitioner gradually achieves the direct service of Śrī Śrī Rādhā-Govinda.

(*bhāva*). That bliss never diminishes, nor does it ever get quenched, because the object of love is eternally new and fresh. At that stage, one has no selfish desire and is only motivated by direct service. Therefore not even an iota of suffering can touch one's heart. The misery that arises out of separation (*vipralambha*) in amorous love is just a transmutation of this ultimate bliss and is not like the suffering one experiences due to the material body.

4 **Śrī-rūpeṇa-samam: Aligned with the teachings of Śrī Rūpa Gosvāmī** Being aligned with the teachings of Śrī Rūpa means to follow the process (*nīti*) that the master-teacher of amorous *rasa*, Śrīla Rūpa Gosvāmī, has taught in *Śrī Bhakti-rasāmṛta-sindhuḥ* and *Śrī Ujjvala-nīlamaṇiḥ*. In this regard he says [in *Bhakti-rasāmṛta-sindhuḥ* 1.2.90–3]:

śraddhā viśeṣataḥ prītiḥ
śrī-mūrter-aṅghri-sevane

śrīmad-bhāgavatārthānām
āsvādo rasikaiḥ saha
sajātīyāśaye snigdhe
sādhau saṅgaḥ svato vare

nāma-saṅkīrtanaṁ śrīman-
mathurā-maṇḍale sthitiḥ

aṅgānāṁ pañcakasyāsya
pūrvaṁ vilikhitasya ca
nikhila-śraiṣṭhya-bodhāya
punar apy atra kīrtanam

With love and full faith one should worship the lotus feet of the Deity (*śrī-mūrti*). One should taste the meaning of *Śrīmad-Bhāgavatam* in the association of pure devotees, and one should associate with the devotees who are more advanced than oneself and who are endowed with a similar type of affection for the Lord. One should congregationally chant the holy name of the Lord and reside in Vṛndāvana. The glorification of these five items is to make known the complete superiority of these five practices of devotional service. (quoted from *Caitanya-caritāmṛta, Madhya-līlā* 22.130–132 and 22.129, purport)

Aṣṭasakhī-līlā Devī Dāsī

One should wear *tilaka* and the Deity's garland, and drink the Deity's foot wash water.

5 **Ijyā: Worship of the Lord** *Ijyā* includes serving the soles of the feet of the Lord's *mūrti* (or the *mūrti* in general); honoring the special day of Lord Hari, Ekādaśī; wearing garlands or necklaces (*mālya*)* and *tilaka*; and taking the vow of accepting remnants of food offered to the Lord and water that has washed the feet of the *mūrti*. Serving *tulasī* and similar services are also included within this category.

6 **Ākhyā: Glorification** *Ākhyā* includes studying devotional literatures, and hearing and chanting the names and pastimes of Lord Hari.

7 **Dhyāna: Meditation** *Dhyāna* is a special category of *smaraṇa* (meditation on, or remembrance of, the Lord), but in this verse, Raghunātha Dāsa Gosvāmī has used *dhyāna* to refer to *smaraṇa* in general. Śrī Jīva Gosvāmī gives a detailed explanation of *smaraṇa* [in the *Bhakti-sandarbha, Anuccheda* 278]:

> *atha pūrvavat krama-sopāna-rītyā sukha-labhyaṁ guṇa-parikara-sevā-līlā-smaraṇaṁ cānusandheyam. tad idaṁ smaraṇaṁ pañca-vidham – yat kiñcid anusandhānaṁ smaraṇam. sarvataś cittam ākṛṣya sāmānyākāreṇa mano-dhāraṇaṁ dhāraṇā. viśeṣato rūpādi-vicintanaṁ dhyānam. amṛta-dhārāvad avicchinnaṁ tad dhruvānusmṛtiḥ. dhyeya-mātra-sphuraṇaṁ samādhir iti.*

Meditation on the Lord (*smaraṇa*) progresses in the following order: First one should meditate on the Lord's holy names (*nāma*), then his form (*rūpa*), his divine qualities (*guṇa*), his associates (*parikara*), one's service in connection to him (*sevā*), and finally his pastimes (*līlā*).

Smaraṇa can be categorized into five stages: 1 To meditate on whatever spiritual topics come easily to the mind is simply *smaraṇa*. 2 To attempt, in a general way, to thoroughly fix the mind on the Lord is *dhāraṇā*. 3 To make a focused attempt to meditate on specific forms, pastimes, etc. of the Lord is *dhyāna*. 4 Meditation on the Lord that occurs spontaneously as a constant flow of nectar is *dhruvānusmṛti*. 5 And when only the Lord (the object of meditation) exists in one's consciousness, it is *samādhi*.

* *Mālya* generally means garlands but could also refer to *tulasī* neck beads (see *Caitanya-caritāmṛta, Madhya-līlā* 24.333)

8 **Śravaṇa: Hearing** Hearing includes listening to saintly people glorify the playful pastimes of the Lord. The cultural system of hearing *purāṇas* in the evenings is a part of this practice.

9 **Nati: Offering Obeisances** One should offer prostrated obeisances (*sāṣṭāṅga-praṇāma**) before the Lord's *mūrti* or any object or place that awakens one's remembrance of the Lord.

10 **Śrī-govardhana-bhajana: Worship Śrī Govardhana** Śrī Raghunātha Dāsa Gosvāmī offers this particular instruction for himself as well as for everyone else. Śrī Caitanya Mahāprabhu, the moon of the sky-like heart of devotees, personally gave his *govardhana-śilā* to Śrīla Raghunātha Dāsa Gosvāmī, who describes this incident in *Śrī Gaurāṅga-stava-kalpataruḥ* (verse 11), from *Stavāvalī*:

mahā-sampad-dāvād api patitam uddhṛtya kṛpayā
svarūpe yaḥ svīye kujanam api māṁ nyasya muditaḥ
uro-guñjā-hāraṁ priyam api ca govardhana-śilāṁ
dadau me gaurāṅgo hṛdaya udayan māṁ madayati

> Although I am a fallen soul, the lowest of men, Śrī Caitanya Mahāprabhu delivered me from the blazing forest fire of great material opulence by his mercy. He handed me over in great pleasure to Svarūpa Dāmodara, his personal associate. The Lord also gave me the garland of small conchshells that he wore on his chest, and a stone from Govardhana Hill, although they were very dear to him. That same Lord Śrī Caitanya Mahāprabhu awakens within my heart and makes me mad after him. (quoted from *Caitanya-caritāmṛta, Antya-līlā* 6.327)

A *govardhana-śilā* is a direct manifestation of the Supreme Lord. Worshipping this *śilā*, or harboring the attitude, "I will never leave Govardhana where Śrī Raghunātha Dāsa Gosvāmī resides," is also service to Govardhana.

* *dorbhyāṁ padbhyāṁ ca jānubhyām, urasā śirasā dṛśā/ manasā vacasā ceti, praṇāmo 'ṣṭāṅga īritaḥ*: "*Sāṣṭāṅga-praṇāma* is defined as paying full prostrated obeisances using one's 1 hands, 2 feet, 3 thighs, 4 chest, 5 head, 6 sight [closed eyes], 7 mind, and 8 speech." (*Hari-bhakti-vilāsa* 8.360)

Aṣṭasakhī-līlā Devī Dāsī

Following the rules, worship Govardhana.

Congregationally chant the holy name of the Lord and reside in Vṛndāvana.

Aṣṭasakhī-līlā Devī Dāsī

Offer prostrated obeisances (*sāṣṭāṅga-praṇāma*) before the Deity or any object or place that awakens our remembrance of the Lord.

Aṣṭasakhī-līlā Devī Dāsī

Taste the meaning of *Śrīmad-Bhāgavatam* in the association of pure devotees.

Aṣṭasakhī-līlā Devī Dāsī

Meditate on the holy names, divine form, divine qualities, Kṛṣṇa's associates, and one's service in connection to him and his pastimes.

This conception of worship to Govardhana has two meanings. The first is that the practitioner should respect and worship a *govardhana-śilā* as one respects the *mūrti* of the Lord. The second meaning is to worship the Lord while residing at Śrī Govardhana, or any of the holy places that surround the hill, where the Lord performed many pastimes. Residence in the holy *dhāma* as indicated here is synonymous with Śrīla Rūpa Gosvāmī's instructions of living in Mathurā.

11 **Nityā: In accordance with the rules of devotion** *Nīti* does not indicate simply *vaidhī-mārga*, or the path where the impetus is scriptural logic and rules. Those who are eligible for *vaidhī-bhakti* will worship according to those rules and regulations. But those on the platform of *rāgānuga-bhakti*, or spontaneous devotional service, will worship by adopting the rules for *rāga-bhakti* as set forth by Śrīla Rūpa Gosvāmī.

ŚRĪLA BHAKTIVINODA ṬHĀKURA'S *MANAḤ-ŚIKṢĀ BHĀṢĀ* – SONG ELEVEN

vrajera nikuñja-vane, rādhā-kṛṣṇa sakhī-sane,
līlā-rase nitya thāke bhora
sei dainandina-līlā, bahu-bhāgye ye sevilā,
tāhāra bhāgyera baḍa jora

Fill yourself with the delectable, intoxicating nectar of Rādhā-Kṛṣṇa's *līlā* with their *sakhīs* in the forest bowers of Vraja, and remain drunk on it eternally. One who serves them according to their daily *līlā* is superlatively fortunate!

mana, yadi cāha sei dhana
śrī-rūpera saṅga la'ye, tān̐'ra anucarī ha'ye,
kara tān̐ra nirdiṣṭa bhajana

Oh heart! If you want that treasure, then along with Śrī Rūpa's associates, become Śrī Rūpa's maidservant, and do worship and bhajana according to Śrī Rūpa's specific instructions.

hṛdaye rāgera bhāve, kālocita sevā pā'be,
sadā rase rahibe majiyā

bāhire sādhana-deha, karibe bhajana-geha,
niḥsaṅge vā sādhu-saṅga laiyā,

In a mood of spontaneous pure love, you will receive a service (*seva*) appropriate to various times [of the day] and become enraptured in the mood of service. Externally, in your form of a practitioner, follow your program of worship (*sādhana-bhajana*) at home, either in seclusion or in the association of saintly persons (*sādhus*).

yugala-pūjana, dhyāna, nati, śruti, saṁkīrtana,
pañcāmṛte seva govardhane
rūpa-raghunātha-pāya, e bhaktivinoda cāya,
dṛḍha-mati e-rūpa bhajane

Perform worship of and meditation of the divine couple, offer obeisance to them, hear about them, dance in *saṅkīrtana,* and bathe Śrī Govardhana with five nectars (*pañcāmṛta*). Bhaktivinoda longs for the lotus feet of Rūpa and Raghunātha. His heart is fixed unwaveringly on doing *bhajana* in this way.

VERSE TWELVE

मनःशिक्षादैकादशकवरमेतन् मधुरया
गिरा गायत्युच्चैः समधिगतसर्वार्थतति यः ।
सयूथः श्रीरूपानुग इह भवन् गोकुलवने
जनो राधाकृष्णातुलभजनरत्नं स लभते ॥

manaḥ-śikṣā-daikādaśaka-varam etan madhurayā
girā gāyaty uccaiḥ samadhigata-sarvārtha-tati yaḥ
sa-yūthaḥ śrī-rūpānuga iha bhavan gokula-vane
jano rādhā-kṛṣṇātula-bhajana-ratnaṁ sa labhate

śrī-rūpa-anuga bhavan—becoming a servant of Śrī Rūpa; *sa-yūthaḥ*—along with Rūpa's companions; *yaḥ*—one who; *madhurayā girā*—in a sweet voice; *gāyati uccaiḥ*—sings loudly; *etat*—these; *manaḥ-śikṣā-da-ekādaśaka-varam*—eleven supreme verses that give instructions to the mind; *samadhigata-sarva-artha-tati*—strives to understand all of their meanings completely; *janaḥ*—that person; *sa labhate*—obtains; *rādhā-kṛṣṇa-atula-bhajana-ratnam*—the incomparable jewel of worship of Śrī Śrī Rādha-Kṛṣṇa; *iha gokula-vane*—here in the Gokula forest.

Becoming a follower of Śrī Rūpa and his companions, one who with a sweet voice loudly recites these eleven supreme verses, which give instructions to the mind, and strives to understand all of their meanings completely, obtains the incomparable jewel of worshiping Śrī Śrī Rādhā-Kṛṣṇa in the forests of Gokula.

Śyāma-vallabha Devī Dāsī

Raghunātha Dāsa Gosvāmī writes *Manaḥ-śikṣā* at the bank of Rādhā-kuṇḍa.

ŚRĪLA BHAKTIVINODA ṬHĀKURA'S *BHAJANA-DARPAṆA* COMMENTARY

ŚLOKĀRTHA: MEANING OF THE VERSE

1 **Sa-yūtha: With your own group** One should remain with Vaiṣṇavas who are similarly disposed, dignified, and more advanced than oneself. Śrī Lalitā and other *sakhīs* (female friends) are independent leaders of their own groups and yet remain subservient to Śrīmatī Rādhārāṇī. Similarly, the *uttama-bhāgavata-vaiṣṇava*, or first class pure devotee, remains a follower of Śrīla Rūpa Gosvāmī even though such a person may be the spiritual master of many disciples. Śrīla Rūpa Gosvāmī elaborates on this point in *Śrī Ujjvala-nīlamaṇiḥ* (*Hari-priyā-prakarana* 3.61):

yūthādhipātve 'py aucityaṁ
dadhānā lalitādayaḥ
sveṣṭa-rādhādi-bhāvasya
lobhāt sakhya-ruciṁ dadhuḥ

> Even though Lalitā and similar *gopīs* are qualified to lead their own separate groups, they choose to remain as Rādhā's *sakhīs* due to their intense desire to ensure Rādhā's pleasure in the groves.

2 **Śrī-rūpānuga: A follower in the line of Śrīla Rūpa Gosvāmī** One should follow the instructions [regarding *bhajana*] that Rūpa Gosvāmī received from Caitanya Mahāprabhu, based on which he performed his own *bhajana*.

3 **Gokula-vane: In the forest of Gokula*** Being "in the forest of Gokula" means to be at any secluded place within the *Mathurā-maṇḍala*. Śrīla Rūpa Gosvāmī describes the glories of *Mathurā-maṇḍala* in his *Śrī Mathurā-stava* in the *Stava-mālā*:

* Bhaktivinoda starts off his commentary with two different Bengali translations of verse twelve. The first one says that the singer of these verses attains the service of Rādhā-Kṛṣṇa in Gokula. The second, which is in simpler prose, says the singer should be in Gokula and will attain the service of Rādhā-Kṛṣṇa.

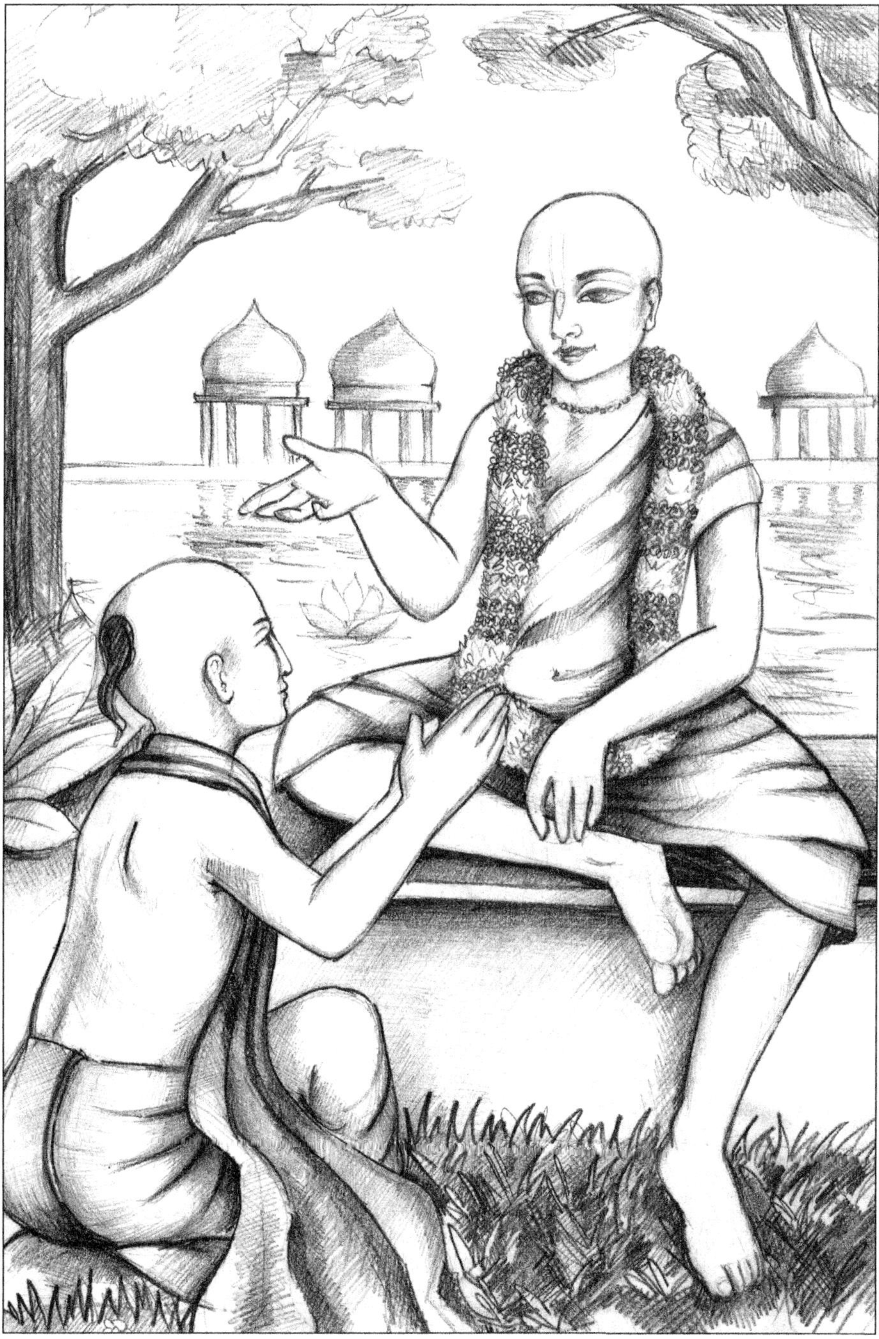

Śyāma-vallabha Devī Dāsī

Rūpa Gosvāmī received instructions from Caitanya Mahāprabhu.

Śyāma-vallabha Devī Dāsī

Follow the instructions that Rūpa Gosvāmī received from Mahāprabhu.

1 *mukter govinda-bhakter vitaraṇa-caturaṁ saccidānanda-rūpaṁ*
yasyāṁ vidyoti vidyā-yugalam udayate tārakaṁ pārakaṁ ca
kṛṣṇasyotpatti-līlā-khanir akhila-jagan-mauli-ratnasya sā te
vaikuṇṭhād yā pratiṣṭhā prathayatu mathurā maṅgalānāṁ kalāpam

Śrī Mathurā is expert in distributing liberation in the form of devotion to Govinda. She is full of eternity, knowledge and bliss. In Mathurā, two illuminating types of knowledge arise naturally – the knowledge to deliver the self from birth and death (*tāraka*), and the knowledge which helps one cross over the material world (*pāraka*). She is a mine of the jewels of the birth pastimes of the crest jewel of the world, Kṛṣṇa. May that Mathurā, more glorious even than Vaikuṇṭha, unfold a host of auspicious blessings for everyone.

2 *koṭīndu-spaṣṭa-kāntī rabhasa-yuta-bhava-kleśa-yaudher ayodhyā*
māyā-vitrāsi-vāsā muni-hṛdaya-muṣo divya-līlā sravantī
sāśīḥ kāśīśa-mukhyāmara-patibhir alaṁ prārthita-dvāra-kāryā
vaikuṇṭhodgīta-kīrtir diśatu madhupurī prema-bhakti-śriyaṁ vaḥ

Mathurā's effulgence is greater than a million moons. She cannot be influenced by the swift attacks of the threefold material miseries. The enchanting glories of residing in Mathurā can easily trouble the enchantments of even the most powerful demigods [in other words, their mystic powers cannot stay here]. The hearts of the great sages [Śukadeva, etc.] are attracted to Mathurā, and they directly witness all the pastimes of Kṛṣṇa here. She can fulfill all desires of her worshipers. Great personalities like Lord Kāśīśvara (Śiva) and Lord Brahmā always pray to be her guardians. May that Mathurā, more glorious even than Vaikuṇṭha, bestow you with devotional love for Kṛṣṇa.

3 *bījaṁ muktitaror anartha-paṭalī-nistārakaṁ tārakaṁ*
dhāma prema-rasasya vāñchita-dhurā-saṁpārakaṁ pārakam
etad yatra nivāsinām udayate cic-chakti-vṛtti-dvayaṁ
mathnātu vyasanāni māthura-purī sā vaḥ śriyaṁ ca kriyāt

Lord Rāma's six-syllabled mantra (*rāṁ rāmāya namaḥ*), known as the *tāraka-mantra*, is the seed of the tree of liberation and delivers one from all *anarthas*. Kṛṣṇa's eighteen-syllable-mantra (*klīṁ kṛṣṇāya govindāya gopī-jana-vallabhāya svāhā*), known as the *pāraka-mantra*, bestows the loving spiritual abode and fulfills all spiritual desires.

However, for the residents of this Mathurā, these two phenomena of *tāraka* and *pāraka* (deliverance from *anarthas* and attainment of all spiritual desires) occur naturally. May that Mathurā destroy your faults and bestow good fortune to all of you.*

4 *adyāvanti patad-grahaṁ kuru kare māye śanair vījaya*
cchatraṁ kāñci gṛhāṇa kāśi purataḥ pādū-yugaṁ dhāraya
nāyodhye bhaja sambhramaṁ stuti-kathāṁ nodgāraya dvārake
devīyaṁ bhavatīṣu hanta mathurā dṛṣṭi-prasādaṁ dadhe

O Avantī (*ujjain-dhāma*), hold the spittoon for collecting betel nut in your hands. O Kāñcī (*kāñcīpuraṁ-dhāma*), hold the umbrella. O Kāśī, stand in front holding sandals. O Ayodhyā, do not fear your mistress. O Dvārakā, please stop reciting her glories. Just see, this queen of Lord Kṛṣṇa, Mathurā, is finally showering benedictory glances on all you maidservants.**

In his *Śrī Vṛndāvanāṣṭakam* in the *Stava-mālā*, Śrīla Rūpa Gosvāmī beautifully explains the glories of Vṛndāvana:

1 *mukunda-muralī-rava-śravaṇa-phulla-hṛd-vallarī-*
kadambaka-karambita-prati-kadamba-kuñjāntarā
kalinda-giri-nandinī-kamala-kandalāndolinā
sugandhir anilena me śaraṇam astu vṛndāṭavī

On hearing the sounds of Mukunda's flute, the creeper of the *gopīs'* hearts blossom, and they enter each and every *kuñja* within the *kadamba* forests of Vṛndāvana. Yamunā, the daughter of Kalinda Mountain, flows here. Lotus flowers in the Yamunā move around due to the fragrant winds. May that Vṛndāvana forest be my shelter.

2 *vikuṇṭha-pura-saṁśrayād vipinato'pi niḥśreyasāt*
sahasra-guṇitāṁ śriyaṁ praduhatī rasa-śreyasīm
caturmukha-mukhair api spṛhita-tārṇadehodbhavā
jagadgurubhir agrimaiḥ śaraṇam astu vṛndāṭavī

* This translation is based on Śrīla Jīva Gosvāmī's commentary.

** In this verse, Śrīla Rūpa Gosvāmī lists six other well known holy places — Avantī, Māyā, Kāñcī, Kāśī, Ayodhyā, and Dvārakā — who also bestow *mukti* (liberation), but who are always busy as maidservants of Mathurā.

Śyāma-vallabha Devī Dāsī

Following the wishes of Rādhikā, the daughter of Nanda's friend Vṛṣabhānu, her *sakhīs* manifest a festival of joy for the moving and non-moving living entities.

The shelter of Vṛndāvana supersedes the shelter of the liberation provided in Vaikuṇṭha by a thousand times, for the shelter of Vṛndāvana provides the ultimate good fortune of the various types of *bhakti-rasa* such as *dāsya, sakhya, vātsalya,* and *mādhurya.* The desire to take birth here as an insignificant blade of grass is expressed even by the excellent four mouths of Lord Brahmā, the spiritual master of the entire world. May that Vṛndāvana forest be my shelter.

3 *anārata-vikasvara-vratati-puñja-puṣpāvalī-*
visāri-vara-saurabhodgama-ramā-camatkāriṇī
amanda-makaranda-bhṛd-viṭapi-vṛnda-vṛndīkṛta-
dvirepha-kula-vanditā śaraṇam astu vṛndāṭavī

Vṛndāvana's fully blossoming creeper-filled forest spreads about an excellent fragrance that amazes even the goddess of fortune. The forest is full of wonderful groups of nectar-dripping, flower-laden trees, which cause the hosts of bees to always offer praises to her. May that Vṛndāvana forest be my shelter.

4 *kṣaṇa-dyuti-ghana-śriyo-vraja-navīna-yūnoḥ padaiḥ*
suvaglubhir alaṅkṛtā lalita-lakṣma-lakṣmī-bharaiḥ
tayor nakhara-maṇḍalī-śikhara-keli-caryocitair
vṛtā kiśalayāṅkuraiḥ śaraṇam astu vṛndāṭavī

Her blades of grass, leaves, and sprouts are luxuriant, and are decorated with marks from the sports of the nail-tips of the superexcellent feet of the lightning and cloud of Rādhā and Kṛṣṇa. Their feet carry a host of beautiful marks such as lightning and lotus. May that Vṛndāvana forest be my shelter.

5 *vrajendra-sakha-nandinī-śubhatarādhikāra-kriyā-*
prabhāvaja-sukhotsava-sphurita-jaṅgama-sthāvarā
pralamba-damanānuja-dhvanita-vaṁśikā-kākalī-
rasajña-mṛga-maṇḍalā śaraṇam astu vṛndāṭavī

In Vṛndāvana, the *sakhīs* of Rādhikā, the daughter of Nanda's friend (Vṛṣabhānu), manifest a festival of joy for the moving and non-moving living entities by her orders. Vṛndāvana is replete with hosts of expert *rasika* animals who are attracted to the sounds of the flute of Kṛṣṇa, the younger brother of Balarāma, Pralamba's enemy. May that Vṛndāvana forest be my shelter.

Śyāma-vallabha Devī Dāsī

Balarāma, Pralamba's enemy, plays a flute and walks through a forest with his *gopīs*.

6 *amanda-mudirārbudābhyadhika-mādhurī-medura-*
vrajendra-suta-vīkṣaṇonnaṭita-nīlakaṇṭhotkarā
dineśa-suhṛd-ātmajākṛta-nijābhimānollasal-
latā-khaga-mṛgāṅganā śaraṇam astu vṛndāṭavī

Here in Vṛndāvana, on seeing the beautiful complexion, like a thick dark cloud, of Nanda's son, the peacocks shout and dance in ecstatic joy. The many creepers, birds, and animals all joyously and resoundingly proclaim the pride of Rādhā, the daughter of the sun-worshiper Vṛṣabhānu. Her pride is, "This forest is mine!" May that Vṛndāvana forest be my shelter.

7 *agaṇya-guṇa-nāgarī-gaṇa-gariṣṭha-gāndharvikā-*
manoja-raṇa-cāturī-piśuna-kuñja-puñjojjvalā
jagat-traya-kalā-guror lalita-lāsya-valgat-pada-
prayoga-vidhi-sākṣiṇī śaraṇam astu vṛndāṭavī

The dazzling groves of the Vṛndāvana forest testify to the love-battle expertise of Śrī Rādhikā, who is the host of unlimited excellent qualities. This Vṛndāvana forest is witness to the beautiful dancing of the lotus feet of Śrī Kṛṣṇa, the lord of all the creative arts in the three worlds. May that Vṛndāvana forest be my shelter.

8 *variṣṭha-haridāsatā-pada-samṛddha-govardhanā*
madhūdvaha-vadhū-camatkṛti-nivāsa-rāsa-sthalā
agūḍha-gahana-śriyo madhurima-vrajenojjvalā
vrajasya sahajena me śaraṇam astu vṛndāṭavī

Śrī Govardhana, who is awarded the fortune of being the best servant of Śrī Hari, resides in the Vṛndāvana forest. This forest is the setting of the *rāsa-sthala*, whose narration amazed even Kṛṣṇa's wedded wives. Vṛndāvana is illuminated by the beauty of the various forests of Vraja-maṇḍala surrounding it. May that Vṛndāvana forest be my shelter.

9 *idaṁ nikhila-niṣkuṭāvali-variṣṭha-vṛndāṭavī-*
guṇa-smaraṇa-kāri yaḥ paṭhati suṣṭhu padyāṣṭakam
vasan vyasana-mukta-dhīra-niśam atra sad-vāsanaḥ
sa pīta-vasane vaśī ratim avāpya vikrīḍati

These eight verses are a meditation on the excellent qualities of Vṛndāvana, the giver of all joy. One who is free from vices, is self-con-

Śyāma-vallabha Devī Dāsī

"Rādhārāṇī's pride is: 'This forest is mine!' May that Vṛndāvana forest be my shelter."

trolled, resides in Vṛndāvana, and recites these prayers in a proper mood, will attain love that can conquer Kṛṣṇa, the wearer of yellow cloth, and will engage in sporting pastimes with him.

4 **Manaḥ-śikṣā-da: Giving instructing to the mind** These verses of *Manaḥ-śikṣā* offer instruction to the mind of those devotees who desire to pursue the spiritual *bhajana* path.

5 **Varam: Super-excellent** These verses of *Manaḥ-śikṣā* are derived from the confidential instructions of Śrī Svarūpa Dāmodara Gosvāmī and Śrī Rūpa Gosvāmī by the grace of Śrī Caitanya Mahāprabhu.

6 **Madhurayā-girā-uccaiḥ: Singing loudly in a sweet, melodious voice** One should loudly and clearly sing these verses of *Manaḥ-śikṣā* with perfect meter, either together with others or alone, in a sweet voice overflowing with loving feeling.

7 **Samadhigata: Thoroughly understanding each and all meanings** One should recite each of the eleven *ślokas* of *Manaḥ-śikṣā* with a clear understanding of the deeper confidential meanings.

yeṣāṁ sarāga-bhajane vraja-rāja-sūnoḥ
śrī-rūpa-śikṣita-matānugamānurāgaḥ
yatnena te bhajana-darpaṇa-nāma-bhāṣyaṁ
sikṣāda-śloka-sahitaṁ prapaṭhantu bhaktyā

Those who have deep attachment for following in the footsteps of the path of opinions taught by Śrīla Rūpa Gosvāmī regarding the spontaneous loving *bhajana* of the son of Nanda should, with great effort and devotion, read carefully this instructive *bhajana-darpaṇa* commentary filled with many instructive verses.

Thus ends the integrated commentaries (*miśra-bhāṣya*) composed by Śrī Bhaktivinoda named *bhajana-darpaṇa* explaining the verses of the *Manaḥ-śikṣā*, offered fully and wholeheartedly to the lotus feet of Śrī Kṛṣṇa Caitanya Mahāprabhu.

PART THREE

Commentaries by contemporary Vaiṣṇavas

VERSE ONE

gurau goṣṭhe goṣṭhālayiṣu sujane bhū-sura-gaṇe
sva-mantre śrī-nāmni vraja-nava-yuva-dvandva-śaraṇe
sadā dambhaṁ hitvā kuru ratim apūrvām atitarāṁ
aye svāntar bhrātaś caṭubhir abhiyāce dhṛta-padaḥ

O dear brother! O mind! Having given up all pride, please develop unprecedented and excessive attachment to Śrī Guru; to Śrī Vṛndāvana, the abode of cows; to the devotee residents of Vṛndāvana; to all the devotees on this planet; to the confidential mantra [given by Śrī Guru]; to the holy names of Śrī Śrī Rādhā-Kṛṣṇa; and to the process of surrendering to the fresh youthful couple of Vraja. Holding your feet, I beseech you with sweet words.

COMMENTARY BY ŚIVARĀMA SWAMI

In his commentary, the question Śrīla Bhaktivinoda Ṭhākura identified as being principal to *Manaḥ-śikṣā* is: what happens when faith, *śraddhā*, in talks of Kṛṣṇa (*kṛṣṇa-kathā*) occurs in the living being? The answer is stated here: that one develops love for the spiritual master, *vṛndāvana-dhāma*, the *vraja-vāsīs*, Vaiṣṇavas, the *brāhmaṇas*, and the holy name, and takes shelter of Rādhā and Kṛṣṇa.

In an overall sense this verse describes the development of faith as being the inaugurator of further activities. Raghunātha Dāsa Gosvāmī explains the natural course of activities for one in whom *śraddhā* has become manifest. *Śraddhā* (faith) is a rare commodity. Śrīla Rūpa Goswami says, *janma-koṭi-sukṛtair na labhyate*: it is not something that can be very easily acquired, but rather may take many millions of lifetimes. It is not a by-product of karma, nor can it be acquired by mental speculation. There is only one real means by which one can acquire faith, and that is solely through the association of devotees.

Śrīla Bhaktivinoda Ṭhākura explains that there is a certain process by which faith (*śraddhā*) develops. He first explains the position of one who does not possess faith. Even by asking what the condition is of someone who doesn't actually possess any faith, the lack of faith is evidenced, and one remains unqualified to actually hear *kṛṣṇa-kathā*, or specifically, unqualified to take shelter of *kṛṣṇa-kathā* and progressive spiritual life.

Secondly, because one's hearing must be based on faith, then without it one is unable to assimilate practical instruction. Therefore Rūpa Gosvāmī says *ādau śraddhā*, that *śraddhā* is the basic ingredient upon which everything else is built. Without it one cannot advance in spiritual life. One may be the greatest philosopher (*jñānī*), or one may be the most elevated personality, but if one is devoid of faith then there will be no progress.

So how is it that faith actually develops? Bhaktivinoda Ṭhākura says that by the association of devotees one will acquire faith. Somehow or other that faith may even come unknowingly. It may start by *ajñāta sukṛti*, a flickering or indirect contact with Vaiṣṇavas. That contact becomes persons' *adhikāra*, or their qualification for getting further association. How does this association actually work? The Ṭhākura points out that such association diminishes the reaction of past sins. In other words, by the association of a Vaiṣṇava one becomes purified of the results of one's past sinful activities, and therefore room in the heart is allowed for *śraddhā* to enter and develop. This word *śraddhā* is very nice. *Śra* means heart and *dhā* means to give. So *śraddhā* literally means to give your heart.

The process whereby the association of faithful devotees, or those who also have *śraddhā*, inspires people to give their heart to Kṛṣṇa is *sādhu-saṅga*. And that results in the development, or the growing, of faith. It will not grow automatically, but only by the proper process. Faith has natural symptoms by which it is marked. If one has a firm conviction, then one's actions will reflect that conviction. It is stated in this verse that automatically if faith is strong, a person will take *dīkṣā* from guru: *sva-mantre, śrī-nāmni*. *Sva-mantra* means Gāyatrī mantra, and *śrī-nāmni* means the holy name. These things refer to the actions that reflect one's conviction because one can only get these things if one is actually initiated by a spiritual master.

We worship by mantra, the Hare Kṛṣṇa *mahā-mantra* and Gāyatrī mantra, specifically, *kāma-gāyatrī*, which is the means by which Lord Kṛṣṇa is worshiped. In *Caitanya-caritāmṛta* it is described, *vṛndāvane 'aprākṛta navīna madana' kāma-gāyatrī kāma-bīje yāṅra upāsana. Upāsana*, or the worship of Lord Kṛṣṇa in Vṛndāvana, transpires by the process of this *kāma-gayatri* mantra, and *kāma-bīja*. These are not ritualistic activities that we are given to perform for some material purpose, but are elaborate processes of worship. Śrīla Prabhupāda uses the words "very sublime." Due to our lack of *śraddhā* and philosophical knowledge we don't appreciate the instruments and the means of worship we have been given.

Sometimes devotees like to do extreme *pūjā* and chant all kinds of elaborate mantras, use *yantras*, or perform *yajñas*, thinking doing so will improve their worship. But these things are foolishness. Everything is there in the Hare Kṛṣṇa *mahā-mantra*. Anything you have ever heard, and anything else that you haven't heard, is all there in the *mahā-mantra. Sarva-vedeṣu dṛśyate*: everything in the Vedas is there. All the procedures are condensed and present in that process of chanting Hare Kṛṣṇa. Therefore any process of worship we have preference for cannot be done in any better way than by this chanting process, which is available to everyone. When one becomes further qualified by the chanting, more *śraddhāvan*, or faithful, then he or she receives Gāyatrī mantra, by which one is considered to be in the mode of goodness and very quickly comes to the transcendental platform.

Gāyatrī mantra is an expansion of the holy name of the Lord, and it gives a clear definition of who is the object of worship through the Hare Kṛṣṇa *mahā-mantra*. Through this worship, one's faith will mature and one will come to render loving devotional service. This term "loving devotional service" is found frequently in Śrīla Prabhupāda's books. It does not simply mean following rules and regulations but rather refers to spontaneous devotional service, or pure devotional service (*rāgānugā-bhakti*).

Thus faith develops further by worshiping both the *śikṣā* and *dīkṣā-gurus*, and taking association with Vaiṣṇavas. Caitanya Mahāprabhu says that associating with Vaiṣṇavas is the *mūla* (the root) of devotional service. One should not think that at any stage in spiritual life one transcends the position of worship of Vaiṣṇavas, or association with Vaiṣṇavas. The quality of the Vaiṣṇavas with whom we associate will reflect the quality of faith we will have. If we associate with devotees who have little or conditional faith, then that will also be the condition of our own faith, unless we are in a position to elevate them. Therefore, we always look for the association of superior Vaiṣṇavas because our whole purpose in association is to increase our faith. If someone in any way whatsoever endangers, threatens, or minimizes our faith in Vaiṣṇavas, guru, mantra, or the process, then we avoid them. At least that should be the position of someone who is serious about spiritual life.

This verse can be understood in depth by analyzing Bhaktivinoda Ṭhākura's words. Firstly, there are four specific questions being answered, so we will address those in summary, and then in detail.

The first question has been asked, what is someone's duty? The word *śaraṇe* answers the second question of what a devotee's duty is when his faith awakens in hearing about Lord Kṛṣṇa. One should take shelter in Kṛṣṇa, *mām ekaṁ śaraṇaṁ vraja*. The ultimate duty of every living entity, every conditioned soul, is to take shelter of Kṛṣṇa. The natural question that arises is, "How do I do that? And what is the method for taking shelter, or what is the practical process?" And the answer is, by developing love for Kṛṣṇa. Taking shelter means that Kṛṣṇa gives us his shelter. But we cannot get Kṛṣṇa's shelter unless we actually have *rati*. This word *rati* is a very nice word, a common word which has multiple meanings and usage. So here *rati* means that one has love of Kṛṣṇa (*prema*). When we have love for Kṛṣṇa then we can receive his shelter. It is something that we have to acquire, that Kṛṣṇa gives. It is not something that we can simply manipulate or achieve by some certain ritualistic or regulated activity.

The third question is how to develop this love. And the fourth: is this love developed exclusively for Kṛṣṇa? No, it is not. Rather, it is stated: gurus, Vraja, Vṛndāvana, *vraja-vāsīs*, the holy name, and Rādhā-Kṛṣṇa. We cannot exclude anyone from the realm of our attachment. If one loves one's father, then one will also love one's mother, brothers, sisters, household – everything else is automatically included. Therefore a devotee is equally disposed, or even more favorably disposed, towards those things that are *tadīya*, related to the Lord, because they are an easier way of achieving Kṛṣṇa.

Tadīya-upāsanam is a science Vaiṣṇavas know, or should know. It is easier to achieve Kṛṣṇa through devotees or through things that relate to him – like the holy name – than it is to achieve him directly. Just like, we worship Caitanya Mahāprabhu, because to approach Kṛṣṇa directly is very, very difficult. But Caitanya Mahāprabhu is that selfsame Rādhā and Kṛṣṇa in the mood of a devotee. A devotee is far more inclined to distribute love for Kṛṣṇa, or is easier to approach, than the Supreme Lord.

So one may ask, how will I develop love for all of these devotees? And here it is stated, *dambhaṁ hitvā*: get rid of your pride. This becomes the main focus in this verse.

In *Manaḥ-śikṣā* 1 it is stated, *gurau goṣṭhe goṣṭhālayiṣu sujane bhū-sura-gaṇe/ sva-mantre śrī-nāmni vraja-nava-yuva-dvandva-śaraṇe*: we should surrender. So what is this surrender? Śrīla Bhaktivinoda Ṭhākura gives a nice definition of surrender which is so very precise and simple. He says that the external indication of one's internal cultivation of love and attraction to Kṛṣṇa is called surrender. The external indication, or one's external activities, correspond to one's internal cultivation of unalloyed attraction to Kṛṣṇa. This is a relevant point because often we hear the argument from Christians that, "I love God." Often we hear it from devotees, too, "Well, I love Kṛṣṇa, I love Śrīla Prabhupāda. And it doesn't really matter what I'm doing. The important thing is what's inside."

But here Bhaktivinoda Ṭhākura says something different. He says that the internal symptom should parallel external behavior, that there should be corresponding external behavior that is symptomatic of an internal attachment. This is surrender. That is the means for loving someone. If we do not have the means, then how can we possibly have the end? Therefore there cannot be a disparity between a devotee's external behavior and their internal advancement.

For instance, we might meet a Christian who has a cigarette in one hand and hamburger in the other and says, "I love Jesus." But by what activity is that person displaying that love? Someone might make a subjective statement that cannot be argued, such as, "I know because I love him." It is a subjective experience, a subjective feeling they are referring to which is obviously beyond the range of anyone else. So it appears we cannot argue the point.

But on the basis of Bhaktivinoda Ṭhākura's definition of surrender and love, then we can argue, and say, "No. Whatever is inside should manifest via external behaviors." There should be external symptoms that evidence one's surrender. There is a process to that surrender, and we will now address that in the following points.

The goal we are striving to achieve is *rati* (attraction) for Rādhā and Kṛṣṇa. We emphasize that it is to Rādhā and Kṛṣṇa that we want to develop our attraction. This point will be repeated over and over again because it requires emphasis, as it is very rarely understood. This is the specific mood of not only Śrīla Raghunātha Dāsa Gosvāmī but also Caitanya Mahāprabhu and our entire Gauḍīya line. That Gauḍīya tradition is to direct all devotees to the loving mood of the inhabitants of Vṛndāvana, and ultimately to engage in the service of Śrīmatī Rādhārāṇī and Śrī Kṛṣṇa. Although there are unlimited incarnations of the Lord, we worship and revere all of them as the Supreme Personality of Godhead, Lord Kṛṣṇa, manifesting his different potencies to varying degrees.

Kṛṣṇa has unlimited potencies, and when Kṛṣṇa as the Supreme Personality of Godhead manifests all to a full extent, he is considered to be most perfect. When he manifests only some of these potencies, all of those in their full depth, then he is considered to be more perfect. When he exhibits only some of his potencies, and those only partially, then he is considered to be perfect.

So there are two things here – one is the extent of Lord Kṛṣṇa's potencies, the quantitative extent, and also the depth of these potencies. Combining the extent and depth, we can have permutations of four. All these other incarnations, *avatāras, guṇa-avatāras, līlā-avatāras, manvanavatāras,* they all fall into these other three categories. And it is the Supreme Personality of Godhead, Śrī Kṛṣṇa, *kṛṣṇas tu bhagavān svayam,* who manifests all of these potencies to an unlimited degree.

He is the original person. And it is he who we are worshiping. Svarūpa Dāmodara Gosvāmī describes that originally Lord Kṛṣṇa is one, and he has eternally separated himself into two. That is *śakti* and *śaktiman*, the potencies of the Lord and the supreme potent.

With our limited perception we see these things as happening in time, but there is no question of time. This is eternal activity. The Absolute Truth therefore is both male and female, or masculine and feminine. The masculine is the energetic and feminine is the supreme energy. And therefore the perfect worship, or the complete worship of the Absolute Truth, is manifest through the worship of Rādhā and Kṛṣṇa. It is developing attachment to Rādhā and Kṛṣṇa which is the ultimate realization, the highest goal of life, and the specific gift of Caitanya Mahāprabhu.

As already mentioned, the process here is developing faith, and developing our love for Kṛṣṇa. Actually redeveloping is perhaps more accurate because in *Caitanya-caritāmṛta* it is described, *nitya-siddha-kṛṣṇa-prema 'sādhya' kabhu naya śravaṇādi-śuddha-citte karaye udaya*: that this *kṛṣṇa-prema* is already there within our hearts. But it has to be brought out, *śravaṇādi-śuddha-citte karaye udaya* (*Madhya-līlā* 22.107). That bringing-out begins by the process of hearing from the spiritual master, from Vaiṣṇavas. This process of redeveloping the dormant love for Kṛṣṇa which is in everyone is true self-realization. It is there in a dormant state. Not only is our love for Kṛṣṇa present in a dormant state, but it is also implied in this verse that our eternal relationship with him is also present in a dormant state.

This important point differentiates the Gauḍīya *sampradāya*, or the *siddhānta-sampradāya* – the followers of Śrīla Bhaktisiddhānta Sarasvatī Ṭhākura – from *bābājīs* who also consider themselves to be Gauḍīyas. Those *bābājīs* believe that *bhakti-latā-bīja* means that you receive your *svarūpa*, or eternal form, from the spiritual master at the time of initiation. We do not accept that. We understand from the explanations from both *Caitanya-caritāmṛta* and Śrīla Prabhupāda what *bhakti-latā-bīja* is. It is knowledge, the process by which one advances in Kṛṣṇa consciousness, and the eternal identity of the living entity that is already present in seed form.

Rūpa Gosvāmī also states in *Bhakti-rasāmṛta-sindhuḥ* (1.2.2), *nitya-siddhasya bhāvasya*, that *sthāyi-bhāva* is already there but it is covered. So we want to redevelop something which is within us. The questions are: if something is already in us, why do we not feel it? What is the problem? What is actually separating us? Śrīla Bhaktivinoda Ṭhākura explains that the problem is due to the influence of the illusory energy of the Lord, which herein is being personified by this word, *dambha* (pride) and we have, by the force of illusion, fallen into this material world. By association with this material world we become further and further covered, and then we become not only covered, but also attached to everything we see around us. We become convinced that this is our home, our eternal place of residence. Thus Rūpa Gosvāmī explains this evolution of the false ego, from falling down, association, conditioning, and attachment. But it is described by Lord Kapiladeva in the Third Canto that this attachment we have for association of home, family, friends, community, wife, and children, that same attachment – when applied to the associates of the Lord, to the association of Vaiṣṇavas – can be the source of our elevation. Attachment becomes the source of our conditioning and bondage in the material world, but when focused onto the devotees it becomes the means by which we can leave this material world.

So what is really required is to spiritualize our attachment, and the process of *sādhana-bhakti* is meant to do just that. Śrīla Prabhupāda uses this word all the time, "dovetailing." It means dovetailing one's particular attachment. When we analyze the different types of devotees that are discussed here, we see for instance *bhū-sura-gaṇe*, which refers to *varṇāśrama brāhmaṇas*. So the entire process – from *varṇāśrama* to the transcendental position of a *śuddha-bhakta* – is meant to draw out that attachment, redirect it in such a way that it does not bind us and cover us, but rather purifies us and ultimately unearths the real love of Kṛṣṇa which is present in our hearts.

Therefore Śrīla Prabhupāda placed so much emphasis on saying that he established this International Society for Kṛṣṇa Consciousness for the purpose of association, because by such association one can actually practice *sādhana-bhakti*. Otherwise it is very difficult. In fact,

Śrīla Prabhupāda points out in *Śrīmad-Bhāgavatam* that one is living in a hallucination if he thinks that outside the association of devotees he can practice devotional service. But there are some basic simple principles in the process of this practice.

Bhaktivinoda Ṭhākura says that the association of devotees diminishes the results of one's karma. Karma is like *hṛdaya-granthi*, a rope that ties us down. So, by association with devotees the knots in this rope become slackened, and one has some ability to maneuver and become free from that tight tying down of the *guṇas*. In this way faith actually starts to develop in a devotee, and then one becomes qualified to hear. By hearing, one assimilates instruction – this is the symptom of someone who really knows how to hear. We should understand this as a very important point. Hearing is not just listening to something and then writing it down. There must be a consequence to that hearing. Kṛṣṇa says to Arjuna:

iti te jñānam ākhyātaṁ
guhyād guhyataraṁ mayā
vimṛśyaitad aśeṣeṇa
yathecchasi tathā kuru

> Thus I have explained to you knowledge still more confidential. Deliberate on this fully, and then do what you wish to do. (*Bhagavad-gītā* 18.63):

Then he says *mām ekaṁ śaraṇaṁ vraja*, "surrender to me." This is the consequence of hearing *Bhagavad-gītā*: surrender to Kṛṣṇa. Therefore one has to be able to assimilate an instruction. "I understand an instruction and practically put it into practice in my own *sādhana-bhakti*, in my own devotional life." When one has understood, ultimately the conclusion is that yes, one should surrender directly to Kṛṣṇa. But surrendering directly to Kṛṣṇa is not possible, therefore one surrenders to guru, or Kṛṣṇa's representative. And that is formalized through the process of *dīkṣā*.

Kṛṣṇa states, *upadekṣyanti te jñānaṁ jñāninas tattva-darśinaḥ*. *Upadekṣyanti*: we come closer by *dīkṣā*. What does *dīkṣā* mean? *Divya-jñāna hṛde prokāśito*, that process by which one receives transcendental knowledge, and by which one's bonds of fruitive or karmic activities are slashed, or purified. When one takes initiation he or she receives a mantra by which to worship the Supreme Lord, and by chanting that mantra service is rendered always in one's mind. One then renders service to Lord Kṛṣṇa, and simultaneously worships gurus and Vaiṣṇavas.

Bhaktivinoda Ṭhākura gives further instruction as to how *sādhana* relates to this attachment that we have to the material world, and to the attachment we want to develop for Kṛṣṇa. As mentioned above, through *sādhana*, the bonds of one's karma become slackened and ultimately dissipated. The result is that one develops an inner spiritual strength. It is something that Bhaktivinoda Ṭhākura refers to in many places, that a devotee should feel inner spiritual strength. Devotees have experience of this. Sometimes when we have practiced Kṛṣṇa consciousness nicely we feel confident and strong. And at other times we feel its absence, or a lacking. Sometimes, for instance, when we sleep through *japa* then we really notice it by its absence, that there is no strength there.

Bhaktivinoda also mentions a related point in *Harināma-cintāmaṇi*, that a devotee can feel the spiritual strength which is bound within the heart of another Vaiṣṇava. Devotees have that experience sometimes when coming into the presence of another devotee. All devotees who have experience with Śrīla Prabhupāda knew of his strong presence. It was not a material presence, or a charismatic presence. It was an overpowering spiritual presence which was sometimes just too much for people to handle, and they would leave. And we still feel that presence here in this temple room. Even if we bring non-devotees into the room, they can still feel a presence. That is an actual spiritual potency. It is a manifestation of the Lord's *hlādinī* and *samvit* potency, which are the manifestations of *śuddha-sattva*.

When a devotee comes to the platform of pure devotional service, or *prema-bhakti*, then this *śuddha-sattva* manifests within that person's heart by the mercy of Śrīmatī Rādhārāṇī. And that *svarūpa-śakti*, that transcendental potency, can then be felt by others who are at least a little sensitive. It has a permanent effect.

The result of this spiritual development is that it attracts the mercy of Kṛṣṇa and devotees. And this is a topic that is recurring in *Śrī Manaḥ-śikṣā*: on one side, the effort of the devotee; on the other side, the mercy of Kṛṣṇa. Both of these are required for advancement in devotional service. And what is the result of this mercy? When we sufficiently attract the mercy of Vaiṣṇavas, guru, and Kṛṣṇa, then this attachment will develop and manifest. It is something that we try to cultivate, but ultimately it is bestowed. What we actually try to cultivate is the qualification for receiving it. Ultimately it is something that is given to us by the mercy of the Vaiṣṇavas and Kṛṣṇa.

Bhaktivinoda Ṭhākura explains what this sublime attachment is, saying that to the degree this attachment is concentrated it is called sublime attachment. In other words, the degree of concentration is the degree to which there are no material impediments, there is no *jñāna-karmādyanāvṛtam*, no other material thing present. To that degree it is called sublime attachment. There are two important qualifications for receiving this attachment. First, one must be very eager, *tatra laulyam ekalaṁ mūlam*. Second, one must be humble. Without these two qualifications one will not be able to attract Lord Kṛṣṇa's attention.

One has to be enthusiastic and constantly maintain oneself in a state of enthusiasm. One should do whatever is required to remain enthusiastic and humble. Without being humble it is not possible to receive Kṛṣṇa's mercy. And what is the disqualification for receiving it? What is the disqualification for development in *sādhana*, for advancing in one's spiritual practices and cultivating this attachment? Lethargy. Lethargy, Bhaktivinoda Ṭhākura says, is thinking, "Oh, it will happen of its own accord. I don't have to do anything." Something may happen, but it won't be what we're expecting or hoping for – advancement in Kṛṣṇa consciousness.

This verse mentions, *dambhaṁ hitvā*, always get rid of this pride. The implication in saying "always" is that we may get rid of it, but it may come back. That means it is a process, not that it's like a shovel filled with dirt and we throw it out and that's it, it's gone. Rather, there is a process for purifying our hearts from pride, and this is the first impediment that we will address here. Raghunātha Dāsa Gosvāmī says *hitvā*, which means to give up or reject. So how do we give up pride?

Bhaktivinoda Ṭhākura says it is by the assistance of the guru. Therefore it is described here that one should always remember the spiritual master first, before all activities, so that one becomes free from one's prideful or envious mentality.

Bhaktivinoda Ṭhākura addresses six different elements of pride: illusion, deceit, pretence, ignorance, deviousness, and offences (or *aparādha*). These are not pride themselves, but are the elements which constitute pride. And sometimes there is difficulty in differentiating between some of them, so they require definition.

Illusion means that one becomes satisfied and complacent by material accomplishments, that we achieve some result which is measured in material terms and become proud. Deceit is that one takes, or is satisfied with, the externals of spiritual life, which may mean one's dress, demeanour, mannerism, birth, and so on, and uses those to portray one's qualification. Pretense is a quality that is clearly defined by Bhaktivinoda Ṭhākura, and that is, cultivating a desire for something else in practising devotional service other than love for Kṛṣṇa. This problem is defined by the words *anyābhilaṣitā śūnyam*. Whereas that verse from where that phrase comes (*Bhakti-rasāmṛta-sindhuḥ* 1.1.11) specifically describes pure devotional service, the converse is pretentious devotional service. So when devotional service is practiced with some other goal in mind other than simply to please Kṛṣṇa's senses, that is pretense. Ignorance is forgetfulness of one's spiritual identity. Deviousness means that some other motivation may arise. And offenses can be made against the holy name, the devotees, and so on. These are all also elements that cause pride.

Śakaṭāsura, the cart demon, personified pride which arose from residual bad habits carried over from previous lifetimes. Tṛṇāvarta exemplified pride from scholarship. Yāmala Arjuna epitomized pride due to aristocracy, or high birth. Kāliya-nāga represented pride which arises due to crookedness or a devious mentality. The sacrificial *brāhmaṇas*, the Vedic *brāhmaṇas*, or the *yajñic brāhmaṇas*, personified pride due to position in *varṇāśrama*. Ariṣṭāsura showed pride which arises due to practising false religious principles. Keśi represented the pride which arises from being materially situated in spiritual life, such as being a guru, *sannyāsī,* or in some big position and becoming proud of that particular situation. From these seven pastimes we can see present the six elements of pride that Bhaktivinoda Ṭhākura speaks of: illusion, deceit, pretence, ignorance, deviousness, and offences (or *aparādha*).

The particular *līlās* that these demons or materialists engaged in with Kṛṣṇa fall under the heading of pride. From our limited perception, reading these *līlās* may not have much deeper value than hearing any other pastime. But a deep insight is illuminated by the directions we read from Bhaktivinoda Ṭhākura, and thus we can understand that while reading these stories we should be very open and pray to Kṛṣṇa that we become free from the illusion of pride which comes due to scholarship, aristocracy and so on.

Raghunātha Dāsa Gosvāmī says, "Throw out pride." But how will we throw it out? Bhaktivinoda Ṭhākura recommends we read all of these seven pastimes relating to pride (*dambhaṁ hitvā*) if we want to become free from pride. Kṛṣṇa will actually remove that pride within our hearts when we have a great desire to be purified by reading and giving careful aural reception to these particular pastimes.

The verse then reads, *ratim apūrvām atitarām. Rati* means love and *apūrvam* unprecedented, so the full meaning is a great unprecedented love. These words in and of themselves are very meaningful. The nature of love of Godhead is that it has no precedent. It has not been freely made available or bestowed until now. Thus it is unprecedented. The word "great" in this context means it is actually the greatest love which a *jīva,* or a living entity, can contain, or possess.

This love, *ratim:* for whom do we want this love? The very beginning of the verse says *gurau. Gurau* means spiritual master in the plural sense. There are two types of spiritual masters, *dīkṣā-guru* and *śikṣā-guru,* and they are described in *Caitanya-caritāmṛta* in detail both in the verses and purports. *Dīkṣā-guru* gives a devotee *sambhandha-jñāna,* by which process one becomes free from *anarthas* and is able to advance on the path of devotional service. *Dīkṣā-guru* is specifically one. *Śikṣā-guru* is that person who gives one *abhideya,* or the process of cultivating one's relationship with Kṛṣṇa. *Dīkṣā-guru* and *śikṣā-guru* may be the same person, although one may have more *śikṣā-gurus* under the guidance or permission of the *dīkṣā-guru*. The *śikṣā-guru* instructs and guides the devotee in confidential service to Rādhā and Kṛṣṇa.

Traditionally in the Gauḍīya *sampradāya,* Sanātana Gosvāmī is the embodiment of *dīkṣā-guru,* and Rūpa Gosvāmī of *śikṣā-guru.* Both are to be considered manifestations of Śrī Kṛṣṇa and are equal in all respects. One should not distinguish or discriminate between one and the other.

Yet there is a clarification to be made between receiving *śikṣā,* and the *śikṣā-guru.* One may receive *śikṣā,* or instruction, from so many individuals, but the *śikṣā-guru* referred to here is different than one who simply gives instruction, no matter how relevant the instruction. *Śikṣā-guru* means the *gosvāmīs* and *ācāryas,* the liberated souls who give us specific instruction in the details of our *sādhana* and service to Kṛṣṇa. It does not simply mean that a temple commander asks us to mop the floor and therefore he is our *śikṣā-guru.* Śrīla Prabhupāda distinguishes between these types of *śikṣā-gurus* in his purport in *Caitanya-caritāmṛta.* He writes, "There are two kinds of instructing spiritual masters. One is the liberated person fully absorbed in meditation in devotional service, and the other is he who invokes the disciple's spiritual consciousness by means of relevant instructions." (*Ādi-līlā* 1.47)

Many people may give us relevant instruction for our advancement or practice in spiritual life, but they do not come under this more specific meaning of the *śikṣā-guru.* In one sense everyone is guru. Mothers are guru, fathers are guru, teachers are guru. We may have so many different types of guru. Anyone who teaches us something, when we use the word guru to mean teacher, that is one category. But when we use guru to mean *jñānāñjana-śalākayā cakṣur unmīlitaṁ yena,* or someone who has opened our eyes with the light of transcendental knowledge and has shown us Kṛṣṇa, then the term refers to this more specific meaning of *śikṣā-guru.*

In either sense, despite the difference in relationship, gurus are to be held in the highest esteem and are objects of worship and service.

Goṣṭhe means pasturing grounds, and here specifically it means Vṛndāvana, Vraja. When Śrīla Prabhupāda came to the West, practically speaking as soon as he unpacked his bags he was immediately making plans for building what he first called his American house in Vṛndāvana, and then later on in Māyāpur, because he wanted devotees to have a home. As long as they did not go to Vṛndāvana they were going to think that their home was somewhere here in the West – in London, or New York, or Paris. These are not our homes. Our real home is in Vṛndāvana. Śrīla Prabhupāda would say, "Wherever I go is Vṛndāvana," but it takes some time for one to come to that advanced stage. So at least one should experience Bhauma Vṛndāvana, or the spiritual world manifest here within this material realm, going to Vṛndāvana and seeing the places of Kṛṣṇa's pastimes and activities. Nandagrāma, Varṣāṇā, Yamunā, Govardhana, Rādhā-kuṇḍa, Śyāma-kuṇḍa – we should see all of these wonderful places where Kṛṣṇa reveals his transcendental pastimes. And our Kṛṣṇa-Balarāma Mandira is situated in Ramaṇa-reti. All these places are very dear to devotees, and one of the symptoms of an advancing devotee, or a second class devotee, is that they become very attached to the holy places. Thus it is very important to become attached and learn how to love Vṛndāvana and Māyāpur.

There are three classes of devotees mentioned here. *Goṣṭhālayiṣu* means pure devotees, or those who are residents of Vṛndāvana. They do not aspire to go to Vaikuṇṭha or to worship any other form of the Lord. They reside in Vṛndāvana. It is not simply that they are residing in Bhauma Vṛndāvana, or this manifest realm, but rather they are in *aprākṛta,* or in the unmanifest Vṛndāvana; either in person they are living there, or by means of meditation. In other words they are partaking in Kṛṣṇa's transcendental pastimes one way or another. That is called *goṣṭhālayiṣu,* and they are considered to be *uttama adhikārīs.*

Gurau goṣṭhe goṣṭhālayiṣu sujane. Su means very good, and refers here to practising devotees, *sādhakas,* or those devotees who are aspiring for perfection in Vṛndāvana. They may also be imbued with awe and reverence. In other words they are not yet fully developed in their intimate relationship with the Lord, or for that matter they may even aspire for service in places like Mathurā and Dvārakā. These devotees are considered *madhyama bhaktas.* They may even worship other Deities. Then there are *bhū-sura-gaṇe,* or *brāhmaṇas* who worship according to the *varṇāśrama* system. They are considered to be *kaniṣṭha,* or third class. This is a different division, a sub-division of first, second, and third class devotees that we generally use.

So in summary, this verse explains how one is developing love for Kṛṣṇa: by worshiping with devotion all the abovementioned, namely *gurau goṣṭhe.* And the last things to be addressed in this verse are *nāma* and mantra: *sva-mantre śrī-nāmni* and then *vraja-nava-yuva-dvandva-śaraṇe.*

Mantra refers to the Gāyatrī mantras, both the twenty-four-and-a-half-syllable Gāyatrī mantra, and the eighteen-syllable Gopāla mantra. Devotees who are *brāhmaṇa* initiated should know the meanings of these mantras, which are discussed in *Caitanya-caritāmṛta* in depth, and they should meditate very seriously and conscientiously on these discussions. This subject is not to be taken lightly. Unfortunately devotees may take it quite lightly. Chanting these mantras is like being requested to do *pūjā* three times a day. We should be thinking, "I am doing *ārati* to Rādhā and Kṛṣṇa." That is what Gāyatrī mantra means, that every day we are worshiping on the altar. That is why devotees are meant to do *ācamana,* or actually purify themselves, before chanting. We should bathe before we go on an altar, and we dress in clean cloth, and apply fresh *tilaka,* and then we worship. But this mantra worship is for advanced people. It isn't simply that we worship with a stick of incense and some ghee lamp and some flower. But rather we are meant to be worshiping *svāhā. Svāhā* means we are offering our heart. So when we don't know how to worship with our heart then we simply get caught up on the mental platform wondering when we can start on our *prasādam.* But this worship is what Gāyatrī mantra means. It is meant as an internal worship which should be very seriously done by *brāhmaṇas. Brāhmaṇas* are actually worshiping Kṛṣṇa by offering themselves to Kṛṣṇa.

The same understanding applies to *śrī-nāmni,* the holy name of the Lord. Chanting the holy name of the Lord is also offering ourselves. "O Lord, O energy of the Lord, please engage me in your service." This is an offering of ourselves, our body, mind, and soul, in service to Kṛṣṇa, to Rādhā and Kṛṣṇa in Vṛndāvana, engaging in their eternal pastimes.

We want to be engaged in that kind of service. We are asking to be engaged in that service.

The first symptom of proper chanting will be that one will be very serious and will beg Kṛṣṇa to accept us and engage us in that service. All of these mantras are meant to be chanted without offense. Even if one does commit offenses, still the best thing to do is simply chant the name of the Lord. But if one wants the real effect of these mantras, they should be chanted properly. We can compare the situation to doing *pūjā*. If when you do your *pūjā* you're going on the altar dirty, or you're doing all kinds of nonsense things, then you will not expect the same result as if you do everything strictly according to the rules.

Aye svāntar bhrātaś caṭubhir abhiyāce dhṛta-padaḥ: now we are falling at the feet of our mind and begging to be able to engage in this type of service, because we are trying to get some very, very great thing, some unprecedented thing. *Ratiṁ apūrvam atitarām:* as previously mentioned, this word "unprecedented" is important. Rādhā and Kṛṣṇa are the supreme lover and beloved. And Kṛṣṇa himself comes to try to appreciate the love that Śrīmatī Rādhārāṇī enjoys in his presence. Even Kṛṣṇa cannot taste that, because he is the object of that love and therefore he cannot taste it. Unless he comes as the actual receptacle of love, he cannot taste it. So he comes as Caitanya Mahāprabhu just for that particular purpose.

There are so many inhabitants in Vṛndāvana, beginning with the blades of grass and the cows, the servants, the cowherd boys, Yaśodā, the *gopīs*, and so on. All of them enjoy a different gradation of loving relationship with Kṛṣṇa. This is all called *rati*. But none of them are *apūrvam atitarām*. They are all fully satisfied in their service, and they are fully satisfied in the loving relationship. But amongst all of the loving relationships which transpire, that which is manifest or exhibited between Kṛṣṇa and the *gopīs* is considered to be the highest, because it is the most complete and the fullest expression of the ability to love without any condition whatsoever.

This is covered in detail in the fourth and fifth chapters of the *Ādi-līlā* in *Caitanya-caritāmṛta*. We know that Rādhā and Kṛṣṇa are surrounded by the *aṣṭa-sakhīs*, who are their most intimate associates. But there are even more intimate associates, those who are assistants to these *gopīs* and who are sometimes known as maidservants. Kṛṣṇadāsa Kavirāja Gosvāmī writes this verse in the *Govinda-līlāmṛta* (11.137):

spṛśati yadi mukundo rādhikāṁ tat-sakhīnāṁ
bhavati vapuṣi kampa-sveda-romāñca-bāṣpam
adhara-madhu mudāsyāś cet pibaty eṣa yatnād
bhavati bata tad āsāṁ mattatā citram etat

This verse explains the position of these maidservants, they have a mood of friendship, but at the same time servitude, to Rādhārāṇī. Just as the author of *Śrī Manaḥ-śikṣā*, Śrīla Raghunātha Dāsa Gosvāmī, exhibited the same unalloyed dependence on Śrīmatī Rādhārāṇī's mercy.

The *gopīs* tend to be in the mood of friendship. But these other maidservants are in friendship and servitude. They are very intimately related with Rādhārāṇī, so whatever particular ecstatic symptoms Rādhārāṇī feels, they also feel. This is the purport, a love that is unprecedented. The unique thing, the reason why it is considered to be great, is because it does not depend upon direct contact with Kṛṣṇa. Rather, by serving Rādhārāṇī and making arrangements for her and Kṛṣṇa to meet, these *gopīs* automatically experience the highest pleasure that Rādhārāṇī feels, even from a distance. So, Rādhā and Kṛṣṇa are dancing and smiling and having a nice time, and these maidservants don't have to associate with Kṛṣṇa in order to experience that same bliss. They experience it from afar.

This is how Śrīla Prabhupāda encouraged us, not to worry about having a direct relationship. Actually the most elevated relationship as described here, *apūrvam atitarām,* is experienced automatically, *tene brahma hṛdā ya ādi-kavaye* (*Śrīmad-Bhāgavatam* 1.1.1). It is manifest through the heart, and all the ecstatic symptoms that manifest on the body of the heroine, Śrīmatī Rādhārāṇī, are automatically also manifest on the bodies of her maidservants as well.

The nature of these devotees of the Lord, the nature of their love, is that it completely brings Kṛṣṇa under control. Not only does it bring Kṛṣṇa under the devotees' control, but Kṛṣṇa becomes purchased. He is respectful and reverential to the love of the devotees who are situated in this particular category of followers of Rūpa and Raghunātha Dāsa Gosvāmīs.

COMMENTARY BY ŚACĪNANDANA SWAMI

After some faith has awakened, how do we become fully Kṛṣṇa conscious? Raghunātha Dāsa Gosvāmī says first of all we must give up *dambha*. *Dambha* is a word that means deceit, religious hypocrisy, arrogance, and pride. This word comes from the root word *dap*, which means endure. It also means to deceive and to go. So when you want to start Raghunātha Dāsa Gosvāmī's guidebook you have to first of all learn to give up pretense, hypocrisy, and deceit.

As long as we pretend to be someone we are not, we cannot enter the path of Raghunātha Dāsa Gosvāmī. We only hurt ourselves by keeping up such a farce. If you want to advance, give up your pride before Kṛṣṇa makes an arrangement for your pride to be taken.

Śrīla Bhaktivinoda Ṭhākura describes a dangerous moment in the life of a devotee. This is when the thought comes, "I am a Vaiṣṇava. I am a devotee." he says that if we think we are a Vaiṣṇava, then we shall look forward to receiving respect from others. If the desires for fame and reputation pollute our hearts, then we shall certainly descend into hell. Therefore, Bhaktivinoda Ṭhākura speaks of this dangerous moment, the thoughts that we are Vaiṣṇavas, that we have done *vratas*, that we have finished extra rounds for Kārtika, or we have distributed extra books or given a very well-acclaimed lecture! If so, then we don't run to Kṛṣṇa – we run in the opposite direction. We run for name, fame, and prestige and our hearts will be polluted. How will love ever come into such a heart? It is not possible.

So Raghunātha Dāsa Gosvāmī's initial instruction is to first give up all pride, because if our *bhajana* becomes *kevala-kaitava* (fully cheating), then we cannot progress. What do we do when respect comes our way? Bhaktisiddhānta Sarasvatī Ṭhākura said that when we are glorified, we should immediately offer the glorification to our spiritual master and the previous *ācāryas*. A servant of a spiritual master should never accept it for themselves but offer it to the previous spiritual master. For example, if someone says, "you gave a nice lecture," you should respond, "I just repeated some points that I learned from my spiritual master and the Vaiṣṇavas; I cannot really accept your praise."

I recently glorified one devotee who did exceptional service and the devotee said something very pleasing. He said, "I had good helpers. I didn't do anything." Immediately when praise comes our way, we should deflect it to where it should go, and it usually goes to the previous *ācāryas*. Bhaktisiddhānta Sarasvatī said this on his 60th Vyāsa-pūjā. Think that the glorifications offered to us really belong to the previous *ācāryas*. We can accept the glorifications and offer all to them. Think, "Those of you who glorify me now are all great personalities. What you are giving to me I am not qualified to accept. So today I am offering it to my guru."

If we don't use this "transparent" technique, the glorification can kill us. If we don't become transparent and let the waters of praise continue on and flow where they belong, then our pipe will burst and blow into pieces and create mishaps. My dear devotees, between us and the Lord is a mountain of *ahaṁ mameti,* the foundations of pride. Prideful thoughts create *saṁskāras* and aggressions from which our whole *svabhāva* is formed.

This is also true with praise and respect that is shown physically. For example, in India people touch the feet of those they hold in high esteem, and when someone accepts this they can fall ill because they take the *karma,* which can burn health and mind. Sometimes Indians are strong wrestlers also; they have hold of your feet and you have to behave like a civilized person as a *sannyāsī* so you can't avoid it. In such a case, one should think, "This person touching my feet is thinking I am a specialist in *bhakti* or because I have white skin, but I am really a mercy case of my spiritual master. Śrīla Prabhupāda, whatever good this person sees in me, it is, by your mercy, your investment into me. It belongs to you." And then we can really see how the *karma* goes through us and does not make us sick. But if it stops at our feet, we can become very ill.

It is said that we should give up all pride. How should we do it? Raghunātha Dāsa Gosvāmī says, "Develop unprecedented love for guru." How do we develop love for our spiritual master or for Śrīla Prabhupāda? We can shout, "Prabhupāda!" until our vocal chords ache, but our mind can still shout "me, me, me!" with the same strength. To cure this problem, we should meditate on something very nice about the spiritual master that is true. Kṛṣṇa is the original guru, the *ādi-guru*, who reaches the conditioned souls through the *vyaṣṭi-gurus* (individual gurus). Now how do these individual personalities become carriers of Kṛṣṇa's mercy? It is because Kṛṣṇa invests his *karuṇā-śakti* (mercy potency) in the spiritual master. This is the way Kṛṣṇa chooses to show his mercy. When water is touched by cold, it becomes ice. So when Kṛṣṇa shows his compassion for the fallen souls, he becomes the *guru-tattva*.

I always like to say that I was a dark end on a dark stone on a dark night in a dark universe. No light in my life. But my spiritual master found me and saved me by bringing me in contact with this process of Kṛṣṇa consciousness. It is simply self-deception to call to the Lord and try to surrender to God by trying to jump over Śrī Gurudeva, who is the tangible form of the Lord's presently-occurring mercy before us.

We can go to God and say, "God, God, God," and tell him so many things, but if we stand before our spiritual master, it is easily seen what is real and what is unreal. Imagination doesn't work when our spiritual master is before us. We can't cheat ourselves.

It is magical. If we turn to our spiritual master with the sincere desire to be helped, we will see how the *karuṇā-śakti* becomes activated and something wonderful will happen. Now what to do if faith in guru is lost? I want to recommend to you if you can't worship your *dīkṣā guru* nicely, go to Prabhupāda or look for a *śikṣā guru*. But take to this principle, because Kṛṣṇa has invested his mercy *śakti* in his devotees.

Bhaktivinoda Ṭhākura tells us how we should see our guru. He says do not see the guru as merely a great sage, but rather see him as your intimate and well-wishing friend. I personally have come to believe that this understanding is very important in our discipleship. We need to come close. If the guru is an abstract concept for us, we won't have that heartfelt connection where we can tell him everything, and we won't call upon him like we call to a friend when we are in trouble.

The first verse goes on to explain that we should love *vraja-dhāma*, the residents of Vraja, and finally Śrī Śrī Rādhā and Kṛṣṇa, who are the eternally youthful divine couple of Vraja.

Kṛṣṇa explains in the *Bhāgavatam* how we can develop love for him. The wives of the *brāhmaṇas* came to him in the forest and offered a meal. They saw Kṛṣṇa standing in the forest twirling a lotus flower with one of his elbows resting on the shoulder of a friend. Kṛṣṇa told them, "Just like I am twirling this lotus, I am twirling your heart. Can you feel it?"

The *brāhmaṇas'* wives said, "Yes." They wanted to walk with him through the forest where he was herding the cows, but that would have been a violation of social etiquette. Highly aristocratic *brāhmaṇa* ladies walking behind a cowherd boy, adoring him, throwing flowers and singing, "O Kṛṣṇa, O Kṛṣṇa," ... the whole society would have been scandalized and Kṛṣṇa did not wish this.

So he sent them home and told them:

śravaṇād darśanād dhyānān
mayi bhāvo 'nukīrtanāt
na tathā sannikarṣeṇa
pratiyāta tato gṛhān

> It is by hearing about me, seeing my Deity form, meditating upon me and chanting my names and glories that love for me develops, not by physical proximity. Therefore, please go back to your homes. (*Śrīmad-Bhāgavatam* 10.23.33)

Kṛṣṇa is serious about these points. He speaks the same verse to the *gopīs*, but there is one difference. The *brāhmaṇa* wives return home and the *gopīs* do not. So, again, *śravaṇād*, it is by hearing about me that you develop love. Women like to stare at men, and men like to stare at women. So do that to the Deity. Then you will develop love for Kṛṣṇa. Stare at him. Meditate about Kṛṣṇa, and chant his names and glories. Then you will develop love, and not by physical proximity.

Kṛṣṇa rested his left cheek on his left shoulder in order to play the *gamakas* (ornamented notes), a vibrato in the ascending and descending modes of the *rāgas*. Kṛṣṇa tilted his head to the left side. At the same time Kṛṣṇa crossed his legs to assume a charming three-fold bending form, which enchanted the three worlds. Kṛṣṇa tilted his neck. He rested the flute on his lower lip, and then he made his eyebrows dance to attract the attention of Subala and others to the skillfulness of his songs. Kṛṣṇa was playing a flute with seven holes, which were covered by his fingers. Because Kṛṣṇa never worked, his fingers were softer than those of other men. But they were somewhat harder than his other limbs because his fingers would cover the holes of the flute. Kṛṣṇa's body is as soft as yoghurt when you touch it. It is cooling and so soft. In this mood, Kṛṣṇa is there in this beautiful form which we can see in the temples, playing his flute and enchanting the mind.

Now we have heard about Kṛṣṇa, so now we should stare at Kṛṣṇa with unblinking eyes. First see his lotus feet. Śrīla Prabhupāda writes:

> The mind of the conditioned soul on account of its association with the material energy from time immemorial contains heaps of dirt in the form of desires to control material nature. This dirt is like a mountain, but a mountain can be shattered when hit by a thunderbolt. Meditating on the lotus feet of the Lord acts like a thunderbolt on the mountain of dirt in the mind of the *yogī*. If a *yogī* wants to shatter the mountain of dirt in his mind, then he should concentrate on the lotus feet of the Lord and not imagine something void or impersonal. Because the dirt has accumulated like a solid mountain, one must mediate on the lotus feet of the Lord for quite a long time. For one who is accustomed to thinking of the lotus feet of the Lord constantly however, it is a different matter. The devotees are so fixed on the lotus feet of the Lord that they do not think of anything else. (*Śrīmad-Bhāgavatam* 3.28.22 purport)

Śrīla Prabhupāda states that if you are a *yogī*, you take advantage of this process of *smaraṇam* and meditate on the lotus the feet for a long time. But the *bhakti-yogīs* (us) take special advantage of the process of hearing and chanting in this *sambandha*, in a relationship where we think of Kṛṣṇa, and make our chanting so wonderful that we feel some devotional feelings.

There is a ladder in our lives. We can go down in the direction of *kāma*, become degraded, sad, disappointed, frustrated, and keep taking birth after birth, or we can go to the same ladder of desire, but go up to the level of love, to the beginning states of gratitude or appreciation of Kṛṣṇa, feeling closeness to the Lord. Then we feel some *bhakti*, and finally some spiritual energy will really start working intensely in us, and then there will be *ruci* and *āsakti* and *bhāva* someday. But we can start now, and it's only a matter of which direction we look.

Do we want to look toward the material energy, or do we want to look toward guru, toward *vraja-dhāma*, toward the *brāhmaṇas*, toward the Vaiṣṇavas, and all these personalities we have heard about in *Manaḥ-śikṣā*? Train the mind to look to these residents of Vraja, the Vaiṣṇavas, and to our *dīkṣā-mantras*, the holy name, and we will see, without any doubt, that we will become free from this *kāma*, this selfish desire that only makes us miserable and disappointed.

When in the association of devotees, something happens. A *sādhu* is someone who practices *bhajana* and who helps us to do *bhajana* also. So when we come together with proper devotees who practice Kṛṣṇa consciousness and who will preach to us nicely, I can guarantee we will faint when we smell the fragrance of the cup full of honey that will be opened in their association. In the association of materialists our heads turn downwards, and down we go. In the association of *sādhus* our heads turn upwards and up we go. It is that simple.

The entire universe is full of miseries and therefore the inhabitants of this material universe are always shedding tears out of intense grief (*Śrīmad-Bhāgavatam* 3.28.32). There is a great ocean of water made from such tears. But for those who surrender unto the Supreme Personality of Godhead, the ocean of tears created by *kāma* and *krodha* (anger) – the all-devouring enemies of this world – is at once dried up. We need only see the charming smile of the Supreme Lord. In other words, the bereavement of material existence immediately subsides when we see his charming smile.

COMMENTARY BY BHAKTIVIJNANA GOSWAMI

Manaḥ-śikṣā by Raghunātha Dāsa Gosvāmī is comprised of twelve instructions to the mind. The author makes the point right at the beginning that these instructions are meant to help us serve Kṛṣṇa based on spontaneity by his use of the term *rāga* (attachment). Everything we're doing should be based on our heartfelt aspiration, not on some heartless planning for gain, but on an emotional impulse.

He further explains how to form such an attachment. Raghunātha Dāsa Gosvāmī offers invaluable instructions on how to acquire taste in devotional service – what should the principles of our service be and what should be happening in our hearts for us to develop this taste.

We need an attachment. In the beginning when we take to devotional service, we develop a taste for it – everything is new and unusual; this novelty thrills us and makes our practice inspirational. But then our practice sometimes becomes a dreary routine because we have already learned how to put on a *dhotī* and apply *tilaka*.

Lord Caitanya said the reason he appeared is that the whole world is following *vaidhī-sādhana-bhakti*. Everyone follows some principles out of fear. We think, "If I do it, I'll be better off than if I don't do it."

There were four schools or *sampradāyas* preaching *vaidhī-sādhana-bhakti* and teaching how it should be followed. In contrast, Lord Caitanya said that he came specially to teach how to develop the kind of attachment that eternally resides in the hearts of the residents of Vraja.

Lord Caitanya set the example. He cried in the *gambhīra* and spent sleepless nights listening to the *bhajanas* sung to him by Rāmānanda Rāya and Svarūpa Dāmodara Gosvāmī. It was actually Svarūpa Dāmodara Gosvāmī who taught this kind of attachment, because the Lord instructed him by saying, "Teach others. Give them a chance to satiate themselves."

Our tradition which Lord Caitanya founded is composed of two schools of thought, or two trends, explaining in a slightly different way the method and principle of developing this attachment. One of the schools originated from the instructions initially transferred by Svarūpa Dāmodara Gosvāmī to Vakreśvara Paṇḍita, who was one of Lord Caitanya's personal associates in Navadvīpa and later in Puri. Vakreśvara Paṇḍita in turn transferred it to Gopāla Guru Gosvāmī, and Gopāla Guru Gosvāmī transferred it to Dhyānacandra Gosvāmī. This is the path called *bahiraṅgā-rāgānuga-sādhana* or the practice to develop attachment by means of external methods. In this school, Svarūpa Dāmodara explained the way we can develop attachment by worshiping Deities.

Gopāla Guru Gosvāmī and Dhyānacandra Gosvāmī wrote a detailed manual (*paddhati*) of how to worship Kṛṣṇa with attachment, what mantras to chant, how to treat the Lord, how he should be imagined, how to meditate while worshiping Deities. In other words, they translated the language of *arcana* into the language of *rāga*, the language of attachment.

The other school also goes back to Svarūpa Dāmodara Gosvāmī, from the instructions he gave to Raghunātha Dāsa Gosvāmī. When Raghunātha arrived in Puri, having finally escaped from household life, he addressed Lord Caitanya through Svarūpa Dāmodara, "I do not know my duty or the goal of my life. Therefore, please personally give me instructions from your transcendental mouth."

Lord Caitanya said, "I don't know; I'm just thinking about Kṛṣṇa. There's no *sādhana* to speak of – I'm just crying for Kṛṣṇa night and day. How can I explain it to you? But if you insist, I can tell you in a few words." And then Caitanya spoke one verse, which explained the fundamental principle. He said: *amānī mānada hañā kṛṣṇa-nāma sadā la'be, vraje rādhā-kṛṣṇa-sevā mānase karibe* (*Caitanya-caritāmṛta, Antya-līlā* 6.237). Externally, we should be humbler than a blade of grass, without an ounce of false pride or desire for honor. In addition, *kṛṣṇa-nāma sada labe*: we should chant the holy name.

We have often heard that we should be humble, and sometimes we walk around bearing a yoke of humility, which lies heavily on us. We walk around harassed and oppressed by this humility. We have been told more than once that externally we should be chanting the mantra but we think everything internal will come automatically. But the school of thought that originated in this verse is about what should be happening in our heart.

Lord Caitanya explains it in the next line of this verse, *vraje rādhā-kṛṣṇa-sevā mānase karibe* "Within your mind you should render service to Rādhā and Kṛṣṇa in Vraja." But what that means and what should be happening in our hearts is not an easy question to answer. Lord Caitanya then told Raghunātha Dāsa Gosvāmī to ask Svarūpa Dāmodara for details.

Certainly, externally we must be humble. Externally, we should try and offer respect to one and all, not expecting it in return. Externally, we should chant the holy name, but *bhakti* is not a mechanical process. We need to think what should be occurring in our hearts. That science is what Raghunātha Dāsa Gosvāmī explains in the *Manaḥ-śikṣā*.

In this first instruction, Raghunātha Dāsa Gosvāmī says, "O my brother, my dear mind, I'm offering my obeisances to you; I'm taking a very humble position. I'm taking hold of your feet and I humbly pray to you. Please, give up all your pride: *sadā dambhaṁ hitvā*."

He then says, "I pray to you, 'O mind, try your hardest to develop attachment.'" The reason for this instruction is contained in the first two lines where he enumerates to whom and to what we should develop our attachment. *Gurau* to Śrī Guru, *goṣṭha* – Vṛndāvana, *goṣṭhālayiṣu* – to the residents of Vṛndāvana. *Sujane* means devotees. *Bhū-sura-gaṇe* means *brāhmaṇas. Sva-mantre* means in our own *dīkṣā-mantras. Śrī-nāmni* – the holy name. *Vraja-nava-yuva-dvandva-śaraṇe* – the shelter of the lotus feet of Kiśora-kiśorī.

Each word or phrase carries an important message, which helps us to have a clearer idea of how we should chant the holy name and perform devotional service.

ADDRESSING THE MIND

First of all, Raghunātha Dāsa Gosvāmī describes his mind. He says – *svāntaḥ bhrātaḥ* – my inner self. It is very important to first of all understand what the mind is. Sometimes it is very difficult to explain to people that they are not their mind. Understanding that we are not the body is easy, but to understand that we are not the mind is difficult.

Raghunātha Dāsa Gosvāmī explains a very important point about *svāntaḥ*. We should understand that in the conditioned state the soul delegates the functions of our personality to the mind. Actually, it is as if there is no soul – it is sleeping. All is delegated to the mind. Therefore, we find it so hard to detach ourselves from our mind. For this reason, Raghunātha Dāsa addresses his inner self with much respect.

The soul is eternal, full of knowledge and bliss. It is pure. So where do the vices reside? The answer is the mind. We have merged with it so tightly that we have delegated to our mind the functions of ourselves. It has a general power of attorney. Whatever we do – it is our mind. All of the past life impressions (*saṁskāras*) make up our personality. A child is born a ready-made personality, with an endless stream of desires. The seeds of these desires are already in the mind. This situation is the reason why we should treat our mind with much respect. Raghunātha Dāsa Gosvāmī demonstrates that respect here by saying, "O my dear brother, my mind. I'm addressing to you *catubhir*." *Catubhir* means with sweet language. In other words, "I want to flatter you," which is a very important point because the mind is very hard to cope with. It is like a sponge absorbing everything. An avid material mind, attached to material things, absorbs everything. We absorb all of these material impressions, living a material life, and we don't know ourselves how we are going to act.

The mind is like a vacuum cleaner. It accumulates material impressions, storing and classifying them. And finally it starts acting, being guided by these impressions that it has absorbed, as if it is us. The 19th century Russian poet Nekrasov, when explaining the nature of the Russian peasant, explained the nature of the mind. He said, "The Russian peasant is like a bull: once an idea has taken hold of the brain, it's almost impossible to eradicate." Arjuna was also speaking about this problem 5000 years ago, how very difficult the mind is to deal with. It has power generated by material impressions.

Therefore, as the *nīti-śāstras* explain, in dealing with the mind we remember that an enemy can be treated in different ways. If we are stronger than the enemies, we punish them. But if we are not sure whether the enemies are stronger or not, we approach them to see if we can win them over.

Some people try to defeat their mind with coercion, trying to rein in their mind through force. But if you just try to rein in the mind, it will kick up like a wild, unbroken horse and throw off its rider.

Therefore, Raghunātha Dāsa Gosvāmī takes a tactful approach. He says, "O my mind, I love you so much. I love you so much; trust me,

I wish you well." This method is very important. Some people try to reform themselves by force, and others say that you should just love yourself, no matter how you behave. But Raghunātha Dāsa Gosvāmī says, "No. I'm addressing you gently, with touching, sweet words – my brother, my mind, you should make some profound changes in yourself, which are bound to be painful."

This very first verse of the instructions to the mind raises the most important problem for anyone attempting to follow a spiritual path, no matter which path they are following. If we are trying to overcome the influence of the material energy, what we first need to overcome is identification with the mind, which is very difficult to conquer.

In Patañjali Muni's *Yoga-sūtras* he explains that a person identifies the self who can see with their ability to see or with their tools of sight. These two concepts are confused: the tool being used and the self who is using these tools. Patañjali explains that this confusion is what is called the false ego, which gives rise to all other difficulties and, in turn, develops into ignorance.

What tools do we possess? These are the mind and senses. When we use these tools we identify with them because we derive pleasure from them. We can run, and since we derive some pleasure in running, we like to identify with the tools that enable us to do so. The same happens when we drive a car. We feel enjoyment associated with the subtle psychology of dominion over this material nature.

We are reluctant to take the position of the observer. In reality, according to the highest spiritual philosophy, we are always the observer. However, we do not like being an observer because the observer cannot really enjoy. Unless the observer identifies with what is going on, there is no enjoyment. The observer does not enjoy, and the enjoyer does not observe.

For example, if we are watching two people fighting, we will not be able to enjoy the fight if we do not identify with one of them. We are given tools and by using them we can experience a feeling or a sensation. But having come to the material world to get various experiences, it is very easy and natural for us to identify with those experiences. In the moment when we identify with the experiences, we may feel nothing but enjoyment. However, the consequences are very sad. Any yoga or any spiritual path teaches that we must withdraw and take the position of observers.

Raghunātha Dāsa Gosvāmī tells us the first thing we must do is detach and look at ourselves with an outward eye. This is very difficult to do precisely because there are two aspects of the Lord's illusory energy – *āvaraṇātmikā-māyā* and *prakṣepātmikā-māyā*. *Prakṣepātmikā-māyā* makes us identify with the body and the senses; *āvaraṇātmikā-māyā* covers the mind and gives us the feeling of happiness.

A very good example of how we voluntarily immerse ourselves even deeper into *māyā* is by drinking alcohol or taking drugs. The chemical substance affects the mind, and the mind changes or transforms. Since we identify with the mind, we immediately identify with this changed mind. This is *prakṣepātmikā-māyā*.

The mind changed by drugs or alcohol is experiencing a pseudo liberation. A drunken man, for example, feels that he can do anything. He identifies with his "liberated mind" that now feels no boundary and, at that very moment, having identified with it, he thinks he is experiencing happiness. To the eye of an enlightened person, we are no less a pathetic image than a drunk is. We are squeezing something out of ourselves, trying to enjoy. But a sober person, a yogī, has taken the position of the observer. Any control of the mind, any kind of yoga, means that we are somewhat recovering from this state of intoxication.

Only when we take the position of observers do we cease to create karma. We all know that the main problem in material life is that anything we do creates karma. But as long as we identify with the body and enjoy what we do, we will continue to create karma, because the impressions of what we do remain in our mind as does the enjoyment we derive from our actions.

There are three possible psychological reactions to the emotions that we experience. The first reaction, for instance, is when someone comes up to us and insults us in some way. A mind identified with all the material qualities immediately becomes filled with self-righteous anger. At such times we can manifest our freedom. We possess freedom, which means that, having become angry, we can still act differently. As a rule, someone who has no freedom, who is completely under the power of the law of karma, who perpetuates the chain of karma, what do they do when they become angry? Depending on their level of culture, they either act through their cognitive or acting senses. But generally there is no difference. If they are intelligent, they will respond, "I am not a fool. You are the fool." An unintelligent person will just start fighting. This action, whether verbal or physical, is the first kind of karmic reaction.

The second kind of reaction of a well-mannered person who is trying to be in control is that they suppress their anger. The first reaction is to give vent to an emotion. The second is to try to suppress it, whether by swallowing the words that are burning to be spoken or clenching fists in an effort not to use them. But have we ceased to create karma in this way? No, because this suppressed emotion goes deeper inside and takes on ugly forms. Sooner or later it will force us to act in accordance with our individual karma.

The third option we have is to start preaching to ourselves. We start explaining to ourselves what we are doing, and in this way we try to overcome our anger. We attempt to somehow explain or justify it.

But all these reactions are wrong. Instead, we merely have to observe. We need to simply stand back, see that the wave of anger has arisen in our mind, and think, "Mmmm. Anger. Hare Kṛṣṇa."

All spiritual paths, in essence, give the same advice to look with this outward eye. The difference which distinguishes the various spiritual paths is in the method in which we can detach from identification with the body and mind.

A most effective way to try to look at ourselves with an outward eye is to tolerate. Just tolerate and perform our duty. When we are tolerating, we are acting as soul. The mind is unable to tolerate. It keeps saying, "I can't. I don't want."

We say, "Shut up, you should!" Tolerance is how we can detach ourselves from the mind. Another way to not identify with all these reactions, with the body, the mind, or with the emotions that take place, is to always be immersed in Kṛṣṇa consciousness and take the standpoint of the scriptures. In the depths of our soul, we should always look at the world from the perspective of Kṛṣṇa's teachings, which he presented in the *Bhagavad-gītā*.

The advice that Raghunātha Dāsa Gosvāmī gives in the first verse is that, having given up *false* identification, we must develop *proper* identification. In other words, the external world we live in constantly forces some role upon us. We play the part of a mother, a father, a spiritual master. But in reality, we are the servant of the servant of the Lord: *gopī-bhartuḥ pada-kamalayor dāsa-dāsānudāsaḥ*.

The path of spiritual life is a way of removing the false identification with the material body and with the roles that we play here. Simultaneously, it is a way of developing our spiritual attachment and attaining our spiritual identity. How do we attain this spiritual identity and whom should we identify with? Raghunātha Dāsa Gosvāmī says that at the beginning we should identify with our attachment to guru. Then we have to identify ourselves with the amazing atmosphere of Vṛndāvana, the atmosphere of pure, selfless love. Then we must somehow or other tie ourselves with the strong threads of friendship and love to the devotees.

We must understand who we are in this spiritual atmosphere of Vṛndāvana and in the spiritual society of devotees, starting this path by identifying with our guru and by developing attachment to him. And then the most important thing that needs to occur will do so, which is to identify with our attachment to the holy name. Attachment to the holy name will become a part of our personality. Ultimately, what all this was started for will take place, and we will take shelter of the eternally youthful couple of Vṛndāvana.

Therefore, cultivating the position of the observer is not enough. In the case of a person following the path of mystic yoga, the ideal is to become an observer. But for *bhakti*, the ideal is to become a servant of Kṛṣṇa. We can remain in this state if a prayer is ceaselessly vibrating within. Inwardly, no matter what's going on externally, we must chant the holy name. We must always be in Vṛndāvana, remembering our spiritual master and the association of devotees. Externally we will go on acting in various ways, playing the parts we have to play, but inwardly we must remain devotees.

ALWAYS GIVE UP PRIDE

At the moment we are the victims of a false program installed in our mind, a program called *karma*. This program causes us to suffer, making other people around us suffer, too, due to all of the vices residing in our mind. And here Raghunātha Dāsa Gosvāmī says, "There is one thing I beg of you: *sadā dambhaṁ hitvā* – cast away all pride." This is the first request everything is supposed to start with. This is the first instruction to the mind.

Sadā dambhaṁ hitvā. Sadā means "once and for all." *Hitvā* means cast away – cast away once and for all. And *dambha* means pride, deception, or propensity for deception, and hypocrisy. Bhaktivinoda Ṭhākura goes on to analyze and explain the anatomy of *dambha*, the anatomy of what we should initially give up. To put it simply, *dambha* is both false ego and the propensity for deception, and not just deception, but self-deception. We have to cast away this tendency towards self-delusion in order to reach our spiritual goals.

For Christians, the mind plays the role of the devil. What we call the mind, they call the devil. The devil appears as the serpent, tempting us to eat the apple so we can become God. This describes our propensity for deception. The mind flatters and charms us, saying we can do anything and be anything. Hence Raghunātha Dāsa Gosvāmī says, "The first step should be *sadā dambhaṁ hitvā*." We should cast away this *dambha* (pride) not just once, but always, because the serpent isn't sleeping, it is there.

Bhaktivinoda Ṭhākura explains that this *dambha* or pride has six constituents. He continues, "First it's *māyā* or illusion." We're all apt to be illusioned, as the famous Russian poet Pushkin said, "Oh, it takes little to assure me! … I am so willingly deceived!" Then Bhaktivinoda Ṭhākura says, "*Chala* – a tendency to deceive." Not everyone allows the cheating tendency to manifest itself externally, but everyone should know that we all have this propensity to cheat. Then there is *kapaṭatā*, which means hypocrisy or pretence, when we're trying to pretend to be something or someone. Then *avidyā* (ignorance). The fifth is *kuṭi-nāṭi* (dishonesty). And the sixth and the last is depravity or corruptness. These make up *dambha,* which Raghunātha Dāsa Gosvāmī implores us to give up.

We have this *dambha* (pride) and sometimes we even take up spiritual practice for the sake of becoming famous. We study the scriptures and quote them to serve our own purposes. That process is what is going on in our minds. So, Raghunātha Dāsa Gosvāmī says, "If you want to have a taste for spiritual life, you should, first of all, dispose of this propensity towards deception. Don't let your mind deceive you."

Śrīla Prabhupāda called his translation and commentary of the *Bhagavad-gītā* "*Bhagavad-gītā As It Is*" and this term has a deep philosophical meaning. It means that we're not trying to interpret the scriptures the way we want to, to please or benefit ourselves. We take it as it is. Honesty is the first rule in order to remove this tendency to deceive.

There was a Muslim living a dissipated life, carousing, drinking, eating and indulging himself. A religious leader, *mullah,* approached him, saying, "My son, don't you know the Quran says that one shouldn't do this because one is going to destroy one's eternal soul? You're carousing, drinking, and corrupting people."

"How come, *mullah,* that you don't know the Quran? It says: eat, drink, and have a good time."

"My son, there's more to that line – 'Eat, drink, have a good time and you will destroy yourself.'"

The debauchee replied, "Holy father, no one can follow the scriptures meticulously. I prefer following the first line of this verse. It says, 'Eat, drink, have fun.'"

The first thing we should understand is that the enemy is within, and it is always ready to deceive us and justify its actions to us. It tells we are the best, and it is finding fault with others, saying the fault lies with others, not us.

One woman who had just joined Kṛṣṇa consciousness said that she loved the *Bhagavad-gītā,* particularly chapter 16, because it describes that there are only two types of people: the demons and the devotees. She said she realized that she was a devotee and the rest are demons.

Śrīla Prabhupāda called the mind the best lawyer. And what is the lawyer paid for? The best lawyer is the one who can lie convincingly.

He's going to win. Within us, there is the best of lawyers working for free. Always lying: you're always right; you can't be at fault.

When two devotees were having an altercation, in an attempt to pacify them, I said that one of you may be at fault but the other party could also be wrong. And one of the devotees replied, "I'm not sure about him, but as far as I am concerned, I'm one hundred percent confident that I am always right." Thinking yourself always right is the foundation of pride. Raghunātha Dāsa Gosvāmī says that until we cast away this *dambha* (pride) manifesting itself through this deception, we will never be able to understand or progress on the spiritual path. Therefore, Raghunātha Dāsa Gosvāmī says – *sadā dambhaṁ hitvā* – always be on your guard and remember that the mind is forever willing to deceive.

We should always remember that the source of *dambha* is within us. *Dambha* means identifying with the material body and even more with the material mind, which plays roles. We all have a split personality. In the spiritual world, there's no difference between the soul, its mind, its feelings. Here, though, there is a difference. Sometimes people start doubting whether they feel something or not, and who feels it – is it my mind or myself? During a *kīrtana* we experience some ecstasy, enthusiasm, and inspiration. Then suddenly we think, "Is it me who is experiencing and feeling this?" And it is hard for people to detach themselves from the mind. It is hard to understand that we are the soul.

I once was on a train with a man who had been drinking. In my compartment there were three other drunken men sleeping and snoring, so there was nothing else for me to do but go out into the corridor and chant *japa*. The other person who couldn't sleep approached me while I was chanting and asked, "What are you Buddhists doing here?" As the conversation went on, I started to explain the nature of the soul.

I said, "You're a soul! Just look: everything about you has changed – your mind, your body. In your childhood, you were different but the soul remained unchanged. You remain unchanged. Try to remember what you were like as a child."

He kept thinking for a while and then said, "No, it wasn't me. It was another soul."

The mind is the source of pride. It makes us play every role possible. In the long run, we try to work these prideful roles into the spiritual realm. There is a very important point we have to understand: even being on the spiritual path and theoretically accepting that we are servants – and any authentic spiritual path teaches this position – we don't always reconcile this within.

Jīva Gosvāmī gives a very interesting explanation of what knowledge is. He says that knowledge is the essence of experience. Knowledge is what we have experienced – it is equal to perception. When Kṛṣṇa begins speaking about what knowledge is, he starts with these two words: *amānitvam adambhitvam* (*Bhagavad-gītā* 13.8–12). To gain true knowledge or true experience, to approach God, we should first of all cast away our passion for honor, *amānitvam*, and this pride, *adambhitvam*, consisting in our ability to deceive and delude ourselves.

There are two forms of pride that exhibit themselves on the spiritual path. At times devotees are naturally naive. As a rule, they come with their hearts open and expect a miracle. Most expect something to happen during or after chanting the *mahā-mantra*. If they experience some miracle, they consider it as proof of genuineness of the spiritual path. However, sometimes miracles do not prove that the spiritual path is true. In southern India, there lives a so-called incarnation of God who works miracles on a regular basis. Although he does some tricks, he can also perform miracles. Many people can attest that he materialized an object in front of their eyes or he came into their dreams or saved them in some situations. At the same time this person claims he is the complete incarnation of God. Some people in their frenzy get stigmata on their hands and begin bleeding. However, this is not at all proof of the true spiritual experience. It is not at all proof of their intimacy with God because the mind can be the cause of all these miracles. We can instill something into our own minds and it will work such wonders, making us think, "God must have come to me." There are lots of examples of false spiritual experiences: 'contactees', psychics, mediums, magicians, and pseudo incarnations.

Sometimes we even see devotees trying to rush a miracle – we are so impatient. We have spent hundreds of lives here in the material world wasting our time, and then at last when we become spiritual, we think, "A miracle must happen now. God must appear before me." And sometimes he may falsely appear to, even with a peacock feather with a blue body.

I remember chanting the *mahā-mantra* for the first time with a devotee who continuously had a big blue finger appear before him. Patañjali describes false ecstacies or false visions as the last of the obstacles on the spiritual path. This is what is done by one category of *sahajiyās*. They sometimes cry, spin, roll on the floor, in the dust. And most surprising is that they sometimes seem to have some love of God. But then they go out and smoke a cigarette. This is how this self-importance manifests itself through illusion or false visions and how we are reduced to the *sahajiyā* level.

Śrīla Prabhupāda warned again and again not to rush things – advancement is supposed to come naturally. Waiting for what is natural is the way the *ācāryas* describe, and it is not easy. It is one type of pride to be impatient. We think, "I deserve more than what I have. I need my spiritual experience right here and right now. God should come to me or I should experience some kind of miracle, or I'll bring myself to some state to make everyone understand I'm the smartest and the most remarkable." This fault resides in the mind.

But there is even a more profound mistake we can make on the spiritual path. When we achieve some success in the practice of our devotional service and learn how to touch people's hearts with the words of the *śāstra*, from Śrīla Prabhupāda, and our initiating spiritual master, all of a sudden we imagine ourselves to be something important. We forget we have received those merits and achievements from our spiritual master and Kṛṣṇa. We should always remember that we owe God and our spiritual master everything we have. On no account should we attempt to claim the credit by saying, "Yes, I made it all happen."

Aside from the above, there is another more profound manifestation of pride, which is vanity and conceit. Bhaktivinoda Ṭhākura gave the most amazing definition of humility, because humility is the opposite of vanity and pride. Sometimes we think we are humble, but we are acting humble only for the sake of showing off how humble we are. The mind sometimes says, "Be humble because this is the way of receiving honor from devotees." So we become humble.

Bhaktivinoda Ṭhākura gives a definition of humility we can use to check whether we are humble or not. He says that true humility is to not expect anything from anyone. Next time when we are going to take offence because someone hasn't done something we expected them to, remember this instruction of Raghunātha Dāsa Gosvāmī – *sadā dambhaṁ hitvā*. Keep renouncing pride because it manifests itself in resentment and the mood that someone owes us something, because we are exceptional.

Caitanya Mahāprabhu came to teach us, "Everyone can see God. Everyone has the way open before them regardless of what family they were born into, regardless of where they come from, regardless of the sins they have committed – even if we are at death's door, we can still see God." He also taught that the important thing is to develop true humility because it is the basis of the genuine spiritual experience. Whatever occurs on the basis of pride is false spiritual experience.

In this verse, Raghunātha Dāsa Gosvāmī says *sadā dambhaṁ hitvā*. *Sadā* – whichever level you've reached be careful of pride. Moreover, the higher level you have attained, the more reason you have to become proud. We should always monitor this carefully. As soon as you become proud, you are bound to fail. This is the instruction Raghunātha Dāsa Gosvāmī gives us.

He says further that we should just cast away our pride. Pride generates attachments; pride is our way to exist in this world; pride is the roles we are playing. It is easy to say, "Cast away your pride." But can we cast away our pride? How can we exist without any kind of self concept in which we feel satisfied? We can't.

Giving up pride means, "Take off all false coverings, all this armor that you have put on. Give up all pride of the roles you are playing here." But what is the problem that we immediately face when we hear this advice? We are told, "Give up all the roles that you are playing here in this world. Stop being a man or a woman, a mother or a father. Stop being a *śūdra, vaiśya, kṣatriya,* or a *brāhmaṇa*."

Essentially, Raghunātha Dāsa Gosvāmī instructs us to 'undress,' because all of these shells are the clothes that we have put on. How would we feel if suddenly we had to, even if not physically, but at least internally, uncover ourselves? We would feel unprotected and defenseless.

Pride is a shield, an armor that we have created, a shell that we have put on. We are like oysters; on top we have a shell and we are inside, thinking, "I am fine. I have protected myself. Let them try to hurt me."

When we hear the advice to become a small, defenseless soul and take shelter at the lotus feet of Kṛṣṇa, completely giving up pride, it is very difficult to follow this advice and abandon our pride, because we have suffered a great deal. We worry that if we become as humble as possible others will exploit us, and that may very well happen. This is why at first glance it may seem that such advice is impractical.

This is the internal work that we must do – *sadā dambhaṁ hitvā kuru ratim apūrvām atitarām*. We must try hard to obtain our spiritual identity. This is the advice of the first verse. We can externally remain what we are and we must remain what we are, playing different roles. But internally we must remain a tiny soul who is constantly linked with Kṛṣṇa by millions of ties and who is always looking for ever-new ties, for ever-new affection for Kṛṣṇa.

In the First Canto of *Śrīmad-Bhāgavatam* Śrīla Prabhupāda tells a story about Nārada Muni that illustrates this verse very well. Nārada Muni is a great preacher, and the power of his words and his purity is so strong that everybody he speaks to becomes a devotee. Once he preached to a cobra who also became a devotee. This reptile was accustomed to biting and hissing and was very spiteful, but when he saw Nārada Muni his heart changed. It turned out the cobra could live without the biting and hissing, and instead he became a happy soul. This is effective preaching. It is the fact that we suddenly see how we can live in a different way without pretending to be something we are not, and no longer having to defend ourselves against anyone. This snake saw Nārada Muni and believed him. The snake's heart was changed. However, the story of his love for, and devotion to, Kṛṣṇa is quite a sad tale because all those who had previously fled in terror at the sight of him, suddenly realized that the cobra had started to behave strangely by constantly smiling.

As a result, the villagers eventually became completely impudent toward him. Once the snake became a devotee, life became absolutely unbearable with everybody humiliating him. Finally the cobra found Nārada Muni and said to him, "What have you done to me? I cannot live like this any more. Everyone is beating me because I can no longer bite anyone. Sometimes I want to, but I just can't."

Nārada Muni, looking at the snake, said, "My dear disciple, I did tell you not to bite, but I didn't tell you not to raise your hood. So from now on you can puff up your hood." He began to behave in this way and, naturally, everyone again started respecting and fearing the snake.

This parable contains a very deep meaning, for the pride we have is like a snake's venom. The advice that Raghunātha Dāsa Gosvāmī gives us is that we should not let the poison of pride reign in our hearts. Externally we can "raise our hoods," and we must go on playing the parts that we have to play, but inwardly we must ceaselessly pray to Kṛṣṇa and chant Hare Kṛṣṇa, Hare Kṛṣṇa, Kṛṣṇa Kṛṣṇa, Hare Hare/ Hare Rāma, Hare Rāma, Rāma Rāma, Hare Hare.

ATTACHMENT TO GURU

Raghunātha Dāsa Gosvāmī also says – *kuru ratim apūrvām atitarām* – develop attachment to the guru. *Gurau goṣṭhe goṣṭhālayiṣu sujane bhū-sura-gaṇe* – try hard to develop attachment to the guru, the Vaiṣṇavas, the inhabitants of Vṛndāvana, to *vraja-dhāma* itself, and the *brāhmaṇas.* What does it mean to develop attachment? It means that having renounced our material roles, we have to accept our spiritual roles. After having broken off our material ties, we should then develop spiritual ties. Here Raghunātha Dāsa Gosvāmī says, "Renounce your material self-designations and develop a spiritual self-designation through attachment to the spiritual." This is his first instruction.

Through a strong attachment to *apūrvām* – an extraordinary attachment to spiritual things – develop your personality in the spiritual world because we are not impersonal there. But what is a personality and actually who are we? How do we designate our real personality? If we are asked who we are in this world, we would say, for instance, "I am the husband of such and such. I am the father of these children.

I was born in such and such country. I have this or that educational background." In other words, our personalities are our relationships.

Raghunātha Dāsa Gosvāmī says to renounce your material ties but develop the spiritual ones straightaway. And he begins by saying that the first attachment we should develop is the one to the guru; he makes it a point that we should make every effort to achieve this. The point of this instruction is that we *can* develop such an attachment.

Here Raghunātha Dāsa Gosvāmī says that we shouldn't remain "warm." If we want to achieve something in spiritual life, we must develop a strong attachment. Where your spiritual attachment begins, there begins the formation of your spiritual personality. Essentially, he is explaining how we can change our material personality for a spiritual one. But first we need to develop this extraordinarily strong attachment to a guru.

Jīva Gosvāmī explains what a strong attachment to a guru is. He first explains why we need an attachment to a guru. He quotes verses from *Śrīmad-Bhāgavatam*, chapter seven, which states that the result of serving the guru is that we can remove our faults. Just by communicating with the spiritual master, or remembering him, we can see our insignificance, because we can see how great our guru is. When we stand before a spotless mirror, which is the heart of our spiritual master, we will see our pride and envy. When we see the person who has no envy, we very clearly see our own.

Narattoma Dāsa Ṭhākura cries, "The only thing I fear is that these faults will go on living in my mind." Therefore, Jīva Gosvāmī says that service to the guru can deliver us from our faults. But that is not all.

Jīva Gosvāmī also says that there is an exclusive perfection that we can obtain by serving the guru and no one else but the guru. According to Nārada Muni, there are different ways of removing faults, but this exclusive perfection is the special mood in which our guru serves Kṛṣṇa, which we cannot obtain from anyone else but from the guru's heart, and only by his mercy. So Jīva Gosvāmī says, "It's the greatest gift we can receive, and it only comes due to personal communication with and service to a guru." Without the right mood, we cannot reach the spiritual world.

We chant this mantra: *śrī-caitanya-mano 'bhīṣṭaṁ, sthāpitaṁ yena bhū-tale/ svayam rūpaḥ kadā mahyaṁ, dadāti sva-padāntikam* (*Prema-bhakti-candrikā*, verse 2, Narottama Dāsa Ṭhākura). When serving someone, we should respect his mind and try to penetrate his heart, understanding his mood and in turn develop his service mood.

If we consider all the things Raghunātha Dāsa Gosvāmī touches upon, we will see that they all possess a certain mood, helping us cast away our enjoying mentality, and developing the true mood of a servant. This channel is first of all supposed to occur between the spiritual master and the disciple, having full faith that he can give all blessings.

A wonderful pastime illustrates this mood. Bihārī, a simple man from Vṛndāvana, was Jagannātha Dāsa Bābājī's disciple. Jagannātha Dāsa Bābājī died when he was 147 years old. He was so old that he needed someone to lift his eyelids for him, which had drooped so much over his eyes due to old age. Bihārī had been carrying his guru in a basket for approximately 40 years, serving him faithfully.

Once Jagannātha Dāsa Bābājī asked his disciple to read *Caitanya-caritāmṛta* because he could not see. Bihārī replied, "Guru Mahārāja, I'd be happy to, but I cannot read or understand Bengali."

His spiritual master replied, "If I told you to read, you should read." With faith in these instructions, Bihārī opened *Caitanya-caritāmṛta*, and suddenly found himself reading the Bengali script. Everything can come by the guru's mercy, *yasya prasādād bhagavat-prasādo* (*Śrī Gurvaṣṭakam*).

Another similar incident occurred that displayed the true guru and disciple relationship. Once Jagannātha Dāsa Bābājī told Bihārī, "Play the *mṛdaṅga*."

He replied, "I can't play the *mṛdaṅga*. I can't even play the *karatāls*, what to speak of *mṛdaṅga*. I can't play this 'one-two-three' beat."

But his guru insisted, "Play the *mṛdaṅga*." Once again he thought that everything is possible by his spiritual master's mercy. He started to play the *mṛdaṅga*, playing beats that even professional *mṛdaṅga* players could not play.

When Jagannātha Dāsa Bābājī was departing this world, he said, "Bihārī, you have been serving me faithfully and unfailingly. You have done so many things for me, whereas I have done none. I feel guilty. Do you want something?"

Bihārī replied, "What can you give to me? I know that you are a mendicant and penniless. You may die in peace and quiet without worrying about me. I will survive somehow; I am still strong."

Jagannātha Dāsa Bābājī said, "If you would like me to, I'll ask Caitanya Mahāprabhu to provide you with five carts laden with gold, right away. What do you want, Bihārī?"

He said, "I don't want anything. I want you. There's nothing else I want, just having you by my side."

Pleased by this, Jagannātha Dāsa Bābājī smiled and said, "Thank God. I was about to give these five carts to you but I wanted to hear it from you first. I'm giving you my blessing that you'll never experience any problems. You are going to have whatever you need. All your desires will be fulfilled; you are going to live to be a 100 years old, and I'll always be by your side. All the time, you will hear my voice within your heart."

According to Rūpa Gosvāmī, after a disciple has been initiated – *viśrambheṇa guroḥ sevā* (*Bhakti-rasāmṛta-sindhuḥ* 1.2.74–75) – they should begin serving their guru and their service should be filled with the spirit of *viśrambha* (unconditional trust). *Viśrambha* is the mood in which Kṛṣṇa communicates with his cowherd friends. It means that the disciple is trying to perceive the spiritual master's mood, trying to feel the way he feels without trying to merely imitate.

Jīva Gosvāmī says that a guru should become like our God, but people find that difficult to understand. But he explains: "For *karmīs*, the guru is God." Why is the guru God for *karmīs*? It is because the spiritual master can fulfill any wish of the disciple. He mentions this verse from the *Śrīmad-Bhāgavatam* (11.17.27) – *ācāryaṁ māṁ vijānīyān nāvamanyeta karhicit*. Kṛṣṇa said, "The *ācārya* is non-different from myself, therefore, you should by no means be envious of him." *Sarva-deva-mayo guruḥ* – the spiritual master is the representative of all the demigods – which means that the guru can fulfill all our material desires. If you want to obtain knowledge, the guru can give it to you. But the most valuable thing the guru can give you is *bhakti*. He can bring us nearer to God.

In another prayer, Raghunātha Dāsa Gosvāmī says, "Everything I have was given to me by my guru. He brought me to Mathurā; he gave me my *svarūpa*. The guru gave me Govardhana Hill and Rādhā-kuṇḍa; he gave me the company of Rūpa Gosvāmī and Sanātana Gosvāmī."

We should understand that Kṛṣṇa acts through our guru and the Lord's mercy only comes through our guru. We should develop loyalty to the spiritual master, trust and love him in our hearts. This is what we should work on consciously.

So here Raghunātha Dāsa Gosvāmī says, "Attachment to guru is the first thing we should achieve to find our spiritual personality in the spiritual world." The process is not about being formally initiated or being presented with chanting beads and a new name. It is about developing love for the spiritual master, who gives instructions and initiates us into the mantra. This is a very important thing for our devotion to develop: love for our spiritual master must be genuine, not false; it should not be a personality cult, but must be based on our spiritual attachment to him.

ATTACHMENT TO THE DĪKṢĀ MANTRA

Raghunātha Dāsa Gosvāmī says that the mind should be taught to grow attached to spiritual things because this is the nature of our mind. It shouldn't be taught how to be attached to material things.

In this verse, Raghunātha Dāsa Gosvāmī says, "My mind, my brother, my friend, my relative, my comrade, my dear, why do you need all these? *Sadā dambhaṁ hitvā* – cast away your pride. Pride is identifying ourselves with the material body, which is essentially identifying with the material world. So he says cast away your pride and all of your perceptions of happiness in this world because our perception of happiness in the material world means *īśvaro 'ham ahaṁ bhogī siddho 'haṁ balavān sukhī* (*Bhagavad-gītā* 16.14). "I am the lord, the enjoyer, I am perfect, I am the strongest; I am the most powerful." Giving up pride is the first step we should take on the spiritual path. Having taken it, we will gradually be able to develop the highest spiritual love, which leaves no place for any kind of contamination in the heart.

Lord Caitanya explains in the last verse of *Śikṣāṣṭaka*:

āśliṣya vā pāda-ratāṁ pinaṣṭu mām
adarśanān marma-hatāṁ karotu vā
yathā tathā vā vidadhātu lampaṭo
mat-prāṇa-nāthas tu sa eva nāparaḥ

He explains, "I am not bothered by my own distress or happiness, but if my distress pleases you, I am ready to suffer it. If my distress will be your happiness, my distress will become my happiness for it pleases you." This is the kind of real self interest we should strive for, because in the material world all of our emotions, all of our feelings, all of our relationships are contaminated and clouded by selfishness. In the long run, we want happiness for ourselves.

Caitanya Mahāprabhu says love conquers all. He gives an example from the *Purāṇas* to explain this text. A faithful wife loved her leper husband sincerely, although he was diseased and a lecher. He had lost sleep and his peace of mind because he had fallen in love with a prostitute. When his wife asked him what he wanted. He answered, "I want the prostitute."

The prostitute was very expensive because she was a royal concubine. Kings lined up for her, taking off their crowns and putting them at her feet. And this leper with a distorted nose, with his hands trembling, wanted to enjoy her company. So, to please her husband, his wife went to serve this woman. And when the latter tried to reward her, his wife said, "I don't need anything. However, if you promise to grant my wish, I will tell you what I want."

"But of course," the prostitute replied. "Whatever you want. If you want jewelry, I have lots; choose whichever you like."

The faithful wife replied, "I don't need anything. Just spend a night with my husband." The prostitute agreed.

So the woman brought her husband in a basket because he couldn't walk anymore. And when her husband saw what his wife had done, he cried out of repentance and love. He said, "Take me back home. I don't want anything else. What have I been chasing while having you by my side?" She put him on her shoulders and took him back.

On the way back the leper happened to touch Mārkaṇḍeya Ṛṣi, contaminating him with his touch. So the *ṛṣi* cursed him, "You are going to die by sunrise."

His wife was resentful. She thought, "This is my husband and some *ṛṣi* has cursed him. He is not going to die. And if it takes the sun not to rise, it won't rise!" And the sun did not rise that day – so strong was the power of her chastity and love.

It is said that at that moment Brahmā, Viṣṇu, and Maheśvara descended and asked her, "What do you want? We'll do anything you want because you've won us with your love." They cured her husband, delivered him from the curse, and sent the sun on its path.

Love can conquer everything but one should learn to love purely. People mistake lust for love. When explaining this verse, Bhaktisiddhānta Sarasvatī says that love rather than lust is what distinguishes true *bhakti* from what *prākṛta-sahajiyās* do. *Prākṛta-sahajiyās* want to enjoy Kṛṣṇa. They come to a spiritual movement, which is like the spiritual world, and take to a spiritual practice because they want to enjoy the Lord. But they don't sacrifice themselves, which turns their spiritual life into a travesty.

When we first receive *dīkṣā*, when we first start chanting the Gāyatrī mantra, we are beginning to restore our true spiritual identity. The beginning of a mantra contains the *bīja oṁ*, or *klīṁ*. This *bīja* already contains the seed of a relationship, which is the seed of a mantra. A mantra ends in *namaḥ* or *svāhā*, meaning we are surrendering and renouncing ourselves. Kṛṣṇa's name is in the middle of a mantra. Any mantra has this structure. Sprouting through chanting of the holy name, this *bīja* or seed of a relationship is supposed to lead to self-surrender.

Caitanya Mahāprabhu speaks about what happens during the *dīkṣā* ceremony. He says: *dīkṣā-kāle bhakta kare ātma-samarpaṇa* (*Caitanya-caritāmṛta, Antya-līlā* 4.192–193). The moment we receive *dīkṣā* and a mantra from our spiritual master, we should do *ātma-samarpaṇa*, which means we should sacrifice. And the moment we surrender, the moment we receive the mantra – *sei-kāle kṛṣṇa tāre kare ātma-sama* – Kṛṣṇa makes one equal to himself. Caitanya Mahāprabhu goes on explaining what is happening. When a person receives a mantra, with it they receive their spiritual body (*siddha-svarūpa*). At that moment our true relationship comes into being.

Bhaktivinoda Ṭhākura's *Jaiva-dharma* describes two heroes, Vijaya Kumāra and Vraja-nātha, receiving this mantra from their spiritual master. Tears came into their eyes and they started to cry, "Gaurāṅga! Gaurāṅga! Gaurāṅga!" Their hair stood on end.

Their guru looked at them and said, "You purified me today when I saw what had happened to you." The moment we receive a mantra, we should undergo a transformation within the heart. After Vijaya Kumāra and Vraja-nātha had received their mantra they summoned all the *brāhmaṇas* of Navadvīpa, the *bābājīs,* and all the devotees there. They made a huge feast for everyone. And while they were sitting modestly aside waiting for everyone to finish their meal in order to take the remains of their food, they saw Caitanya Mahāprabhu and his associates come to participate in that celebration.

This is a process that has two conditions. Both parties must make the effort. In our case we may take a little longer to see Lord Caitanya. But, in the long run, a mantra is to change our consciousness so that we begin to see the world in a different way, because we are removing the cataracts of selfishness. We chant: *oṁ ajñāna-timirāndhasya, jñānāñjana-śalākayā. Śalākayā* means a surgical instrument used to remove a cataract. Even in the distant past, they performed eye surgeries and removed this clouding. It is like we have a cataract on our eyes removed by our guru. And the guru removes it with this mantra instrument and opens our eyes with *jñānāñjana-śalākayā,* or the torch of knowledge.

Receiving a mantra is called *dvija* (second birth) and the person who receives this mantra is called a *dvija* (twice-born). Birds are also twice-born. First a bird is born in an egg and its second birth is as a bird coming out of the egg. What is the difference between the first and the second births? The second one enables a bird to fly. During our first birth we are figuratively inside a shell, bound hand and foot. We are struggling in this conditioning shell wanting to break free. We are naturally free souls. We want to love, we want to fly, but we are trapped inside an egg. Therefore, we need a guru who'll break this shell of material conditioning. The difference between the first and the second birth is that during the second birth one gets unlimited freedom and can fly. He gets the whole sky. During his first birth he gets a shell. He feels much better in this egg than in the mother's body, but still it is cramped.

Gopa-kumāra is another example of the power of a mantra. He had seen the guru and began to serve him on Govardhana, providing him with milk. Once his guru was chanting a mantra and as soon as he had chanted half of it, he got a lump in his throat. He hardly finished the mantra and then fainted. Gopa-kumāra ran to fetch some water to bring him to his senses. But when he returned his master had vanished. So, Gopa-kumāra started chanting the mantra. Gradually, the seed, which a mantra is often compared to, sprouted.

In other words, there are two things that occur during initiation. First, our guru puts his spiritual experience into the mantra; when receiving the mantra we receive *brahma-niṣṭhā*, or our spiritual master's spiritual experience. All this spiritual experience is supposed to sprout in our heart if our heart is ready to have something sprout within. As a rule, a conditioned soul's heart is barren – nothing grows there whether you plant anything or not. Our heart should be fertile. The spiritual master puts certain energy into these words, the energy of his understanding, his realization and spiritual experience. Secondly, we make a commitment to grow what we've received. A small seed contains the energy necessary to make a tree out of it. But if this seed falls down into barren soil, the tree won't grow – this energy is going to be wasted.

For example, one lady told me that she had read *Bhagavad-gītā* by Śrīla Prabhupāda. When she was reading it for the first time, she was crying from beginning to end. When I was reading her letter, I thought, "Why am I not crying?" I've been reading *Bhagavad-gītā* for years, but I've never gotten tears in my eyes. She explained why; she said it was because she had immediately understood that each word in that book was true. That is what she realized. This is the power that Śrīla Prabhupāda had put into his words; this same power is put into the words of the mantra by the spiritual master. But at the same time, the person who has received the mantra should possess certain qualities for this power to manifest itself. As I have already mentioned, the heart, or the soil of our heart, should be fertile.

Śrīla Prabhupāda explained that receiving a mantra is *divya jñāna hṛde prokāśito*. When we are speaking about *divya jñāna*, or transcendental knowledge, the seed of that spiritual knowledge is within the mantra. In fact, the whole spiritual knowledge is within the mantra. The essence of *divya jñāna* is that when we chant a mantra, Madanamohana, who is a personification of the spiritual master, and gives *sambandha-jñāna*, becomes attracted to it. When chanting the mantra received from the spiritual master, we should understand that our spiritual body is supposed to be growing.

Śrīla Prabhupāda often laughed when speaking about how Vivekananda received divine knowledge. In one of his books, Vivekananda wrote about how he once visited Ramakrishna. He said, "Master, give me the knowledge." Ramakrishna touched his forehead and at that moment, as if an electric discharge occurred between them, Vivekananda fell down to the ground, unconscious, and Ramakrishna fell too. Then when they both came to their senses, Ramakrishna said, "I have given you all of my knowledge – there is nothing left in me."

Śrīla Prabhupāda questioned, what kind of knowledge can you give away, leaving nothing for yourself? This is nonsense. *Vaiṣṇava ācāryas* say that knowledge (*divya jñāna*) comes with the sound of a mantra. But for the chanting of the mantra to be really effective and for us to get a response, it is said that we should have four qualities. When we are chanting a Gāyatrī mantra the first thing we should have is *śraddhā* – deep faith that the mantra is capable of saving us and creating our spiritual bodies; that, in the long run, it will take us to the spiritual level equal to God himself. The second is *śaraṇāgati* – we should surrender; we should be putting into the mantra the power of our surrender. The third is *mantra-dhyāna* – we should be mediating on the mantra and be deeply focused on the sound of the mantra in our mind. And the fourth one is the spirit of self-sacrifice – *svāhā* – when we are losing ourselves in the mantra. These are the ways we should be chanting the words of the mantra.

When we have these four qualities and chant the main 18-syllable mantra, *klīṁ kṛṣṇāya govindāya gopī-jana-vallabhāya svāhā*, we are going to feel the mantra responding. In *Bṛhad-bhāgavatāmṛta* Sanātana Gosvāmī says that a mantra can take one to any level of existence. For example, Gopa-kumāra visited all the planets and became Indra. He would go to a planet; he'd like it at first because he saw how they worshiped Kṛṣṇa. Then a revolution or something would happen, and Indra would be displaced and Gopa-kumāra would become Indra only because he chanted his mantra attentively.

Then he reached the planet of Brahmā and something happened to Brahmā too; he was displaced and Gopa-kumāra became Brahmā. He moved from one level to another, from one planet to another. He was going up all due to the mantra. Sanātana Gosvāmī explains that his mantra was leading him all the way. Sometimes his guru would come to him. It is said that we first get a mantra from the guru and then it becomes our guru, our guide. It leads us.

Sanātana Gosvāmī says that a mantra contains the highest relationships. If the guru has put these highest relationships into the mantra and we chant it, what level will we reach? We tend to be pleased with whatever we reach – Indra or Brahmā. In fact, we can be pleased with a million dollars or a skyscraper, or maybe a mansion somewhere in California. We will forget about everything else. When Gopa-kumāra would reach a place, he would feel initially satisfied. He would also continue to chant the mantra, and at some point a terrible pain would start to break his heart. He would begin to feel that the level he reached wasn't what he wanted. He became Indra – it wasn't what he wanted; he became Brahmā – it wasn't what he wanted. He reached Vaikuṇṭha – again, it wasn't what he wanted. He needed to go further.

This moving forward is where the power of a mantra lies. If we chant a mantra in the proper way, it will prevent us from resting on our laurels or being content with something inferior. We will always be striving to get higher and higher; it will help us achieve the highest goal. Such is the power of a mantra. But for power to become manifest, we should be attached to it; we should chant it properly. That's what happens during the initiation (*dīkṣā*). Raghunātha Dāsa Gosvāmī says we should have *rati* for *sva-mantre* – how we should be attached through understanding what a mantra is. And then he says – *Śrī-nāma*. This is the very last thing Raghunātha Dāsa Gosvāmī says regarding the beginning of the relationship with the guru. *Śrī-nāma* is the holy name. This is what we should get attached to before getting attached to the shelter of the lotus feet of Rādhā and Kṛṣṇa.

If we consider *gurau goṣṭhe goṣṭhālayiṣu sujane bhū-sura-gaṇe*, we can understand that all the things Raghunātha Dāsa Gosvāmī enumerates here: the guru, Vṛndāvana where the land is made of philosopher's stone, where desire trees grow, and where the residents, the *Vaiṣṇavas*, the *brāhmaṇas*, your *dīkṣā-mantras* and, finally, the holy name have one quality in common. They can fulfill any of our desires. Our *dīkṣā-mantra* can fulfill any of our desires.

ATTACHMENT TO THE HOLY NAME

Nāma (the holy name) may fulfill any of our desires. *Nāma* is *cintāmaṇi*, the philosopher's stone, which can elevate us to any level.

nāma cintāmaṇiḥ kṛṣṇaś
caitanya-rasa-vigrahaḥ
pūrṇaḥ śuddho nitya-mukto
'bhinnatvān nāma-nāminoḥ
(Padma Purāṇa)

But Raghunātha Dāsa Gosvāmī appeals to us to develop pure attachment, to change our attitude from, "How can I benefit from it?" to, "What am I supposed to want?" I am supposed to want the highest love, not anything else, only love for Kṛṣṇa. The true attachment to the holy name is when I chant it in such a mood. But there can be *bhukti-nāma*, which is when the holy name gives *bhukti* (material enjoyment), and there is *mukti-nāma* – when the holy name gives us liberation.

When we are chanting the holy name, we should be asking Kṛṣṇa, "Kṛṣṇa, Kṛṣṇa, Kṛṣṇa, bring me closer to you. Kṛṣṇa, purify my heart." Bhaktivinoda Ṭhākura says that when chanting the holy name, we should not have any desires. But we can still have one desire – the desire to purify ourselves. At first *prema-bhakti* seems like a very abstract thing. If love is too abstract then, at least, when we are chanting the holy name, we should have this desire, "Kṛṣṇa, make my heart pure."

When we chant the holy name, we should feel that something is saving us. Rūpa Gosvāmī glorifies the holy name in *Nāmāṣṭakam* as the only thing that can save us. He says, "O Kṛṣṇa! You manifest in two forms: *vācya* and *vācaka*. You can be an object of description – *vācya* – like Kṛṣṇa himself. And your second form is *vācaka* – the name." They are non-different, but, nevertheless, there is some difference. The difference is that the name is more merciful than Kṛṣṇa himself. We can offend Kṛṣṇa, but if we start crying Hare Kṛṣṇa, Hare Kṛṣṇa, Kṛṣṇa Kṛṣṇa, Hare Hare/ Hare Rāma, Hare Rāma, Rāma Rāma, Hare Hare we can get tears of ecstasy. We can offend Kṛṣṇa, and we can offend the holy name but the holy name can even forgive the offence we committed towards God. The holy name can deliver us from numerous offences. Therefore, when we are chanting the holy name, we should have this feeling that something is saving us.

Jīva Gosvāmī says that in Kali-yuga persons can only become great devotees under the condition that they serve the holy name and give it to others. We should give the holy name out of mercy, out of compassion, and in the right way, in a joyful way.

It is said that the holy name is the *aṅgī* of devotional service. In *Nectar of Devotion*, Rūpa Gosvāmī enumerates 64 *angas* (limbs) of *bhakti*. But chanting of the holy name is not an *aṅga*, it is *aṅgī*, the body itself. Chanting the holy name is the most important part of devotional service and the most essential thing we can do. If we do it properly, in a proper mood, in a proper state, we can get everything.

Rāmānanda Rāya and Svarūpa Dāmodara asked Lord Caitanya, "How should one chant the holy name to receive *prema*? What is the method of chanting the holy name? What is supposed to be happening in the heart? We also chant the holy name, but feel no *prema*."

Caitanya Mahāprabhu smiled and said, "What is the method of chanting the holy name to receive *prema*? *Tṛṇād api sunīcena taror api sahiṣṇunā/ amāninā mānadena kīrtanīyaḥ sadā hariḥ*. (*Śrī Śikṣāṣṭaka*, verse 3) If I chant the holy name in this humble state of consciousness, in this state of mind, *prema* becomes attracted by this chanting of the holy name."

ATTACHMENT TO THE DIVINE COUPLE

Raghunātha Dāsa Gosvāmī says, "O my mind! Take the shelter of the divine couple of Vṛndāvana Śrī Śrī Rādhā-Kṛṣṇa." Such shelter is the reason why Caitanya Mahāprabhu came to this world. Nowhere else can we get what we can get from Lord Caitanya, because lots of people worship Kṛṣṇa. The Śrī and Madhva *sampradāyas* worship Kṛṣṇa, the Rāmānuja *sampradāya* worships Kṛṣṇa, and the Nimbārka *sampradāya* worships Rādhā and Kṛṣṇa. But nowhere are Rādhā-Kṛṣṇa worshiped as Lord Caitanya's followers do.

What's the difference between worshiping Kṛṣṇa and worshiping Rādhā-Kṛṣṇa? When he is by her side his heart is all syrup. When he is by her side, he gets sweeter. When Śrīmatī Rādhārani is by his side, he is even sweeter because he feels she loves him. And when he feels her love, he is eager to become sweeter. It is said that when Rādhā is approaching Kṛṣṇa, she makes him get sweeter. And when Kṛṣṇa gets sweeter she loves him even more. And Kṛṣṇa becomes even sweeter. This is a chain reaction. Kṛṣṇadāsa Kavirāja Gosvāmī says that this situation is the paradox of love. He says one of the paradoxes of spiritual love is that it is eternal. But despite being eternal, it is ever growing. It is impossible to understand how something infinite may be ever expanding. How can Kṛṣṇa's everlasting sweetness become even sweeter?

Here Raghunātha Dāsa Gosvāmī says, "Try to understand that you should get attached to them, not just Kṛṣṇa." We should get attached to Rādhā and Kṛṣṇa because in this case Śrīmatī Rādhārani enables us to taste Kṛṣṇa's sweetness more than we can. Prabhodhānanda Sarasvatī compares Kṛṣṇa's sweetness with a drop of the ocean of sweetness one experiences when seeing Kṛṣṇa and Śrīmatī Rādhārani together. The miracle that Caitanya Mahāprabhu brought and gave us is a chance to worship this love. In *Caitanya-caritāmṛta, Ādi-līlā,* Śrīla Prabhupāda writes that Caitanya Mahāprabhu didn't come to give people ordinary religion. Caitanya Mahāprabhu doesn't care. He is indifferent to ordinary religions.

During a Rathayātrā celebration in Ivanovo, I got a glimpse of what the Lord's indifference to ordinary religion might be like. Ivanovo is a poor town. According to statistics, it is the poorest town in Russia. For the parade, a businessman who had arranged for the Rathayātrā to be held brought boxes of bananas and oranges to be distributed from the chariot. The guest of honor was supposed to give the bananas and oranges to the crowd of hungry Ivanovo residents, who had only seen bananas in picture books and had eaten oranges only in their early childhood, which they had received from Santa. Everybody was quite indifferent to the festival until we started to throw the bananas, and then the crowd became really enthusiastic. Immediately the people developed *apūrva-rati* – an extraordinary attachment in their hearts, and everyone went running after the chariot. In the first six minutes I relished handing out the fruit – I felt like God. There was a crowd around me stretching out their hands crying, "Give me! Give me!" People were smiling, praying, quivering – and you couldn't help but feel so generous, magnanimous, and able to make anyone happy.

Finally, if I wasn't giving in the way they wanted, people start pulling and poking me as if saying, "Can't you see? I want a banana." And it went on for two hours until the bananas were gone. And then suddenly all at once they lost interest in me. Nobody cared about me anymore. I remained the same, but the bananas were gone.

Therefore, Caitanya Mahāprabhu says ordinary religion – where people serve God just to get something from him – is not interesting. No one needs such religion; we only need pure love. It is pure love that can make us happy. Here Raghunātha Dāsa Gosvāmī is begging his mind, "My mind! Try and understand what you need. You don't need anything else – you don't need bananas, dates, pears, diamonds, emeralds – you only need love for Kṛṣṇa. You can only get pure love if little by little you develop attachment."

COMMENTARY BY ŪRMILĀ DEVĪ DĀSĪ

In his book *Jaiva-dharma*, Bhaktivinoda Ṭhākura writes, "*Śrī Manaḥ-śikṣā* has laid down a systematic procedure (*paddhati*) for one to enter into and become absorbed in the pastimes of Śrī Śrī Rādhā Kṛṣṇa; one should follow it without guile." A *paddhati* is a kind of instruction manual. Verse one first of all establishes the audience for these verses—who is qualified to take up these instructions and follow this procedure. Those who study and practice these verses are expected to be initiated by a spiritual master into the chanting of the holy name and the Gāyatrī mantras. Otherwise, there is no possibility of having "unprecedented and excessive attachment" for what one does not have. A reader who does not yet have a guru, or one whose guru has not yet given initiation (*dīkṣā*) is not, however, forbidden from studying this work to know what is ahead. Certainly, anyone even somewhat interested in this subject can put into practice some portions of the book, on the principal of *sv-alpam apy asya dharmasya, trāyate mahato bhayāt* (*Bhagavad-gītā* 2.40), even a little progress on this path protects from fear and is not lost.

Raghunātha Dāsa Gosvāmī joins together the concepts of having great love for others with giving up our inner pride. If we explore that relationship, we will find that love and humility must go together. Even in ordinary life, when we are convinced that we are great and so deserve to have others serve us, we can neither serve them selflessly nor appreciate and value the service they do for us. Thus, the essence of love—being fascinated by the beloved, valuing the beloved, and caring for the beloved—cannot happen authentically in the presence of pride. Certainly in the spiritual realm, *saprema-bhakteḥ paramānukūlaṁ dainyaṁ mahā-puṣṭi-karam* (*Bṛhad-bhāgavatāmṛta* 3.5.74), utter humility nourishes pure love.

We should note, however, that the giving up of pride required to begin following this instruction manual cannot be absolute, because the last obstacle we must abandon—the desire for fame and honor as explained in verse seven—undoubtedly involves pride. After all, Śrīla Prabhupāda writes in his purport to *Bhagavad-gītā* 13.8–12, "Humility means that one should not be anxious to have the satisfaction of being honored by others."

First, we have already explained that any authentic love at all, even a small degree of love, demands at least some measure of humility. Indeed, our depth of humility and depth of love are proportional. Second, because this path of *bhakti*—as we will see in verses four through seven – involves facing and rejecting deep, ugly, and embarrassing evil in our heart, a lack of pride is essential. Proud persons rarely admit fault in their actions, what to speak of faults in their motives and desires. Third, one of the main methods of spiritual progress that Raghunātha Dāsa Gosvāmī repeatedly gives is to beg for mercy, to cry out for help. Proud persons cannot do so, as Queen Kuntī explains (*Śrīmad-Bhāgavatam* 1.8.26):

janmaiśvarya-śruta-śrībhir
edhamāna-madaḥ pumān
naivārhaty abhidhātuṁ vai
tvām akiñcana-gocaram

Considering how the lack of pride is essential in these three ways, with each step in the procedure given in *Manaḥ-śikṣā*, we must let go of at least enough pride to take that step. By the time someone has followed the instructions to arrive at verse eight, no further pride remains at all.

We should especially note that we are told in verse one to have great love for our gurus, the spiritual masters who show us the path, instruct us, and initiate us into the chanting of mantras. Kṛṣṇa tells us in the *Bhagavad-gītā* that we must serve a guru to receive transcendental knowledge. Such service, however, is not merely official, nor in the mood of an employee. As Śrīla Prabhupāda explains in his purport to *Caitanya-caritāmṛta, Madhya-līlā* 17.15: "The words *snigdha* (very peaceful) and *su-snigdha* (affectionate) are used in verses fourteen and fifteen respectively, and they are also found in *Śrīmad-Bhāgavatam* (1.1.8): *brūyuḥ snigdhasya śiṣyasya guravo guhyam apy uta*. 'A disciple who has actual love for his spiritual master is endowed, by the blessings of the spiritual master, with all confidential knowledge.' Śrīla Śrīdhara Svāmī has commented that the word *snigdhasya* means *prema-vataḥ*. The word *prema-vataḥ* indicates that one has great love for his spiritual master." Thus the exchange of service and knowledge between guru and disciple is that of love.

Raghunātha Dāsa Gosvāmī also instructs us in the principle that everyone who loves God should love all persons and places connected with God. We may ask how to have "the concept of kinship completely reposed" (*Nectar of Devotion*, chapter 19) in Kṛṣṇa if we are to spread our love among the list given here in verse one. The answer is found in the *Śrīmad-Bhāgavatam*, (11.11.43–45):

> My dear Uddhava, ... one may worship me among the *brāhmaṇas* by respectfully receiving them as guests, even when uninvited. I can be worshiped within the cows by offerings of grass and other suitable grains and paraphernalia for the pleasure and health of the cows, and one may worship me within the Vaiṣṇavas by offering loving friendship to them and honoring them in all respects. ..., and one may worship me within all living entities by seeing the Supersoul within all of them, thus maintaining equal vision.

If we want to know more about how to love the Vaiṣṇavas, then we can study the six loving exchanges that Rūpa Gosvāmī lists in his *Upadeśāmṛta*, verse four.

It is of particular interest how Bhaktivinoda defines the beginner, intermediate, and advanced devotees in his commentary to verse one. We may note that understandings of devotees' levels of realization are described according to different parameters in various parts of the *śāstras* and by various *ācāryas*. These descriptions are not necessarily parallel. In other words, an intermediate devotee according to one set of criteria may not be an intermediate devotee according to another set of criteria. Just as in embodied life a human matures physically, socially, intellectually, and so forth, but maturation in one area may not be equivalent to maturation in another, so spiritually someone might be understood as a beginner in one way, and an intermediate in another way. Such is explained in *Mādhurya Kaḍambinī*. *Niṣṭhā-sādhana-bhakti* must be achieved in body, mind, and words, and this steadiness in each generally happens sequentially, not simultaneously. The general order is to first achieve steadiness in body, then speech, then mind. However, the order of where steadiness is achieved may vary from one practitioner to another. Of course, it is expected that at some point a person is at the highest level overall.

VERSE TWO

na dharmaṁ nādharmaṁ śruti-gaṇa-niruktaṁ kila kuru
vraje rādhā-kṛṣṇa-pracura-paricaryām iha tanu
śacī-sūnuṁ nandīśvara-pati-sutatve guru-varaṁ
mukunda-preṣṭhatve smara param ajasraṁ nanu manaḥ

Indeed, do not perform any pious acts prescribed in the Vedas and supporting literature, or sinful acts forbidden in them. Staying here in Vraja, please perform profuse service to Śrī Śrī Rādhā-Kṛṣṇa. O mind, unceasingly remember the son of Śacī as the son of Nanda Mahārāja, and Śrī Guru as the dearest servant of Lord Mukunda.

COMMENTARY BY ŚIVARĀMA SWAMI

The first verse dealt with the question of what one should do when faith in *kṛṣṇa-kathā* rises within the heart of the *jīva*. And the answer to that was *gurau goṣṭhe goṣṭhālayiṣu sujane bhū-sura-gaṇe sva-mantre śrī-nāmni,* that one should take *dīkṣā* mantra by accepting a spiritual master, serve Vaiṣṇavas, and worship Rādhā and Kṛṣṇa. There are certain implied questions in that first verse, namely, that if one is always worshiping Rādhā and Kṛṣṇa chanting Hare Kṛṣṇa, how is one meant to maintain oneself or live within this world. So the answer to this is covered in the second verse, as well as how to see the position of Śrī Caitanya Mahāprabhu, the position of the spiritual master, and how this process of worship should be done.

COMMENTARY BY ŚACĪNANDANA SWAMI

This *paddhati* is a guidebook for those who have developed faith in Kṛṣṇa as their complete shelter, including their maintainer. It answers the question, "If I have now developed my faith in Kṛṣṇa, then what is my duty?"

Once, Caitanya Mahāprabhu went to Śrīvāsa Paṇḍita and asked, "Paṇḍita, you are only reciting the *Gītā* or holding *kīrtana* festivals at your house and this doesn't bring money. How do you maintain your family with its numerous members?"

Śrīvāsa Paṇḍita said, "If we serve you, if we have trust in you, if we have faith in you, you have said that you will maintain us. If for one day you don't maintain us, no problem. For the second day you don't maintain us, also no problem. Even for the third day we can still keep on fasting – we can fast three days, no problem. If on the fourth day nothing comes, we will all go to the Gaṅgā and drown ourselves because you have failed on your promise."

The *dharma* (function) of the conditioned soul is to run around in the world and make many arrangements for maintenance according to pious rules given in the Vedas. The ignorant cannot work without such rules and regulations; otherwise, their activities become inauspicious and immoral. But those who possess knowledge of the soul and their *sambandha* (relationship to Kṛṣṇa) do not require such scriptural rules and regulations. They are called wise. They are ready to embrace the path of surrendering to Lord Kṛṣṇa.

However, *gṛhasthas* need to maintain their families and also try to support the *brahmacārīs* or the renunciates. This is the old tradition. Such earning of livelihood should be done while we make ourselves absolutely dependent on Kṛṣṇa; then it works. A friend of mine married and took to the profession of astrology. But it didn't work; no money came. So he went one day to Bālajī, and said, "Bālajī, whenever someone comes to me for astrological consultations, I promise to give you one-tenth of the income."

He made himself dependent on Bālajī, and customers came, but he forgot to give the tenth. His business ran down, and one day his good wife said to him, "The reason why you are so poor is you don't make yourself dependent on Bālajī. You keep everything for yourself. You don't donate. Donate! So he gave the tenth and now he is one of the richest *gṛhasthas* in ISKCON.

With this somewhat clumsy example, I am saying our life situation may change, but we should not change the idea of making ourselves dependent on Kṛṣṇa. How to have this dependence? This verse tells us that we should meditate on Śrī Caitanya Mahāprabhu. It is so important, because Śrī Caitanya Mahāprabhu opens for us the road of mercy. Because of Mahāprabhu's appearance in this world we have access to these highly exalted subject matters. Śrī Caitanya Mahāprabhu has given us the key: just chant the holy name, avoiding the ten offenses, and then we enter the road of *prema*, and we go upwards. There is a song by Vāsudeva Ghoṣa where he asks: Would anyone have ever heard of something known as *prema* as the ultimate aim of mankind if Caitanya Mahāprabhu had not come and been compassionate? Could anyone know of the divine power of the holy name if Gaurāṅga Mahāprabhu didn't come? Had anyone ever entered the sweet charming forest of Vṛndāvana without Gaurāṅga Mahāprabhu? Did anyone know that Śrī Rādhā is the embodiment of the highest transcendental ecstasy?

Then this second verse of *Manaḥ-śikṣā* says you should see Caitanya Mahāprabhu as non-different from Rādhā and Kṛṣṇa, and when you meditate about Gaurāṅga Mahāprabhu, Kṛṣṇadāsa Kavirāja tells us that we should think of Gaurāṅga Mahāprabhu as Kṛṣṇa, but as Kṛṣṇa in a special mood. He has descended in the mood of Śrīmatī Rādhārāṇī to teach us how to develop devotion.

Once* Kṛṣṇa sat with Rādhārāṇī in the forest of Vṛndāvana. He took Rādhā's hand in his own and said, "Would you please give me something today?" Rādhārāṇī was in a very special mood. Her heart had melted. Kṛṣṇa said, "Could you give me this love?"

Rādhā said, "This love would be too heavy for you to bear."

Then Lalitā chimed in, "This will be too heavy. When our Svāminī has this type of love in her heart, her everything goes to you, Kṛṣṇa. She cannot be pacified when you are not there. We put sandalwood paste on her body, but it falls off like leaves of paper that are dried. We put her on a bed of damp lotus petals, but the lotus petals burn up. This would be too heavy for you."

Then Kṛṣṇa took the other hand of Rādhārāṇī. "I want to experience this love."

* This story is from *Naraharira-viśeṣa-parichaya* by Ānanda-nārāyaṇa Maitra, a disciple of Śrīla Narahari Cakravartī. The *Naraharir-viśeṣa-parichaya* is a rare appendix to the *Narottama-vilāsa*.

Rādhā said, "All right, Śyāma, I will give you this love. But in addition to this, I will cover your beautiful blackish body with my golden complexion. Then, when you stumble and fall and bruise your body, you will be protected by my effulgence, and in this way you will not harm your soft body, which is so dear to me."

So Kṛṣṇa came with a golden complexion, and he danced, calling like Rādhā, "O Kṛṣṇa, where are you? Where are you, O moon who has risen from the dynasty of Nanda Mahārāja and Yaśodā? Where are you?" When Kṛṣṇa had this love, which would make him cry so much that the stones melted, he would crash down like a tree that was felled by a gale. Then that beautiful golden shining effulgence of Rādhā would protect him. This is how we meditate on Gaurāṅga Mahāprabhu if we follow the footsteps of Raghunātha Dāsa Gosvāmī and Bhaktivinoda Ṭhākura.

Verse two of the *Manaḥ-śikṣā* says how to meditate about the guru, and I find this very practical. You should think of the guru with this attitude: he is dear to Mukunda, the Lord who gives liberation. See him as a dear friend of Kṛṣṇa, doing Kṛṣṇa's work. There's a verse in the Fourth Canto of the *Śrīmad-Bhāgavatam* where the Pracetās address Lord Śiva. Lord Śiva had taught them a special mantra called the *Śiva-gīta,* the song of Lord Śiva. It is a beautiful song, describing attractive features of Kṛṣṇa as glistening like a rain cloud lit up by a flash of lightning. The Pracetās sang this song, meditating upon it. They saw the Deity of this song, Viṣṇu, and said to him, "Dear Lord, by virtue of a moment's association with Lord Śiva, who is very dear to you and who is your most intimate friend, we were fortunate to attain you." (*Śrīmad-Bhāgavatam* 4.30.38)

It is important to see your guru as a friend of Kṛṣṇa, or *mukunda-presta,* very dear to Mukunda. See his essence even when he chastises. The spiritual master wants to give you Kṛṣṇa and he wants to bring you to Kṛṣṇa, because that is what Kṛṣṇa wants. Kṛṣṇa wants you. Of course, the guru will help in Kṛṣṇa's mission. That is the meditation we should have.

Verse two of *Manaḥ-śikṣā* also says, "Staying here in Vraja, please perform profuse service to Śrī Śrī Rādhā-Kṛṣṇa." If you want to worship Rādhā and Kṛṣṇa in Vraja, there are six ingredients that are very important.

First of all, you must learn to offer obeisances. When you are in Vraja offer sufficient obeisances. Bow down and touch the dust. This is a *sādhana* on the path of *bhajana*. Raghunātha Dāsa Gosvāmī paid 2000 obeisances to the Vaiṣṇavas every day. This practice is important.

When I was introduced to *daṇḍavat parikramā*, I decided to do it at midnight so no one would see me. In Rādhā-kuṇḍa, I readied myself; there was no one on the streets, so I started. At first I thought how advanced I am, and so on. But then, very quickly, I noticed it was strenuous. I said to myself, "Maybe there is another mode of consciousness here that is more appropriate."

Immediately just by placing my body on the pilgrim's path with prostrated obeisances, I remember a feeling of humility swept over me – and then came my challenge. I came to a herd of pigs blocking my path. First of all, my false ego sprung up and I said to the superior pig, "I am the son of a director. Get out of my way please." The pig didn't even look at me, so I then thought, "Okay, I learned to be a street fighter when I was very young; he can have it the other way." So I went with my hand "Bang!" on the pig because I really wanted him to go out of my way for my glorious bowing-down exercise.

The pig just gave me a smile that made me think, "This pig might bite me and then I'll have to go to the hospital, so better I don't hit him." So I really prostrated myself, and thought, "Again my false ego has appeared. This time I will pray very hard to Rādhārāṇī and Kṛṣṇa." I paid my obeisances and came again to that head pig who studied me very carefully. I said to the pig, "Please, let me do this service. I know you are a great soul. You have been sent by Rādhārāṇī to test me and I failed my first test." I really prayed, *tapta-kāñcana-gaurāṅgi rādhe vṛndāvaneśvari*, because I was going around Rādhā-kuṇḍa (the lake of Rādhā). The pig then ran to the side, leading the other pigs to the side as well. So I went through the pigs easily. I have never felt so cleansed in my life as I felt among the *saṅga* of pigs, because they had told me in their own graphic way that I have to be humble. I had to do it for Rādhārāṇī otherwise they would bite me.

We may not offer so many obeisances as in a *daṇḍavat parikramā*, but we should offer a sufficient amount of obeisances. Especially we can use the time when we start and end the Gāyatrī mantra, and when visiting the holy *dhāmas*, to pay obeisances. This is the *mārga* (path) of devotion.

The second ingredient is prayers. The Gosvāmīs wrote prayers one after the other, because they would sing these wonderful prayers that encourage devotion in the heart. Their prayers are full of devotion, and when we chant them we will also be overwhelmed with devotion.

The third item is to offer our activities. That means to do something for Kṛṣṇa. When visiting the holy *dhāma*, for instance, do some broom *sevā*. That is a wonderful service to just sweep the holy *dhāma*. Clean Vraja, like you clean a place before you sit down. Do something practical.

The fourth is similar to the third: offering the fruits of all your activities, which means perhaps giving a donation to the Deities and to good *sādhus*, or offering your services.

Fifth is to learn how to meditate on the lotus feet of the Lord, called *smaraṇam*. Finally, sixth is to hear the topics of the Lord sufficiently.

Śrīla Bhaktisiddhānta Sarasvatī Ṭhākura writes that we should learn to do these six when we want to do *bhajana* or worship. These six items are also referenced in *Śrīmad-Bhāgavatam* Seventh Canto, chapter 9, verse 50, where Prahlāda Mahārāja describes them to us.

Now, at this verse of *Manaḥ-śikṣā*, where we have been introduced to dependence on Kṛṣṇa, meditation on Lord Caitanya Mahāprabhu and the guru, we might ask what would be wrong in practicing some eclectic spirituality from various spiritual schools and paths – reading different books, going to a variety of lectures, maybe listening to the Dalai Lama. We could just construct our own spirituality with bits and pieces that we have collected from here and there. We could ask whether or not it is possible to attain residence in *vraja-dhāma* and execute devotional service with this intense attachment and love by accepting *dīkṣā* and *śikṣā* from other *sampradāyas*, from other spiritual schools. This question will be addressed in verse 3.

COMMENTARY BY BHAKTIVIJNANA GOSWAMI

ONE-POINTED IN OUR GOAL

This second verse of *Manaḥ-śikṣā* contains a very important element – the principle of a single goal. Raghunātha Dāsa Gosvāmī explains how a person who lives in the world and performs the duties associated with the world can attain this unity of spiritual direction.

In the early verses of *Manaḥ-śikṣā*, Raghunātha Dāsa Gosvāmī speaks of the various obstacles that arise on the *sādhaka*'s way. One obstacle is that our minds are many-branched. We are accustomed to setting many goals and pursuing them, but by doing so we can never reach Kṛṣṇa, because as the saying goes, "If you chase two rabbits, both will escape." Unfortunately, we are practiced at trying to accomplish many things at a time. This is the same obstacle that Kṛṣṇa speaks about in the second chapter of the *Bhagavad-gītā*.

For a person who follows the path of conventional religion, *dharma*, there are many regulations one of which is the instruction to worship God. The prescription for the person who has chosen *bhakti* and wants to attain *bhakti* is just one, however. God is not merely included; the only goal is to attain God. It should be the only goal and everything else a means to attain this goal. In other words, we should develop chastity to God.

As Kṛṣṇa says in the *Bhagavad-gītā* (18.66), *sarva-dharmān parityajya mām ekaṁ śaraṇaṁ vraja*. Kṛṣṇa also says that foolish people worship the demigods and their minds are stolen by illusion, *māyā*. Ultimately a person must have one goal, which is love of God, not just worship of God. When we worship God for material gain, then the gain we want to get is more important to us than God himself. In essence, we put this material goal above God. For us God is nothing but a means or a tool of fulfilling our desires.

Raghunātha Dāsa Gosvāmī is stressing that a person must clearly understand that they have only one goal and everything else serves that goal. For example, Droṇācārya, marveling at Arjuna's accuracy, asked him, "How do you hit the target so precisely?"

Arjuna explained by saying, "First I see the bird and along with the bird I see the tree in which the bird is sitting, and I see the branch on which it is sitting. Then I see only the branch on which the bird is sitting and the bird. Then I see only the bird. But I do not shoot the arrow until I stop seeing everything else but the eye of the bird. The arrow then flies there by itself because I do not see anything else."

It is this quality that we need to develop. When we look, we should not see anybody except Kṛṣṇa. In conditioned life, we look and we see *māyā*. As we practice as Raghunātha Dāsa Gosvāmī speaks about in this verse, we gradually stop seeing everything else – *ekānta*. *Ekānta* means a person who has only one goal. And when we do not see anything else, then our hearts are filled by faithfulness towards God, just like a faithful wife towards her husband. After all, God is *īśvara*, the Supreme *pati* or husband. When we scatter our minds over various goals, it is as if we were being unfaithful to him.

This unfaithfulness manifests itself in various ways, either subtle or gross. Vedic culture first teaches a person to be chaste in an ordinary way, but the highest chastity consists in reducing everything else to this goal, in seeing how everything else brings us to this goal. And here Raghunātha Dāsa Gosvāmī says: *na dharmaṁ nādharmaṁ śruti-gaṇa-niruktaṁ kila kuru*. Reject all *dharma* and all *adharma* for Kṛṣṇa's sake.

We wear a *kānti-mālā*, and eat with our right hand instead of a fork because it pleases Kṛṣṇa. Kṛṣṇa, believe it or not, likes it when we sit on the floor and when we wear neck beads. A chaste wife decorates herself with ornaments only for her husband. An unchaste wife also puts on ornaments, but she wears them for everyone. In the same way we must adorn ourselves with our virtues and qualities, not for the sake of the virtues themselves or to make a show of these virtues, but so that Kṛṣṇa enjoys them. We keep this secret deep in our heart: I am following this *dharma*, all that Kṛṣṇa wants me to, for the sake of pleasing him.

It is said that there are different categories of *gopīs*. When Śyāmasundara Gopīnātha stands under the Vaṁśīvaṭa, playing his flute, the *gopīs* run to him, but they face different obstacles on the way.

There are impediments that some *sādhana-siddha-gopīs,* of which there are different categories, meet on their way to the forest. Some run to Kṛṣṇa and face no obstacles because they have no obstacles in their hearts. But there are other *gopīs* who hear the sound of the flute. They want to rush to Kṛṣṇa, but their husbands bolt the doors, stand before them and exclaim, "Where are you running to?" These *gopīs* remain at home and die of love for Kṛṣṇa.

Some *gopīs'* husbands seem non-existent and do not bolt their doors. Those *gopīs* run out and come directly to Kṛṣṇa. However, with other *gopīs* there are husbands and bolts. The restricted *gopīs* still have an attachment to *dharma,* to their righteousness; attachment to the idea, "I am such a righteous *gopī,*" and, "Yes, Śyāmasundara is playing his flute and I want to run to him, but here is my husband."

Immediately the husband turns up and says, "Did you call me?" and he bolts the door.

When a person retains even the slightest attachment to the notion of being something other than a person who loves Kṛṣṇa, this is attachment to pride. This attachment to pride can become manifest even as attachment to virtues and it will create an obstacle on the way.

In the process of spiritual practice, we must overcome all these hindrances, and when we overcome these internal obstacles, the external ones will disappear. Then when we hear the sound of Kṛṣṇa's flute, we will run and dance and embrace Kṛṣṇa.

We should clearly understand that we have only one goal, which is love for Kṛṣṇa. And the only way to achieve this goal is by chanting: Hare Kṛṣṇa, Hare Kṛṣṇa, Kṛṣṇa Kṛṣṇa, Hare Hare/ Hare Rāma, Hare Rāma, Rāma Rāma, Hare Hare. We do not need anything else.

GURU AND LORD CAITANYA

Ragunatha Dāsa Gosvāmī says: *vraje rādhā-kṛṣṇa-pracura-paricaryām iha tanu* – I start worshiping Rādhā and Kṛṣṇa. Then he says *śacī-sūnuṁ nandīśvara* – how I should see Lord Caitanya. Lord Caitanya, son of Śacī, I should see as the son of Nanda Mahārāja. When we worship Lord Caitanya, we worship him as Kṛṣṇa. We see him as Kṛṣṇa who brought us love of God and came to teach us to love God.

My guru I should see as *mukunda-preṣṭa*. In other words, Raghunātha Dāsa Gosvāmī says to learn to see one goal in everything we do. If we worship guru, worship him as someone who is most dear to Kṛṣṇa. Worshipping guru should not turn into a personality cult. Sometimes people, blinded by their so-called love for guru, start worshiping him apart from God. We worship guru only because he is dear to Kṛṣṇa and because through him we can come to Kṛṣṇa.

We want to come to Kṛṣṇa; we don't want to come to anything else, because there is nothing else we need except Kṛṣṇa. We need love for Kṛṣṇa. We need chastity in our hearts. This is what Raghunātha Dāsa Gosvāmī asks his mind in the second verse. He says, "Give up everything else. You need Kṛṣṇa. Everything else should not become an end in itself for you. You should learn this art of how to connect everything you do to a single goal, to see that at the end of everything is Kṛṣṇa, who is bent at three places, with his flute to his lips, who is calling us all to dance."

SATTVA-GUṆA, DETACHMENT, FAITH, AND LOVE

Kṛṣṇa establishes some principles, adherence to which allows us to gradually purify our hearts. When our hearts are pure, what should then appear in our hearts? Love won't immediately appear, but gradually, by following the principles of *dharma*, the four regulative principles, and the other principles of Vedic culture, we will rise to the level of *sattva*.

In *Śrīmad-Bhāgavatam*, Eleventh Canto, Kṛṣṇa says that *sattva* and *dharma* are synonyms; that *sattva* strengthens *dharma;* and religiosity strengthens goodness. Purity, or adherence to the principles of purity, following the principles of sattvic life, will make a person more religious, and religion makes a person live in more purity. These are integrally related to each other. If we simply live a pure life, we will become more inclined to God, and this inclination will, in turn, make us live an increasingly pure life.

But we do not need merely material purity or material *sattva*. Ultimately, purity will certainly result in love of God, but love is preceded by something else – faith.

Therefore, Kṛṣṇa explains to Uddhava in the *Bhāgavatam* (11.20.9):

tāvat karmāṇi kurvīta
na nirvidyeta yāvatā
mat-kathā-śravaṇādau vā
śraddhā yāvan na jāyate

If a person performs some *dharma,* some Vedic rituals, then gradually something wonderful happens – *na nirvidyeta yāvatā.* Detachment from the material world appears in our hearts. If a person follows the principles of Vedic *dharma* what they attain is indifference to the temptations of the material world, the sign of purification of the heart. A pure heart is the heart that is gradually drifting away from the temptations of the material world.

As a result of detachment, faith in *kṛṣṇa-kathā* will spring into our hearts. As we become more aloof from the stories of the material world, from all this *jaḍa-kathā* or *māyā-kathā,* proportionally faith in *kṛṣṇa-kathā* appears. By watching the news on TV, for instance, we actually strengthen our faith in *māyā-kathā.*

I do not know how many thousands of *ślokas* there are describing *māyā-kathā,* but every day there are more mundane stories in the form of films, the news and everything else. But if a person begins following the principles of *sattva,* rising early in the morning, chanting *japa,* following other principles, then gradually they feel detachment from mundane *kathā* and faith in *kṛṣṇa-kathā.*

GIVING UP ADHARMA

There are general fundamental principles of renouncing *adharma* that apply to everyone which we should follow. In our practice these are called the four regulative principles, which Śrīla Prabhupāda called the regulative principles of freedom. These are the foundation of Vedic culture.

In 1983, there were some attempts to recruit me into the KGB. I was promised various benefits if I worked for them, and I was also threatened with dire punishments if I refused. I did not want at all to work for them in any way, but at the same time I was frightened. Finally I plucked up the courage and went to the person who had threatened me, to give him my final answer. I stood in front of him, a man twice my size. I was a graduate student then, and was trembling. As I stood before him shaking like an aspen leaf, I took a deep breath and said, "I thought about it and decided that I will not work for you because this does not correspond to my principles."

When he heard this, he cried out, "What principles do you have except for the four regulative?" I was shocked by the fact that even the KGB knew about the four regulative principles.* But in essence, these four are the basis for the development of *bhakti* in our hearts. These are the basis of *dharma*, the basis of a happy life in this body, not to mention life in the next world. We must clearly understand where this foundation is because sometimes we have deeply hidden doubts that can make us stray far away.

We hide what we treasure most, so we hide our values. We hide our doubts about Kṛṣṇa deep in our hearts as something most treasured. As long as I have these doubts, I can enjoy in this world. When there are no doubts, there are no more chances. In a sense, we should have no doubt in the regulative principles. They are the basis of a normal life in this world.

The first regulative principle, no meat-eating, is obviously foundational. Our hearts become cruel if we eat meat because we become contaminated by living at the cost of another being's life. Any person with even a little intelligence understands that meat-eating should not be done.

I knew a boy, now a young man, who became a vegetarian because

* He was at his appointment with the KGB, feeling cool and confident. The secret meeting was in one of the city's international hotels, which were under the government's close watch. In a small room, the colonel and another man sat, smiling.

"So," the colonel said lightly, "did you think about my offer?"

"I am not going to work for you, because it is against my principles."

The colonel jumped from his chair and yelled, "What principles do you stupid fools have besides four regulative? Go home now, but you should know you are finished."

Bhaktivijnana Goswami walked calmly out of the room and traveled to the empty apartment a friend had given him in Moscow. He decided all would be fine, somehow or other.

his mother accidentally put a rabbit's eye in his stew. He saw the eye and he then realized where meat was coming from and he stopped eating it. Usually devotees have no problem with following this principle.

I also know a five-year-old boy who became a vegetarian under someone else's influence. Since then, he has been saying to his grandmother, "Grandma, why are you eating corpses? How can you eat these corpses?" His grandma replies, "Why are you always spoiling my appetite?"

But there are principles that are harder to accept, such as no gambling. The three remaining principles (gambling, intoxication, and illicit sexual relations) have something in common. Our future in Kṛṣṇa consciousness depends on how well we understand this point. They have passion and attachment to the body in common. Because of attachment to the body, a person does many things that tie the person to the body. Therefore Śrīla Prabhupāda calls these principles the regulative principles of freedom. All the four sinful activities enslave us, forcing us to become addicted to the body, so much so that ultimately there is no self-control. Whether we take intoxicants, gamble, or have illicit sex, we will ultimately become slaves to that activity.

It may seem like the price we pay isn't so high, but the price is suffering. We may spend some money gambling, but the winnings can be huge. Drugs may cost a certain amount, but we think the result is worth it. But when we want to buy something very big for a very cheap price it is called cheating – and we cheat ourselves. Therefore the ultimate result is pain and suffering, and the inclination to deception becomes increasingly stronger.

Yes, a person has the right to experience the material pleasures of sex, but what price must be paid for it? Because of lust, children will need to be cared for and worried about over the next twenty-five years. If we want to be happy and have a peaceful mind free from any worry, what price should we pay for it? We could meditate and purify the mind. But why should someone do that if they can go and buy some LSD or similar substance and imagine that they are already there in the spiritual world, having visions, and blue-complexioned Kṛṣṇa is there, too.

But all this is deception; we are only deceiving ourselves. When we drink or take drugs we do not become happy. We simply turn into slaves. If we engage in illicit sex what we get eventually is pain and terrible things happen to us. Leo Tolstoy's wonderful novella *The Kreutzer Sonata* describes this very deception underlying illicit sex. But since the result, at first glance, is huge and the price seems very small, we become attached to these activities.

Therefore, these four principles are the basis of civilized life (just like there are the four pillars of religion: *satyam* – truthfulness; *tapa* – ascetism; *daya* – charity; *śaucam* – purity). We must follow the regulative principles, and if we do not, then we are cheaters and rascals, as Śrīla Prabhupāda used to say.

Since by following the four principles we are trying to avoid sin in our lives so that our hearts become purified, we need to clearly understand the nature of sin. There is a lie behind the sin and that is why Raghunātha Dāsa Gosvāmī implores his mind in the first verse, "Give up the lie that makes you pretend to be something that you are not."

In our so-called normal life, when we pretend in one way or another to be God, the enjoyer, we commit certain actions that reinforce this proclivity to deceitfulness. This attempt to deceive God and take something very valuable without paying a proper price for it, unfortunately, lives in the heart of every conditioned living being. Not all conditioned living beings are deceivers, but the proclivity to be deceitful is there in us all. In other words, not everyone is a cheater, but everyone is a potential cheater. If we allow this tendency to become manifest, we turn from being potential cheaters into actual cheaters.

GIVE UP ATTACHMENT TO DHARMA

The second verse makes us think about how to go on playing our role in the material world and simultaneously inwardly find ourselves in the spiritual world, in Vṛndāvana. Again Raghunātha Dāsa Gosvāmī is instructing his mind, saying, "O mind – *na dharmaṁ nādharmaṁ śruti-gaṇa-niruktaṁ kila kuru*." You must stop acting in accordance with the *dharma* described in the *śruti*, in the scriptures, and you must stop acting in accordance with *adharma*, that is, violating your *dharma*.

In other words, you should not follow *dharma* and you should not follow *adharma*.

From the beginning Raghunātha Dāsa Gosvāmī says, *śruti-gaṇa* (Vedic scriptures). The scriptures describe every possible responsibility of a living being, both *dharma* and *adharma*. There are two categories of living beings. The first is the intelligent, who are enlightened, possess spiritual knowledge, and who live in accordance with the philosophy of *Śrīmad-Bhāgavatam* (*vijña*). The second is the ignorant, the unenlightened (*ājñā*). Raghunātha Dāsa Gosvāmī's instruction *na dharmaṁ nādharmaṁ śruti-gaṇa-niruktaṁ kila kuru* is addressed to the *vijñas*, the enlightened people.

Jīva Gosvāmī gives an interesting definition of the ignorant person, or the person with materialistic tendencies as someone who identifies with the body. In essence, most of us are faced with the same problem. We do not understand that we are a soul, and we identify with the body, despite the numerous instructions that we have heard.

Jīva Gosvāmī also gives a slightly different definition that allows us to understand more clearly how to stop being an ignorant person. He explains that an ignorant person is someone whose mind and intelligence are not absorbed in the message or teachings of the Supreme Personality of Godhead, Kṛṣṇa. These people are not fully focused on the teachings set down in the *Bhagavad-gītā* and *Śrīmad-Bhāgavatam* and have not learned to see the world through the prism of these teachings.

The only way to remove the ignorance of identifying with the body, as we explained in verse one, is to stand back and look at ourselves with an outward eye from the point of view of the *Bhagavad-gītā* and the other scriptures. We take to take Kṛṣṇa's standpoint. Why does Śrīla Prabhupāda call our path "Kṛṣṇa consciousness"? It is because of how we should look at everything.

For example, the first time Śrīla Prabhupāda flew on a plane, he was going from New York to San Francisco. The plane started approaching San Francisco and he saw small houses and cars moving on the roads, which fascinated him. He started saying, "Look, they're like matchboxes." Then he called his servant and pointed at the tiny houses through the window which delighted the servant to look at all this together with Śrīla Prabhupāda. Then Śrīla Prabhupāda looked at him and said, "Now imagine how this entire world looks from Kṛṣṇa's perspective if it appears so small even from a plane. And the people running around are very insignificant, so imagine what all this looks like to him."

The path of Kṛṣṇa consciousness means that we look at everything from Kṛṣṇa's perspective and that we try to see everything in terms of Kṛṣṇa. If we have learned to see the world from his viewpoint, then we move from the category of the ignorant to the category of the enlightened.

What does an ignorant person need to do in order to move into this other category? We have already established with certainty that we fall into the category of the ignorant. What do we need to do while we are still ignorant? We need to follow *dharma*.

We can't identify with philosophy. We cannot see this world from Kṛṣṇa's perspective, so what can we do? Focusing on Kṛṣṇa isn't so simple. We should focus on how to observe the rules of the scriptures that constitute *dharma*, and this is something that anyone can do.

We must now very clearly understand at what point we can and must reject all these instructions of *dharma*. Here Raghunātha Dāsa Gosvāmī says that we must do it: *na dharmaṁ nādharmaṁ śruti-gaṇa-niruktaṁ kila kuru*. However, we need to understand when we must do that, because we must be careful not to do it prematurely. If we do that too early, the result can be very unfortunate.

What Caitanya Mahāprabhu brought is not just *bhakti*, but a special form of *bhakti* that we all must aspire to as the highest religious principle. He came to give people *rāga*, a form of practice that should develop in our hearts as a burning desire to serve Kṛṣṇa, just like the inhabitants of Vṛndāvana have done and are still doing. The instructions of *Manaḥ-śikṣā* are to be followed so that ultimately this *rāga*, attachment to Kṛṣṇa, is awakened in our hearts.

The first verse introduced us to the sphere of spiritual attachment, explaining the major obstacle to the development of this attachment, which is *dambha* (pride). Pride forces us to identify with this body and the roles we play in life. It forces us to become attached to the material world. This is the weakness of the heart. Later Raghunātha Dāsa Gosvāmī describes specific forms in which this pride manifests itself. But at the very beginning he says that in order to develop attachment we must overcome our pride, and simultaneously we must start forming our spiritual identity, which consists of spiritual emotions. From his first instruction, Raghunātha Dāsa Gosvāmī explains that we should try to attain our spiritual selves, being attached to the spiritual world, Vṛndāvana, the inhabitants of Vṛndāvana, the spiritual master, the holy name, the mantra, which the spiritual master gives us, and ultimately to the ever-youthful couple of Vraja.

Beginning from the second verse, he explains step by step what we should do. The first step Raghunantha Dāsa gives to his mind is, "O mind, give up attachment to *dharma* and *adharma*." Give up attachment to following religious principles and non-following of religious principles.

Although this is a seemingly paradoxical statement, Bhaktivinoda Ṭhākura resolves this contradiction. On the one hand we are told to follow the principles of *dharma* and we promise our guru that we will follow the four regulative principles. Yet on the other hand we are told, "Well, give it up; all this is nonsense." *Sarva-dharmān parityajya mām ekaṁ śaraṇaṁ vraja* (*Bhagavad-gītā* 18.66).

Even if you are an absolute ignoramus, you can still go back to Kṛṣṇa. Even if you are a *mleccha* and have nothing to do with brahminical culture, you can still go back because these things are unimportant. Yet it is easy to become confused whether *dharma* is important or unimportant. We may oscillate from one extreme to the other.

Vedic culture, true culture, is so important because it actually reflects the laws of the spiritual world.

The principles of brahminical culture, strictly speaking, are not just some fanciful conventions. These are profound laws that help us tune into the right mood, which is very important because the law of the spiritual world is to always be in the right mood, the basis of which is to surrender to God. The materialistic *brāhmaṇas* forget about this detail of mood, although they observe everything else. Therefore, any religious preacher or true messenger of God comes and says, "*na dharmaṁ nādharmaṁ śruti-gaṇa-niruktaṁ kila kuru"* – all this good and bad is just nonsense. However, it is very important not to throw the baby out with the bathwater because these principles are nonetheless essential.

The primary principle is love of God; we should forget about ourselves and give up our selfishness. We must purify our hearts so there will be an outpouring of pure love to serve Kṛṣṇa. But there are also secondary principles. The secondary principles mean, for example, that we should eat with our right hands and use our left hands to take care of what comes out as a result of our food intake, or we should not give or accept anything using our left hand, which is the behavior of someone familiar with Vedic culture. But in no way should we confuse the primary and the secondary principles with each other.

In *Śrī Caitanya Śikṣāmṛta*, Bhaktivinoda Ṭhākura gives us a recipe or an algorithm that we must follow. He explains all these secondary principles and says that a person who does not follow them develops hardheartedness, an adverse condition. In one way or another, if a person does not follow these principles of the Vedic culture their attachment to the modes of passion and ignorance grows stronger. Therefore, Bhaktivinoda Ṭhākura explains in which way the secondary principles should be combined with the primary principles.

First of all he says a person should follow all the primary principles. There are only five main principles of devotional service (*pañcāṅga-bhakti*): *sādhu-saṅga, nāma-kīrtana, bhāgavata-śravaṇa, mathurā-vāsa, śrī-mūrtira śraddhāya sevana*. Those are, the association of devotees, chanting the holy name of the Lord, studying the scriptures, living in a holy place, and faithful service to the Deity form of the Lord.

We should always, at least in our minds, live in a holy place; we should hear the scriptures, first of all *Śrīmad-Bhāgavatam*; we should chant the holy name; we should associate with the Vaiṣṇavas; and we should worship a Deity. Therefore, Bhaktivinoda Ṭhākura says that first we should adopt these five principles. They must become the center of our lives because in any situation – whether it is a conditioned situation or a situation in spiritual life – they are the basis of spiritual existence. In the spiritual world we will do the same.

What do devotees do in the spiritual world? Where do they live first of all? They live in a holy place; they live in the spiritual world. Do they worship a Deity or not? They do – Kṛṣṇa. They take care of him, they feed him, and they bathe and dress him. What else do they do? Do they hear *Śrīmad-Bhāgavatam*? They do, constantly; they constantly speak about Kṛṣṇa, and that is it. Do they associate with *sādhus*? Certainly. Do they associate with materialists? No, because there are none. Do they sing the holy name? Yes, they do.

In other words, those five items are both *sādhana* and *sādhya* at the same time. These principles constitute not just the method, but also the goal of our spiritual practice. When we attain the goal, we will do the same, but in the right state of mind and heart, when our hearts will be absolutely pure and overflowing with love. Therefore, when asked, "What is the result of your chanting the holy name Hare Kṛṣṇa, Hare Kṛṣṇa, Kṛṣṇa Kṛṣṇa, Hare Hare/ Hare Rāma, Hare Rāma, Rāma Rāma, Hare Hare?" Śrīla Prabhupāda would reply that we will chant even more.

But at the same time, Bhaktivinoda Ṭhākura says that along with these five basic principles of *bhakti*, we must decide what to do with the secondary principles. Some of us choose the option to follow what we want. Others follow all the principles, or others follow only the principles that they have been taught. But Bhaktivinoda Ṭhākura says that from the very beginning, never mind how difficult it may be and no matter how long it takes, we should try to follow all the secondary principles. From the very beginning, not only should we adopt the basic principles, but also we should study and achieve perfection in following all the details.

As *bhakti* develops in our hearts, Bhaktivinoda Ṭhākura explains, we must give up those principles that contradict *bhakti*. What is most surprising is that at the beginning he suggests we follow all the principles, even those that contradict *bhakti*.

There are actually many principles of *varṇāśrama* that contradict *bhakti*. When we talk about Vedic culture, the first item that comes to mind is worship of the demigods. We are advised to worship this demigod or that demigod. For instance, Śacīmātā used to worship the goddess who protects children. She worshiped this goddess of snakes to prevent reptiles biting her little Nimāi. Yet worshiping *devatās* contradicts *bhakti*.

Another principle of Vedic culture that contradicts *bhakti* is that we must respect a person according to their *varṇa* or their social position. Following a similar principle of *bhakti*, we respect a person not because of their *varṇa* or their external position, but because of their devotional qualities.

Nevertheless, Bhaktivinoda Ṭhākura says that at the beginning we must follow all the principles. This is because, first of all, we are attached to the body and, secondly, because we do not yet have sufficient *bhakti* ourselves to see *bhakti* in the others. Therefore, from the very beginning, when we just begin our path of devotional service, we must follow the maximum of what is possible of secondary principles. We must not neglect any details and nothing should be considered trifling.

The second step is that we renounce that which interferes with our *bhakti*. And the third step is that we give up everything and become a pure soul. The third stage, Bhaktivinoda Ṭhākura says, is when we begin to understand that all the principles of *varṇāśrama* are servants of the main principle. It is in this way that we follow these principles of *varṇāśrama* and understand which ones we ignore and which ones we do not ignore.

In other words if we return once again to the main thesis, we must first follow the maximum principles of *dharma* for our stage of advancement. Only as *bhakti* develops in our hearts may we gradually give up some small things and see whether or not they hinder the development of the basic principle.

There are also other very important points related to the principles of Vedic culture which we should consider. In the Eleventh Canto of *Śrīmad-Bhāgavatam* (11.11.32), Kṛṣṇa formulates the attitude to Vedic culture. These are the words of Kṛṣṇa himself, addressed to us. Kṛṣṇa explains to Uddhava who is the best of men:

ājñāyaivaṁ guṇān doṣān
mayādiṣṭān api svakān

dharmān santyajya yaḥ sarvān
māṁ bhajeta sa tu sattamaḥ

"A person who, understanding good and bad aspects of *dharma* as taught by me gives up all his duties and simply worships me is the best of all." Kṛṣṇa states that the best human being is the person who perfectly knows that the Lord has given the principles of Vedic scriptures to purify their heart, and that the principles of Vedic scriptures are beneficial. The best person knows that someone who rejects these principles begins to degrade and eventually goes to hell. But despite knowing that Kṛṣṇa himself has given these principles to purify our hearts and that those who neglect these principles go to hell, such a person rejects these principles and starts worshiping Kṛṣṇa.

What Kṛṣṇa defines in this verse is exemplified by the *gopīs*. We can reflect on their rejection of all principles, even those that are not rejected in decent society. They rejected not just some detailed dharmic principles, but they in fact abandoned their husbands and their children. They abandoned everything they could and ran away to Kṛṣṇa. In the dark, at night, they ran to the forest – to a stranger, to some cowherd boy who started playing his flute. The *gopīs* gave up everything. However, in the above verse Kṛṣṇa makes an extremely important statement that the best of humanity is not the person who rejects the value of *dharma*. At the outset, Kṛṣṇa says that the best persons are they who know that it is Kṛṣṇa who has given the numerous principles of the Vedic scriptures, that these principles purify our hearts, and that if we violate these principles we will become degraded. Despite this, the person gives up everything and sees these principles as an impediment to serving Kṛṣṇa.

For example, when Kṛṣna had a headache, at his request Nārada Muni started asking different people, "Please give Kṛṣṇa the dust of your feet, because only the dust of your lotus feet can save him."

What did they say? "We can't do that; we'll go to hell. This is a violation of *dharma*."

However, when Nārada Muni found the *gopīs*, they said, "Here, take the dust from our feet immediately!"

Nārada asked, "Aren't you afraid that you will go to hell?"

"Who cares about hell? The main thing is that Kṛṣṇa will stop having a headache."

Therefore, we should know all the principles of *dharma* knowing that they are meant to purify the heart. We can have such knowledge only in practice, not theoretically, understanding that these principles purify our hearts and nevertheless still give them up at the right time. In other words, first we have to understand that following Vedic culture is good.

The first aphorism of the *karma-mīmāṁsā-sūtra* by Jaimini Ṛṣi is: "*Athāto dharma-jijñāsā.*" Now that we have obtained a human form of life, we should ask questions about *dharma*. We must ask ourselves what is good and what is bad; what is religion and what is not religion; what we should follow and what we should not follow.

The simplest definition of *dharma* is that by observing certain rules we get benefit in this life and in the next. If people follow the laws of *dharma* consistently and as a principle, they will reap the benefit both now and in the future. If they do not follow these principles, they are engaged in *adharma*; and if someone violates these principles and acts against them, it is called *vikarma, kukarma,* or *ugrakarma*. Such a person then is engaged in terrible activities which bring pain even in the present and bad reactions in the future.

An important point here is that principles of morality need to be applied realistically. For example, we can say that sex is bad and that the highest principle of morality is not to engage in sex at all. But it is an unrealistic goal for most people. Therefore the Vedas say that we should marry and perform *vivāha-yajña*. Sex should be done as a *yajña,* as a sacrifice. We should focus our love on one person and develop a relationship with that person. In the Eleventh Canto of *Śrīmad-Bhāgavatam,* in the third chapter, Kṛṣṇa says that if a person has not curbed their senses and has also given up the principles of the Vedas, they will inevitably fall down from spiritual life.

If by our inner state of *bhakti* we have not yet developed our love to such an extent that we can renounce everything, but we still try to live according to the principles of renunciation, the result is very unfortunate. Therefore, the Vedas try to make allowances for conditioned nature and operate in such a way that the conditioned nature does not impede the development of *bhakti*. The Vedas offer the opportunity for a *vivāha-yajña* so we can live with our lawful wife or husband and there will be no sin attached to it. The result is actual moral principles. This is the glory of the Vedic principles – they try to give us an opportunity to actually progress and simultaneously cleanse our hearts.

Kṛṣṇa says that if you want to be rich, if you want to be happy, if you want to have a nice family life, then follow the principles of *dharma*. Along with this candy, Kṛṣṇa also gives a medicine inside the sweets. A person swallows the candy and thinks, "How sweet!" Eventually when they reach the center, the very essence, they suddenly realize that they did not need the other part they had been sucking.

Despite this greatness of Vedic *dharma*, Raghunātha Dāsa Gosvāmī says: *na dharmaṁ nādharmaṁ śruti-gaṇa-niruktaṁ kila kuru* – give up all *dharma*. In the end attachment even to *dharma* is unfavorable for three very important reasons.

First, when we are attached to *dharma*, we start to naturally depend on it. In other words, when attached to *dharma*, to the law in our lives, we tend to put *dharma* above God. We can see this flaw in the classical religions, such as Judaism or Islam. A Jewish rabbi once said that the best religion is Judaism, because to be an exemplary Jew one does not even need to believe in God. All Jews need to do is simply follow all the Jewish principles and rules. Faith in God is not required. If a person becomes used to this, they become what Jesus Christ called them – a legalist, a Pharisee, a scribe – when the law displaces God from the heart. Instead of depending on God, such a person starts to depend on the law and becomes a *karmī*. That is why we speak disdainfully of *karmīs*. But remember that *karmī* does not mean the general populace in the material world, who are not *karmīs*. *Karmīs* are those who actually follow all the principles of *dharma*.

Sometimes we may speak derisively of the *gṛhamedhīs*, but *gṛhamedhī* literally means a person who perfectly follows all the principles of *dharma*. They perform sacrifices every day, pour ghee onto the fire, chant mantras, and so on. A *gṛhamedhī* is a high term for a person who follows all the principles, but who nevertheless has forgotten the most important thing that these principles are meant for.

The second reason why attachment to *dharma* prevents us from attaining the supreme goal is a natural consequence stemming from the fact that, as we become attached to the adherence to *dharma*, simultaneously we become attached to the pleasures that come from *dharma*. As explained in *Śrīmad-Bhāgavatam* (1.5.15): *jugupsitaṁ dharma-kṛte 'nuśāsataḥ svabhāva-raktasya mahān vyatikramaḥ* – Nārada Muni came to Vyāsadeva and started rebuking him, saying, "You have brought about the ruin of human society. You have given them all these Vedic scriptures and so have ensured their degradation." He said this because people will follow and become attached to the result, after which they ultimately forget about these very rules or *dharma*. In this way human society becomes abased.

Bhaktivinoda Ṭhākura explains the third reason. He says that human psychology is such that we try to follow principles which are higher than our capability or qualification. What drives such action is pride, because people want to prove as soon as possible to everyone that they are the greatest devotee.

I was once approached by a man who said that he had wanted to be great three times. Once was when he finished school and did not yet know what kind of a great man he would become. Then he decided to join the armed forces to become a great military man. He did not succeed in achieving greatness that way, so his third attempt was when he decided to become a great devotee.

Therefore, Bhaktivinoda Ṭhākura says that first we must achieve stability in initially following some principles, such as chanting the *mahā-mantra*, before going any further. For instance, I may have started chanting six rounds, but I should not immediately try to chant sixteen rounds if it is difficult for me. First, I must become very stable in chanting six rounds; then further on, I must become stable in chanting eight rounds. Bhaktivinoda Ṭhākura says that in order to move successfully from stage to stage, I must first be firmly established on the current platform and not jump over three or more stages.

So we must achieve stability on a certain stage before we raise the bar too high. Another problem is that when we achieve stability at this level, we can become attached only to this level. We may think that we don't have to advance any further. This attachment or pride to following the standard of a particular stage we have achieved becomes manifest in our attitude towards others. We despise those below us, and, more importantly, we despise those who are higher than ourselves. We develop attachment to our particular level and say, "My level is the best. Those who are below me do terrible things."

Bhaktivinoda Ṭhākura says that we can see this tendency at all different levels of development of human consciousness. Consider the attitude of those who are living uncivilized lives to those who live by specific rules and principles. They often think, "They are wasting their precious human life. Human life is so rarely achievable and we can enjoy anything that no one else can enjoy, yet they spend their lives by following rules." And people who follow certain rules, have a contemptuous attitude towards those who believe in God. Those who just believe in God hold those who are very devoted to God in disdain. They say, "These *bhaktas* do not understand anything." The *bhaktas* who follow the principles of *vaidhī-bhakti*, think of the *rāgānuga-bhaktas* as mere sentimentalists.

Therefore, we must equally take care of our own hearts and neither hurry too much nor linger too long at each stage. When we have reached a certain level, we must go higher. And that is why the *śāstras* describe going the whole way up. Sometimes we may wonder whether we need to hear descriptions of *prema*, but we need to know what the supreme goal is. Occasionally the description of *prema* may even frighten us. However, the principle should be that we gradually move from one stage to the next and therefore attachment to *varṇāśrama* can be a hindrance. So Raghunātha Dāsa Gosvāmī says here, *na dharmaṁ nādharmaṁ śruti-gaṇa-niruktaṁ kila kuru* – do not get attached to either *dharma* or to *adharma*.

COMMENTARY BY ŪRMILĀ DEVĪ DĀSĪ

Raghunātha Dāsa Gosvāmī advises us to abandon both *dharma* and *adharma*. Such is not a call to become an *avadhūta* who appears crazy to the world. Indeed, Rūpa Gosvāmī tells us in *Bhakti-rasāmṛta-sindhuḥ* "not to be neglectful in ordinary dealings."

Rather, the point in verse two is to absorb our mind in eternal truth, *tattva*, rather than in the details of what is right or wrong in a karmic sense. Such details are hard to discern even for the wisest persons. We can easily be diverted from love of God trying to unravel those complexities. Ultimately, the underlying natural desire of the soul for balance, harmony, and goodness, which prompt our dedication to justice, morals, and ethics, is only found completely by transcending those concerns to come to full spiritual realization. Nor should we calculate as to what actions of ours are likely or unlikely to bring us good results in a material sense. As stated in *Śrīmad-Bhāgavatam* (11.7.8):

> One whose consciousness is bewildered by illusion perceives many differences in value and meaning among material objects. Thus one engages constantly on the platform of material good and evil and is bound by such conceptions. Absorbed in material duality, such a person contemplates the performance of compulsory duties, non-performance of such duties and performance of forbidden activities.

Generally, Kṛṣṇa wants his devotees to act in ways equivalent to material piety, and to avoid behaviors equivalent to material impiety. After all, such rules of piety and impiety originate with him, *dharmaṁ tu sākṣād bhagavat-praṇītaṁ* (*Śrīmad-Bhāgavatam* 6.3.19). A serious practitioner of *bhakti* should act to please Kṛṣṇa as foremost, whether externally it appears that such a person's actions are fully in line with pious karma or not. After all, only low-level clerks enforce company rules blindly; at higher levels employees know the essence of company policy and can adjust externals according to the specific time, place, and circumstances.

Indirectly, therefore, here in the second verse we find a further implied description of the intended audience for this instruction manual.

These verses are intended for persons disinterested in karma, or the attempt to better oneself through enjoying the fruits of material action.

yadā yasyānugṛhṇāti
bhagavān ātma-bhāvitaḥ
sa jahāti matiṁ loke
vede ca pariniṣṭhitām

> When a person is fully engaged in devotional service, he is favored by the Lord, who bestows his causeless mercy. At such a time, the awakened devotee gives up all material activities and ritualistic performances mentioned in the Vedas. (*Śrīmad-Bhāgavatam* 4.29.46)

Furthermore, verse two indicates that this book is intended not only for persons who aspire to the service of Kṛṣṇa in Vṛndāvana, but also specifically for those who follow the teachings of Śrī Caitanya Mahāprabhu.

VERSE THREE

yadīccher āvāsaṁ vraja-bhuvi sa-rāgaṁ pratijanur
yuva-dvandvaṁ tac cet paricaritum ārād abhilaṣeḥ
svarūpaṁ śrī-rūpaṁ sa-gaṇam iha tasyāgrajam api
sphuṭaṁ premṇā nityaṁ smara nama tadā tvaṁ śṛṇu manaḥ

Listen, O mind. If you desire, in every birth, to reside in the land of Vraja with loving attachment and to serve the youthful couple Śrī Śrī Rādhā-Kṛṣṇa in close proximity, then clearly remember and offer obeisances to Śrī Svarūpa, to Śrī Rūpa and his associates in Vṛndāvana, and to Śrī Rūpa's elder brother, Śrī Sanātana.

COMMENTARY BY ŚIVARĀMA SWAMI

This process of worship taught in verse one is *ratim apūrvām atitarām*, or unprecedented great love. The unique nature of this love is that it is practiced by the inhabitants of Vṛndāvana. It's not practiced in any other place: not in Vaikuṇṭha, nor in any other quarter of Goloka such as Dvārakā, Mathurā, or Gokula. Only the inhabitants of Vraja have this extraordinary type of devotional service. They are also called *rāgātmikā-bhaktas*.

So verse three dealt with a question which was implied in verse one, of whether someone taking *dīkṣā* and *śikṣā* outside of the Gauḍīya *sampradāya* can actually achieve *rati* or *rāgātmikā-bhakti*. In order to answer that question, the definition of *rāgātmikā-bhakti* must be understood: is it is specifically achieved by *rāgānugā-bhakti* or *rāgānugā-sādhana*, which is one of the two process of *sādhana-bhakti*.

Vaidhī-bhakti and *rāgānugā-bhakti* are divisions or elements of *sādhana-bhakti*. The general method by which practitioners in Kṛṣṇa consciousness achieve the perfectional platform is to practice *vaidhī-bhakti* under the direction of elevated Vaiṣṇavas. One will then enter into the platform of *rāga*, spontaneous devotional service, by which one is then able to approach or enter into the realm of *rāgātmikā*. So this process, although very rare and difficult to achieve, is very easily attained by the mercy of Caitanya Mahāprabhu. *Svarūpam-śrī-rūpam-sa-gaṇam iha tasyāgrajam api*: by the mercy of Rūpa Gosvāmī, Sanātana Gosvāmī, and *sa-gaṇam*, by all their associates.

COMMENTARY BY ŚACĪNANDANA SWAMI

In my simple language, I call this verse "the flowerpot verse." A culture of nourishment is needed if you wish to develop something. Look at a flower. What would be the future of a flower without appropriate soil? There are minerals just suited to the needs of each particular flower. It is very important if we want to develop something very special, then we must provide the right nourishment. We must learn to put a living culture around our lives so we will nourish what we want to attain. The information, the habits, the way of dealing with each other, eating styles, everything should be conducive for what we want to reach. Otherwise, taking just a little bit of Hare Kṛṣṇa, Hare Rāma – this medicine for Kali-yuga – may not work so much.

I have a doctor called Naram. Dr. Naram told me that the greatest challenge in his profession as an Ayurvedic *kavirāja* didn't come from the direct victims of 9/11, but the firefighters who had breathed in the poisonous vapor. He treated them without charge and made them healthy. As a result, he received much benefit and became very famous.

He could cure almost anyone until he came across a boy from slums of Mumbai who had bronchitis. Despite treatment, the child was wasting away more and more. One day the doctor went to the boy's home in an attempt to find out why the child was becoming increasingly sicker, although he was being treated. Finally, Dr. Naram found out the cause. This boy worked three hours a day in a chemical factory, where they had a pool of chemicals. To mix them they had this little boy swimming in it, and by his froglike swimming movements he stirred up the chemicals to produce the proper mix. This is Indian technology. Then Dr. Naram understood, "I can give him medicine, but if the culture around him is not supportive to his growth, he will waste away and won't survive."

So, yes, you can chant Hare Kṛṣṇa, Hare Rāma, but if you don't have the proper culture, the proper examples, and the proper role models in your life, *vraja-bhakti* may not come to you. Therefore, Raghunātha Dāsa Gosvāmī very clearly says that if we are eager to reside in *vraja-dhāma* and execute service on the platform of *bhakti* with love, if we yearn for the direct service of Śrī Śrī Rādhā and Kṛṣṇa, then we must have the right examples. We must learn from the right people. "Clearly remember and offer obeisances to Śrī Svarūpa, to Śrī Rūpa and his associates in Vṛndāvana, and to Śrī Rūpa's elder brother, Śrī Sanātana."

We have to have an alliance to a spiritual school. We have to stay with that school and dig deeper and deeper. If we drill for water, after half an hour we may think, "Water has not come, let me drill somewhere else." Then again we go three meters deep in another place and find no water. "Let me now go to the camp of *rasika-bhakti* times one million at Rādhā-kuṇḍa and drill there." Four meters, still no water. "Okay, let me drill somewhere else. Let me drill now at *rasa-bhakti* times ten." We drill at this other institution, and still no water. We will end up drilling for the rest of our life. If we would have stayed at one bona fide place and drilled there, we would have gone very deep and found an abundance of water. Stay with a line of Gaurāṅga Mahāprabhu and drill deep. That way we will find a proper environment, proper minerals, and receive the flower of *bhakti*.

COMMENTARY BY BHAKTIVIJNANA GOSWAMI

The *Manaḥ-śikṣā* is a methodology by which a person can overcome their internal obstacles and gradually develop love for Kṛṣṇa. This is our goal, and Raghunātha Dāsa Gosvāmī has written these verses for us. These prayers are addressed to his mind, but actually they are more relevant to our minds than to his. If we follow these recommendations step by step and try to apply them in our lives, success is guaranteed.

We may think that there are more important things to think about, like our marriages. At the end of the day, however, the most important thing will be the extent to which we have managed to develop attachment for Kṛṣṇa. At the end of our lives everything else will be unimportant and devoid of meaning, and what will stay with us is our attachment to Kṛṣṇa. We will see how everything else slips through our fingers – our health, happiness, wealth, beloved ones, relatives and friends – they will all be gone, but this wealth of attachment to Kṛṣṇa will remain with us. No matter what position we are in now, it is important to know how to develop this attachment to Kṛṣṇa. Otherwise, when faced with the last test, we may prove bankrupt when we no longer have anything material, and neither do we have any spiritual wealth.

Raghunātha Dāsa Gosvāmī specifically says here that if you have two desires: to live with love in Vraja life after life and directly serve the eternally young couple, then you should *svarūpaṁ śrī-rūpaṁ sa-gaṇam iha tasyāgrajam api sphuṭaṁ premṇā nityaṁ smara nama tadā tvaṁ śṛṇu manaḥ*. Then (*tadā*) you should remember (*smara*). *Sphuṭaṁ premṇā nityam. Nityam* means incessantly, all the time. *Premna* means with love. *Sphuṭam* means very clearly. He says that if you have these two desires you have to constantly, with love and very clearly, remember *svarūpaṁ śrī-rūpaṁ sa-gaṇam iha tasyāgrajam api*. We need to remember Svarūpa Dāmodara Gosvāmī and Śrī Rūpa Gosvāmī. *Gaṇam iha, sa-gaṇam* – all their associates, all their followers. *Tasyāgrajam* – the elder brother of Rūpa Gosvāmī, Sanātana Gosvāmī. It is them that we should always think of with love.

Several important questions arise which we will try to answer. First, why does Raghunātha Dāsa Gosvāmī say *prati-januḥ,* for many many lifetimes? The first thing we have been promised is that this will be our last life, and now it turns out that we have to live for many lifetimes in Vraja.

But the first word of this verse means "if you want to." Raghunātha Dāsa Gosvāmī says the goal is *bhakti,* which does not require liberation from birth. Real devotees do not think that they deserve to be born anywhere in particular. Such devotees says that they are ready to be born here, again and again; that they have no merits to be in the spiritual world. If we have *rāga,* attachment to the Lord, then life in Vṛndāvana, even here on earth, is amazingly beautiful.

His Holiness Bhakti-tīrtha Mahārāja, despite his severe pain, shows us a great example of the beautiful picture of life in Vṛndāvana. One of his last pastimes is perhaps the most amazing one. Just before his departure from his body he was in terrible pain. The pain was so agonizing that no drugs could suppress it. Sometimes he would be placed in a bathtub to relax, but the pain would be burning his entire body from within. During one such attack, Rādhānātha Mahārāja was next to him. As Bhakti-tīrtha Mahārāja was writhing in pain, tears streaming from his eyes, Rādhānātha Mahārāja began telling him about Vṛndāvana, where everyone loves Kṛṣṇa and where Kṛṣṇa loves everyone, and where there is nothing but love. This went on for a long time, with Rādhānātha Mahārāja whispering in his ear and Bhakti-tīrtha Mahārāja listening. Suddenly he smiled and said, "I have never felt so good in my life."

Raghunātha Dāsa Gosvāmī is drawing this picture, because he is ready to take birth and to die, to be sick and to suffer here on earth as long as it is in Vṛndāvana. In this way he glorifies Vṛndāvana and *prema* itself, which makes a person willing to take birth again and again, because the happiness of *prema* is so intense it overshadows any material pain. This picture of life in the earthly Vṛndāvana is presented by Śrīnivāsa Ācārya in a song glorifying the six Gosvāmīs (*Ṣaḍ-gosvāmy-aṣṭaka*, verse 8):

he rādhe vraja-devike ca lalite he nanda-sūno kutaḥ
śrī-govardhana-kalpa-pādapa-tale kālindī-vane kutaḥ
ghoṣantāv iti sarvato vraja-pure khedair mahā-vihvalau
vande rūpa-sanātanau raghu-yugau śrī jīva-gopālakau

Let us imagine this scene for a moment: the Gosvāmīs of Vṛndāvana are clad in nothing but loincloths and shawls, consisting of nothing but patches, living there in the land of Vraja crying, *he rādhe vraja-devike ca lalite he nanda-sūno kutaḥ* – where are you? Where are you Rādhārāṇī? Where are you, Lalitā? Where are you, son of the king of Vraja? Where are you all? Have you gone to Govardhana or to the banks of the Kālindī? They are running there, filling Vṛndāvana with their cries. Are we willing to live like that in Vṛndāvana, life after life?

Raghunātha Dāsa Gosvāmī says *prati-januḥ*, that he is ready to take birth again and again because he has experienced happiness in

Vṛndāvana. We can also experience this happiness. Such is the answer to the first question.

The second, and most important, question is answered by Bhaktivinoda Ṭhākura's explanation of this verse. Why does Raghunātha Dāsa Gosvāmī mention *svarūpaṁ śrī-rūpaṁ sa-gaṇam iha tasyāgrajam api* – with all their associates? The Sanskrit means Svarūpa Dāmodara Gosvāmī, Śrī Rūpa Gosvāmī, Sanātana Gosvāmī (*tasyāgrajam*) and all their associates as being the persons we should remember clearly with love. Why doesn't he say, instead, "Remember Nityānanda?"

Rūpa and Sanātana discovered Vṛndāvana, but that was by the mercy of Nityānanda. Raghunātha Dāsa Gosvāmī received the mercy of Caitanya Mahāprabhu by first receiving the mercy of Nityānanda. By the mercy of Nityānanda he received Mahāprabhu's mercy; by the mercy of Mahāprabhu, he received the mercy of Rādhā and Kṛṣṇa. But he does not say Nityānanda. He described that we should always clearly remember *svarūpaṁ śrī-rūpaṁ sa-gaṇam iha tasyāgrajam api*. It is this difficult question that I will try to answer.

We know this famous verse (Śrī Rūpa Gosvāmī's *praṇāma-mantra*):

śrī-caitanya-mano-'bhīṣṭaṁ
sthāpitaṁ yena bhū-tale
svayaṁ rūpaḥ kadā mahyaṁ
dadāti sva-padāntikam

We know that it was Rūpa Gosvāmī who is our *sampradāya-ācārya* or the *ācārya*-founder of the entire Gauḍīya *sampradāya*.

The *Caitanya-caritāmṛta* begins with:

pañca-tattvātmakaṁ kṛṣṇaṁ
bhakta-rūpa-svarūpakam
bhaktāvatāraṁ bhaktākhyaṁ
namāmi bhakta-śaktikam

This verse, written by Svarūpa Dāmodara Gosvāmī, describes Lord Caitanya, Nityānanda, Advaita Ācārya, Gadādhara Paṇḍita and Śrīvāsa Ācārya. However, none of them are mentioned in Raghunātha Dāsa Gosvāmī's third verse. On the one hand, these are the five *tattvas* who came to give us love of God, yet, Raghunātha Dāsa Gosvāmī does not tell his mind to remember them. We know that in *Caitanya-caritāmṛta*, again in the words of Svarūpa Dāmodara, who states the nature of this most merciful *avatāra* (*Madhya-līlā* 19.53):

namo mahā-vadānyāya
kṛṣṇa-prema-pradāya te
kṛṣṇāya kṛṣṇa-caitanya-
nāmne gaura-tviṣe namaḥ

Śrī Kṛṣṇa Caitanya, who came to give *prema* to everyone, had two missions: to give *prema* to everyone and enjoy *prema* himself. The Pañca-tattva helped him primarily with the first mission. The Pañca-tattva gave him the opportunity to spread this *prema*. We know Lord Nityānanda, Advaita Ācārya, Gadādhara Paṇḍita, and Śrīvāsa Ṭhākura all preached the holy name, but here Raghunātha Dāsa Gosvāmī teaches us the inner *bhajana*, the inner culture of *bhajana*; the culture of emotions or *rāga* that was taught by *svarūpaṁ śrī-rūpaṁ tasyāgrajam*. The most important thing they did was to explain spiritual experience, allowing us to join the spiritual experience of the great devotees of the past.

We want to obtain the same feelings and the same emotions that they did. After all, we want the same love to be burning in our hearts in such a way that nothing else will be burning there. At present what is burning there is a soup of *kāma, krodha, lobha, moha, mada* and *mātsarya*. Rūpa Gosvāmī, above all, gave a roadmap or guidebook to these feelings, explaining how spiritual emotions can be attained, how one emotion leads to another, and what causes the emotions in the first place.

This is what Nityānanda Prabhu did not do, but not because he had a mission of his own. For instance, in Locana Dāsa Ṭhākura's song *Akrodha paramānanda*, he sings that Nityānanda Prabhu goes from house to house, knocking on every door and, holding a straw in his mouth, says: "Do you want to buy me? Chant the holy name." Having said this, he then falls in the dust, and starts crying and rolling about in it, his hair standing on end. This is what he did – he let people see and feel a spritual experience and he gave the main method to attain that experience: Hare Kṛṣṇa, Hare Kṛṣṇa, Kṛṣṇa Kṛṣṇa, Hare Hare/ Hare Rāma, Hare Rāma, Rāma Rāma, Hare Hare.

He gave people the holy name. He did not explain what we should feel or how the holy name should work in our hearts. At a certain level we can just chant the holy name without thinking about anything, without knowing what it stands for, without understanding all this science, without realizing who Kṛṣṇa is – but sooner or later we may get lost. Even if we start feeling something, we may not understand what it is or what the next step is. We can get lost in this spiritual experience. For our advancement, we very much depend on how clearly we understand where we are going.

Sometimes, even in ISKCON, we have various points of view. One perspective is that there is no need of much ado to attain Vraja. Chant Hare Kṛṣṇa, Hare Kṛṣṇa, Kṛṣṇa Kṛṣṇa, Hare Hare/ Hare Rāma, Hare Rāma, Rāma Rāma, Hare Hare. There is no need to do anything else. We must just dedicate ourselves to the holy name. We must just knock on every door and shout to them, holding a straw in our mouth or a book in our hand, "You, rogues, chant the holy name, otherwise you will go to hell!" And sometimes we dance ecstatically, then get up and go on and knock on a door again. This is the method, and we should have absolute faith in it.

But we also need to know the spiritual science so that eventually we come to Vraja. Lord Caitanya infused the holy name with *prema*, and when we hear the holy name we feel this love. From the very beginning our hairs may stand on end and our tears may flow. A good example is when a new product is being released on the market, it is often given away for free. A company I once saw in Sweden had marketers handing out free samples of its new product. People were taking these, and some were repeatedly going up for more. In this way they were given a taste of the new item.

Similarly, Caitanya Mahāprabhu, the *prema-avatāra*, came and brought *prema* with him, and began distributing it for free. Although *prema* is free, it is absolutely free only at the beginning.

We are given this small bottle of *prema*, and we are told, "Drink a little; you'll like it." And we do like it. But then we are told, "Now you have to shell out and pay the price." Now we must work on our *anarthas* and engage in *sādhana*.

Caitanya Mahāprabhu is the most merciful (*mahā-vadānyāya*). He gave *prema* to everyone, and each and every one of us has experienced *prema*. From the very beginning our path is based not on *vaidya* but on *rāga*. He gave us this *prema*, but at the same time he sent Rūpa Gosvāmī to explain to us the obstacles that we will encounter on this path because, like on any spiritual path, we will be besieged by a dark night. The dark night of the soul is when despair brings us down, when it gets tough, when we are unable to understand what is going on, why this taste that we felt is now gone, where it has gone and why. To guide us, Rūpa Gosvāmī wrote an amazing guide to the spiritual emotions, *Bhakti-rasāmṛta-sindhuḥ*, explaining how they should evolve in our hearts.

Recently I met a *bhakta*, a simple-hearted man in his early sixties, who had been practicing Kṛṣṇa consciousness for a couple of years. He told me, "I sometimes chant 16 rounds and I am eager to quickly finish these 16 rounds so that I can chant the holy name properly. Because to chant 16 rounds is a must, I must do it and I am eager to quickly finish them so that after that I can chant freely and with love." He continued, "I chant and chant. I chant a lot, and then it starts! I look forward to the moment when I can chant just because the heart wants to do it. And chanting, all of a sudden I feel tears welling in my eyes. Sometimes suddenly a sad melody comes to me that I've never heard before. When I hear it tears begin to flow from my eyes." And then he stopped and said, "This must be *ābhāsa*, right? I was told that what I feel is *ābhāsa*."

Clearly, he does not know what *ābhāsa* (a reflection of pure chanting) is, but he said, "This *ābhāsa* comes to me and makes the tears flow from my eyes. And I do not know where that melody comes from. I once sang it and I was told that it sounds like some Muslim melody, a very poignant one; no one appreciated it. But I know it comes from there, from Kṛṣṇa. When I hear it all of a sudden, it comes by itself; I have not invented it. I do not remember anything else. I just remember that Kṛṣṇa is God and that I'm there, next to him."

When I sat there with him, listening to all this, I thought, "What *ābhāsa*? It's not *ābhāsa*. He's an uninitiated *bhakta*, but he has *bhāva* in his heart."

In fact, we should not think that *bhāva* is somewhere far away. We have all felt a small sample of *bhāva*, as I said, but Rūpa Gosvāmī came to explain to us what it is, because otherwise we can get confused very easily. Tears will flow and we won't know where they are from, whether it is *ābhāsa* or true tears.

Rūpa Gosvāmī has created the amazing book, *Bhakti-rasāmṛta-sindhuḥ*, which is a guide to the realm of spiritual emotion. This is why we must remember Rūpa Gosvāmī with focus. To remember him clearly means to remember what he taught us, and understand the way, so we do not get lost again in the forest of material life.

Bhakti-ratnākara is a book on the history of Gauḍīya Vaisnavism and the final years of Raghunātha Dāsa Gosvāmī's life. The account begins by stating that the feelings he was experiencing while living on the banks of Rādhā-kuṇḍa defy description. He was always feeling the pain of separation from Kṛṣṇa, a fire burning him from the inside. He was swimming in tears and rolling in the dust as he constantly cried, "Where are you, Śrī Svarūpa Dāmodara, Śrī Rūpa, and Śrī Sanātana?" He was repeating these three names because they are a treasure for all Gauḍīya Vaiṣṇavas. In Narottama Dāsa Ṭhākura's *Bhajana-lālasāmayī-prārthanā* (from *Śrī Prārthanā*, 4) he also sings *rūpa-raghunātha-pade haibe ākuti*, "When will I be so eager to understand the words of Rūpa and Raghunātha, so that by their virtue the treasure of love for Rādhā and Kṛṣṇa, and the understanding of this love, will awaken in me?"

In fact, even ordinary love is very difficult to understand. Pushkin, a great authority in mundane love, used to speak about it. Even with ordinary love it is impossible to understand how it appears and disappears, and what causes and destroys it. What can then be said of understanding the love between Rādhā and Kṛṣṇa? But at the same time such an understanding is our goal.

Caitanya Mahāprabhu appeared on earth and has made that love possible and achievable. Of course, sometimes the goal seems very lofty and almost unreachable; nevertheless, it *is* achievable. Therefore, this third verse tells us that after we have cleared pride from our mind, we should meditate on Svarūpa, Śrī Rūpa and Sanātana Gosvāmīs, because it is only through them that can we understand the pastimes of Rādhā and Kṛṣṇa, and truly understand the meaning of the holy name.

In itself the holy name contains a powerful impetus for change. We hear the holy name, and we hear that the holy name is God himself and we realize that we can no longer live as we lived before. There are books, like the *Bhagavad-gītā*, and there are teachings and words that carry this impetus in themselves: I must not live like this anymore; I must transform my life. Sometimes people get this feeling of needing to change at the first sound of the holy name, perhaps seeing devotees on *harināma*.

Sometimes people underestimate the holy name as a form of spiritual practice and preaching, because they do not understand what it is. I was once told a story about a *harināma* on the Arbat in Moscow. A girl came up and stood in the crowd, then suddenly started sobbing after hearing the sound of the holy name. She began clapping her hands, tapping her foot and singing along. When the *harināma* moved on, she followed behind and, as if spellbound, sang along with the devotees, Hare Kṛṣṇa, Hare Kṛṣṇa, Kṛṣṇa Kṛṣṇa, Hare Hare/ Hare Rāma, Hare Rāma, Rāma Rāma, Hare Hare. She walked and walked and then she came with them to the temple. In a couple of hours she was dressed in a sari, with beads in hand.

It is Rūpa Gosvāmī, along with Svarūpa Dāmodara and Sanātana Gosvāmī, who explained this personal spiritual experience to us and gave it a particular form. There is a story about the moment Rūpa Gosvāmī *became* Rūpa Gosvāmī. We chant this mantra: *śrī-caitanya-mano-'bhīṣṭaṁ sthāpitaṁ yena bhū-tale svayaṁ rūpaḥ kadā mahyaṁ dadāti sva-padāntikam.* It says that Rūpa Gosvāmī had entered the mind of Śrī Caitanya Mahāprabhu and by special mercy he could understand what was going on in Lord Caitanya's heart.

It was at a Rathayātrā, and year after year during Rathayātrā the same thing happened over and over again that nobody could understand. When the devotees pulled the chariot of Lord Jagannātha, Lord Caitanya danced in front of that chariot, repeating strange words: *seita parāṇa-nātha pāinu yāhā lāgi' madana-dahane jhuri genu* (*Caitanya-caritāmṛta, Madhya-līlā* 1.55). Over and over again he said, "I have gotten that lord of my life, for whom I was burning in the fire of lusty desires." *Madana-dahane* means the fire of passion. The devotees could not understand why he was saying this verse. After that Lord Caitanya would repeat a Sanskrit verse from the romantic collection of one hundred verses by the poet Śrī Amaru. Caitanya Mahāprabhu would repeat this verse over and over again (*Caitanya-caritāmṛta, Madhya-līlā* 1.58):

yaḥ kaumāra-haraḥ sa eva hi varas tā eva caitra-kṣapās
te conmīlita-mālatī-surabhayaḥ prauḍhāḥ kadambānilāḥ
sā caivāsmi tathāpi tatra surata-vyāpāra-līlā-vidhau
revā-rodhasi vetasī-taru-tale cetaḥ samutkaṇṭhate

He was saying that the same young man who stole my heart in my youth has come back to me and these are the same moonlight nights of the month of Caitra. The month of Caitra is a very hot month, and at night when the full moon is shining and there is a cool breeze, people become peaceful. In this verse Caitanya Mahāprabhu was saying that he can smell that same fragrance of *mālatī* flowers. He mentions fragrance here deliberately because smell has a special potency. It is able to carry us back to a situation that we have almost forgotten. Suddenly, smelling a particular fragrance, we are transported to where we once were, even if the situation only existed in our mind.

Caitanya Mahāprabhu says, "It is that same smell that was there once in my youth, and the young man that stole my heart then, is back again. The same breeze is blowing and the same fragrance of *mālatī* flowers is wafting from the *kadamba* forest; and I am the same, too. Nevertheless, I am unhappy, and I want to go back again to the place of our first meeting on the bank of the Reva, under a Vetasī tree."

Everyone honored and respected Caitanya Mahāprabhu, but no one could understand what he was saying, except for Svarūpa Dāmodara, who was admitted into the depths of his heart. He was the first to write in his memoirs who Caitanya Mahāprabhu is.

Some time later, during Rathayātrā, Rūpa Gosvāmī was there and heard this verse. When he heard it, he returned home and wrote another verse on a palm leaf, his handwriting as even and beautiful as a string of pearls. He attached the palm leaf to the roof of his hut and then went to bathe in the ocean.

Meanwhile, Caitanya Mahāprabhu came to see him but found no one. He went to the hut and saw the verse attached to the roof. When he read it, his hairs stood on end and a shiver of ecstasy ran over his skin. He wondered, "How does he know what is going on in my heart? Svarūpa Dāmodara knows because I have told him. He spends his sleepless nights with me. But Rūpa Gosvāmī has just come to Purī, so how does *he* know everything?"

He grabbed the leaf in ecstasy, embracing Rūpa Gosvāmī, who had returned from his bath. Then Mahāprabhu ran to Svarūpa Dāmodara, told him the story about the verse, and asked him, "Svarūpa, how does Rūpa know what is going on in my mind?"

Commenting on this story, Śrīla Prabhupāda said that once he had a similar personal story. He had written an offering to his spiritual master in the form of a poem. When Bhaktisiddhānta Sarasvatī Ṭhākura read it, he was so pleased that he called his closest companions and servants and had them read this offering again and again, explaining to them that his intention had been understood. Śrīla Prabhupāda asks, "I wonder how I could have understood his intention?"

It is the same question that Caitanya Mahāprabhu asked Svarūpa Dāmodara, "I wonder how he could understand my mind?"

Svarūpa Dāmodara replied: "He could understand only because he had received your mercy. He could not have understood it in any other way."

Caitanya Mahāprabhu confirmed this, saying, "I was so pleased with Rūpa Gosvāmī that when I embraced him near Siddha Bakula in Jagannātha Purī, after reading this verse, I invested him with all the *śakti* needed for preaching *bhakti* and revealing the nature of *bhakti* to everyone else."

We see that Rūpa Gosvāmī understood everything by mercy. Although certainly he already had Caitanya Mahāprabhu's mercy, the Lord further invested his spiritual *śakti,* or energy, into Rūpa Gosvāmī so that he could explain it to us. After saying that Rūpa Gosvāmī understood his heart, Mahāprabhu instructed, "Now, Svarūpa Dāmodara, go and explain everything to him." He already understood everything – he had written that verse because Caitanya Mahāprabhu had invested him with his *śakti*. Nevertheless, even if we have understood everything and our hearts are overflowing with love of God, we should go to our spiritual master and hear him explain to us even what we have already understood.

We should do this because the spiritual master will explain what we have learned or felt in our hearts to us on the level of rational understanding. Our intuitive perception can then remain and be established in our hearts. This is a very important point that we must understand. It is the exampleRūpa Gosvāmī set for all of us.

This is the contribution of our *sampradāya* that we cannot find elsewhere. Rūpa Gosvāmī has explained *bhakti* as *rasa*. In order to understand what spiritual *rasa* is, let us first understand what *rasa* is in the worldly sense. Caitanya Mahāprabhu was repeating a verse from a mundane *rasa-śāstra* – a verse that is an example of worldly love. But Mahāprabhu has explained that *bhakti* in the highest sense must ultimately lead to *rasa*.

There are two fundamental concepts: *bhāva* and *rasa*. *Rasa* is the transformation of *bhāva*. *Bhāva* is an emotion. Let us first examine *bhāva* and *rasa* not in the spiritual sense, in terms of our philosophy, but in the worldly sense so we can all relate to it.

Bhāva is the emotion that a person experiences, such as an actor, a poet, or a writer. The actor who is expressing an emotion on the stage, or a writer who is expressing it in the words of his poems, is expressing *bhāva*. This *bhāva* can be expressed even in a gesture.

Worldly *rasa* is the result of transformation of worldly *bhāva*. *Bhāva* is what is expressed. A writer, a poet, or an actor reflects or represents their emotions. Someone has experienced some feeling and I, as the reader or observer, feel the same but as a reflection. This reflected feeling that has no relation to myself. I have not been in that situation, yet I still feel this emotion – the aesthetic sense of perception of another's emotions is called *rasa*.

It is very important for us to understand these two terms so that we are able to comprehend in what way spiritual *bhāva* and spiritual *rasa* correlate with each other. Material *rasa* is a product of transformation or purification of another person's *bhāva*. Someone is experiencing some emotion or feeling and we might have also felt them in a more coarse state.

Those who listened to The Beatles were going crazy because of what was going on in their hearts. The Beatles themselves were not going crazy; they just expressed some feelings in their songs. The hair of those who heard them was standing on end, tears were streaming from their eyes, and they were rolling on the floor. The fans were dying to go and tear their idols to shreds for souvenirs because they were able to awaken in their hearts feelings that no one else could awaken. This is how worldly *rasa* functions and how powerful it is. In Vedic culture, beginning with Bharata Muni, this theory of *rasas* was developed. Vedic philosophers possessed an amazing, unique ability to classify every possible condition.

Vedic literature and culture describe how feelings arise even on the mundane level, what they consist of, what the stimulus of emotion is, and how all this takes place so that this emotion can be reproduced.

This science of *rasa* is Rūpa Gosvāmī's contribution. He has described, demonstrated and explained that *bhakti* should turn into the sublime spiritual emotion of love for Kṛṣṇa, not just into service to Kṛṣṇa. At the first level, we serve Kṛṣṇa using our senses – we are trying to serve the lord of the senses using our own senses in order for them to be purified. At a higher level, we serve not with our senses but with our emotions. In fact, what is embodied in *Śrīmad-Bhāgavatam* is the picture of the spiritual world, which cannot be found anywhere else. If someone tries to draw some image, it will be a picture of perceptions or states. Suppose we were shown advertisements of the spiritual world; it would still be a picture of perception. Yes, it is a beautiful sight that you can keep looking at for forty years, but there is something lacking. It is a static image where a person is described as a kind of a motionless being who is staring at that sight and enjoying it. But the inner experience is missing.

Śrīmad-Bhāgavatam's descriptions of the spiritual world are unique and not found in any other scripture. *Śrīmad-Bhāgavatam* describes a dynamic account of a constantly expanding love experienced by the *bhakta* and Bhagavān, and the reciprocation of that love. This love swelling in the heart of the *bhakta* is reflected in the heart of God, and because of the happiness that he feels from his *bhakta's* love, it starts to be reflected in the heart of the devotee and become even greater. It is an autocatalytic reaction that takes place between them, the reaction of love.

This is the spiritual picture that *Śrīmad-Bhāgavatam* describes, and there is no question of time whatsoever, because when it is experienced, time is unnoticed. When someone says he can look at the same picture for forty years, it means that he is aware that time is passing by. One thing that distinguishes *rasa* from wordly *rasa* is that there is no question of time.

You can love eternally, because you are never bored with love; it is ever fresh and always burning in your heart; it is always reflected in a new way; and always brings new surprises. Those who enter into these pastimes of Kṛṣṇa in Vṛndāvana and due to their *sādhana* gain access to these pastimes, see new pastimes that no one else has described.

Visvanatha Cakravarti Ṭhākura describes pastimes that are not found anywhere else, neither in *Śrīmad-Bhāgavatam* nor in any other *Purāṇa*. There have been, and there still are, those who, by entering these pastimes, can see them. Rūpa Gosvāmī and Sanātana Gosvāmī were in these pastimes or in this *rasa*.

There's another aspect of *rasa* that we should now understand. The characteristic of worldly *rasa* is that *rasa* or the aesthetic bliss is pleasing even when the emotion someone feels is so-called negative. It is an amazing law of *rasa*. In tragedies like *Hamlet*, for example, the Western scholars tried to give some explanation to the emotions felt. They introduced the concept of catharsis when a person going through a tragedy feels purification of the heart. In fact, this understanding of catharsis is the dawn of the understanding of *rasa* or the aesthetic sense.

So the characteristic of *rasa* is that even if the emotion is negative, it still makes us blissful; I feel grief together with the characters of the play or the singer who sings about how his girlfriend left him, but that grief makes me feel bliss.

Now the difference between that material *rasa* and spiritual *bhakti* as *rasa* (Rūpa Gosvāmī describes *bhakti* as *rasa*, taught by Svarūpa Dāmodara Gosvāmī) is that with the spiritual we are not talking about a spectacle. We are not the spectators of the relationship between Kṛṣṇa and his devotee. We enter these relationships and we feel these emotions, and these emotions are called *rasa*, because the object of my emotions is *rasa* itself.

Taittirīya Upaniṣad (2.7.1) defines God as *raso vai saḥ* – he is *rasa* or pure emotion. Kṛṣṇa is *rasa* and *rasa* is impossible to be translated in any way or by any words; it is not just a taste or emotion or anything else. *Rasa* is *rasa*. *Rasa* is a special state that we must clearly understand. Kṛṣṇa is a fountain of *rasa*. He is *akhila-rasāmṛta-mūrti*. He is the infinite source of all kinds of *rasas* and all kinds of relationships. He is constantly inviting us to love, and Kṛṣṇa becomes the object of our love. The love that we feel at some point turns into *rasa*. In its early stages it is called *bhāva* or simply a feeling, but when the relationship becomes real, when Kṛṣṇa becomes the real object of our love, it transforms into *rasa*.

Spiritual *rasa* is always beautiful and always blissful for one simple reason. Even in worldly relationships when we experience love in the material world, that love is always fraught with either fear or other negative emotions because the object of our love is material, and the relationship can hurt. In the material world, love is always defiled. Śrīla Prabhupāda said that the purest manifestation of love in the material world is a mother's love for her child. But in the material world love is not always blissful because the child is not always blissful. When the child is suffering, the mother suffers, even more than her child. Therefore, material love always contains this duality between love and suffering. But when we love Kṛṣṇa, he feels happiness. Kṛṣṇa is always happy, even when he is crying and saying, "Why have you abandoned me?" He is happy all the same. Therefore when we love him, our love is always blissful. Kṛṣṇa is always *rasa*. Kṛṣṇa himself is *rasa*. Just like the nature of *rasa*, the nature of the aesthetic sense is always bliss. Kṛṣṇa is *raso vai saḥ*; he is the pure sense of eternal bliss. And when we fall in love with him, our feeling is *always* blissful. Only love for Kṛṣṇa can make a person truly happy, and this love is attainable thanks to Rūpa Gosvāmī.

We must understand literally that Caitanya Mahāprabhu *gave* us *prema*. For example, if a piece of wood fell into the Ganges, it would end up sooner or later in the ocean, even if for some time it became stranded on the bank, thinking, "How nice it was when I was floating in the Ganges, but for the time being I will take some rest on the bank."

Sometimes, people think "I've had enough of devotional service; that's it for this lifetime." But Lord Caitanya has already given *prema* to all of us, like it or not, and sooner or later the Ganges will burst the banks and that piece of wood will be carried to the ocean. The piece of wood may shout again, "Enough, enough, I want to get to the shore again and dry out a little bit."

And the Ganga will say, "If you want to lie down a bit, you can." But then it will rise again, and sooner or later carry that wood to the ocean.

From the very beginning, by the mercy of Caitanya Mahāprabhu, we were given that *prema*. Sooner or later we will get it in full if we do what Rūpa Gosvāmī has explained to us. If we follow this path, we'll eventually reach the ocean of this *rasa*. Kṛṣṇa will then appear right before us, and at that moment our emotion, our *bhāva*, will develop into *rasa* and will become *prema* because *rasa* is a synonym of *prema*. The combination of these *rasas* turns into this feeling and this emotion.

It was Rūpa Gosvāmī who explained to us how to cultivate emotions. *Sādhana-bhakti* means that we imitate those who have love. They do everything that we do. And we do everything that they do. But we do everything that they do in order to become like them so that ultimately love awakens in our hearts. Rūpa Gosvāmī has given us this roadmap to the realm of spiritual emotions, which will turn into pure spiritual *rasa*, into pure spiritual love.

Rūpa Gosvāmī made use of the worldly *rasa* theory, the theory of aesthetic bliss or aesthetic pleasure that a person experiences contemplating some display of emotions.

He made use of this structure to explain the mystical experience of *bhakti*. He did not give a new definition of *bhakti*. *Bhakti* is *bhakti* and *bhakti* always has the nature of *rasa*. Kṛṣṇa is Kṛṣṇa and Kṛṣṇa is always *rasa*. The *Taittirīya Upaniṣad* (2.7.1) has declared since time immemorial: *raso vai saḥ* – Kṛṣṇa is pure *rasa*, pure bliss. Rūpa Gosvāmī made use of this structure to explain to us in what way we can approach the pure original *rasa*, the *ādi-rasa* that is Kṛṣṇa, as quickly as possible.

Rūpa Gosvāmī developed this structure so that we could attain this experience in the right way. There are people who, inspired by Lord Caitanya's example of extraordinary ecstatic love for Kṛṣṇa, try to imitate him. Of course, that is one way to try to experience it by throwing yourself into some kind of artificial emotional state – just go and start rolling on the floor or rub your eyes with an onion.

But this would be *dambha*, a manifestation of deception or pride, as discussed earlier in reference to the first verse of *Manaḥ-śikṣā*. We need a genuine experience, and Rūpa Gosvāmī has given us the structure through which we can attain true experience.

Soon after Lord Caitanya's departure, the tantrics who dressed in Vaiṣṇava attire, the *sahajiyā* sects, were trying to transfer their tantric experience into the sphere of love of God.

We have seen how easy it is to stumble in this very delicate, subtle sphere of spiritual experience and misinterpret our emotions. An example of this is the direct associates of Lord Caitanya. In Orissa (now Odisha), when Lord Caitanya resided in Purī, there were several devotees who were close to him. They are still the object of worship in Odisha, the so-called *pañca-sakhīs* or the five closest friends. If you go to Odisha, the cult of these *pañca-sakhīs* is very prominent in Jagannātha Purī. From our point of view, these five people were *sahajiyās* of the lower sort. We do not hold them in high regard, although these people saw Lord Caitanya and touched him. They saw the tears streaming from his eyes, but they did not understand; they deviated and their experience turned into a cheap imitation that we, as orthodox Vaiṣṇavas, see as a pitiful imitation.

The difference between them and us consists of one thing only: that we follow in the footsteps of Rūpa Gosvāmī. Rūpa Gosvāmī described the yoga of emotions as a science. What is very important for us to understand is that although we strive for the manifestation of absolute spontaneous unrestrained love, in order to attain it we must submit to a strict discipline. We follow the path of yoga based on discipline and on a most profound rational philosophy – the philosophy describing the mystic experience in categories of reason.

This is the watershed that runs between the so-called mainstream of our movement of Lord Caitanya and the various sects, which are still appearing nowadays. Do not think that ISKCON will be an exception to the rule that many other religious movements have been spawning sects but we will remain absolutely united and non-sectarian. Sects are appearing as they have always done along with charismatic leaders, prophets and "*avatāras*" – even in ISKCON.

Rūpa Gosvāmī has come to prevent us from making this mistake, so it is imperative that we follow in his footsteps. When Raghunātha Dāsa Gosvāmī says, *svarūpaṁ śrī-rūpaṁ sa-gaṇam iha tasyāgrajam api; sa-gaṇam* means "all associates or followers of Svarūpa and Śrī Rūpa." We must remember not only Rūpa Gosvāmī but also any follower of Lord Caitanya who strictly follows in his footsteps.

Sa-gaṇam iha tasyāgrajam api is about all the devotees who are in one way or another connected with Lord Caitanya, starting with Svarūpa Dāmodara, Śrī Rūpa Gosvāmī, Sanātana Gosvāmī, and their closest associates. Raghunātha Dāsa Gosvāmī emphasizes that remembering them is the condition for attaining love and there is no other way to obtain love, except through them and by remembering them.

In the history of our *sampradāya*, there was an important event held in Kheturī, which was the first Gaura Pūrṇimā celebration, personally organized by Jāhnavā-mātā, Lord Nityānanda's wife. Narottama Dāsa, Śyāmananda Prabhu, and Śrīnivāsa Ācārya, who had come from Vṛndāvana to Bengal with the books written by the six Gosvāmīs of Vṛndāvana, also attended.

The purpose of this festival was, above all, to establish the doctrine developed by Rūpa Gosvāmī and Sanātana Gosvāmī in Vṛndāvana and bring it to Bengal, which at that time was flooded by a huge number of Vaiṣṇavas who followed various practices in various forms. The event took place approximately forty or fifty years after Lord Caitanya's departure, and by that time those who knew him personally had started to leave this world. As it happens, those who were inspired by his personality had become confused and began to speculate. The movement as a result began to disintegrate into small sects because there was no single strict doctrine.

The Gosvāmīs of Vṛndāvana created this doctrine, but it also had to be established. This act of establishment took place in Kheturī. The exact date of the festival is unknown, but what is known without doubt is that during the festival Lord Caitanya personally returned and danced with Lord Nityānanda. During the *kīrtana* the devotees suddenly saw that Lord Caitanya and Lord Nityānanda were dancing with them. In this way, they sanctified the festival and approved of everything that took place there. During this celebration, Narottama Dāsa Ṭhākura was the chief *kirtaneer.* The wife of Lord Nityānanda herself presided over it. Śrīnivāsa Ācārya, along with his disciples, helped coordinate the event. Narottama Dāsa Ṭhākura's stepbrother, who was the King of Kheturī, personally built accommodation for all the visiting Vaiṣṇavas who came from all over Bengal, and he also assisted with the organization.

Jāhnavā-mātā was the *ācārya* and is credited with the fact that she united the movement of Lord Caitanya, which had started to fall apart, channeling it again into a single direction. She had previously gone to Vṛndāvana where she studied from Jīva Gosvāmī personally the full conclusion of the Gauḍīya Vaiṣṇava doctrine. Thanks to Jāhnavā-mātā's extraordinary energy and influence – she had thousands and thousands of disciples – she gathered all the Vaiṣṇavas in Kheturī. Thousands of people came and danced and sang, officially "following in the footsteps of Rūpa Gosvāmī."

As a result of the Kheṭari festival, it was recognised that the immediate associates of Lord Caitanya directly received his mercy which they then transmitted. In the wake of the festival at Kheṭari, Narottama Dāsa Ṭhākura wrote a famous song – *Gaurāṅgera saṅgi-gaṇe, nitya-siddha kori māne* (*Sāvaraṇa-śrī-gaura-mahimā*). He says that one must consider all of Lord Caitanya's associates to be *nitya-siddhas,* and through these *nitya-siddhas* we are given the opportunity to return to the spiritual world.

It was then that the tradition of remembering the names of Vaiṣṇavas originated. In another of his songs, Narottama Dāsa Ṭhākura mentions several times that it is the dust of the Vaiṣṇavas' feet in which he bathes. He writes, "Chanting the names of Vaiṣṇavas is the source of my happiness." He writes that when he hears the names of Vaiṣṇavas he is overwhelmed with ecstasy.

The Vaiṣṇavas' names in our tradition are called *prātaḥ-smaraṇīyam* – that which must be remembered in the morning. In other words, when we rise early in the morning we must remember the names of the devotees of the Lord. We must remember: *svarūpaṁ śrī-rūpaṁ sa-gaṇam iha tasyāgrajam api*. We must remember Raghunātha Dāsa Gosvāmī, Lokanātha Dāsa, Narottama, Śyāmānanda, and Śrīnivāsa Ācārya. We must remember them all.

Imagine having woken up early in the morning and the first thing we think of is not the terrible dreams we were having, not the stomach ache, not anything else but *vaiṣṇava-nāma*: Svarūpa, Śrī Rūpa. When we wake up each morning, we can say: *svarūpaṁ śrī-rūpaṁ sa-gaṇam iha tasyāgrajam api*.

Raghunātha Dāsa Gosvāmī says here that remembering the names of Vaiṣṇavas is the condition for attaining love of God. When we remember the devotees, attachment to Kṛṣṇa appears in us by itself, because Vaiṣṇavas are eternally linked with God.

Now let us return to *rasa* and the theory of *rasa* and how the mystical experience of *rasa* comes. Rūpa Gosvāmī gives a definition of a *sādhaka* in *Bhakti-rasāmṛta-sindhuḥ* (2.1.276) in terms of the elements of *rasa* or mystical experience. He says that there are two kinds of devotees: *siddhas* (devotees who have attained perfection) and *sādhakas*.

utpanna-ratayaḥ samyaṅ nairvighnyam anupāgatāḥ
kṛṣṇa-sākṣāt-kṛtau yogyāḥ sādhakāḥ parikīrtitāḥ

Sādhakāḥ parikīrtitāḥ – a person is praised as a *sādhaka* if *utpanna-ratayaḥ samyak* – if he has fully awakened his love for Kṛṣṇa (*samyak* means completely). *Nairvighnyam anupāgatāḥ* – but there are still some obstacles on his way. *Vighnyam* – they are not yet fully destroyed. *Kṛṣṇa-sākṣāt-kṛtau yogyāḥ* – but still he is *yogyāḥ* (*yogyāḥ* means worthy). *Kṛṣṇa-sākṣāt-kṛtau* – to directly see Kṛṣṇa. Such a person is called a *sādhaka*.

In *Śrī Caitanya-caritāmṛta*, Kṛṣṇadāsa Kavirāja Gosvāmī says that the *svarūpa-lakṣaṇa* (essential definition, the essence) of *sādhana* is *śravaṇaṁ kīrtanam*. *Śravaṇādi* – everything that we do is inspired by hearing, and everything that is triggered by our hearing about Kṛṣṇa is *sādhana*.

Now, he says that the *taṭastha-lakṣaṇa* (secondary characteristic) of *sādhana* is that it gives *prema*. Why is the main feature of *sādhana śravaṇaṁ kīrtanam*, and the secondary characteristic is that it gives *prema*? It is the main feature because the essence of *sādhana* is to hear and glorify Kṛṣṇa. Why *prema* or attainment of *prema* is the secondary feature of *sādhana* is because it sometimes gives *prema* and sometimes it does not at that stage.

Rūpa Gosvāmī explains that as we perform *sādhana*, as we chant the holy names, we hear and preach. When we tell others about Kṛṣṇa, when we sing the holy names loudly: Hare Kṛṣṇa, Hare Kṛṣṇa, Kṛṣṇa Kṛṣṇa, Hare Hare/ Hare Rāma, Hare Rāma, Rāma Rāma, Hare Hare, our *bhāva* or attachment to Kṛṣṇa gradually deepens.

The essence of our practice is that the attachment that dawned at the very first moment of our start of devotional service in the form of *śraddhā* (faith) completely transformed our lives. The word *śraddhā* in Sanskrit comes from the word *śrad*, which means truth. It is said that one of the functions of the intellect, our *buddhi*, is the ability to recognize truth. In the Third Canto of *Śrīmad-Bhāgavatam* (3.26.30), Kapiladeva says that intelligence has a function called *niścaya*. *Niścaya* means that at a certain point I recognize the truth, but not by any logical process. I understand: this is truth. Obtaining *śraddhā* is when suddenly the veil is removed from our eyes, we realize that there is God, and we need no evidence whatsoever. We suddenly understand that he exists, because it just cannot be otherwise. Faith is precisely this feeling. It is not because there is some logical chain that has led me to this understanding or because somebody told me something, but simply because it cannot be otherwise. I can recognize God, I can see this truth inside, and I fully recognize God by my intelligence or *buddhi*.

When we obtain *śraddhā*, we are overwhelmed by an extraordinary exaltation that sometimes lasts for years. Recently someone wrote to me saying, "I have been chanting Hare Kṛṣṇa for two years and it seems that the *utsāha-mayī* (the first ecstasy) is not over yet. When will it be over?"

If a person tries to avoid offenses and serve the Vaiṣṇavas, this ecstasy or euphoria can last infinitely and ultimately will lead us all the way to *prema*. The entire path from the very beginning to the very end is infused with ecstasy, and we obtain a taste of this experience of ecstasy at the level of *śraddhā*. As we practice *śravaṇam* and *kīrtanam*, we must deepen this ecstasy, this *bhāva* towards Kṛṣṇa.

I received another letter that said, "When I met the devotees I became happy. I tried to understand why I became happy." This is the way the mind works. The intellect understands something and then the mind starts interpreting it asking why, how, and what is happening. The letter continued, "And at a certain point I realized that I have suddenly found the meaning of my existence, that previously everything was pointless."

This ecstasy comes because of the fact that God is in our lives, that he loves us, that he is a personality and wants our love and nothing else. He is not some evil despot who sends everyone to hell if they do not love him. This ecstasy can and must last and deepen in the course of our *sādhana*. Everything we do is only for the purpose of deepening this ecstasy. When this ecstasy reaches the stage of attachment, *āsakti*, or the stage of *bhāva*, it is called *sthāyi-bhāva*, and it becomes permanent.

At the level of *bhajana-kriyā* this ecstasy is sporadic; it is like a sinusoid (a curve having the form of a sine wave) – now it is here and the next moment it is gone. Moreover, most of this sinusoid is below zero. Sometimes the sinusoid wave elevates us somewhere, then again ... bang! This is called *aniṣṭhā-bhajana-kriyā*, or when we have no stability. When we reach stability, our *bhakti* is somewhere on the zero mark in the form of a flat line. It is a smooth zero *bhakti*, and now and then small explosions of ecstasy overwhelm us and again there is a flat line where we feel good, calm, and pure. At the level of *ruci* the ecstasy gets stronger and we slightly rise above zero. But at the level of *bhāva* or emotion, love for Kṛṣṇa, the ecstasy becomes a permanent *sthāyi-bhāva*.

Rūpa Gosvāmī explains how *sthāyi-bhāva* becomes manifest externally. *Sthāyi-bhāva* means permanent *bhāva* or permanent love for Kṛṣṇa and is the main component of *rasa*. At the level of *bhāva* there are, nevertheless, things to help this ecstasy manifests itself externally.

One of the elements of *rasa*, when *sthāyi-bhāva* turns into *rasa*, is *vibhāva*. Rūpa Gosvāmī explains that *vibhāva* consists of three things: *viṣaya-ālambana, āśraya-ālambana,* and *uddīpana*. It is sometimes said that Kṛṣṇa is *uddīpana*; sometimes it is said that Kṛṣṇa is *viṣaya-ālambana*; and sometimes that Kṛṣṇa is *āśraya-ālambana*. It is also sometimes said that the devotees are *uddīpana*; sometimes *āśraya-ālambana*; and sometimes that the devotees are *viṣaya-ālambana*.

However, Rūpa Gosvāmī means a very simple thing: *āśraya* means one with whom love rests, *viṣaya* means object of love, and *uddīpana* means stimulus of love, something that reminds us of Kṛṣṇa. When we hear about Kṛṣṇa or see a picture of him as the object of love, or we hear a description of Kṛṣṇa as the object of love (as the *viṣaya*, the one who is loved), then love, or *rasa*, can awaken in us. When we hear how a devotee loves (*āśraya-ālambana* – the one who carries love within), then *rasa* can be awakened in us, too. When we hear of some things associated with Kṛṣṇa, they are incentives or *uddīpanas* that awaken love or the experience of *rasa*.

When Rūpa Gosvāmī says that there are two kinds of love carriers who are capable of generating the experience of *rasa* in our hearts, he means that a love carrier can be either a *siddha* or a *sādhaka*. We can either hear about how Lalitā and Viśākhā and Rūpa Mañjarī associate with Kṛṣṇa, or we can listen about how a *sādhaka* associates with Kṛṣṇa. By listening about the *sādhaka* we begin to experience *rasa*. When we hear how the *sādhaka* loves Kṛṣṇa, *rasa* is awakened in our hearts. Therefore Rūpa Gosvāmī says that a *sādhaka* has already reached the level where his love for Kṛṣṇa has become fully manifest and he is eligible to directly associate with Kṛṣṇa; however, at the same time there is some obstacle in his way. And when we hear how he overcomes those obstacles on his way to Kṛṣṇa, *rasa* appears in us. Our love for Kṛṣṇa, our *sthāyi-bhāva,* the dormant love for Kṛṣṇa, starts manifesting itself.

When we see what a devotee does out of love for Kṛṣṇa (a devotee who has reached the highest level of attachment and who is ready to see Kṛṣṇa), how he or she is overcoming the obstacles standing in his way, ready to sacrifice everything – when we remember this, attachment to Kṛṣṇa or the experience of *rasa* comes to us.

We thus understand another meaning of this verse when Raghunātha Dāsa Gosvāmī says, "Remember clearly Rūpa Gosvāmī." Because who is Rūpa Gosvāmī? Is he a *siddha* or a *sādhaka*? He is a *siddha* playing the role of a *sādhaka*. He is a *sādhaka-āveśa* – in the body of a *sādhaka*. He runs around Vṛndāvana and cries: *he rādhe vraja-devike ca lalite he nanda-sūno kutaḥ* (*Śrī Ṣaḍ-gosvāmy-aṣṭaka*, verse 8) Where are you? I cannot see you!

We think of Sanātana Gosvāmī and we think of the obstacles he had to overcome in order to come to Lord Caitanya, of Lord Caitanya seeing him and his expensive *cādar,* of the Lord telling him, "Give away this expensive blanket," of how he nearly got killed in an inn by the owner, and how Husain Shah sent him to prison. We read about this and see how love manifests itself in the pure devotees.

When Rūpa Gosvāmī explains *āśraya-ālambana,* he explains how a pure devotee loves Kṛṣṇa and how he responds to him. Śrīla Prabhupāda's love for Kṛṣṇa manifested in his renunciation of everything, including his wife, and going out to preach; in the fact that he carried the order of his spiritual master in his heart throughout his life and that the order of his spiritual master was the thread upon which Śrīla Prabhupāda's entire life was strung. That was the manifestation of his love for Kṛṣṇa. What should happen in our hearts when this inspires us? Love for Kṛṣṇa should come – an experience of *rasa* should appear.

Raghunātha Dāsa Gosvāmī says, "O mind, if you want to attain attachment to Kṛṣṇa, then constantly remember." He says to remember the *sādhaka* devotees who have spent all their lives in Vṛndāvana and who were willing to go through anything for the quest of God. Remember Śrī Rūpa, Svarūpa, and Sanātana Gosvāmī who have given up everything in order to come to God; and all the other devotees who can generate in our hearts that same attachment and cause tears to come to our eyes.

COMMENTARY BY ŪRMILĀ DEVĪ DĀSĪ

Raghunātha Dāsa Gosvāmī gets even more detailed in verse three about whom this book is meant for, namely those who follow Svarūpa Dāmodara and Rūpa Gosvāmīs. In *Caitanya-caritāmṛta, Madhya-līlā* 19.20, we read about Rūpa Gosvāmī:

yaḥ prāg eva priya-guṇa-gaṇair gāḍha-baddho 'pi mukto
gehādhyāsād rasa iva paro mūrta evāpy amūrtaḥ
premālāpair dṛḍhatara-pariṣvaṅga-raṅgaiḥ prayāge
taṁ śrī-rūpaṁ samam anupamenānujagrāha devaḥ

> From the very beginning, Śrīla Rūpa Gosvāmī was deeply attracted by the transcendental qualities of Śrī Caitanya Mahāprabhu. Thus he was permanently relieved from family life. Śrīla Rūpa Gosvāmī and his younger brother, Vallabha, were blessed by Śrī Caitanya Mahāprabhu. Although the Lord was transcendentally situated in his transcendental eternal form, at Prayāga he told Rūpa Gosvāmī about transcendental ecstatic love of Kṛṣṇa. The Lord then embraced him very fondly and bestowed all his mercy upon him.

Svarūpa Dāmodara Gosvāmī's mood and position is explained in *Caitanya-caritāmṛta, Ādi-līlā*, chapter 4, text 105 as follows: *svarūpa-gosāñi – prabhura ati antaraṅga*, "Svarūpa Gosāñi is the most intimate associate of Lord Caitanaya." In text 109, it is stated: *rātre pralāpa kare svarūpera kaṇṭha dhari 'āveśe āpana bhāva kahaye ughāḍi*, indicating that Lord Caitanya spoke to Svarūpa Dāmodara in the evenings about his most ecstatic and esoteric feelings. Then, *yabe yei bhāva uṭhe prabhura antara, sei gīti-śloke sukha dena dāmodara* (text 110), explains that Svarūpa Dāmodara would reciprocate by singing songs or verses in the same mood. The fact that only he knows the deep conclusion of *rasa,* and anyone who says they also know certainly learned from him is given here: *atyanta-nigūḍha ei rasera siddhānta, svarūpa-gosāñi mātra jānena ekānta. yebā keha anya jāne, seho tāṅhā haite, caitanya-gosāñira teṅha atyanta marma yāte* (111–112).

Our following of Svarūpa Dāmodara and Rūpa Gosvāmīs is not just theoretical, in terms of intellectually accepting their philosophical conclusions. Nor does following them, in the context of *Manaḥ-śikṣā,* imply merely external adherence to the practices of *bhakti* under scriptural rules, *vaidhī-sādhana bhakti.* Raghunātha Dāsa Gosvāmī's use of *sa-rāgaṁ* in verse three indicates that the intended audience for these verses is a practitioner of *bhakti* for whom a particular, individual emotion of love towards Kṛṣṇa has awakened. Such a person is on the path of loving attachment, as a *rāgānuga-sādhaka.* Only such a person can fully use *Manaḥ-śikṣā* as a guidebook. However, *Manaḥ-śikṣā* is not forbidden to others, as it's not a description of intimate *līlās.* Therefore, those whose inner spiritual disposition has not yet awakened can certainly apply many of the principles Dāsa Gosvāmī gives, as well as gain some understanding of their goal.

Among the society of devotees of Kṛṣṇa, we often find three common misconceptions about *rāgānuga-sādhana bhakti.* The first is that all persons on this path will share the same specific mood of Rūpa Gosvāmī, namely being a *mañjarī-gopī* assistant to Śrīmatī Rādhārāṇī. The second misconception is that an awakening of one's inner, eternal mood can only occur at a state of perfection or complete purity, at *prema* or *bhāva.* The third is regarding the way in which a person comes to understand his or her particular inner mood.

Regarding the first misconception, Bhaktivinoda quotes *Bhakti-rasāmṛta-sindhuḥ* 1.2.292 in his commentary to verse three. In *Caitanya-caritāmṛta* (*Madhya-līlā* 22.155), Śrīla Prabhupāda translates this verse as follows:

> When an advanced, realized devotee hears about the affairs of the devotees of Vṛndāvana – in the mellows of *śānta, dāsya, sakhya, vātsalya and mādhurya* – he becomes inclined in one of these ways, and his intelligence becomes attracted. Indeed, he begins to covet

> that particular type of devotion. When such covetousness is awakened, one's intelligence no longer depends on the instructions of *śāstra* [revealed scripture] or on logic and argument.

A practitioner will naturally feel attracted to one of the five primary relationships with Kṛṣṇa – servant, friend, parental/superior, or amorous. Undoubtedly the instructions in *Manaḥ-śikṣā* lean towards those who awaken to a desire to serve as Rādhā's *mañjarī-gopīs*, perhaps including those whose mood is as Rādhā's *sakhī-gopīs*. Readers whose inner mood is different will use Raghunātha Dāsa Gosvāmī's instructions as a template for their own mood.

Regarding the second misconception, a simple look at Sanskrit should dispel it. The person practicing *rāgānuga-sādhana-bhaki* must be a *sādhaka*. These terms directly tell us the path of *rāgānuga* starts before attaining the *sādhyā*, or goals, of *bhāva* and *prema*. In *Bhakti-rasāmṛta-sindhuḥ* 1.2.292–293, both of which Bhaktivinoda Ṭhākura quote in his commentary on the third verse, *rāgānuga* and *vaidhī-bhakti* are contrasted. In the former, reliance on scriptural rules for impetus diminishes as soon as a practitioner has genuine attraction for a particular mood of love. In the latter, reliance on scriptural rules for impetus continues until at least the stage of *bhāva*. Clearly, *rāgānuga-sādhana-bhaki* starts before *bhāva*.

Additional evidence is that here in *Manaḥ-śikṣā*, after verse three with the word *rāga*, there are four verses (four through seven) where the practitioner gets free of a number of progressively subtle forms of contamination. Also, those on the path of *rāgānuga* are enjoined to engage in ever-increasing meditation in terms of scope and concentration as explained in Bhaktivinoda's commentary to verse eleven.

Someone may argue that particularly Śrīla Prabhupāda and Śrīla Bhaktisiddhānta warned that the awakening of one's eternal specific position happens only to those who are liberated. It is true that both of these *ācāryas* have made strong general statements to that effect. At the same time, both of them, following Svarūpa Dāmodara and Rūpa Gosvāmīs, consistently present *rāgānuga* as a *sādhana* done by *sādhakas*. Therefore, the purity that almost always is necessary for an awakening is not absolute. In this connection, Śrīla Prabhupāda defines the stage for the eligibility for *rāgānuga-sādhana* in *Nectar of Devotion*, chapter 16: "In following the regulative principles of devotional service, there is a stage called *anartha-nivṛtti*, which means the disappearance of all material contamination." *Anartha-nivṛtti* is a stage in the middle of practice; it is not a stage of perfection. From the point of view of a gross materialist, such persons are liberated and free from all material desires. From the point of view of the eternally perfected *rāgātmikā-bhaktas*, such persons are in a gradual process of awakening and still harbor some subtle *anarthas*. Therefore, in the same chapter of *Nectar of Devotion* Śrīla Prabhupāda writes of the *rāgānuga-sādhakas*: "By spontaneous nature they become attracted to some of the eternal devotees such as Nanda or Yaśodā, and they try to follow in their footsteps spontaneously. There is a gradual development of the ambition to become like a particular devotee, and this activity is called *rāgānugā*." We note the word *gradual* in Prabhupāda's statement.

The third misconception concerns how a person comes to know what is his or her eternal inclination. The following verse from *Bhakti-rasāmṛta-sindhuḥ* (1.2.2) gives an indication:

kṛti-sādhyā bhavet sādhya-
bhāvā sā sādhanābhidhā
nitya-siddhasya bhāvasya
prākaṭyaṁ hṛdi sādhyatā

Each of us already has an eternal individual relationship with Kṛṣṇa and his eternal associates. That relationship is of the nature of desire and emotion much more than intellect. Therefore, it is the desire and emotion that must awaken. That awakening is natural, spontaneous, and due to mercy. It may happen while hearing or reading Kṛṣṇa's *līlā*, as Śrīla Prabhupāda explains in his purport to *Caitanya-caritāmṛta, Ādi-līlā* 4.34: "Special natural appreciation of the descriptions of a particular pastime of Godhead indicates the constitutional position of a living entity." It may happen while chanting in *kīrtana* or *japa*. It may happen while serving the Deity. There is no absolute formula, and each individual is different. For everyone, however, an authentic experience will be undeniable and persistent. An authentic awakening is also always within the boundaries of *sādhu-śāstra-guru*, free from improper mixing of mellows. Furthermore, the person who has an authentic awakening feels unqualified for such revelation. The irony is that those who feel qualified are thus disqualified!

Regarding inauthentic attempts to awaken one's identity, no one should intellectually decide after reading something in the *śāstras* or commentaries, "Oh, I think I would like to be such-and such," and then take such a decision as something serious. No. Nor can one person so-called assign an identity to someone else. Such assignments have no meaning. Nor should anyone so-called choose an identity because of thinking a particular service to be higher or lower based on *śāstric* glorifications. Such apparent distinctions are not material. Everyone's inherent personality is perfect and the highest for that person. In fact, artificially assuming a spiritual identity greatly hinders the authentic identity from revealing itself.

According to verses one through three, those who are qualified practitioners have at least a general idea of their particular inherent disposition towards service. Full revelation awaits relinquishing the progressively deeper and more elusive, hidden material attachments outlined metaphorically in the next four verses.

VERSE FOUR

asad-vārtā-veśyā visṛja mati-sarvasva-haraṇīḥ
kathā mukti-vyāghryā na śṛṇu kila sarvātma-gilanīḥ
api tyaktvā lakṣmī-pati-ratim ito vyoma-nayanīṁ
vraje rādhā-kṛṣṇau sva-rati-maṇidau tvaṁ bhaja manaḥ

O mind, abandon the prostitute of mundane talks, who plunders all intelligence. Do not listen at all to the stories of the tigress named *mukti* (liberation), who devours all souls. Moreover, also give up attachment to the husband of Lakṣmī, Śrī Nārāyaṇa, who only leads one to Vaikuṇṭha. Instead, here in Vraja, serve Śrī Śrī Rādha-Kṛṣṇa, who give one the jewel of their own love.

COMMENTARY BY ŚIVARĀMA SWAMI

The first three verses are in a sense the introduction to *Manaḥ-śikṣā,* and the following five verses deal with the practical methodology for advancing in spiritual life in Kṛṣṇa consciousness, rising to the realm of spontaneous devotional service and appreciation of the Lord. Raghunātha Dāsa Gosvāmī speaks in these verses about different obstacles which arise in devotional service. These obstacles are of an internal nature in terms of *anarthas,* external nature in terms of bad habits, and those imposed by the forest of material energy upon the living entities. How are these obstacles overcome? That answer is of great importance in our achieving our particular goal and destination. Verse four specifically relates to the gross obstacles, external obstacles, which impede the cultivation or practice of sublime transcendental love for Śrī Śrī Rādhā and Kṛṣṇa.

We discussed in the commentary for verse one how Raghunātha Dāsa Gosvāmī says *dambhaṁ hitvā* (to get rid of pride). We have already touched on some different demons and obstacles which were destroyed by Lord Kṛṣṇa that relate to specific types of pride they represent in the aspiring devotee's progress in devotional service. Other related obstacles are also described by Raghunātha Dāsa Gosvāmī.

Part of our method for trying to purify these obstacles within our hearts is to remember the particular pastimes of Lord Kṛṣṇa killing these demons. To read them in *Kṛṣṇa* Book is a specific means to removing these *anarthas*.

Verse three deals with the question of who is eligible to achieve the perfectional stage of worshiping Rādhā and Kṛṣṇa in Vṛndāvana. But we may be very far away from that, so the question that arises here in verse four is how to achieve that eligibility. Even though we try, we see there are practical difficulties, obstacles. If we don't have guidance from *ācāryas* then we will have to find out what the obstacles are ourselves by trial and error, rather than have them pointed out to us. Even if we know what they are, we will not be able to overcome them simply by our own effort. We need guidance and direction. So Raghunātha Dāsa Gosvāmī and Bhaktivinoda Ṭhākura both explain in detail what these obstacles are, what their effects are, and how to remove them.

In this particular verse, we will also come across a concept which is not new, and should not be clarified specifically as being an *anartha*, but is a particular path which Gauḍīya Vaiṣṇavas do not walk down. That path is *lakṣmī-pati-ratim ito vyoma-nayanīṁ*, or service and association with Lord Nārāyaṇa in the Vaikuṇṭha planet. There are many incarnations of Godhead, many forms of the Supreme Lord, and ultimately Vaiṣṇavas have to choose a particular Deity, *iṣṭa-deva*, whom they eternally serve. Raghunātha Dāsa Gosvāmī is giving his opinion of what one's direction and aspiration has to be. Therefore, he always repeats the same thing, *vraje-rādhā-kṛṣṇa*. Throughout the book we will always see that he mentions these three words: Vraja, Rādhā, and Kṛṣṇa. He never simply talks about just Kṛṣṇa being the goal, nor does he simply say only Rādhā and Kṛṣṇa are the goal, but he always qualifies, Rādhā and Kṛṣṇa in Vṛndāvana.

So what are the obstacles being discussed? The first is *asat-vārtā*, or speaking with non-devotees. *Vārtā* means speaking. *Sat* means truth, so *asat* means those who are against the truth. *Asat* means *asādhu*. *Sādhu* means pure devotees or those who are aspiring to know the Absolute Truth. *Asat* are those who embody just the opposite. *Kathā, gramya-kathā,* idle talk is the second one. *Mukti* or impersonal liberation, the desire for merging into the Brahman effulgence, or into the body of the Supreme Lord, or the other types of liberation, is the third one. The fourth is *lakṣmī-pati-ratim*, love for Lord Nārāyaṇa.

Obviously the first one, *asad-varta*, is an obstacle. In *Caitanya-caritāmṛta*, Mahāprabhu explains the essential feature and characteristic of a Vaiṣṇava, how to recognize a Vaiṣṇava, as *asat-saṅga-tyāga, ei vaiṣṇava-ācāra. Vaiṣṇava-ācāra*, or Vaiṣṇava behavior, is *asat-saṅga-tyāga*. A Vaiṣṇava rejects the association of the *asat*.

Let us examine the nature of this *saṅga*. The principle of enjoying in this material world is the characteristic of the *asat*. They see this temporary material world as their home and within it so many different things which they have many plans to enjoy. When one associates with such people one will become like them. There is one nice verse here which Bhaktivinoda Ṭhākura quotes in this connection from the *Hari-bhakti-sudhodaya*. Believe it or not, the quote is from Śrīmān Hiraṇyakaśipu, who says to Prahlāda Mahārāja, "Just as a transparent crystal takes on the colors of nearby objects, the association of a person determines one's qualities. Therefore, the intelligent take shelter in like-minded, similarly practicing groups for the sake of bringing auspiciousness and prosperity to their group." Of course, he is talking about the high class materialist, atheists like himself, but the point is also applicable in the spiritual way. Like a crystal, whatever you hold it near it automatically reflects. So it's a very nice analogy. Association is like that. If you associate with a thief you become a thief. If you associate with saints, you will become a saint. If we associate with pseudo-spiritualists, materialists, Māyāvādīs, or enjoyers of sense gratification, we will certainly become influenced by them. Therefore a devotee does not live with non-devotees, because these people encourage the acquisition of wealth and association of women, and such encouragement will simply destroy our aspiration for spiritual life. Śrīla Bhaktivinoda Ṭhākura says that two things will be lost. It is stated here, *asad-vārtā-veśyā visṛja mati-sarvasva-haraṇīḥ. Sarvasva* means treasure, and *mati*, refers to the heart. So, in our heart there is a treasure. What is that treasure? It's that little desire there for advancing in spiritual life. We have a little *śraddhā*. We began with a little faith, and even from the very beginning of Kṛṣṇa consciousness, there is some *rati*, there is some love. We feel some *ānanda*, some pleasure from practicing Kṛṣṇa consciousness. There is some attachment to the Deity and devotees. These are very valuable things that have to be protected, but if we don't protect them, then *haraṇīḥ*, they will be stolen.

How will this wealth be lost? Bhaktivinoda Ṭhākura says it is two things: first one's knowledge becomes covered, and then one loses one's resolve – or in the advanced stage, one's greed, *lobha*. Such greed is not for material things but is greed for achieving one's destination in spiritual life. The example in this verse is *asad-vārtā-veśyā*. *Veśyā* means prostitute. The example is a prostitute apparently shows so much love and affection for some customer. She relieves him of all his money and then he is finished. His money is gone and the pleasure is over. It's all finished. Similarly the association of these people relieves us of the treasure of our hard-earned devotional service. The word treasure implies something very valuable that we want to protect. So even though this treasure is in our hearts, by the wrong association we will lose it. We should be very careful.

The next thing is *kathā, gramya-kathā*. Caitanya Mahāprabhu gave this instruction to Svarūpa Dāmodara:

grāmya-kathā nā śunibe kāne
grāmya-vārtā nā kahibe

The first instruction he gave is, "Do not talk like people in general or hear what they say." And in this fourth verse of *Manaḥ-śikṣā* it is stated *kathā vyāghryā*. Raghunātha Dāsa Gosvāmī uses the word, *kathā*, with *mukti*, which is very interesting. They are both side by side, *kathā mukti-vyāghryā na śṛṇu kila sarvātma-gilanīḥ*. *Vyāghryā* is a tigress. All devotees know how seriously detrimental *mukti* is, or the desire for impersonal liberation. Caitanya Mahāprabhu says *māyāvādī kṛṣṇe aparādhī*, that Māyāvādīs are offenders to Lord Kṛṣṇa. It is stated in *Caitanya-caritāmṛta* that even a *mahā-bhāgavata* will fall down by associating with Māyāvādīs. So we all know what a horrible thing the desire for impersonal liberation is, and we are trained, but we don't have a real appreciation of how serious *grāmya-kathā* is.

But here Raghunātha Dāsa Gosvāmī emphasizes by putting the two side by side: *kathā mukti-vyāghryā, mukti* is like a tigress. A tigress is a very fierce animal, because she is desperate to get some food for her cubs. So tigress means a fierce animal, a relentless, ruthless animal. The male tiger is a little more laid back. He just has to feed himself, but the female also has to feed her cubs. Therefore she doesn't spare anyone. So Māyāvāda philosophy is like that. It will destroy one's devotion even at an advanced level. But this *gramya-kathā* is in the same category, this talking about frivolous things, and hearing about these things. Ultimately by this type of hearing and talking one ends up not only talking about mundane subjects but begins to talk unnecessarily about Vaiṣṇavas, and the result is that one speaks and hears *vaiṣṇava-aparādha*. Raghunātha Dāsa Gosvāmī says, *na śṛṇu* — don't hear these things. Both *anarthas* are committed through the process of hearing, Māyāvāda philosophy and *gramya-kathā*. So he says, *na śṛṇu sarvātma. Sarvātma,* everyone give it up, or it will devour you. He uses *sarvātma,* meaning every person. We might think, "Oh! That's all right. It's not so dangerous for me." But Raghunātha Dāsa Gosvāmī is saying, yes it is: *sarvātma-gilanīḥ*. This tigress will devour. One should be very careful, otherwise the effect will be that these talks and desires will destroy our greed for devotional service.

The desire for impersonal liberation, or *mukti,* is *kṛṣṇa-aparādha*. Māyāvāda philosophy is offensive to Kṛṣṇa. Every devotee should be familiar with the basic elements of Māyāvāda philosophy. They are extensively described in practically all of Śrīla Prabhupāda's books and purports. But Bhaktivinoda Ṭhākura emphasizes that this philosophy makes the heart very hard. In *Bhakti-rasāmṛta-sindhuḥ,* Śrīla Rūpa Gosvāmī talks about the condition of a devotee's heart. He explains that some people have hearts that are very noble like gold, others are considered to be soft like shellac, and others are like honey, which is already molten. So the condition of the heart, especially of a Vaiṣṇava heart, should be very soft. This is practically one of the first characteristics Śrīla Prabhupāda talks about in *Bhagavad-gītā,* that Arjuna feels compassion because he is soft hearted, because a Vaiṣṇava is by nature soft hearted. But even if a soft hearted Vaiṣṇava hears Māyāvāda philosophy then his heart will become hard. Why? Because Māyāvāda philosophy is offensive, and by *aparādha* the heart becomes hard.

Māyāvāda philosophy makes one callous because there is no longer any ability for loving exchanges when everything is all *kevala-advaita*. Everything is one. There is no lover and there is no beloved, but it's all one, and there is no exchange. So, one becomes very hard hearted. The result is that a hard heart makes devotional service impossible to blossom. Some seed is there, the *bhakti-latā-bīja*, but it will be stunted or destroyed. Therefore *gilanīḥ* means devour. This Māyāvāda philosophy devours, just like a tigress devours some little deer or rabbit, some innocent little thing.

For the next obstacle, Raghunātha Dāsa Gosvāmī makes another very radical statement and appeal, *tyaktvā*, meaning you should also reject. What should we reject? It is *lakṣmī-pati-ratim*, love for Lord Nārāyaṇa. Lakṣmī-pati, the husband of Lakṣmī. He says you should also reject this love for Lord Nārāyaṇa *iti*, here, *vyoma-nayanīm*, in Vaikuṇṭha. So why does he says to reject it? Is it something bad? Of course love for Lord Nārāyaṇa is not bad. However, although Lord Nārāyaṇa is non-different than Lord Kṛṣṇa, still the manifestation of the qualities of the Personality of Godhead are only partially revealed through Lord Nārāyaṇa, only ninety-six percent. Specifically the most important attributes of Lord Kṛṣṇa, that last four per cent, are his extraordinary pastimes such as the *rāsa-līlā*, his playing of the flute, his extraordinary beauty, and his unique loving exchanges with devotees. These are not present in Lord Nārāyaṇa. You never see a picture of Lord Nārāyaṇa playing a flute. You never see Lord Nārāyaṇa on the lap of his mother. Any relationship with him is a formal relationship with the Supreme Personality of Godhead. Therefore intimacy is missing, and there is an absence of the sweetness which is present in Vraja, and in the relationship of worshiping and serving Rādhā and Kṛṣṇa.

Those who are followers of Gauḍīya Vaiṣṇava *sampradāyas* are generally in the mood that they do not worship Lord Nārāyaṇa nor any other incarnation, plenary incarnation, or any other expansion of Lord Kṛṣṇa. Simply Kṛṣṇa is their only goal. They have no other goal or object of their love. There are some counter-examples. For instance Rūpa Gosvāmī's brother, Anupama, was a worshiper of Lord Rāmacandra, and he simply could not divert his mind from Lord Rāma, although both Rūpa and Sanātana tried to get him to do so. A similar example is of Murāri Gupta, but these are rare exceptions. Gopal Bhaṭṭa Gosvāmī and his uncle, Prabhodhānanda Sarasvatī Ṭhākura, as well as their whole family, were worshipers of Lord Nārāyaṇa. Caitanya Mahāprabhu converted them into worshipers of Kṛṣṇa.

So *sva-rati* is the jewel that we want to have. What is that? *Vraje rādhā-kṛṣṇau sva-rati-maṇi-dau tvaṁ bhaja manaḥ*: that we should worship Rādhā and Kṛṣṇa. Why? Because here it is stated so nicely that they are two philanthropists who give away the jewel of pure love. Rādhā and Kṛṣṇa are distributing this jewel. Awe and reverence for Lord Nārāyaṇa is an obstacle to spontaneous pure love for Lord Kṛṣṇa, to *rāgānugā-bhakti* and ultimately *rāgātmikā-bhakti,* which is the abode of the highest *rasa.*

Bhaktivinoda Ṭhākura explains the *brahma-vimohana-līlā* where Lord Brahmā's bewilderment actually represents the misconception that one should favor *aiśvarya,* or opulence, over *mādhurya.* So by hearing this pastime one will also become free from such a misconception.

COMMENTARY BY ŚACĪNANDANA SWAMI

The mind is a storehouse of so many pollutants, and these contaminations are stirred by *prajalpa* or *asad-vārtā-veśyā* – nonsense topics that are like prostitutes. Prostitutes pretend a loving excitement, but they are really after the man's wealth. That is their motive; they want money. They don't want the person, and they don't want the relationship. So all of us devotees have a wealth, which is our inclination and determination to engage in devotional service. Then why invite a prostitute in our lives by talking *prajalpa*? This nonsense talk will steal our inclination and determination to serve Kṛṣṇa.

The type of *prajalpa* that is the most effective to steal our determination to engage in devotional service is to criticize others. This is the luxury prostitute, the really expensive one, because she steals everything. When we criticize devotees or when we talk so bitterly or gossip about this one or that one's fall down, after some time, we think, "Oh, Kṛṣṇa consciousness doesn't work." We feel less inclined to sit down and chant Hare Kṛṣṇa. That's the negative energy *prajalpa* creates.

What else is *asat-vārtā* or *prajalpa*? Bhaktivinoda Ṭhākura says it's discussions of temporary things, while Śrīdhara Svāmī says it's village religion. When we have close association with illicit sexual partners, or TV, radio, films, magazines, and newspapers, or mundane songs, they certainly all fill our consciousness so that we forget Kṛṣṇa. But the worst *prajalpa* is describing the faults of others. That's the worst, because that is the most determined prostitute.

I know that a lot of devotees go to movies and look at magazines and newspapers, and so on. This is too much and it pulls our consciousness down. It is very important to reduce non-devotional literature, outside movies, and other mundane entertainment. They leave permanent impressions in the consciousness if one is not careful. There are some movies, for example, that do explain a point in a good way, but each person knows exactly when it gets too much and one's consciousness suffers, and there is remembrance of movies instead of Vraja *bhakti*.

Those who have taken *brahmacārī* vows of celibacy and renunciation should not look at mundane movies at all. But, those who are in other directions may want to see if there is something that helps in understanding and, in the spirit of *yukta-vairāgya*, can be used in service. But be careful. You are playing with fire, and some unfavorable impressions might enter your mind. As a result of this activity, you might remember the wrong things and not the right things.

This whole verse four is giving a list of the wrong things that will prevent us from developing Vraja *bhakti*. We need to provide the proper culture so that our plant of *bhakti* can grow. *Manaḥ-śikṣā*, or the instructions to the mind, is all about this one point, to provide the proper earth, which has the right elements in it so that our own *bhakti* plant can grow very nicely.

COMMENTARY BY BHAKTIVIJNANA GOSWAMI

ATTACHMENT THROUGH MERCY

Raghunātha Dāsa Gosvāmī ends verse 4 with a similar instruction to that he has given in other verses: *vraje rādhā-kṛṣṇau sva-rati-maṇi-dau tvaṁ bhaja manaḥ* – O mind! Worship Rādhā and Kṛṣṇa." But this time he explains why we should worship Rādhā and Kṛṣṇa. He says, "Rādhā and Kṛṣṇa give us something very important: *sva-rati-dau.*" *Dau* means give. They give us attachment to themselves – *sva-rati-dau.*

In the *Bhagavad-gītā,* Kṛṣṇa explains in great detail that all our problems arise from our indifference, our lack of attachment, to God. Jīva Gosvāmī also, at the beginning of the *Bhakti-sandarbha,* says, "All our problems begin from the fact that a person turns away from God."

The majority of people fall into this category, not caring whether God exists or not. What they care about is what happens to themselves. We turn away from God, often saying, "I do not care whether God exists or not." We may not even be atheists, but sometimes it is better to be militant atheists, like Kaṁsa or Hiraṇyakaśipu, than be merely indifferent. From reading *Śrīmad-Bhāgavatam,* as well as from our own life experiences, we can understand that our main problem is that we have no attachment to Kṛṣṇa, and as a result we are wandering unhappily in this material world.

So again, in this instruction to his mind, Raghunātha Dāsa Gosvāmī says: *vraje rādhā-kṛṣṇau sva-rati-maṇi-dau tvaṁ bhaja manaḥ* – "O mind, worship Rādhā and Kṛṣṇa in Vraja, because they can give *maṇi.*" *Maṇi* means a gem, a jewel, treasure. He says, "To solve all your problems you need attachment to Rādhā and Kṛṣṇa" This cannot be obtained by some artificial means or by force, but only bestowed upon us by mercy. Therefore, "Worship Rādhā and Krsna in the hope that someday they will give you this attachment."

We must understand that the path of *bhakti* is one of mercy; it cannot be taken by force or achieved by our own efforts, but *bhakti* is given to us by Kṛṣṇa. *Bhakti* is independent and on the level of God himself. Therefore *bhakti* is self-willed. God may either come to us or not. Similarly, *bhakti* will either come or not – but one way we can receive *bhakti* is by someone giving it to us.

Nevertheless, it does not mean that we should not do something ourselves to get *bhakti*. As a rule, people have a strange attitude, thinking that either I'm doing something completely myself, or this will be given to me completely by mercy. Actually, we like to say that *bhakti* should come by itself, by mercy, because then we can make the exuse that we don't have to do anything.

An example of this attitude is the Catholic Church and its Indulgences. When the Catholic Church was building St Peter's, it had to raise funds for it. Someone had the brilliant idea to accept donations in return for forgiving sins. It was the most brilliant technique for collecting donations that has ever been created. Accordingly, Indulgences appeared: you did not have to do or believe in anything; you just had to give some money to God's work and you would be saved.

Hence one of the most popular religions originated in the 16th century as the result of one honest monk called Luther, who resented this trading of Indulgences. When Luther saw this hypocrisy and abuse of religion, he was inwardly outraged. He hung a memorandum on the wall of a cathedral saying that a person is saved not by deeds but by faith alone. His statement was made in an honest way and with good intentions. He wanted to stop the abuse where people were told, "Just do something, and you will be saved." As a result, the Church declared him a heretic.

For the Indulgences you had to at least pay some money. Now with Luther you don't have to do anything. Declare, "I believe" – and that's it! People have carried this idea of mercy to the point of absurdity. When people are told that everything comes only by God's mercy and that they just have to believe, they immediately say, "Everything's fine with me. I have already believed and now I will just wait for the mercy."

But the point is that a person should wait for the mercy and simultaneously do everything they can. People cannot understand this point because they think that if I wait for mercy and rely on God, then why should I do anything else? If we are on the ocean in a fragile boat and there is a storm raging should we just pray? We must pray and simultaneously row because God helps those who help themselves. Mercy is the source of everything, but this does not mean that we should not make any effort.

MUNDANE TOPICS

In this verse, Raghunātha Dāsa Gosvāmī explains that we should act so that this precious jewel, the treasure of the attachment to Rādhā and Kṛṣṇa, comes to us. The first most important instruction for action that he gives in this verse is: *asad-vārtā-veśyā visṛja mati-sarvasva-hariṇīḥ*. The first thing a person should do is to get rid of *asad-vārtā-veśyā visṛja mati-sarvasva-hariṇīḥ*. *Asat* means temporary or unreal. It also means illusory, non-existent, without true substance. Thus *asat* is something that does not exist in reality. *Vārtā* means news (a newspaper in Sanskrit is called *vārtāpatrika*). *Patrika* means a sheet where the news is shown. *Asat-vārtā* means unreal news, some things related to the material world. *Veśyā* means a prostitute, *asad-vārtā-veśyā visṛja*.

His first instruction, then, is that in order to attain this precious treasure of attachment to God – *asad-vārtā-veśyā visṛja* – I must turn away and leave this prostitute or woman of easy virtue who is *asad-vārtā-veśyā* because she steals, *hariṇīḥ*. Such women may rob their customers when they have relaxed and fallen asleep.

Raghunātha Dāsa Gosvāmī says, "What does the unreal news of this world do to us? It robs us of spiritual intelligence – *mati-sarvasva-hariṇīḥ*." *Mati* means "mind." He says, *asad-vārtā-veśyā visṛja mati-sarvasva-hariṇīḥ* – if you do not give this up, it will deprive you completely of your spiritual intelligence. Actually, we need to understand how this happens because if we do not understand, then we will sooner or later be deprived of our spiritual intelligence. We know that most prostitutes usually look attractive, and in the same way the news of this world is also attractive. When you open the newspaper or start watching TV, everything is so attractive. Our minds are drawn to it, but the news of this world is just like a prostitute who must first seduce the person. And how do prostitutes do that? They have special manners, they dress in a particular way, and they put on special make-up. But what is actually their essence? Their intention is to rob and turn their client into a pauper.

The story of Akbar and Birbal nicely illustrates this point. Akbar was a great Muslim emperor and Birbal was his advisor. Akbar once asked him, "I have heard from the Indian scriptures about Apsarās." (Apsarās are celestial courtesans, the most beautiful women in the universe.) "And it is also mentioned that there are witches." And Akbar said, "You can do anything, Birbal. Bring an Apsarā and a witch here to the palace. I want to see them."

Birbal thought and thought and finally found a way out. He took his wife and went to a prostitute. Then he told both of them, "Cover your face and your bodies entirely tomorrow when we are going to the courtroom, where the great Sultan sits."

Next day, Akbar, seated on his throne, asked, "Well, Birbal, have you brought me an Apsarā and a witch?"

He said, "Yes, I have, your Majesty. Here are the two of them."

The Sultan said, "Show me the Apsarā first. I want to have a look. It is always nice to see someone beautiful first."

Birbal went up and told his wife to remove her veil. The emperor saw an old wrinkled woman wearing ordinary clothes. He said, "This is an Apsarā? Who is this ugly old woman?"

Birbal said, "Your Majesty, this is an Apsarā. Believe it or not, she is my wife and is so chaste, so kind, and so affectionate. My wife takes such nice care of me like no Apsarā would ever be able to. She is a true Apsarā."

He said, "Okay, well, show me the witch now." He went up to the prostitute, removed her veil and saw a beautiful woman and then said, "Here is the real Apsarā! Whom did you show me before?"

Birbal said, "No, your Majesty, this is a witch, because as soon as you are left alone with her she will get her teeth into you and won't let you go until she has sucked all your blood."

Here Raghunātha Dāsa Gosvāmī says – *asad-vārtā-veśyā* – the news and events of this world, the things of this world, seem very attractive and we fall easy prey to them all.

An aspiring disciple came to me once and begged for forgiveness because he said that a woman had seduced him. At the same time, I could see that he very much liked the fact that he had been seduced. There wasn't a trace of remorse on his face, although he was saying, "Please forgive me; I could not resist."

We are so easily beguiled because we *want* to be. This desire for fleeting pleasures resides deeply in our hearts. We begin to justify ourselves in various ways. For example, the man who said that he had been seduced, then hopefully asked me, "Well, may I continue this relationship or not?" I told him no, to which he said, "What if I make her a devotee?"

This is how our mind works. We have this deeply hidden desire, or even just a hope, to enjoy in the material world and this is the main problem. Why does a person so easily fall prey to a prostitute (*asad-vārtā-veśyā*)? Precisely because a hope lives in his heart that he will be able to be happy. By fair means or foul, we have been struggling to be happy for a very long time, despite all of our experiences to the contrary.

When we invite this material happiness, we also invite misery, because material happiness and unhappiness are two sides of the same coin. But so long as the hope for enjoyment and material happiness is hidden deep inside us, temptation remains. The moment we are faced with temptation, this hope for enjoyment immediately pops up in front of us and says, "Yes, that's it! You have never had that."

Śrīla Prabhupāda made a very nice comparison about the nature of the manifestation of temptation in our lives. He explained what our subconscious mind looks like by using a contemporary example. He says that our subconscious mind is like photographic film. Of course, nowadays such film is practically a thing of the past, but not so long ago there were no digital cameras but only those that required film. This kind of film had silver crystals and when the film was exposed to light for some time, these silver crystals underwent a reaction. In areas where the silver was, everything goes black.

But what else needs to be done to the film to create the photograph? It must first be developed and then it must be fixed. At the beginning there is no image visible, and this situation is like our material life. The whisper of enjoyment of material life, so to speak, leaves impressions or *saṁskāras* imprinted on our subconscious mind. These *saṁskāras* are like the undeveloped image on a film. There is a long film inside us with many, many shots. We have "photographed" everything that has happened to us for so long. All the images of our enjoyments are there in our subconscious mind, and it is a very large album. However, the major part of these images are not yet developed, but the *saṁskāras* are there in the form of original imprints.

Just like the image develops on film after being immersed into the developer, the developer for the film of our subconscious mind is the environment or *prajalpa*. Words or vibrations serve as the most powerful developer through which memories of sensual pleasures emerge from the subconscious mind. We need to hear about some sense gratification and immediately the image appears that had been hidden there before.

For example, people read novels describing indecent or obscene scenes. Fools write and complete idiots read them. Readers devour these types of books because as soon as sound comes, it brings along an image. Along with that image, an image of our own sensual pleasure pops up and the *saṁskāra* becomes activated. This *saṁskāra* has been sleeping but is nevertheless alive in the subconscious mind for a long time and now emerges. This is the "film developer" of our subconscious mind.

Another example is that when the spiritual master sows the seed of *bhakti* in our hearts, the seed of faith, it needs watering in order to grow. Hearing and chanting, *śravaṇaṁ* and *kīrtanaṁ*, is the water for our seed of faith: Hare Kṛṣṇa, Hare Kṛṣṇa, Kṛṣṇa Kṛṣṇa, Hare Hare/ Hare Rāma, Hare Rāma, Rāma Rāma, Hare Hare.

Unfortunately, there are many other seeds in our hearts growing alongside the small seed of *bhakti*, the *bhakti-latā-bīja*. We have been planting them there for a long time. To grow, these desire seeds also need watering. Hearing and chanting about mundane things is the water that germinates these seeds of material desires. For instance, advertising is often based on sound. In our minds, sound is linked to the image of material enjoyment and when we hear that vibration it evokes a desire in us. The sound in an advertisement for Pepsi, for instance, makes us feel like drinking a Pepsi.

Using the same process – *śravaṇam* and *kīrtanam* – the seeds of material desires grow rapidly in our heart. Therefore Raghunātha Dāsa Gosvāmī states *asad-vārtā-veśyā*. We must stop listening to the news of the world because otherwise these images of material pleasures will be constantly growing in our subconscious mind. Kṛṣṇa also speaks of the same thing (*Bhagavad-gītā* 2.52).

yadā te moha-kalilaṁ
buddhir vyatitariṣyati
tadā gantāsi nirvedaṁ
śrotavyasya śrutasya ca

When our consciousness and *buddhi*, or intellect, go beyond the boundaries of this material world, or when we are free of the illusion of this material world, then *śrotavyasya śrutasya ca* – we remove the desire to hear this *grāmya-kathā* (material talk). We have to train our minds in accordance with what Raghunātha Dāsa Gosvāmī teaches us in the fourth verse, and how he has explained to the mind what we must meditate and focus our mind on.

The essence of all these appeals to the mind are, as Raghunātha Dāsa Gosvāmī says in the very first verse, *sadā dambhaṁ hitvā*, to "once and for all cast away this pride that is manifested in our life as the false ego in its various forms and guises." This *dambha* or arrogance, the attempt to lie to God and to ourselves, spoils our lives. Therefore, appealing to the mind, where an infinite number of intricate self-deception mechanisms are contained that enhance our pride, Raghunātha Dāsa Gosvāmī instructs his mind to eradicate false attachment.

In this world we easily develop affection and become attached to various things. But mostly we grow attached to what gives us pleasure or that we can exploit. A woman may be very attached to her husband, if he can be exploited. If he can't be exploited, she is not so attached to him. But the meaning or the principle that lies behind this attachment is the desire to dominate or rule over. Therefore, in the very first verse

Raghunātha Dāsa Gosvāmī advises his mind: "Mind, become attached to that in relation to which even the thought of enjoying will not occur."

Raghunātha Dāsa Gosvāmī explains that as a result of association with saintly persons *rati aṅkura* appears, which means the seed or germ of spiritual attachment. However, when a person begins hearing or repeating empty and meaningless talk, nothing is left of this spiritual attachment. We are squandering the precious intelligence that we have.

Our entire life follows our tongue – what our tongue speaks about, there goes our consciousness. As a result of worldly talks, without even our noticing it, our consciousness focuses on the mundane and the ephemeral. We think it is acceptable to gossip a little and perhaps talk about some devotee's difficulties in following the regulative principles.

Śrīla Jīva Gosvāmī explains that as a result of mundane talk we first become indifferent to *bhakti*. In the beginning we find the practice of *bhakti* to be like a life-preserver. We understand that *bhakti* is something that can save us from the ocean of material existence, but when we waste our intelligence on worldly talk we become indifferent. Conversely, the taste for worldly news grows more powerful. We can see that the so-called progress of humanity, especially in Kali-yuga, is the progress in the amount of worldly news. First, people wrote books by hand. Then they invented the printing press, first to print the Bible, but then mainly to print nonsense, because previously people wrote down only what was most valuable. Then the radio was invented. But that wasn't enough – then they invented television. Television is another hotbed of *asat-vārtā*. And, finally, the most remarkable achievement of Kali-yuga, the Internet. The very meaning of the word "net" means to catch, and it catches our minds and consciousness. There are statistics from 2013 that revealed more than a 100 people died from the Internet simply because they could not stop – they forgot about eating, sleeping, mating and defending, just surfing the Internet for days on end.

Therefore, followers of the spiritual path must remember *asad-vārtā-veśyā visṛja* – they need to exercise extreme caution. Śrīla Jīva Gosvāmī says that when we commit an offense in our practice of devotional service, one of the effects of these offenses is that we become attached to the very things that destroy our *bhakti*. Many devotees love watching television, but it is a most dangerous invention. Perhaps we should introduce a fifth principle in ISKCON that everyone receiving initiation should follow – no watching TV.

Mati-sarvasva-hariṇīḥ – here Raghunātha Dāsa Gosvāmī says that spiritual intelligence is completely gone. The most dangerous and despicable form of worldly news that completely destroys our spiritual intelligence or consciousness is when we begin criticizing others.

In the Eleventh Canto of *Śrīmad-Bhāgavatam* (11.28.2) is a very important verse:

para-svabhāva-karmāṇi
yaḥ praśaṁsati nindati
sa āśu bhraśyate svārthād
asaty abhiniveśataḥ

Kṛṣṇa says *para-svabhāva-karmāṇi yaḥ praśaṁsati nindati* – when we start to either glorify or censure the activities or the nature of other people, we very quickly (*āśu*) fall down and forget our true interest as a result of mundane criticism and offences. The reason is *asaty abhiniveśataḥ*. Kṛṣṇa says, "Because his mind is immediately devoured by the ephemeral." Our consciousness is devoured by this illusion and we forget what we truly need. This is the meaning of what is happening when we start critizing others.

In this verse, Kṛṣṇa also says that even glorifying others is bad, because both are actually food for the false ego. As soon as I critique or reproach others, especially behind their backs, my false ego is nourished and becomes stronger and stronger. When we praise others, we often do so to receive some benefit for ourselves. Praising someone is also food for the other's false ego, for almost every person can be bought by flattery, no matter how renounced they are.

When Abraham Lincoln, one of America's early presidents, was a boy, on the way to school one day he visited a blacksmith's forge. He went to the blacksmith and watched as he worked. It so happened that day that the blacksmith's assistant had not come. Seeing the boy, the blacksmith thought: "Let me make use of him." And so the blacksmith began to praise Abraham, saying, "Oh, what a clever boy. He hasn't gone to school. Instead he has come here. This is where exciting things happen. What a good boy! Come, give me a hand here; hold this." Young Abraham Lincoln started helping the blacksmith as the praise went on and on. "What a boy! Amazing! I've never seen such an obedient boy."

Abraham Lincoln said, "I spent four hours in that shop and I was constantly praised. I thought I'd never escape from there. Since then, when someone praises me I know that he needs something from me."

Kṛṣṇa says, *asaty abhiniveśataḥ*: "Whether someone criticizes or praises others, his mind begins to be devoured by the ephemeral. Such a person loses his spiritual intelligence." Both praise and blasphemy are based on the fact that we envy that person. We either want to praise and glorify someone for something material which is not really theirs, or we criticize them because of envy. *Caitanya-caritāmṛta* explains the mechanism of how human consciousness focuses on matter as a result of *prajalpa*, and especially as a result of the false so-called pleasure we get from doing so. The result of criticizing someone is that our material desires gain strength and our false ego is nourished. Criticism is the best vitamin supplement for the false ego, because as soon as we start criticizing our material desires grow stronger.

Śrīla Prabhupāda explains this with the story of Rāmacandra Purī, narrated by Paramānanda Purī to Lord Caitanya. On his deathbed, Mādhavendra Purī was experiencing the ecstasy of separation from Kṛṣṇa, and he kept repeating the same verse that somehow or other he had not attained his lord, the lord of Mathurā. He was crying, "Where are you, Kṛṣṇa?"

Rāmacandra Purī approached his spiritual master and said, "Why are you crying? You're supposed to be a pure devotee. Kṛṣṇa says of pure devotees (*Bhagavad-gītā* 18.54): *brahma-bhūtaḥ prasannātmā na śocati na kāṅkṣati*. Kṛṣṇa says that a pure devotee – *na śocati na kāṅkṣati* – neither laments nor desires anything. You must just lie there and be in complete bliss."

Paramānanda Purī explained that as soon as Rāmacandra Purī uttered those words, he committed an offence to his guru, because one is not supposed to give instructions to his guru. The disciple should not be so stupid as to approach his guru and say, "You do not understand. You are doing something wrong. Instead of rejoicing in life you're crying."

Śrīla Prabhupāda, commenting on the story, cites Jīva Gosvāmī in his *Bhakti Sandarbha* where he says, "Even for one who has attained liberation, as soon as he commits an *aparādha* (offence) his *vāsanās* become stronger." *Vāsanās* are the material desires hidden in our subconscious mind. In material life, the *vāsanās* or the material desires have practically full control over us.

The *vāsanās* or *saṁskāras* that are dormant in our subconscious mind become weaker as a result of spiritual practice. We chant Hare Kṛṣṇa, Hare Kṛṣṇa, Kṛṣṇa Kṛṣṇa, Hare Hare/ Hare Rāma, Hare Rāma, Rāma Rāma, Hare Hare, and what was once a problem no longer exists. Even such terrible habits as heroin addiction can be given up as a result of chanting the *mahā-mantra.*

Śrīla Jīva Gosvāmī explains that even if a person has reached the stage of liberation and is at the level of a *jīvan-mukta,* as soon as he or she commits an offense, especially against a devotee, and especially against a pure devotee, the strength of that offense is such that immediately, out of nowhere, the demon of material desires becomes overwhelmingly strong.

When we commit an offense our material desires emerge, yet we continue to think that in one way or another we are devotees. We may continue to lead a certain way of life and maintain our reputations as devotees. These material desires in a perverted way are then exhibited in the form of a new desire – criticism of others. Our material desires will manifest themselves in that we will be pulling down others again and again. There is nothing more unfortunate than the fate of a person who was following the spiritual path, and who made offenses, and who, in order to compensate for the offenses instead of honestly admitting them, starts criticizing and offending others. Unfortunately, someone who has committed an offense is again victimized by material desires.

In an attempt to remove this material desire and to justify themselves and these material desires, they start offending everyone. Frequently they start offending even their spiritual master, holding him responsible for the predicament they have found themselves in.

When we follow the spiritual path, we feel that our consciousness elevates, and the more it improves, the happier we feel. But if we do not want our minds to again degrade to the material level, we should never sell our mind once more to the harlot of mundane talk, and especially material criticism or material praise.

LIBERATION

After Raghunātha Dāsa Gosvāmī explains that if you value your spiritual intelligence, stop talking on material topics, he says, *kathā mukti-vyāghryā na śṛṇu kila sarvātma-gilanīḥ*. The next *kathā* which is highly dangerous to those following the spiritual path is *mukti-kathā*, or talk of *mukti* (liberation). He says that these conversations are like a tigress that will devour everything. She can devour your soul, your mind, and your intelligence, because all this is *ātmā* and he says *sarvātma* – she devours you whole. In a sense this *mukti-kathā* or talk associated with liberation, is even more dangerous than *grāmya-kathā* – talks of material enjoyment or benefits, worldly religion or worldly material duty.

To explain false topics, the author of *Caitanya-caritāmṛta*, refers to the second verse of *Śrīmad-Bhāgavatam* where Vedavyāsa says, *dharmaḥ projjhita-kaitavo 'tra paramo nirmatsarāṇāṁ satāṁ*. In the *Bhāgavatam* there is no *kaitava-dharma*, no cheating or telling lies. Kṛṣṇadāsa Kavirāja Gosvāmī begins explaining all this, and he says that false, deceptive *dharma*, or the false goals pursued by people, which will squander their human form of life, are *dharma, artha, kāma,* and *mokṣa*.

Of these four, Kṛṣṇadāsa Kavirāja Gosvāmī says that the greatest deception is liberation, *mokṣa*. This is because, when a person pursues the goals of *artha, kāma,* or *dharma,* they at least try to become the ruler of only a limited scope in this material world. When a person starts pursuing the goal of *mokṣa,* they are no longer satisfied to rule over a limited scope in this world. They want to rule over everything – they want to be God. As Śrīla Prabhupāda says, this is the last trap that the mind can fall into.

Our *ācāryas* do not skimp on biting remarks about *mokṣa*. For example, Śrīla Rūpa Gosvāmī wrote his famous verse in the *Bhakti-rasāmṛta-sindhuḥ* – *bhukti-mukti-spṛhā yāvat piśācī hṛdi vartate*. The desire for *bhukti* and *mukti* is a witch. Witches seize us and suck out everything from us.

Vallabhācārya, the great founder of his *sampradāya*, came to read the manuscript of *Bhakti-rasāmṛta-sindhuḥ* and said, "Everything is written so sweetly, but I do not like this verse. How can you call *mukti* a witch? So many people want liberation and the goddess Mukti Devī bestows liberation. Kṛṣṇa himself is called Mukunda. Mukunda is one who bestows liberation."

Rūpa Gosvāmī said, "Yes, of course, I will correct that. I will edit this verse and write something else."

Jīva Gosvāmī was standing nearby, fanning Rūpa Gosvāmī. Jīva Gosvāmī ran out after Vallabhācārya and said, "Dear *ācārya*, you are wrong!"

Vallabhācārya said, "How am I wrong?"

Śrīla Jīva Gosvāmī continued, "Dear *ācārya*, what is bad is the desire for liberation, not Mukti Devī herself. Rūpa Gosvāmī, my spiritual master, has written *bhukti-mukti-spṛhā* – the desire for *mukti* is bad, because it is a witch!"

Why is it a witch? What does it deprive us of? The desire for liberation deprives us of our own nature. When we become obsessed by this desire of liberation, we forget who we are, that we are servants and that we can be truly happy only in relationships. When that desire to somehow or other eradicate suffering becomes very strong, then we forget Kṛṣṇa and devotional service. What remains within us is this single false desire, and we think, "That's it! I will now become God! I just have to realize that I am God!"

Śrīla Rūpa Gosvāmī explains that a devotee may accept liberation, but only those forms of liberation acceptable to Kṛṣṇa. Lord Caitanya says *mama janmani janmanīśvare bhavatād bhaktir ahaitukī tvayi* (*Śrī Śikṣāṣṭaka*, verse 4) – "I am willing to stay here life after life." At the same time, we know that we need to go to the spiritual world because that is where devotees live. In the material world are those who want liberation, who are envious of each other. In this world it is difficult to practice devotional service. Therefore, we can accept liberation (*mukti*), in order to get to a place where everyone is engaged in devotional service. Man is a gregarious animal. It is easier for humans to do something everyone else does, and when we are here, we start doing what everyone else is doing.

Therefore, our goal is to reach the spiritual world and serve Kṛṣṇa there. As Kṛṣṇadāsa Kavirāja Gosvāmī says, we accept liberation only to be able to serve Kṛṣṇa in a better way, not for any other purpose.

One devotee, a professional psychologist who often offers consultations to devotees, said that to his greatest surprise ninety-five percent of the devotees actually want liberation rather than *bhakti*. In fact, he said, they do not want *bhakti*. *Bhakti* is too ephemeral and intangible, whereas *mukti* is clear. We do not really understand the extent to which this desire for liberation (*mukti*) is driving us.

Often devotees wonder, for example, how we can be aware of the desire for liberation in our consciousness. Here is a simple example. When some devotee has material trouble, if we say, "But he's a devotee! Why has misfortune come to him?" This means that we became devotees in order to alleviate suffering and are driven by the motive of *mukti*. When a person strives for *mukti*, Raghunātha Dāsa Gosvāmī says that this desire devours everything – *sarvātma-gilanīḥ*. This tigress of desire for *mukti*, or *mokṣa*, is all-consuming. People lose not only their intelligence, but ultimately they develop the desire to be a "nobody," to turn into a nonentity.

Ultimately, Māyāvāda often gets reduced to this foolish statement: "Everything is fine; there is no need to do anything or aspire for anything." When people read this kind of thing, they take it at face value. They are told that at the end of the day you have to become God and that there is no goal. We just need to go on and on, progress all the time and broaden our experiences, acquiring increasingly more until our experiences become so great that we become God. This is the deception. Everything will be spoken with a smile and we will think that everything is fine.

At one time I read various Māyāvāda books. They are all nonsense but sound so beautiful and poetic. Talk of *mukti* ultimately deprives us of our true selves in which we can exist eternally. They deprive us of our inner purpose, that we are always an eternal servant of Kṛṣṇa. Therefore Raghunātha Dāsa Gosvāmī warns us against this.

VAIKUṆṬHA

Raghunātha Dāsa Gosvāmī further writes, *api tyaktvā lakṣmī-pati-ratim ito vyoma-nayanīm* – give up even the attachment for Nārāyaṇa, the lord of Lakṣmī. He goes as far as saying that worship of God with awe and reverence is bad because it will take you to Vaikuṇṭha.

Why does he say that worshiping *lakṣmī-pati* is bad? What is wrong with Vaikuṇṭha? Kṛṣṇa in his form of Nārāyaṇa is there. There is order there. Law reigns there. But when devotees of Kṛṣṇa find themselves there they feel ill at ease.

In the second part of the *Bṛhad-bhāgavatāmṛta*, Sanātana Gosvāmī describes how Gopa-kumāra went to Vaikuṇṭha. On first arriving, there was no end to his happiness. He saw the wealth of Vaikuṇṭha – the palaces of philosopher's stone and gemstones and everything was of the nature of *sat-cit-ānanda*, eternity, knowledge and bliss.

Gopa-kumāra was walking around and looking, but decided that he did not feel like dressing in such fancy clothes with so many gemstones like the other residents. By nature he was a cowherd boy. He went up to Nārāyaṇa and shouted, "Hey! Gopāla, Gopāla! I'm here!" but he was hushed. Several inhabitants of Vaikuṇṭha approached him, took him aside and corrected him. It is then described that when he was playing the flute for Nārāyaṇa, the Lord was looking at Gopa-kumāra and smiling.

Gopa-kumāra expressed, "Nārāyaṇa is seated there on the throne and I am standing nearby playing the flute. I sometimes fan him. We are next to each other. There is no one happier than me. But when I called him 'Gopāla!' I was taken aside." Public pressure. The public of Vaikuṇṭha was disturbed.

The inhabitants of Vaikuṇṭha took Gopa-kumāra to the side and said, "What you say is wrong. He is God! Being a cowherd boy is just his pastimes. He is playing a role on earth. Yes, we know, Gopāla, Gopāla – he is pretending to be a cowherd. He is God! You must praise him in Sanskrit. Let us teach you the way you should glorify him. Come, we'll tell you how he should be glorified."

Others started saying, "No, no, do not chastise him. This is one of the *līlās* of our Nārāyaṇa, too. There is nothing wrong. Let him call him Gopāla. We've heard about that."

Still others began saying, "In fact, Nārāyaṇa is willing to do anything for his devotees, even to become a cowherd boy. He is rightly glorifying our Nārāyaṇa for saving his devotees from the tyranny of Kaṁsa."

The Nārāyaṇa in Vaikuṇṭha guessed Gopa-kumāra's heart. One morning Nārāyaṇa woke up and said, "Today we are going to herd the cows."

He jumped off his throne, Lakṣmī turned into Rādhā, Dharā into Candrāvalī, and the other inhabitants, all his courtiers, and the entourage surrounding Nārāyaṇa, turned into cowherd boys. "If the Lord plays, we are also supposed to play." They quickly changed dress, decorated themselves with flowers, and ran away in a crowd, Nārāyaṇa ahead.

Gopa-kumāra was delighted, "At last, that's the real thing!" In an instant this *līlā* was over and again the Lord was sitting on the throne. Gopa-kumāra thought, "I do not understand anything. On one hand I am happy, on the other there is something wrong. In meditation, I go up to him and embrace him, but here I cannot approach him for he is sitting on the throne. In my thoughts I go up to him and kiss him because he is mine! He's my friend! But here you can't do this, they will hush you up, and you will get expelled from Vaikuṇṭha."

Nārada Muni came to Gopa-kumāra and said, "You look so sad! What's wrong, Gopa-kumāra?"

He replied, "I do not know what's wrong with me. I seem to be fine. I seem to be happy. Nārāyaṇa is sitting here, the God I worship. I can play with him. However, something is missing."

So Nārada Muni told him, "Go, you do not belong here. You belong elsewhere." Because when intimate devotees see the Lord's greatness, they cannot express their love and be themselves. Fear, awe, and reverence is the exact opposite of intimate love. Gopa-kumāra cannot be himself in Vaikuṇṭha and neither can Kṛṣṇa fully express his love.

In the Tenth Canto of *Śrīmad-Bhāgavatam* there is the pastime of Kṛṣṇa and Balarāma going to Mathurā. We know that Kaṁsa had organised a great celebration on the occasion of their arrival. The best priests and fighters were invited, and there was going to be lots of entertainment for the entire public because all sacrifices are entertainments.

At that time Kṛṣṇa was only a young cowherd boy. Everyone stared at him, unable to take their eyes away. Wrestlers were looking at him and thinking, "Our death has come to us." Kaṁsa was looking at him, his eyes red with anger. In the end Kṛṣṇa pulled Kaṁsa down from his throne and destroyed him.

Devakī and Vasudeva started trembling because God himself had come. They had just seen how he manifested his power and killed Kaṁsa before their eyes. They started praying, "O Supreme Personality of Godhead, you have come to us to save us from Kaṁsa's wrath."

Kṛṣṇa listened for a while but then started crying. He said, "My dear parents, what is wrong with you?"

In Mathurā the devotees see his greatness and that greatness carries their minds away from their loving relationships. In Vṛndāvana they see his greatness, but think, "I must be seeing things. It must be just some kind of hallucination." Yaśodā Mātā looked into Kṛṣṇa's mouth where she saw the whole universe: all the material elements, all the planets, everything. She was sitting and staring, thinking that she must be sick. "I'm seeing things. My son's mouth is full of amazing wonders." Kṛṣṇa did not like her mood, either. Yaśodā then forgot what she saw, sat him on her lap and said, "You're my Gopāla!" She thought, "No one is dearer than him."

Sanātana Gosvāmī explains the way *Bhāgavatāmṛta* comments on this story of Gopa-kumāra. He says that the mood of Vaikuṇṭha kills intimate love. Raghunātha Dāsa Gosvāmī says here, "The Vaikuṇṭha mood will poison your love within. It will kill the love in you!" That seedling will die and all we will feel will be just respect. Therefore in the end Raghunātha Dāsa Gosvāmī says, *vraje rādhā-kṛṣṇau sva-rati-*

maṇi-dau tvaṁ bhaja manaḥ – "O mind, worship Rādhā and Kṛṣṇa who can give you the greatest treasure."

After all, the only thing we have to understand is that love for Kṛṣṇa is the greatest treasure. Kṛṣṇa appears in the form his devotee wants to see him in. Kṛṣṇa himself says, *ye yathā māṁ prapadyante tāṁs tathaiva bhajāmy aham* (*Bhagavad-gītā* 4.11). The deeper our love, the more fully God will manifest himself to us. If our love is mixed with reverence, then God will also appear in that way. If we need love and love only, Kṛṣṇa will appear before us in his most complete form as *svayam-bhagavān*.

There is a story in this connection, well-known in Ranabari, north of Sūrya-kuṇḍa. (The story is also in A. W. Entwistle's book, *Vaiṣṇava Tilakas*.) Śrī Kṛṣṇadāsa Bābājī lived in a village near Varṣāṇā, India. He had gone to Vraja as a boy and performed his *bhajana* in this village for many, many years. He had blessed that village that there would be no hunger or epidemics in the village and that it would prosper. When he was fifty years old he thought, "Half of my life is over. Who knows how long I am going to live? Everyone is going on pilgrimage to the holy places and I have never been to any other holy places."

There are four main holy places in India: in the south it is Rāmeśvaram; in the west it is Dvārakā; in the east it is Purī, and in the north, Badarikāśrama. He decided to tour the whole of India, visiting these four sacred places. As Kṛṣṇadāsa was about to leave, Śrīmatī Rādhārāṇī came to him in a dream and said, "Why leave? You are here, in Vraja. I will give you everything you need! There is nothing you will find in the other places."

He woke up and thought, "Oh, I must have imagined it all. The dream can't be true. After all, I just want to go to a holy place and become purified."

He left and traveled everywhere. Finally he came to the temple of Dvārakādīśa in Dvārakā. He received a mark on his body as evidence that he had been there. Kṛṣṇadāsa Bābājī finally came back to Vraja. When he fell asleep on his first night back in Vraja, Śrīmatī Rādhārāṇī again came to him in a dream and said, "Go away. Go away. I do not need you. Satyabhāmā has taken you into her entourage. You are now her servant – you have that mark on your shoulders. Get out of here; otherwise you will just be bothering everyone, poisoning the atmosphere of Vraja."

Kṛṣṇadāsa went to his friends, the other *mahātmās* and holy men, and asked them, "What shall I do?"

Listening to him, they all became frightened, saying, "Well, Śrīmatī Rādhārāṇī does not want to know you. What can we say?"

He said, "Please, accept me. I want to be here with you!"

They replied, "How can we go against her will? Śrīmatī Rādhārāṇī herself has rejected you." Then he realized that there was no hope.

Disheartened, Kṛṣṇadāsa sat in his hut and began to fast. He was fasting and chanting the holy name, Hare Kṛṣṇa, Hare Kṛṣṇa, Kṛṣṇa Kṛṣṇa, Hare Hare/ Hare Rāma, Hare Rāma, Rāma Rāma, Hare Hare. He was chanting with all his heart. In his heart, he was praying and weeping, repentance burning him inside. He was appealing to Śrīmatī Rādhārāṇī, imploring her. He fasted for three months, remaining in his hut. After three months, he suddenly saw that his body was wrapped in flames. Jagannātha Dāsa Bābājī was in Vṛndāvana at that time. He sent his servant to see what was going on with Kṛṣṇadāsa. The servant saw his body literally burning, like that of Satī, while he was sitting and chanting Hare Kṛṣṇa.

All the villagers came running. They crowded around and began peeping into his window where they saw that their saint, whom they worshiped, was burning. As the flames reached his throat, he raised his hand so that he could chant the *mahā-mantra* holding his beads out of the flames. Suddenly there was a flash, and there was nothing left of him except for a handful of steaming ashes.

Jagannātha Dāsa Bābājī, who had also gone to see what was happening, began crying out to Kṛṣṇa, "*Vipralambha, vipralambha*. He has burnt in the flames of separation from Kṛṣṇa." This Bābājī's disappearance day is still celebrated in springtime in that village.

Someone who hears this story may have some doubts. Śrīmatī Rādhārāṇī is the *hlādinī-śakti* of the Lord and the manifestation of his mercy. Why would she do that? We may think what was so terrible in his going to Dvārakā?

By way of explanation, the *ācāryas* say that Rādhārāṇī even rebuked Kṛṣṇa himself. For example, when Kṛṣṇa was at Kurukshetra, Rādhārāṇī said to Kṛṣṇa, "What are you doing? Why have you come here? Here horses are neighing, pounding the ground with their hooves, and elephants are trumpeting. Your wives are here, also! Everything is so disturbing. Let's go to Vṛndāvana, because everything here prevents me from loving you. I am the same; so are you. I love you – you are my beloved. But I cannot love you here, because there are so many obstacles. Only in Vṛndāvana can I love you."

When an opulent, reverential consciousness appears in a devotee's mind, Śrīmatī Rādhārāṇī will not allow that person into Vṛndāvana. She is the Mistress of Vṛndāvana. She does not recognize anything other than the ultimate, infinite, absolute intimacy that is based on the ultimate, infinite surrender to Kṛṣṇa. Nothing else will she accept. Therefore, giving instructions to his mind, Raghunātha Dāsa Gosvāmī says, *api tyaktvā lakṣmī-pati-ratim ito vyoma-nayanīṁ vraje rādhā-kṛṣṇau sva-rati-maṇi-dau tvaṁ bhaja manaḥ* – worship Rādhā and Kṛṣṇa, and as a result of that, you can attain the greatest treasure in the world. That is your goal.

The nature of the soul is to be a servant of God, fully surrendered to him. This ideal of our inner nature can only be realized in Vṛndāvana. This is what Śrī Caitanya Mahāprabhu came to give us. No one else has ever given that. Thanks to him we can attain *sva-rati-maṇi,* the gem of attachment to Rādhā and Kṛṣṇa. We must understand that this is the greatest treasure. This is the meaning of the instructions given by Raghunātha Dāsa Gosvāmī in this verse.

COMMENTARY BY ŪRMILĀ DEVĪ DĀSĪ

In his *Bhakti-rasāmṛta-sindhuḥ,* Rūpa Gosvāmī compared desires for mundane pleasure (*bhukti*) and liberation (*mukti*) to two witches. In verse four of *Manaḥ-śikṣā*, not only does Raghunātha Dāsa Gosvāmī use the analogies of a prostitute and a tigress, respectively, but interestingly he also writes of each in terms not exactly of our desires, but of our speech. It is *talking* about mundane things which is a prostitute stealing one's wealth with a promise of pleasure. It is *talks* of liberation which is a tigress eating our very self.

Raghunātha Dāsa Gosvāmī's analogies also focus on what is valuable. Both the prostitute and the tigress *take* what is valuable from us. Whereas, if we choose to instead serve Rādhā and Kṛṣṇa, we *receive* wealth as their own love in the form of a jewel.

Often in *śāstra* and the works of the *ācāryas* we are told to engage in Kṛṣṇa's service with body, mind, and words. In this verse the emphasis is on words – what we hear and what we talk about. At this point in *Manaḥ-śikṣā*, the reader has already relinquished attachment to ordinary *dharma* and *adharma*, being firmly on the path of love and attachment to guru, Vaiṣṇavas, and Kṛṣṇa in Vṛndāvana. Yet here we see that Dāsa Gosvāmī warns even such a person about what topics are appropriate for hearing and speaking.

Rūpa Gosvāmī identifies such talk as one of the destroyers of *bhakti*. In his purport to *Nectar of Instruction*, verse two Śrīla Prabhupāda comments: "Old men, retired from active life, play cards, fish, watch television and debate about useless socio-political schemes. All these and other frivolous activities are included in the *prajalpa* category. Intelligent persons interested in Kṛṣṇa consciousness should never take part in such activities." Today we could add so many modern electronic means of *prajalpa* to Prabhupāda's list.

The reason talking – hearing and speaking – can have such a devastating effect lies in the nature of sound in general. As Śrīla Prabhupāda writes,in his purport to *Śrīmad-Bhāgavatam* 3.26.32, "The entire material manifestation began from sound, and sound can also end material entanglement, if it has a particular potency. ... Our entanglement in material affairs has begun from material sound. Now we must purify that sound in spiritual understanding." On the grand cosmic scale, we know that it is sound which creates space, then matter in a gaseous form, then radiant energy, then matter in liquid form, and finally matter in solid form. Sound is the basis of everything. As Prabhupāda writes in the above referenced Third Canto *Bhāgavatam* purport, it's also our own individual material situation which has started from sound. Hearing and talking about mundane enjoyment or impersonal liberation are therefore not harmless, incidental diversions.

Hearing and talking lead to contemplation, to attachment, and then to a life spent in pursuit of those attachments. Ultimately, what we hear about molds our destination after death: *pitṛ-yānaṁ deva-yānaṁ, śrotrāc chruta-dharād vrajet* (*Śrīmad-Bhāgavatam* 4.29.13).

Furthermore, what we talk and hear about reveals the deeper attachments already within. Perhaps it's primarily for that latter reason that this obstacle is first on Raghunātha Dāsa Gosvāmī's list, which goes from gross to subtle. The ultimate symptom of what is dear to our heart, our real goals, is revealed in our speech. We may think that we aspire for pure service to the divine couple in Vraja. The evidence is how much time and energy we spend hearing and talking about them and their service. Jesus also spoke about the relationship between treasure and the heart in Matthew 6:19–21:

> Lay not up for yourselves treasures upon earth, where moth and rust doth corrupt, and where thieves break through and steal. But lay up for yourselves treasures in heaven, where neither moth nor rust doth corrupt, and where thieves do not break through nor steal. For where your treasure is, there will your heart be also.

To conquer the *prajalpa* problem, as well as the problem of deep affection for the opulent form of Nārāyaṇa, we need to do active service for Rādhā and Kṛṣṇa. That service has to be in a servant's mood, which means without pride. The divine couple then share with us the most valuable jewel of their own love! What a beautiful parallel literary ornament Raghunātha Dāsa Gosvāmī has written! Be a false enjoyer – lose the treasure you have. Be a real servant – gain the greatest treasure possible.

VERSE FIVE

asac-ceṣṭā-kaṣṭa-prada-vikaṭa-pāśālibhir iha
prakāmaṁ kāmādi-prakaṭa-patha-pāti-vyatikaraiḥ
gale baddhvā hanye 'ham iti bakabhid-vartmapa-gaṇe
kuru tvaṁ phutkārān avati sa yathā tvāṁ mana itaḥ

"While here on the revealed path of devotion, I have been attacked by the gang of my own lust, etc., who have bound my neck with the troublesome dreadful ropes of wicked deeds. I am being killed!" Cry out piteously like this to the devotees of Śrī Kṛṣṇa, the destroyer of Baka. O mind, they will save you from these enemies.

COMMENTARY BY ŚIVARĀMA SWAMI

This is a very important verse because in verse four gross obstacles were explained, but now more subtle obstacles are being described, *asac-ceṣṭā-kaṣṭa-prada-vikaṭa-pāśālibhir iha prakāmaṁ kāmādi.*

Śrī Caitanya Mahāprabhu says to Sanātana Gosvāmī:

nitya-siddha kṛṣṇa-prema 'sādhya' kabhu naya
śravaṇādi-śuddha-citte karaye udaya

> Pure love for Kṛṣṇa is eternally established in the hearts of the living entities. It is not something to be gained from another source. When the heart is purified by hearing and chanting, this love naturally awakens. (*Caitanya-caritāmṛta, Madhya-līlā.* 22.107)

Śravaṇādi means beginning with hearing. Our *anarthas* are purified through hearing and chanting. Everything in *bhakti* begins with hearing and chanting. The same with *kāmādi,* which means beginning with lust, *kāma.* The word *kāmādi* means the problem doesn't end just with *kāma,* or *kāma* is not the one or principal obstacle, but there are others. So what are these next obstacles or *anarthas* towards our advancement in Kṛṣṇa consciousness?

Kāmādi begins with *kāma,* and the other things headed by *kāma. Kāma* is leading the charge. *Kāma* means lust, and what follows lust is anger, greed, illusion, arrogance, and envy. These are the six main enemies or *anarthas* which are represented by this word *kāmādi*. So they are *vyatikaraiḥ*, likened to highwaymen or thugs. The example is very nice because even a materialist can appreciate it. We are on our path back home, back to Godhead. Then there are highwaymen who are there to stop you, obstacles on the path. They want to steal your wealth. We have already discussed that this wealth is our devotional treasure. Whatever little is there we want to protect it. But there are these *anarthas* present who are actually trying to steal our wealth.

They steal our wealth in very exacting ways, sometimes in very subtle ways, which Bhaktivinoda Ṭhākura illuminates. He says that we become tormented. They torment us. They catch us. How do they catch us? *Vikaṭa-pāśālibhir*, they have ropes. How can we get away from these anarthas, *kāmādi* (lust) and their friends? They're in the heart and even if we say "Get rid of them! Throw them out!" they're really tied on to us. Even if we get away, they come back again, just like a yo-yo that comes back again. You can't get rid of it. We're very tightly bound. *Vikaṭa-pāśālibhir iha*. How are they tied to us? *Gale*, means around the neck. *Baddhvā*, we are bound by the neck by *asat-ceṣṭā*, the rope of wicked deeds. The *kāmādi* are the cause and result of wicked deeds. They are very difficult to unravel. Where is the beginning? Where is the end? We are bound with ropes around the neck and are being strangled. Bhaktivinoda Ṭhākura says the result of this strangling is we feel great pain. We are put into all kinds of distressing situations, and sometimes forced into so many futile endeavors even against our will. This is Arjuna's question:

atha kena prayukto 'yaṁ
pāpaṁ carati pūruṣaḥ
anicchann api vārṣṇeya
balād iva niyojitaḥ

Aniccha, against my desire. "Why am I being forced to do something?" Very, very strong, these ropes.

So walking along the highway are all these dacoits. They have their ropes of past sinful activities around our neck strangling us, almost killing us. What will we do? *Phutkārān* means that we will have to cry out, scream; the actual word is scream. Scream very loudly. Whom do we scream very loudly to? *Bakabhid vartmapa-gaṇe*. We call for Bakabhid. *Baka* means Bakāsura, and Bakabhid is the person who killed Bakāsura – Kṛṣṇa. We must scream for help. These highwaymen of lust and and his cohorts have bound me by the neck with painful, horrible, strong ropes of many wicked deeds. We must beseech our mind to scream out to the devotees of Kṛṣṇa, the killer of Baka, "Help! I am being killed!" Not that we simply whisper. Someone has to hear us. So why Baka? Bakāsura embodies deceit, and we will see later that this deceit is the most difficult problem to unearth.

Kāma comes in so many different alluring and attractive forms: women, children, home, husband, paraphernalia, all kinds of things, and they are very deceiving. All of these things seem to be so very attractive but in the Fifth Canto, Śukadeva Gosvāmī gives the analogy that all the family members are like thieves. Even though we might think, "Oh, this is my dear husband," or "this is my dear wife and children," actually they are all thieves, stealing our hard-earned treasure – not money but actually one's hope for advancement in spiritual life.

This is the meaning of Baka, duplicity where a friend is really an enemy. How will we be saved? What should we do? First we have to be convinced that we are in a dangerous situation. Sometimes we think, "It's all right. I will handle it myself. It's not such a big thing to get away with it. I may learn more later in Kṛṣṇa consciousness." So if we are not aware of the danger, we don't think it is such a bad thing. If we recognize the dangers then automatically we want to be saved. Then *phutkārān*, we scream out, *baka-bhid vartmapa-gaṇe*, to the unalloyed devotees of the Lord. Bhaktivinoda Ṭhākura says they are like Kṛṣna's police force, and just as a police force guards a certain place, devotees are the guardians of our path of devotion. That is their service. That is a responsibility of a Vaiṣṇava, to guard the path of devotion.

We saw that nature often with Śrīla Prabhupāda. He was like a policeman. As soon as he saw some deviation in devotees in his society, that they had gone towards Māyāvāda or *sahajiyāism*, or most especially philosophical deviation, Prabhupāda would immediately be like a policeman, immediately arresting the person, correcting the situation, eradicating and purifying any anomaly he came across. So devotees who are *baka-bhid vartmapa-gaṇe*, which indicates that they are free from deceit, can assist us. If they themselves are deceitful then how can they assist somebody? They protect the path of *bhakti* from deceit. Otherwise deceit becomes a very great obstacle, and we will read later on why it is so. The nature of deceit is not only that one tries to deceive others but one also deceives oneself. Therefore, one loses sight of which path is the real path. We need real association. By association one becomes free of this deceitful mentality. This is the method of purification.

Bhaktivinoda Ṭhākura summarizes that devotees guard against pretenders and deceit, which prey on innocent Vaiṣṇavas practicing devotional service. The purport is that the heart and consciousness cannot be purified by sacrifices, yoga, or any other activity, but only by the association of pure devotees. Narottama Dāsa Ṭhākura also says that not only will these problems go away with the particular demons identified with each *anartha*, but they can also be engaged or purified. What is the method of purification? He says he will offer his lust in service of Lord Kṛṣṇa. The examples are given in *Śrīmad-Bhāgavatam*. Anger – what do I do with anger? Prabhupāda gives the example of Hanumānji and Arjuna. My greed, I am very greedy. What to do with this greed? I should become very greedy for the association of Vaiṣṇavas and to hear *kṛṣṇa-kathā*. Delusion or bewilderment, how to purify both? I should be deluded, or completely bewildered, if I am in the absence of devotees. In other words, I should feel great separation from Kṛṣṇa, thinking, "Where is Kṛṣṇa?" And pride, how to purify pride? I should be very proud that I have such a wonderful Supreme Person, such a wonderful master, whom I am serving. He is full of wonderful opulences, transcendental glories, so beautiful and wise and kind. I should be proud of these things. This type of dovetailing of these particular qualities will naturally bring them to the pure state.

COMMENTARY BY BHAKTIVIJNANA GOSWAMI

This is a very important verse for all of us. *Asac-ceṣṭā-kaṣṭa-prada*. *Ceṣṭā* means efforts, *asat-ceṣṭā* means false, futile, meaningless efforts. *Kaṣṭa* means suffering, *prada* means yielding. *Asac-ceṣṭā-kaṣṭa-prada* – Raghunātha Dāsa Gosvāmī says that our life consists of futile efforts.

In Soviet literature there is a famous piece by Illya Ilf and Yevgeni Petrov called *The Golden Calf*. It pictures the fate of a man who has been striving after a million rubles all his life. He did get a million and then said, "The dream of an idiot has come true." Raghunātha Dāsa Gosvāmī says the same thing: *asac-ceṣṭā-kaṣṭa-prada vikaṭa*. *Vikaṭa* means very severe suffering. The efforts we make and the labor we expend in this world makes us suffer, but both our effort and the fruit are actually *asat* – something that has no reality or meaning. *Pāśālibhir*: *pāśa* means rope. He says, "These ropes have tied me." The karma we create has tied us hand and foot causing us excruciating pain.

We may think, "Now, I need just a little money. I'll first earn a million and then I will peacefully perform *bhajana*." Thus, we start to work, saying, "I need some money, just a little. I just have to reach my financial goal!" Thirty years pass by and we have made little or no spiritual progress. These meaningless efforts bind us hand and foot, and we create more karmic debts. Decades later, instead of millions, we have only increased these debts.

Therefore, Raghunātha Dāsa Gosvāmī says that by these ropes here, *iha*, I am tied up. *Prakāmaṁ kāmādi-prakaṭa-patha-pāti vyatikaraiḥ*. There is a gang of thugs (*vyatikaraiḥ*) and it is they who have tied us.

LUST

Prakāmaṁ kāmādi, the chief of that gang is *kāma*, lust. *Kāma* has five underlings: *krodha, lobha, moha, mada,* and *mātsarya*. In fact, there's a whole clan, a family succession of thugs working together. Raghunātha Dāsa Gosvāmī says that gang has attacked me. I was walking along the spiritual path and suddenly, out of nowhere, *kāma, krodha, lobha* jumped out. Crying out and encircling me, they started tying me up.

Here in this verse Raghunātha Dāsa Gosvāmī gives us highly practical advice on how to defeat our lust, anger, greed, illusion, pride, and envy. He says that these highwaymen are not just robbing us, but killing us. *Kāma, krodha, lobha, mada, moha,* and *mātsarya* strangle us.

What gives rise to *kāma* (lust)? We need to know from which lair *kāma* leaps out at us. Everything can appear as being so perfect – the sun is shining, the air clear – then suddenly, out of nowhere, *kāma* appears and drags us somewhere, forcing us to act, and we say, "Yes, I need to do that!"

In the *Bhagavad-gītā* Kṛṣṇa explains the origin of *kāma*. He says "*saṅkalpa-prabhavān kāmān*." Material desire or *kāma* (lust) comes from *saṅkalpa*. *Saṅkalpa* is something more subtle than lust itself. Lust is already the specific desires that stifle us. *Saṅkalpa* means determination. Desire arises from the determination to enjoy. Before the specific desire, we have this focus on enjoyment in this world: *saṅkalpa-prabhavān kāmān*.

Śrī Caitanya-caritāmṛta (*Ādi-līlā* 4.166) says that if we simply want to gratify our senses, we have a deeply rooted purpose.

> *kāmera tātparya – nija-sambhoga kevala*
> *kṛṣṇa-sukha-tātparya-mātra prema ta' prabala*

Kāmera tātparya – the interpretation or explanation of *kāma* is that it is *nija-sambhoga*, the desire to please our own self and our self only, *kevala*. The root of lust is, ultimately, the desire for our own satisfaction, which in its turn is derived from the fact that we have left Kṛṣṇa and turned away.

The main problem is that lust is the most difficult to be rid of, and the strongest manifestation of lust is sexual desire. As long as a person has a body and a mind, lust will more or less be there. We have received a body and a mind to enjoy, if not grossly, then in a subtle way. At the bottom of it all lies our original sin – that we have turned away from Kṛṣṇa. We do not want to look at him. Even when we are trying to turn to him, we constantly turn back to ourselves. We love ourselves and we want to satisfy our own senses. Therefore, in any spiritual discipline a person must somehow or other solve this problem. Different spiritual disciplines offer different solutions.

In the sixth chapter of the *Bhagavad-gītā*, Kṛṣṇa gives us very interesting advice (verse 24). This is the same verse to which I have already referred. *Saṅkalpa-prabhavān kāmān*, that lust is simply the personification of all our material desires, subtle and gross.

sa niścayena yoktavyo
yogo 'nirviṇṇa-cetasā
saṅkalpa-prabhavān kāmāṁs
tyaktvā sarvān aśeṣataḥ
manasaivendriya-grāmaṁ
viniyamya samantataḥ

This is the advice that Kṛṣṇa gives. He says, *saṅkalpa-prabhavān kāmān* – when a person sees some sense object and wants to enjoy it, this gives rise to all kinds of material desires, and the advice he gives is to give up all sense objects. In essence, we must simply close our eyes to all sense objects, we must stop listening, we must stop gratifying our tongue, our nose, *tyaktvā sarvān aśeṣataḥ*; stop all the endless desires. *Aśeṣataḥ* means without end, all these arising desires. *Manasaivendriya-grāmam* – with the help of the mind we must master our senses. *Viniyamya samantataḥ* – with the help of intelligence we must master our mind.

Kṛṣṇa is describing the meditative stage of *dhāraṇā* in yoga. He says that to get rid of *kāma* we have to give up all sense objects along with the *vāsanās*, all the imprints of pleasure. In my mind, I have endless memories of all the pleasures that I carefully store there. I can look into my memory and see all the things I have enjoyed.

Therefore, Baladeva Vidyābhūṣaṇa, explaining verse 6.24, says that we have to give up all these *vāsanās* with the help of the mind. He explains we should begin to mentally analyze material enjoyments and think, "Well, what good are they?" Thus gradually we force our intelligence to meditate on the *ātmā*, the pure soul, which is full of eternity, knowledge and bliss, taking it away from the meditation on sense objects.

In his purport to verse 6.24, Rāmānujācārya explains this point in a very interesting way. He says that there are two kinds of desires:

those generated by the mind and those arising from contact between the senses and the sense objects. Desires generated by the mind can be easy to give up by using the mind. For example, our desire for mundane relationships, because we enjoy through these relationships, is one of the first things we should give up, understanding that they are temporary and ultimately unbeneficial.

When death is upon us, no one from among our many relationships can help at that point. Even if we have children, they cannot help us. Even if there is a loving wife, still no one can help us. We are face-to-face with the terrible problems resulting from our karma. At that point we can cling to the tiny island of Kṛṣṇa consciousness that we have and start chanting, Hare Kṛṣṇa, Hare Kṛṣṇa, Kṛṣṇa Kṛṣṇa, Hare Hare/ Hare Rāma, Hare Rāma, Rāma Rāma, Hare Hare. Then we can rise above all material desires.

This is the advice that Kṛṣṇa gives. He says with the help of your mind ponder over the futility and uselessness of all these material pleasures, because ultimately you do not need them. They are not going to save you. Further on, Rāmānujācārya says we should give up the enjoyments arising from the contact between the senses and their objects, also by reflecting on the fact that despite of all our efforts, we have not got anything in the end.

THE RELATIONSHIP BETWEEN THE ENEMIES

This gang of thugs has been friends with us over a long time, so much so that, generally, we have almost become a member of that gang. Raghunātha Dāsa Gosvāmī says: *prakāmaṁ kāmādi-prakaṭa* – they have appeared out of nowhere and are led by *kāma*.

In the *Bhagavad-gītā*, Śrī Kṛṣṇa calls this enemy of ours *kāma-rūpaṁ durāsadam*. *Kāma-rūpa* means an enemy in the form of lust, but *kāma-rūpa* also means a ghoul. *Kāma-rūpa* means one who can take any form he wishes. *Kāma* means desire; *rūpa* means form. So, this *kāma-rūpa* is the main enemy of the living being, especially the living being who is trying to attain a spiritual nature and has taken to the spiritual path. Sometimes lust comes to us in undisguised forms, but it may also come to us as a Vaiṣṇava with a *tilaka* and beads saying, "Let's chant!" because sometimes a person engages in spiritual practice for the sake of some mundane fruits. Therefore, Śrī Caitanya Mahāprabhu says, *na dhanaṁ na janaṁ na sundarīṁ kavitāṁ vā jagad-īśa kāmaye*: "I want neither money nor followers, nor beautiful women; *kavitām* – neither do I want respect; I want nothing."

Kāma generates four types of *anarthas* – those generated by sinful activities; by pious activities; by offenses; and those generated by *bhakti*. All these things represent obstacles to our *bhajana*.

The *anarthas* generated by pious or sinful activities are classified in various ways: ignorance, false ego, attachment to something, aversion to something, fear of death. *Avidyā*, ignorance, is the original problem of the living being, when the living being, which is spiritual in nature, identifies itself with this bag of flesh and blood. All this is the result of our past activities whether sinful or pious.

Offenses generate the most horrible *anarthas*. Ultimately, it is precisely our independent, capricious desire to do only what I want that is at the heart of committing offenses. If I am driven by this desire, I begin committing offenses to the guru or the Vaiṣṇavas because they are an obstacle to the realization of my independent desires, my *kāma* (lust). As a result, I start considering them to be ordinary people.

Finally, the *anarthas* generated by *bhakti* are the desire for gain, and the desires for honor and respect. These are also the result of *kāma*.

Sometimes people, being aware of this problem of *kāma*, try to overcome it by applying additional efforts in practicing renunciation (*vairāgya*). They may fast a lot or perform some extreme form of austerity. But actually *vairāgya* is not our practice. Those who practice *vairāgya* as a means of achieving something in spiritual life are just torturing themselves, getting nothing but suffering. Rūpa Gosvāmī was a renounced man, but did he practice *vairāgya*? No, he did not. For him *vairāgya* was not an end in itself; for him it was the natural state of his heart.

The principle of renunciation, *vairāgya*, begins with austerity. Austerity does not mean that a person is standing on one leg or fasting. Let us consider our attachment to food. Everyone, even modern scholars who study the human physiology, agree that the average person eats more than needed from a physiological point of view. Why are we so attached to food? For enjoyment or greed? To get strength? No. As soon as we are born, we start eating milk. Since very childhood, even in those who have been raised on artificial milk, an inner psychological association between food and love takes place in a person. Mother's milk is a manifestation of her love and the baby sucks and sucks. Usually a baby wants to suck beyond the need for food. The baby sucks for love. So, whenever we lack love, we start eating. There is a strong emotional or psychological association inside us that food means love. What we are looking for in life is not food – what we are looking for is love. When we have love we do not need much food or sleep, what to speak of other things, to satisfy our lusts. Thus *vairāgya* appears in a natural way and we do not need anything else, because our needs are satisfied.

Raghunātha Dāsa Gosvāmī would drink a glass of buttermilk every other day and was in perfect health, because he was getting energy from another source, from love. Therefore, when we artificially try to protect ourselves from the sense objects, from the stimuli, then, Kṛṣṇa says:

karmendriyāṇi saṁyamya
ya āste manasā smaran
indriyārthān vimūḍhātmā
mithyācāraḥ sa ucyate

If we are restraining our senses but all the while thinking about sense objects, we are a hopeless fool because we are cheating themselves. (*Bhagavad-gītā* 3.6)

In his purport to verse 5 of the *Manaḥ-śikṣā*, Bhaktivinoda Ṭhākura refers to a series of verses from chapter 2 of the *Bhagavad-gītā* (verses 62-63). They describe how degradation takes place in eight steps. There is an eight-step yoga that has eight ascending steps, and there are also eight descending steps. Everything is symmetrical – eight steps up and eight steps down:

dhyāyato viṣayān puṁsaḥ
saṅgas teṣūpajāyate
saṅgāt sañjāyate kāmaḥ
kāmāt krodho 'bhijāyate

krodhād bhavati sammohaḥ
sammohāt smṛti-vibhramaḥ
smṛti-bhraṁśād buddhi-nāśo
buddhi-nāśāt praṇaśyati

These eight steps leading down start when we begin to meditate on something material. By nature, we are meditators, and if someone doubts it, pay attention to what we do. We contemplate, we reflect, we begin to look. We are painfully trying to find an object that will make us happy as we scan the world. This is something only a human being is capable of. This is because other entities do not have a choice. All the other species see only what they need to see.

For example, a frog's vision is created in such a way that it does not see slow-moving objects, but only fast-moving objects like flies. If you slowly touch a frog it will not see you. The mosquito perceives only warm objects emitting carbon dioxide. Everyone has their own vision and each species sees only what it needs. But mankind sees everything. Therefore, a person can develop any desires. A person sees something, starts meditating on that object, and thinks, "Maybe that is what I've been missing." A person focuses on something and gains more and more confidence that, "Yes, that is what I need!"

The nature of meditation is that the more we meditate on something or someone, the greater our *saṅga* or attachment becomes to that object or person. Those who practice *vairāgya* may say that if you take some sense object, someone of the opposite sex, for example, and try to see them through a large magnifying glass, they will not look so beautiful. Such persons ignore the way we are created – *saṅgas teṣūpajāyate saṅgāt sañjāyate kāmaḥ* – a person first meditates and then develops attachment, *saṅga*. When attachment is developed, then comes *kāma*.

Kāma means our intelligence is set to work. It means desire, and desire means that the scheme of getting that object has already appeared in our mind. Very powerful mechanisms are set to work. I go into the supermarket, for instance, and see something I want. If I do not have the money, then I start thinking about how to get the money. When I start making plans of how to get it, lust enters my intelligence.

After that a number of various physiological mechanisms turn on because intelligence sets to work on our senses and that's the end. *Kāma* (lust) has devoured the mind. First there is a desire that appears simply in the mind, *saṅga*; then that desire appears in the intelligence, then it appears in our senses and that's it.

Kāma is also a huge burst of energy. Have you noticed what a surge of energy we feel when *kāma* appears? The days have been dragging slowly, you have been feeling bored with no desire for anything, you have been feeling depressed... but *kāma* appears and you spring to life. Then we get fed up with that particular sense object, and again the days are dragging and boring, and then there is a new object again, there is a new *kāma*, and a new life.

Now, when we are trying to achieve that sense object, when we are trying to get what we need, we inevitably encounter obstacles. To destroy these obstacles we need anger. It is a special energy that destroys obstacles. If something stands between me and the object of my desire, I am ready to destroy it all. "Who has dared to prevent me? Who has dared to come between me and what I want, what I love?!" In my anger I am prepared to do anything.

This gang of highwaymen that Raghunātha Dāsa Gosvāmī speaks of consists of *kāma, krodha,* anger, *lobha, moha, mada,* and *mātsarya*. First is lust, the most respected progenitor of the clan. *Kāma* gives rise to *krodha*. Another name for *krodha* is *kāma-anuja*. *Kāma-anuja* means *kāma's* younger brother. *Krodhā* means anger. The river of anger begins to surge. We start screaming, we start destroying, we clench fists and our eyes turn red. This energy can sweep anything on its way. Another result of *kāma* is when we satisfy *kāma,* then *lobha* (greed) appears. If *kāma* is not satisfied, then there is *krodha,* one is outraged and ready to kill everyone. And if we satisfy *kāma,* then there is greed. Greed is another kinsman – the fat guy in their gang. When this gang comes to you, you should know them by their looks. The *kāma* that has grown fat is *lobha*, greed. The *Hitopadeśa* says that due to *lobha*, we lose all shame. When this greed of satisfied desires develops, we cannot stop it.

And there is a third result that is not mentioned among these six sins or six vices. If the obstacles are too strong for our anger to remove, then fear comes. Sometimes Kṛṣṇa speaks about it; he says, *vīta-rāga-bhaya-krodhā*. *Rāga* means *kāma* or lust, *bhaya* means fear, and *krodha* means anger. These are three emotions associated with each other. Accordingly, as a result of fear, greed, and anger, we are seized by illusion (*moha*), identifying ourselves with our possessions.

What is illusion? *Moha* is when we forget ourselves to such a degree that we are ready to kill someone. Normally, we would never do that. Again, this is a purely psychological reaction, because anger, fear, or greed inside produces an extremely strong drug that obscures consciousness, and we may act in a way entirely out of character, because we forget who we are.

Kṛṣṇa explains that this is how the downfall takes place where we do something we would not otherwise do. Eventually, at the heart of it all is *kāma*. Because of *kāma* we degrade more and more. We commit a sin we would never imagine being able to commit. But then everything goes like clockwork, everything is perfect, because *moha* has covered our intelligence and our conscoiusness. We do not understand who we are, or what we are living for.

The *Viṣṇu Purāṇa* defines illusion (*moha*). It is said there, "This is my father and this is my mother, this is my wife, and this is my house." But this is not your dad and your mom, this is not your wife and this is not your house, and this is not your body. We think that it all belongs to us. Actually, nothing belongs to us. We expand our 'I', and *moha* makes us expand our ego over all.

We are studying the kinship between *kāma, krodha, lobha, moha, mada,* and *mātsarya*. What comes after *moha*? *Mada* means pride and madness. We start to be proud, "All this is mine! This is mine and that is mine! I have so many things, and they are all mine!" So, we start to expect that all others should respect and honor us, because we have become very important. We cannot tolerate even the slightest humiliation.

There is a nice example in *Śrīmad-Bhāgavatam* when Dakṣa was insulted. As a result of disrespecting his son-in-law, Lord Śiva, Dakṣa was decapitated and his head burned to ashes. He was later restored to life when he was given a goat's head as a replacement.

In this way *moha* is transformed into *mada* and as a result of this the ripe fruit, the most beloved youngest son in this family is born. And who is this – *mātsarya*. *Mātsarya* means when we start to envy someone for being better than we are, even in something small. It seems to us that the very fact of their existence is humiliating us. Our dignity suffers. We feel hurt and we rejoice when another person is suffering. When someone is suffering we do not show it of course, but inside we think, "Ah! Kṛṣṇa has punished him!"

This is how these enemies are related to each other and at the bottom of it all is *kāma,* lust. Usually we consider *kāma* to be our friend. There are even special training courses that teach people to develop *kāma*. There are motivational training courses where people are told to write down all of their desires and then meditate on them. Every evening they go through all of their desires and tick off each one. But *kāma* is a terrible thing and generates all human sins. The most surprising of all is that *kāma* is impossible to satisfy. Even if one has everything, one will still be not satisfied. Therefore, Kṛṣṇa calls this enemy, *kāma,* voracious, devouring everything, *mahā-aśanaḥ*.

BAKA, THE PRETENDER

Raghunātha Dāsa Gosvāmī calls the police or the Vaiṣṇavas a team or an army of *baka-bhid,* Kṛṣṇa who has ripped the hypocritical demon Baka into two halves. The *yogīs* also try to tear their senses from the sense objects, reflecting on the futility and temporality of it all.

Kṛṣṇa explains in the *Bhagavad-gītā* (3.6):

karmendriyāṇi saṁyamya
ya āste manasā smaran

indriyārthān vimūḍhātmā
mithyācāraḥ sa ucyate

Mithyācāraḥ means pretender, one who seemingly renounces sense objects, but constantly thinks about them. The problem of most kinds of yoga is that people are striving by their own efforts, but all the while in their mind there lives the memory, the *vāsanās,* sensations and enjoyments of material life. This memory is constantly pulling us here and there, even if we are ninety years old. When we get older it may be even more difficult because in old age the desires will be as strong as ever, but we will have no more strength. Cāṇakya Paṇḍita said that in old age the liver ages, the teeth fall out, there is no more strength, but the desires can remain as strong as in youth.

Externally we may seem completely renounced. Our eyes are closed to facilitate thinking, and we are sitting in the lotus pose, externally chanting with our tongues, but the mind is enjoying! What happens in this case is most important. The *saṁskāras* or *vāsanās,* which remain in the mind, grow stronger. Sometimes people think that if I give up something, then gradually this *saṁskāra* or memory of past pleasures will diminish. To some extent that is what happens, but only if we do not meditate on them. If we dwell on them, the *saṁskāras* grow even stronger. At some point such persons break down and start trying to enjoy as much as they can. They have been tolerating it, but their *saṁskāras* have been growing stronger and stronger and finally such persons get into trouble. For example, someone who fasts without any real reason, at some point loses control and begins eating everything. Therefore, Śrīla Prabhupāda said that instead of fasting it is better to eat something. He said that rather than fasting on Ekadasi, eating nothing all day long but thinking about food, you'd better eat something and not think about food.

Therefore, Raghunātha Dāsa Gosvāmī calls Kṛṣṇa *baka-bhid.* Baka is Bakāsura. *Baka* means a heron. That heron is figuratively a *yogī.* It demonstratively stands on one leg, elegantly holding up the second leg. It has no problems whatsoever with keeping balance. On one leg, like a true *yogī*, it meditates with completely closed eyes. However, as soon as a frog jumps the heron eats it up. Again it meditates, and again it looks completely self-absorbed, eyes closed, standing on one leg. That is why *baka* means a cheater. In his purport to *Bhagavad-gītā* 3.6, Śrīla Prabhupāda says that it is better to be an honest householder than a cheating meditator. People are trying to meditate, to externally withdraw from the sense objects, but if the material desires within remains, they turn into charlatans and nothing good comes out of it.

Another example from *Śrīmad-Bhāgavatam* is Saubhari Muni. He was a *yogī* who submerged himself under the Yamunā River so he would not see the objects of the senses. For many, many years underwater he held his breath, performing severe austerities. At one point, he saw some fish mating, which completely disturbed his mind. And he thought, "What am I doing here underwater?" He rushed to the nearby palace in Mathurā and said to King Mandhātā, "I want to marry your daughter!"

The king had fifty daughters and he said, "My daughters are princesses, so they must choose their husband by themselves. Go, and if they choose you, I'll give you my blessing!" Saubhari Rsi used some of the power from his penance to turn into a handsome and attractive young man and all the fifty daughters wanted to marry him. In that way he became a servant of lust.

We have eagerly taken up the spiritual path, but the highwaymen attacked us in the dark and began strangling us. *Gale baddhvā hanye 'ham* – if that has happened to you, you have to cry out, "They're killing me! Help! Save me! Help! *Hanye 'ham*! They're strangling me! *Gale baddhvā!*"

Raghunātha Dāsa Gosvāmī says *vartmapa-gaṇe (vartma* means path, *vartmapa* means policemen). There are *patha-pāti*, robbers, and there are *vartmapa*, the police, *vartmapa-gaṇe*, and we must call them. But it is a special police. The police, like the gang, has its leader, whose name is *baka-bhid*, the one who ripped Bakāsura apart. That is Kṛṣṇa.

Kuru tvaṁ phutkārān; kuru means O mind, *phutkārān* means shout loudly, "Help! Help!" *Avati sa yathā tvaṁ mana itaḥ* – we will be rescued by Kṛṣṇa himself when we call for the devotee police officers.

VAIṢṆAVA POLICE SAVE US

Raghunātha Dāsa Gosvāmī says that when we are overcome by these enemies, we must shout for help, crying, "They're killing me! They are dragging me to hell! I am in trouble!" And we must call the Vaiṣṇavas who will save us. He says here that what can actually save us is the society of Vaiṣṇavas.

There is one devotee friend of mine who used to take very addictive drugs over many years. He became a devotee, and for some time he stood firm, but then gave in again, and also started to deal in drugs because addicts like to get others addicted as well. He was sent to prison for three years or so and then released. This devotee came to one of our festivals. When I saw him I went up to him and started asking how he was doing. He said, "As long as I am here with the devotees I do not want anything. I feel no desire and it's nice. But I know as soon as I leave here I will get addicted again."

This is what happens if we meditate on the sense objects – at one point our desire will grow so strong that we can do nothing but cast prudence to the wind. Therefore, Raghunātha Dāsa Gosvāmī says that conquering the enemies headed by lust is not going to work by our own efforts. We have to call to those who can save us from hypocrisy, to those who serve the *baka-bhid*, the one who can rip the hypocrisy within us in two.

We must remain in the association of devotees. When we are with the devotees, all problems are solved; lust goes away, material desires go away, and the only desire that remains inside is to serve Kṛṣṇa and his devotees. To be constantly situated at the lotus feet of the Vaiṣṇavas is the only safe place in this world, where we can feel fully protected against all enemies. If there are no Vaiṣṇavas near us physically, then another type of *sādhu-saṅga* is reading books and listening to lectures. Hear their words, read what they have written, and think about the verses they have left to us. Doing this will give us the strength to resist the most frightening and powerful enemies that we have inside. Therefore, thanks to modern advances, we can be with the Vaiṣṇavas twenty-four hours a day.

Sādhu-saṅga is life-saving; it can save us from all these problems. All our problems in spiritual life are due to a lack of spiritual taste. If we had a spiritual taste there would be no need for any seminars or festivals; we would all be running around like crazy, chanting, Hare Kṛṣṇa, Hare Kṛṣṇa, Kṛṣṇa Kṛṣṇa, Hare Hare/ Hare Rāma, Hare Rāma, Rāma Rāma, Hare Hare. But as long as our *anarthas* remain in our heart, we cannot go mad with love. Rather, we have gone mad but in a different way. Rūpa Gosvāmī and Sanātana Gosvāmī would run around Vṛndāvana with hearts overflowing with love. Our heart is also overflowing with love for material objects, lust. What prevents us from relishing this taste are the *anarthas*. But when we meet a *sādhu*, they help us develop the taste for *sādhana-bhakti*.

The following story about Jīvana Ṭhākura is a very enlightening example of this principle. Jīvana Ṭhākura was a very pious man who lived his whole life in his village during the time of Sanātana Gosvāmī. He was engaged in some spiritual activities, but he was very poor. When he grew old, Jīvana Ṭhākura decided that he would not be able to live in such poverty any more. He came to in Kāśī, Benares, to see Viśvanātha, a powerful Deity who fulfills all the desires of those who come to him. So, Jīvana Ṭhākura prayed to Lord Śiva in the following way, "I have been worshiping you all my life. All my life I remained poor, and now I am too old to be poor. Make me rich at least at the end of my life."

He returned to where he was staying overnight. Viśvanātha Śiva came to him and said, "Go to Vraja. There lives a *bābājī*, a *sādhu*, called Sanātana Gosvāmī. Find him and he will make you rich."

Jīvana Ṭhākura happily thought, "Wow, it works! Viśvanātha has showed mercy to me!" He went to Vraja where he found Sanātana Gosvāmī and said to him, "Sanātana Gosvāmī, *prabhu*, help me! Śiva himself told me that you can make me rich. Please, make me rich."

Sanātana Gosvāmī replied, "How can I make you rich if I myself am a beggar? Look at me, all I have is a loincloth."

"Well, Śiva could not be mistaken; make me rich!"

Sanātana Gosvāmī remembered that he has a philosopher's stone. One day as he was walking along the road, he had stumbled over a philosopher's stone. He had picked it up, but thought, "Well, it will be of no use to me. It will only be an impediment." So, he hid it in his garbage, thinking, "It might come in handy for someone." So, now he remembered and said, "Yes, I have something for you over there in my pile of garbage." He picked up the stone, gave it to him and said, "Jīvana Ṭhākura, this is for you! Now you can fulfill any desire. If you touch it to iron, the iron will turn into gold. You can get rich. No one has such a stone."

Jīvana Ṭhākura was delighted. He walked away, holding the stone in his hands and admiring it. He was thinking about what desires it would fulfill and how even kings would envy him. But then, suddenly, he began thinking about why Sanātana Gosvāmī readily gave him this stone without regret. He thought, "He must possess something more valuable, otherwise why would he give it to me so easily?" He took the philosopher's stone and threw it far into the Yamunā. He thought, "I do not need it! I will go back to Sanātana Gosvāmī and ask him to teach me what he knows!"

So, this is how association with a *sādhu* works, though not always immediately. Like in the case with Jīvana Ṭhākura, he came to the *sādhu* to get something tangible. Instead, he got an instant of association with a *sādhu*, and that instant of association impressed him in such a way that he began thinking, "Why is he so happy? He is wearing nothing but a loincloth. Why is he so happy? He does not need that philosopher's stone, the greatest jewel of all! Why had he thrown it into the garbage pile?" So, at some point he felt relieved because *kāma* had gone from his heart, greed had gone, lust had gone, everything else had gone from his heart. That is the effect of *sādhu-saṅga*.

When Rūpa Gosvāmī explains the mechanism of this influence of the devotee, he quotes Hiraṇyakaśipu who says that our mind is like a crystal and when something comes close to that mind it gets reflected there. Rūpa Gosvāmī says that when we approach a *sādhu*, the qualities of the *sādhu* begin to be reflected in our minds – we begin to feel a pale shadow or shade of what the *sādhu* feels.

So here Raghunātha Dāsa Gosvāmī says that if lust is strangling you, call the Vaiṣṇavas, call the sā*dhus* and you will immediately feel relief.

Lust will go away and all these thugs will flee in different directions. As soon as they see that a *sādhu* is coming, they begin to disperse. They run away in fear because Vaiṣṇavas, as Raghunātha Dāsa Gosvāmī calls them here, are the police who guard the spiritual path.

We may ask why Raghunātha Dāsa Gosvāmī does not say, "Call Kṛṣṇa," or, "Cry out the holy name." Instead he says, "Call the Vaiṣṇavas."

Viśvanātha Cakravartī Ṭhākura explains the principle in his commentary on verse 1.2.228 of *Bhakti-rasāmṛta-sindhuḥ*. There, he says that in one sense the Vaiṣṇavas are stronger than Kṛṣṇa. He gives a very powerful explanation, quoting a verse from the Third Canto of *Śrīmad-Bhāgavatam* where Kapiladeva says that there are two forms of unwanted association: association with a woman and association with a man who is attached to a woman. The second type of unwanted association is the most dangerous. When we associate with a woman we might or might not get attached depending on whether she is beautiful or not, but when we associate with a man who is attached to a woman, we begin to feel his taste. This taste is so strong that we will inevitably get attached. When we associate with those who are attached to sex, to base things, it is very difficult to stand firm because we think, "Why am I wasting my time? Others are enjoying!"

Similarly, Viśvanātha Cakravartī Ṭhākura says, therefore, association with Kṛṣṇa is not so important, for association with Kṛṣṇa may or may not give you a taste. Association with Vaiṣṇavas who have a taste will impart that taste to us, because we will feel their taste reflected in our consciousness. The taste they have will make us contemptuously regard all the temptations of the material world. Those who associated with Śrīla Prabhupāda felt that liberating or cleansing association. They felt how, being near him, they were getting free from the passions that used to torment them before.

Therefore, the only way to protect ourselves from degradation is to call out to the Vaiṣṇavas. And if there are no great Vaiṣṇavas, we must call the ordinary Vaiṣṇavas; if there are no ordinary Vaiṣṇavas, we must call the lowest Vaiṣṇavas – and even they can teach us their taste. Therefore, when we associate with the devotees, we must not in any case take them for granted. This is a *saṅga* that will help free us of all vices and purify our hearts. Never, under any circumstances, should we offend the Vaiṣṇavas. The Vaiṣṇavas are our saviors.

The Vaiṣṇavas are those who give us freedom from lust, envy, anger, greed, illusion, and pride. They can save us and can free us. Therefore, we must at every moment of our lives thank Śrīla Prabhupāda for giving us the opportunity to associate with the Vaiṣṇavas, to come to festivals and together engage in *sādhana*, being able to chant Hare Kṛṣṇa, Hare Kṛṣṇa, Kṛṣṇa Kṛṣṇa, Hare Hare/ Hare Rāma, Hare Rāma, Rāma Rāma, Hare Hare. The main lesson of this verse is that Vaiṣṇavas can give us a taste and there is no other source for that taste. The only source of spiritual taste is the heart of a Vaiṣṇava who has *bhakti*.

COMMENTARY BY ŪRMILĀ DEVĪ DĀSĪ

In the fifth verse practitioners of *bhakti* are on the shining path of service to the divine couple of Vraja but are not not progressing much because they are anchored by strong ropes. Bhaktisiddhānta Sarasvatī used to tell the story of a family crossing a river to attend a wedding. Their boat made no headway all night because of failing to pull up the anchor. The oars are moving, everyone is in the boat, but they are standing still. In a similar way, if those on the path of devotion are still slaves to lust, anger, greed and so forth, those evil masters will bind the devotees with ropes of evil deeds, making their apparent progress on the surface of *bhakti* either very insignificant or nonexistent in the depths.

Having conquered the difficulties explained in verse four, the persons described in verse five speak of spiritual things, but have actions not in harmony with their words. As Śrīla Prabhupāda writes in his purport to *Bhagavad-gītā* 3.33, "There are many so-called spiritualists who outwardly pose as advanced in the science but inwardly or privately are completely under particular modes of nature which they are unable to surpass."

We find a similar concept in Caitanya-caritāmṛta (*Antya-līlā* 4.102): *āpane ācare keha, nā kare pracāra, pracāra karena keha, nā karena ācāra,* "Some behave very well but do not preach the cult of Kṛṣṇa consciousness, whereas others preach but do not behave properly. This problem of preaching nicely but behaving improperly may be due to weakness, hypocrisy, or some of both. If preachers are honest and humble about failures to live up to what they teach, the situation is not so dangerous. Indeed, even those devotees who both preach and act perfectly generally present themselves as being far less than the ideal they teach. Such a presentation comes from their genuine humility. The greatest danger, however, is the hypocrite who cheats others. Such persons often cheat themselves as well.

The cheating hypocrite is struggling with pride. Pride prevents us from admitting our problems, even to ourselves. Who wants to admit being a slave to lust, greed, or envy? No one wants to confess, "There's a rope around my neck, and Master Envy is dragging me like a pet dog on a leash to one wicked deed after another!" Out of pride, we instead try to cover our real motives with something more socially acceptable.

Therefore, we return again to verse one where we are told to give up pride and love the devotees of the Lord. As soon as we reject pride, we will notice that along with the robbers on the road are police officers. The police are servants of Kṛṣṇa the killer of Baka, personified hypocrisy. Baka takes the form of a crane. The crane appears to meditate peacefully in a yogic pose on one leg. The crane's real meditation, however, is on eating fish. Quickly it dives for a fish and then returns to its posture.

We may think the thick ropes of our attachments, bad habits, and private weakness are insurmountable. But the servants of Baka's killer can cut the ropes of wicked deeds through their own humble and honest mood, which gives us the courage to follow their example. They also cut the ropes through their instructions, including what they have written in their books.

These Vaiṣṇavas will only destroy the robbers and break our bonds if we ask them to. Like Kṛṣṇa himself, they respect free will. If we want to be a hypocrite and remain tied, they will not force us to change. So we must call to them with desperation and sincerity. Such a call requires an absence of pride – a willingness to admit that we are weak slaves who require the help of those more powerful than we.

When we are released from these wicked masters, our love and humility will grow. We will give all the credit to Kṛṣṇa, as Nanda Mahārāja does in chapter 46 of *Kṛṣṇa* Book, saying, "How wonderful it is that he has killed all the demons like Pralambāsura, Dhenukāsura, Ariṣṭāsura, Tṛṇāvarta and Bakāsura! They were so strong that even the demigods in the heavenly planets were afraid of them, but Kṛṣṇa killed them as easily as anything."

VERSE SIX

are cetaḥ prodyat-kapaṭa-kuṭināṭī-bhara-khara-
kṣaran-mūtre snātvā dahasi katham ātmānam api mām
sadā tvaṁ gāndharvā-giridhara-pada-prema-vilasat-
sudhāmbhodhau snātvā tvam api nitarāṁ māṁ ca sukhaya

O ruffian mind! Why do you burn yourself and me [the soul] by bathing in the trickling urine of the great donkey of full-blown hypocrisy and duplicity? Instead, you should always bathe in the ocean of love emanating from the lotus feet of Śrī Śrī Gāndharvikā-Giridhārī, thereby delighting yourself and me.

COMMENTARY BY JAYĀDVAITA SWAMI

In the *Bhagavad-gītā*, Kṛṣṇa says,

kāma eṣa krodha eṣa
rajo-guṇa-samudbhavaḥ
mahāśano mahā-pāpmā
viddhy enam iha vairiṇam

The big enemy of the conditioned soul is lust. But Raghunātha Dāsa Gosvāmī says that even if you're done with that, there's still another problem to deal with. Deeply embedded within the human heart are four defects, and one of them is the propensity to cheat. Therefore it is said, *dharmaḥ projjhita-kaitavo 'tra paramo nirmatsarāṇāṁ satāṁ*. The Bhāgavatam kicks out *kaitava-dharma*, "cheating religion." Śrīla Śrīdhara Svāmī says that *kaitava-dharma* means *dharma, artha, kāma, mokṣa* – material objectives, culminating in impersonal oneness.

Raghunātha Dāsa Gosvāmī has some pungent words for this deceit and hypocrisy: *prodyat-kapaṭa-kuṭināṭī-bhara-khara-kṣaran-mūtre snātvā* – "bathing in the donkey urine of full-blown hypocrisy and duplicity." One may ask, "Why donkey urine?" Well, to begin with, it's not cow urine. Cow urine is purifying. Some people clean their kitchens with it. It's antiseptic. But this verse talks about donkey urine. There's a difference. Donkey urine doesn't seem to be held in high esteem. Śrīla Prabhupāda said that the donkey, the ass, is the symbol of stupidity, as in the expression "work like an ass." In America a common insult is to call a person an ass, a stupid ass.

TYPES OF DECEIT

Śrīla Bhaktivinoda, in his commentary, says, "There are three categories of spiritual practitioners (*sādhakas*)." He calls two types of householder devotees as *sva-niṣṭha-sādhakas* and *pariniṣṭha-sādhakas,* and the renounced devotees *as nirapekṣa-sādhakas.* He further writes, "All three types are benefited only when they become thoroughly honest and give up deceit, pretense, and hypocrisy; otherwise, they are surely vanquished. Each type of *sādhaka* has distinct ways of exhibiting a deceitful nature."

Śrīla Bhaktivinoda writes that householders may be deceitful by indulging in sense enjoyment on the pretext of *sādhana-bhakti.* For example, a person might offer opulent food for the pleasure of the Lord – thinking of eating it later. Bhaktivinoda also suggests that a renunciant man may want to train ladies in Deity worship so that he can have their association. These are some of the different ways Bhaktivinoda lists to enjoy sense gratification under the pretext of *sādhana-bhakti.*

Bhaktivinoda Ṭhākura warns against the deceit of housholders "serving rich influential materialists instead of serving simple *nirapekṣa* servants of Kṛṣṇa." He lists similar pitfalls for the renunciants – for example, the deceits of "staying with materialistic people with the expectation of receiving wealth" and "being inwardly anxious and worried about collecting more wealth, while making a pretense of performing devotional service or chanting." In a similar vein, Śukadeva Gosvāmī says, "Aren't the trees giving fruits? Isn't the river giving water? Then why are *sannyāsīs* going to the homes of materialists just to flatter them?" Of course, we have seen this behavior to an almost absurd extent in Indian culture, but it happens in the West also. Whether initiated Vaiṣṇavas or "professional" Vaiṣṇavas, supposedly saintly devotees go around from one rich man's home to another, collecting donations, mainly to support their families. Meanwhile the rich materialists flatter them, saying, "O Mahārāja!" until the preacher starts to believe he *is* "mahārāja." And then it's "By the way, where's my elephant?" This kind of preacher is basically a businessman who is in "the Vaiṣṇava business."

Such a mentality can be also be institutionalized. If your institution becomes solely interested in courting the wealthy and influential, then you have a problem. An ordinary guy walks in, and you size him up. When you see he doesn't have any money you go on to the next man, neglecting the sincere candidates for devotional service. That's to be avoided.

Bhaktivinoda Ṭhākura talks about yet another kind of deceit, "enthusiasm for meaningless temporary gains, even at the cost of envying and harming others." We see this in devotees who get enthusiastic about a more or less mundane project of no great importance. Often the enterprise is simply self-indulgent. One indulges one's mundane propensities under the banner of devotional service. A common example is becoming a rockstar again, "for Kṛṣṇa." The devotee may be very enthusiastic about it, but it really has no value, except for self-indulgence.

One common form of deceit Bhaktivinoda lists for the *pariniṣṭha-sādhaka* is "making an external show of strictly following rules and prohibitions while inwardly being very attached to material subjects unrelated to Kṛṣṇa." From my reading of a book by a friend of mine who's a Christian professor, it seems that the Christians deal with the same tendency, which they call "legalism." It's quite a good term, legalism. The legalist is punctilious, very attentive to following rules and regulations, but his heart is all junk. He makes an outward show of being a very *pakka* devotee but inwardly allows all sorts of *anarthas* (weeds) to grow. Easier than purifying the heart is to make a show of crossing your t's and dotting your i's. You make sure that you circumambulate the *tulasī* plant exactly four times, that you chant such-and-such verse in exactly the right meter, that you bow facing the right direction – all the details you can possibly think of, but without a real connection and purification of the heart.

The internal and the external are not mutually exclusive. But when the rules and regulations become the point, or when we make a show of rules and regulations, that's what Rūpa Gosvāmī calls *niyamāgraha:* missing the point. If we think rules are the most important thing, we're fooling ourselves: self-deceit. Then again, if others think the rules are the most important thing, we may deceive them by making a show of following the rules, but without having the substance.

Some *sādhakas* are deceitful by preferring the association of people who are materially impressive in some way. Bhaktivinoda writes of "preferring the association of non-devotees rather than Kṛṣṇa conscious devotees." Whether it's intellectually sophisticated company or high-society types or mode of goodness people, such a *sādhaka* prefers their association to that of genuine devotees. That's another type of cheating.

Recognizing the various types of deceit helps us guard against materially motivated religion and contaminated consciousness.

DEVOTION OR PROFESSION

Impediments to spiritual progress may also come because we maintain our householder life by what is essentially professional *kīrtana*. That is a subject that deserves careful thought because there are so many statements in our literature advising against meeting one's family expenses by speaking *Śrīmad-Bhāgavatam* or by becoming a professional preacher. The danger is that it becomes a business. Someone may be a car mechanic, a teacher, or an accountant, and someone is a preacher. Everybody has a way to maintain his family life, and it becomes exactly that: a business. And this may occur in any department: Preaching becomes a way to maintain your family, being a *pūjārī* becomes a way to maintain your family, and devotional service becomes a way to maintain your family. It becomes a profession. Since our interest lies in building up our bank account, we are interested in preaching to the wealthy or preaching where people give us good money. And we collect money not for a preaching project, to distribute books or to spread *kīrtana* but to pay the rent, to save money for the kid's education, all of that.

A devotee may sometimes accept some modest contribution for maintenance, but when our program is meant mainly for maintaining our family by professional Vaiṣṇava service, then the situation needs to be looked at.

When we first went to Vṛndāvana, we saw the Deities being maintained very poorly. Basically Deity worship was a family business. Prabhupāda's evaluation was that the pujaris just keep the temples open to collect some money and don't really care about the Deity, except as a gimmick or tool for making money.

Sometimes we see that people are willing to serve but everything they do has a price to it. We then have to ask, Is that devotional service, or is that a job? And if it's a job, is this really what Prabhupāda wanted? Is this really what Caitanya Mahāprabhu came to teach – that devotional service is a means of earning your livelihood? That's not really the idea. Better to earn your livelihood by honest means – and do service. You can have a career, make money, and meet your family expenses, so that everything that you do for the temple or for the preaching is actually devotional service. It's not mixed. You don't have to ask, "Okay, what's my compensation package?" No, you can say, "My family expenses are met, and this is what I do for service." So much of our time is taken up with the responsibilities of family maintenance, but they don't take up all our time. So the balance of our time we can use for Kṛṣṇa's service. We won't waste it watching television, talking *prajalpa,* and hanging out. We can invest that balance of our precious time, when we're not earning a livelihood, in devotional service. There's a strong case to be made for that approach.

On the other hand, Prabhupāda approved of book distribution. "As a business, it's a good business," he said. "Best business." A full-time book distributor can keep aside some quota for personal and family maintenance.

You can also use your occupation for serving. If you are an accountant, then do temple accounts. If you are a lawyer, help get documents registered. Whatever you are. A cook? Cook for the Deity. But not with the mentality of "How much they will pay me? How much will I collect if go to this engagement? How many hours do they want me to serve? Can I make the same amount but do less? Maybe I can get a few more dollars per hour." None of that comes into consideration when you cover your own family expenses separately.

Taking payment for service to maintain your family can also create unhappy relations. For instance, the *brahmacārīs* are giving selflessly of their time, they are bringing in money – and you are spending it to maintain your household. Or the congregational householders are working hard and making money and giving it to the temple – and it goes to you to maintain your family. How good are people going to feel about that? We also need to ask if this is how we want our temples to operate, basically employing people to do service.

KĪRTANA

We are advised not to hear from professional *bhajana* singers. They are singing for money, not for the pleasure of the Lord. It's their profession, their way of earning a livelihood, and they cultivate a beautiful voice for public gratification. One can say these people are Vaiṣṇavas, but that's not our standard of a Vaiṣṇava – someone who doesn't really follow the principles of devotional service or practice but is a great singer. Some of the most popular bhajana singers are based in Bombay, and we know about them quite well. So we know that in their private life they are drinkers, womanizers, and so on. They don't follow the four regulative principles an ISKCON devotee is expected to follow. So we are advised, *avaiṣṇava-mukhodgīrṇa-pūta-hari-kathāmṛtam:* Do not hear from a person who is not a Vaiṣṇava.

Apart from that, devotees who listen to professional *bhajana* singers often start to sound like professional *bhajana* singers themselves. Instead of immersing themselves in the transcendental sound vibration sung by the pure devotee of the Lord, they immerse themselves in the beautiful music sung by the professional *bhajana* singers. But although fancy tricks with tunes and notes may turn the public on, that's not what pleases Kṛṣṇa.

There's a passage in *Jaiva Dharma* about a spiritual aspirant who has had training in classical music. When he has been in the association of devotees for a while, he takes the opportunity to sing *kīrtana* in beautiful classical style. All the devotees get turned off right away. "What is this?" Here is a guy with a professional background and technical training, but he doesn't have *bhāva,* he doesn't reflect genuine devotion. His music reflects his cultivation of professional technique. And we see that a lot, unfortunately: *kīrtana* lacking devotion but overflowing with technique.

I was in some *kīrtana,* and the *mṛdaṅga* player was all beats. If there was a moment of space, it had to be filled with *alaṅkāras* (decorative sound vibrations). There wasn't enough space in the *kīrtana* for all of the beats one can play, so the player had to fill in as many as possible. And I noted the difference between that kind of *mṛdaṅga* playing and the expert playing of Śrīla Prabhupāda's godbrother Kṛṣṇa Dāsa Bābājī Mahārāja. When Bābājī Mahārāja wanted to do something extra, he could do it. But for most of the *kīrtana* it would be *boom, boom-boom,* simple, simple, simple, because the thing he wanted to hear was the holy name. The *mṛdaṅga* was only to give a little shape or support to the holy name, not for a *mṛdaṅga*-playing exhibition. Śrīla Bhaktisiddhānta Sarasvatī Ṭhākura, at the time of leaving this world, wanted to hear *śrī rūpa mañjarī pāda* sung by someone *other* than a big *kīrtanīya* who was present. "Śrīdhara Mahārāja is there. Let him sing." Śrīdhara Mahārāja was not known as a silver-voiced *kīrtanīya,* but the technique wasn't what was wanted – it was the feeling.

Once in Māyāpura, the devotees and the managers in 1976 or '77, arranged a *kīrtana melā* (a *kīrtana* competition). The idea was to attract more people to Māyāpura from surrounding areas. There are *kīrtana* groups that roam around and do *kīrtanas* at weddings, birthdays, and festivals and then get paid something. So at this *melā,* various *kīrtana* groups were invited to come. They would perform and be judged by the panel of judges on their *mṛdaṅga* playing, their dancing, and their dress. These guys could play *kartālas* with their hands behind their backs. They could play *mṛdaṅga* with their elbows. They were fantastic. Prabhupāda was in the Lotus Building in his quarters. At that time he was feeling indisposed; his health was deteriorating. So he sent word down from the Lotus Building, "Turn off the amplifiers." Prabhupāda wasn't interested in hearing them at all. He said, "They are simply singing for money."

Our *kīrtana* is different. What Kṛṣṇa wants is your feeling. *Bhāva-*

grāhi janārdana: What the Lord accepts is the feeling of the devotee. After Hiraṇyakaśipu was killed, the demigods offered prayers to pacify the Lord, but still the Lord was roaring in fury. Then Brahmā pushed Prahlāda Mahārāja forward, saying, "You speak something." Prahlāda Mahārāja thought, "All the demigods have offered their prayers in beautiful Sanskrit" – again so many *alaṅkāras* – "and they are all big demigods. What will I say? When all these demigods have failed to satisfy the Lord, what can I do?" Then Prahlāda thought. "But I can offer my feelings." That's the thing, not how great a singer you are.

EXPERTISE AS PART OF DEVOTION

Now, it's not that we have to be a culture of incompetence. When Acyutānanda Prabhu compiled ISKCON's first song book, Śrīla Prabhupāda appreciatively wrote in a foreword, "He has learned how to sing in Bengali and play *mṛdaṅga* like an expert professional." But, on the other hand, if externally someone is a great singer or a great speaker or a great *pūjārī* or a great *yajña* performer or whatever but internally the heart is all trash, then we have a problem, the one Raghunātha Dāsa Gosvāmī is speaking about in this verse. It's a deceit problem.

Raghunātha Dāsa Gosvāmī balances his verse by saying on the one side to give up all this affectation, this urinary interest you have, and on the other side develop your love for Rādhā and Kṛṣṇa. That's the real business of life.

In the early days of Jaduräṇī's painting, at one point she was applying techniques from the great masters and trying to become really professional. She wasn't trying to become as good as Rembrandt, but because all the great masters studied anatomy carefully, she painted a very muscular Nārada Muni. And Prabhupāda said, "If you want to go down this path, I will pray to Kṛṣṇa to save you." Save her from what? From becoming like a professional artist.

Śrīla Prabhupāda sometimes detected a problem with devotees who had learned some Sanskrit. A devotee may have wanted to serve by editing Sanskrit, so he decides to go university and take an introductory Sanskrit course. Now he knows a little Sanskrit. But Prabhupāda said, "As soon as he knows a little Sanskrit, he think he is better than

Guru Mahārāja." You absorb the mundane mentality that these people have. You start to become a rationalist, and you start to think you're hot stuff because you know the rules of *sandhi* and all these incompetent ISKCON *brahmacārīs* are chanting without the correct pronunciation. And then you think you can correct your guru. You become puffed-up and then you are finished. In any category, whether it is academics, art, music, business, or anything, when people start to think they are God's gift to the Vaiṣṇava community, deceit will arise. So professional training can be a pitfall. There are valuable things we can learn. On the other hand, when you pick up the head, you get the tail also. So one has to be very careful.

Academically, if a product is up to a certain standard it's good, no matter what rubbish the actual content is. But if something is not up to that standard, then it is rubbish, no matter how exalted it is. Academics with this point of view are fools because their emphasis is on what doesn't matter and they are missing the point. Someone is crying out that there's a fire, and you are analyzing the grammar of their sentence.

Prabhupāda wrote in regard to his translations and commentary on Śrīmad Bhāgavatam that somehow he had to get his message across in a foreign language although there would be so many discrepancies. He said that if there's a fire in the house, then the residents will somehow or other make it known to the neighbors, even if they don't speak the same language.

Of course, you have to know your level of capability and also be humble. If you approach a big Sanskrit professor, it doesn't really pay to come off like you're the world's greatest Sanskritist. Therefore it is advised that one be humble but at the same time clear about one's principles. Academics who are honest will appreciate that you've got something.

THE LORD AND HIS INTERNAL ENERGY

The contamination of deceit and hypocrisy can lodge in the heart of the aspiring devotee. Raghunātha Dāsa Gosvāmī says to stop this hypocrisy, this deceit, this cheating.

What is the impetus for this deceit? The material energy. We may think, "I may not be able to come to the real standard, but I am getting some nourishment from what's within reach. I may not have purified my heart and developed love for Kṛṣṇa, but I can be a sharp Vaiṣṇava dresser and play spiffy *mṛdaṅga* beats and sing like a professional, and then all the perks come in. Women are looking at me, and people are giving me money. And if I am coming from India to America, the green card is within reach." One hardly needs a greater impetus for cheating than that. The green card is like the next best thing to an entry ticket to Indraloka.

But if we tell the mind to give up deceit, the mind will say, "Then what am I supposed to do? I have to be active. You're torturing me; you're going to make me stop everything. You don't want me to bathe in donkey urine, but I have to bathe somewhere." So Raghunātha Dāsa Gosvāmī describes the real business of the mind. He says, *gāndharvā-giridhara-pada-prema-vilasat sudhāmbhodhau snātvā*, "bathing in the ocean of love emanating from the lotus feet of Śrī Śrī Gāndharvikā-Giridhārī." Śrīla Bhaktivinoda Ṭhākura says, "Gāndharvā refers to Śrīmatī Rādhikā, who is the internal energy of the Supreme Personality of Godhead. Giridhārī refers to Śrī Kṛṣṇa, the Supreme Personality of Godhead, who possesses all unlimited inconceivable potencies, and is thus known as *śaktimān-puruṣa*. Here one is advised to bathe in the *viśuddha-cid-vilāsa*, the ocean of nectar of transcendental spiritual transformation. This nectar arises from love of the shelter of Gāndharvā-Giridhārī's lotus feet."

Here *śakti* and *śaktimān* indicate energy and the possessor of energy. *Parāsya śaktir vividhaiva śrūyate*. The Absolute Truth is possessed of energies, *vividhaiva* – so many different kinds of energies. Kṛṣṇa has three principal energies – the material energy, the marginal energy and the spiritual energy. Without energy, you have impersonalism. Without energy there is no meaning to "Personality of Godhead;" you just have a homogeneous substance. But the *śāstras* say otherwise. The Absolute Truth has so many different kinds of energies.

viṣṇu-śakti parā proktā
kṣetrajñākhyā tathā parā

avidyā-karma-saṁjñānyā
tṛtīyā śaktir iṣyate

There are three kinds of energies – material, spiritual, and marginal.

eka-deśa-sthitasyāgner
jyotsnā vistāriṇī yathā
parasya brahmaṇaḥ śaktis
tathedam akhilaṁ jagat

Say you have a fireplace. If there were a fire in that fireplace, then heat and light would spread throughout the room. Although the fire is in one place, the energy is distributed . The heat of the fire wouldn't just be in the fireplace.

There must be heat. There must be light. Otherwise, what is the meaning of fire? Can it be cold? No, there must be heat and light. Then it's called fire. Just as "sun" means there must be sunshine, and "sunshine" means there must be sun, "Kṛṣṇa" means Kṛṣṇa with his energies. Without energies there's no meaning of Krsna, and without Krsna how can the energy exist? So now we're hearing of the *svarūpa-śakti* (the internal energy). That energy is Śrīmatī Rādhārāṇī, the pleasure potency of the Personality of Godhead. And Śrī Kṛṣṇa is *śaktimān*, the person to whom the energy belongs. Together, they are described as Gāndharvā-Giridhārī, Rādhā-Kṛṣṇa *yugala*. Together they are the complete Absolute Truth. Their activities are *viśuddha citta vilāsa; citta vilāsa* (spiritual activities) and *viśuddha* (completely pure). Not only *śuddha* but *viśuddha* (absolutely pure). So this energy is exactly the opposite of the energies of the material world. In the material world everything is motivated, contaminated, and unconstitutional because those who are meant to give enjoyment to Kṛṣṇa are trying to enjoy independently, as if they were Kṛṣṇa. They're trying to do that through the medium of the material energy, which they are trying to exploit while at the same time getting entangled. *Manaḥ-ṣaṣṭhānīndriyāṇi, prakṛti-sthāni karṣati* (*Bhagavad-gītā* 15.7). The soul struggles with the mind and senses – the physical body, and the mental, subtle body. *Prakṛti-sthāni karṣati* – struggling and trying to enjoy. But the loving dealings of Rādhā and Kṛṣṇa are manifestations of purity. They have nothing to do with the contaminated business of this material world. Therefore Śrīla Raghunātha Dāsa Gosvāmī advises us (or advises his mind) to turn away from hypocrisy, from deceit, from the false project for enjoyment in the material world, and turn toward the service of the Absolute Truth: Kṛṣṇa with his spiritual internal energy. That's the plea to the mind, the direction to the mind, the instruction to the mind.

Śrīla Bhaktivinoda, in his commentary, says that Śrī Rūpa Gosvāmī himself prays in *Śrī Prārthanā-paddhatiḥ* of his *Stava-mālā*:

śuddha-gāṅgeya-gaurāṅgīṁ
kuraṅgī-laṅgimekṣaṇām
jita-koṭīndu-bimbāsyām
ambudāmbara-saṁvṛtām

> O Śrī Rādhā, I offer obeisance to you. You have a complexion of pure golden hue, possess of a pair of doe-like restless eyes, have a face that conquers the beauty of millions of full moons, and dress in dark cloud-like garments.

Rūpa Gosvāmī gave up all material wealth and opulences (*tyaktvā tūrṇam aśeṣa-maṇḍala-pati-śreṇīṁ sadā tucchavat*) and took up the life of a beggar (*bhūtvā dīna-gaṇeśakau karuṇayā kaupīna-kanthāśritau*). Yet here he is describing the beautiful qualities of a woman – beautiful limbs, beautiful eyes. That means he's not talking about a woman of this material world. The Gosvāmīs had had everything. Raghunātha Dāsa Gosvāmī's wife, for example, was a young, aristocratic, beautiful girl, comparable to the goddess of fortune, but he gave her up. The Gosvāmīs had no business going to Vṛndāvana and then discussing the features of a beautiful young girl. But Rūpa Gosvāmī glorifies Śrīmatī Rādhārāṇī, because her entire existence is a manifestation of Kṛṣṇa's spiritual energy.

As Kṛṣṇa is glorious, so his *svarūpa-śakti* is glorious and their pastimes are glorious. The Gosvāmīs are teaching us this. This material world is the reflection of that reality, a perverted reflection. The mind is attracted to that reflection. Why should you be so captivated by the reflection of reality? Here is the actual reality, but not for enjoyment:

for service. Not "This is mine, this is mine." The energy is Kṛṣṇa's energy. When Hanumān went to Laṅkā, he saw beautiful women lying in the palace, half-drunk, vulnerable, but he wasn't attracted. He thought, "I have come here not to enjoy but to serve." And the most beautiful of all the women was Śrīmatī Sītā-devī. Hanumān's concern was not to enjoy but to see Sītā restored to the side of Lord Rāmacandra. That's an example of pure consciousness. In pure consciousness the devotee has no interest in enjoying; he is interested in serving.

AVOID IMITATION

Rūpa Gosvāmī prays, "[O Śrīmatī Radhika] I, a distressed soul belonging to you, beg you with sweet words while rolling on the banks of the Yamunā!" These are signs of advanced devotional service. Raghunātha Dāsa Gosvāmī was situated on that platform of pure Kṛṣṇa consciousness, and his pleas to the Lord and his energies originate out of pure desire to be engaged in the service of the Lord. The *sahajiyās* imitate these things. They cry, they roll on the ground, they express their deep longings for Kṛṣṇa – and then they go smoke or go looking for their mistress, because it's all so-called *prasādam*. It's that deceit and hypocrisy that Raghunātha Dāsa Gosvāmī condemns in the first part of the verse. They want to be known as advanced devotees. They want to get prestige and fame, so they superficially imitate Raghunātha Dāsa Gosvāmī and Haridāsa Ṭhākura.

There's a story that Gaurakiśora Dāsa Bābājī was chanting Hare Kṛṣṇa in a secluded place and some imitator thought, "I will get prestige by also chanting Hare Kṛṣṇa in this sacred place." So he set up a shop, so to speak. He got himself a little *bhajana-kuṭīr*, not so far away, and he was chanting. But Śrīla Gaurakiśora Bābājī Mahārāja commented that you can't have a child just by going to the maternity room and making noise. The *sahajiyās* want to be seen as great devotees, but they don't want to follow the path of devotional service. The path of devotional service is to be followed step by step (*kramenaiva*). But *sahajiyās* want to jump from where they are to where they want to be without doing the work, without taking the steps in between. Therefore they don't have foundation or substance.

Śrīla B.R. Śrīdhara Mahārāja commented one time that if you skip some step, the part you skipped will remain hollow. In India, buildings sometimes crumble because the cheapskate building contractors don't build according to code. To save a rupee, they use less sand and cement, fewer steel rods – whatever they can skimp on. The building looks really good, and they book it all out, but then one day it crashes. So if we don't follow the step-by-step process, that's what will happen. One can look really good, but there is some hollow portion, and under pressure everything will come crashing down.

REAL HUMILITY

Bhaktivinoda quotes Rūpa Gosvāmī's verse:

kṛtāgaske 'py ayogye 'pi
jane 'smin kumatāv api
dāsya-dāna-pradānasya
lavam apy upapādaya

Although I am unfit, an offender with a crooked mind, please bestow on me a fragment of the gift of service to you.

Śrīla Sanātana Gosvāmī comments that this mood is the necessary qualification for Kṛṣṇa consciousness: extreme humility. The Gosvāmīs weren't just "being humble." It wasn't just that they knew that they were supposed to be humble so they said things like "I am the lowest. I am the most fallen." As Prabhupāda said, "You're not the most anything!"

Kavirāja Gosvāmī wrote, "I am lower than the worm in the stool." Prabhupāda says it's not just that he is writing poetry – he genuinely feels that. The Gosvāmīs genuinely feel that they are unqualified when they write this way. It's not just adherence to some traditional formula: "You are supposed to say something humble." They genuinely felt that way. Sanātana Gosvāmī avoided the main path to the Jagannātha temple and took the long way around the beach, walking over the hot sand, because he thought he might otherwise come in touch with *pūjārīs* and contaminate them. Who can imagine the level of Kṛṣṇa consciousness the Gosvāmīs were speaking and acting from? He writes, "I am an offender. I am unqualified. I have crooked intelligence." When he looks at himself he sees these things, but we see a pure devotee. We see a devotee of the highest caliber, but the devotee of the highest caliber doesn't think, "I am a *paramahaṁsa*; I have attained perfection." Bhaktivinoda also quotes this verse of Rūpa Gosvāmī: "This unhappy soul is not fit to be neglected by you, for you have a butter-soft heart that melts constantly by the warmth of your compassion."

Narottama Dāsa Ṭhākura also says, *patita-pāvana-hetu tava avatāra, mo-sama patita prabhu nā pāibe āra:* "I have some qualification that I am fallen and you are the *dīna-bandhu*. You are *patita-pāvana*. So what about me? What about me?"

PRACTICAL ABSORPTION OF THE MIND

Prabhupāda pointed out that this is *samādhi,* to absorb the mind in these pastimes, these topics. And Prabhupāda's slogan was "Work now. Samādhi later," the purport being that if we try to go to Vṛndāvana and imitate Raghunātha Dāsa Gosvāmī, it will not turn out right because we are not fit to do that. "Now I will get a little cottage, and I will meditate day and night on the divine loving pastimes of Rādhā-Madhava." Śrīla Rūpa Gosvāmī in *Upadeśāmṛta* says that one should spend day and night by the side of Rādhā-kuṇḍa in one's spiritual body, serving Rādhā Kṛṣṇa. This instruction is for those on the platform of *viśuddha-sattva*. On the platform of pure consciousness one can be absorbed in this way. But if one is still infected by *anarthas,* by contamination in the heart, and at the same time wants to imitate this process of Śrīla Raghunātha Dāsa Gosvāmī, then the attempt will be a failure because one has not yet reached that platform. Prabhupāda gave the example of one devotee who went to Māyāpura. Back in the days when Māyāpura was all fields, he built himself a hut and he was out there in the fields in his hut chanting sixty-four rounds a day. But after three or four days he was gone and no one ever saw him again, because that was not the platform on which he was situated.

Gurudāsa tells the story of the first time he went to Vṛndāvana. He was traveling from Delhi to Vṛndāvana in a car with Prabhupāda,

Kṛṣṇa's pure devotee, anticipating reaching Vṛndāvana, and wondering what Prabhupāda must be thinking about. But Prabhupāda wasn't speaking. Finally, after an hour and a half of driving, Prabhupāda said, "Cement. We have to get cement." Prabhupāda was thinking of service: "We have to build the temple. We have to spread Kṛṣṇa consciousness to Western boys and girls. They need a place to come," and so on, whatever Prabhupāda's conception was. And to do all that, he needed cement. Practical.

In *Nectar of Instruction* Prabhupāda says, "Kṛṣṇa consciousness is not a matter of imaginative ecstasy." One wants to catapult himself into Vṛndāvana by imagining, picturing oneself there. You play a role and then you are there. Prabhupāda said that's not what it is. "It's not imaginative ecstasy." What does he say it is? "Devotional service is not a matter of sentimental speculation or imaginative ecstasy. Its substance is practical activity." Practical activities in the service of the Lord. Even in Vṛndāvana, Yaśodā is in ecstasy, but it's not that she's thinking, "What do I have to do to be in ecstasy?" or "Let me absorb myself in ecstasy." She is thinking of how to get the butter together and what to cook for Kṛṣṇa. She's wondering if he's getting into trouble with the monkeys. She is thinking about practical activities for the service of the Lord, and in that mood she is naturally in ecstasy. But she is not thinking, "You know, I should be in ecstasy because this is Vṛndāvana and, after all, Kṛṣṇa is my son."

In all of Vṛndāvana, everyone is thinking, "What can I do to please Kṛṣṇa?" Practical activities. They are holding a meeting, discussing, "Too many demons are coming. I think we have to move. It's not safe for the children here." Practical, that's Kṛṣṇa consciousness: not imaginative ecstasy, and not dry speculation, but serving. We have to serve the order of the spiritual master with dedication. Therefore, Prabhupāda said, "Work now." The spiritual master wants me to do something. How can I do it? Prabhupāda was thinking, "I got this order. I have to spread Kṛṣṇa consciousness in English. How do I do that? How do I do that?"

It's not that only a neophyte devotee thinks, "How do I get the practical business done," whereas the advanced devotee thinks, "How can I relish these topics of *līlā*?" Rather, the advanced devotee thinks, "How can I carry out the order of my spiritual master? How do I please guru and Gaurāṅga by service, by practical activities?" The two songs Prabhuapda wrote on the Jaladuta are very instructive. In these songs, he is thinking about the charge that's been given to him. Fake devotees, less advanced devotees, think about how they're going to "get a charge," how to get ecstasy. But we follow the Gosvāmīs by following the follower of the Gosvāmīs and serving them. In due time that stage will come, in which one becomes absorbed in thoughts of Kṛṣṇa and qualified to think of and appreciate these things, but without material contamination. Otherwise, Prabhupāda said, "They will think of these things and they will simply think of sex." So, therefore, *viṣaya chāḍiyā kabe śuddha habe mana:* When will I give up this spirit of sense gratification so that my mind will become pure?

PRABHUPĀDA'S BOOKS

Once, Śrīla Prabhupāda instructed the editors of *Back to Godhead*, "These topics – *rāsa-līlā* and such things – are not for public." He said, "When I describe Kṛṣṇa's life in *Kṛṣṇa* Book, I cannot avoid these topics. In the course of narration everything is there." But Prabhupāda takes care to explain or contextualize these pastimes. He presents not just those five chapters of the *rāsa-līlā* but the whole picture of Kṛṣṇa's life. Prabhupāda presents the whole story of Kṛṣṇa – his killing of demons, his pastimes as a cowherd boy, his pastimes in Dvārakā with the Pāṇḍavas, everything. And in the course of that, these *līlās* with the *gopīs* are also there within the context that Kṛṣṇa is the Supreme Personality of Godhead who performs all these wonderful activities. It's not that we just print these five chapters: "That's what is really going to attract the public, and besides, this is the essence of everything." No.

Even *Bhagavad-gītā* is too much for most people: "You are not this body." But if they just come in contact with Kṛṣṇa's subject matter it will purify their hearts. Prabhupāda gave an example: If someone is sleeping and someone else is calling "Mr. John! Mr. John! Wake up!" because he is hearing the vibration again and again, he finally wakes up. Prabhupāda therefore said that if people even touched the book they would be purified. And we see that. People read *Kṛṣṇa* Book and become devotees. They read *Teachings of Lord Caitanya* and become devotees. They read *Bhagavad-gītā* and become devotees. How is it possible? Look at the market. Look at what sells. What do people like to read? Prabhupāda's books are the furthest thing from what the world wants to read. And yet, we distribute our books and people read them and they have an effect.

Mundane books are all alike. After a while, you see they are empty. Despite all of their decorations and big names and sex scenes, there is no substance. Prabhupāda's writing is not the writing of a professional writer, but he has the substance, and that substance will act. In the end, what the soul wants is that substance. We can see, practically, that our whole movement has grown on the basis of books, chanting, and *prasadām*. They act. If you go to the so-called spirituality section of a book store, there are so many books about feeling good and getting in touch with your feelings and all this kind of cotton candy stuff. No one is telling people the real story. Hardly anyone is "letting 'em have it." It's all a compromise – what the authors think the reader wants to hear. Prabhupāda didn't care. In Prabhupāda's books you read, "You are fools. You are *mūḍhās*, you are asses, you are demons. Surrender."

As a preacher, you can tell people, "You are *mūḍhā*." You are authorized. You can say, "Don't mind, but – Kṛṣṇa says ..." They need to hear that they are wasting their lives. This is the message, and it acts. It may be that we don't exactly understand how it acts. Rationally, we might have a different plan or some better approach, a more tactful approach. A writing or marketing coach would probably say, "Uh, Mr. Svāmī, you might want to tone that part down a little bit. You might lose your reader." But we see that it acts. This sound has potency, transcendental potency. It acts not exactly by an intellectual process, but a transcendental process.

How do we remain humble when we are telling someone that their intelligence is stolen by illusion? We should remember that we are just messengers. In the *Mahābhārata*, Uluka was sent to the Pāṇḍavas with a very unpalatable message. And when he spoke, the Pāṇḍavas were furious – but not at him. He was just the guy who brought the message.

That's our job. We should not think that because we preach to people we are better than they are. If that's how we think of ourselves, then people will sense that we are just puffing ourselves up by putting everyone else down. But out of genuine concern for people, and as a matter of duty, we have to say these things. It's not humility to compromise and pussyfoot and say what people want to hear so that they will think we are nice guys. Sooner or later, we have to tell them the truth.

COMMENTARY BY ŚIVARĀMA SWAMI

Both this verse and the next are quite interesting in the sense that they deal with the psychology of *anarthas* or impurities within the heart. We will see how exact a science *bhakti* is that it purifies these things from within. In this and the next verse, Raghunātha Dāsa Gosvāmī will be using very graphic, strong language. This is called contrast. On one side you have been burnt by bathing in the trickling urine of an ass, a donkey, and on the other side is bathing in the nectarean ocean of love for Rādhā and Kṛṣṇa. Generally such strong language is used in order to make a point, and specifically to make a point to people who don't understand a message in more subtle ways.

So this contrast is for us, because we are infected by different gross impurities, and the result of these gross impurities is that we become covered by ignorance. In order to penetrate this ignorance, strong language is used. Just like when the child is playing, you tell him, "Stop playing! Stop playing!" If he won't listen because he is so absorbed, ultimately you have to raise your voice and then it pierces through the child's ignorance. In the same way, Raghunātha Dāsa Gosvāmī starts to pierce through our ignorance by using some strong and graphic language. It's effective, because it's something that we don't forget once we hear it. "Why do you burn yourself and me [the soul] by bathing in the trickling urine of the great donkey of full-blown hypocrisy and duplicity?" So you can just imagine a huge ass, and we take a bath in his trickling urine. Furthermore, he says it burns. This is the nature of urine; it is acidic. So we'll address these things specifically later.

In verse five, we discussed *kāmādi*, and Raghunātha Dāsa Gosvāmī says, *prakāmaṁ kāmādi-prakaṭa-patha-pāti-vyatikaraiḥ,* that along with lust comes a host of other unwanted characteristics. So these things need to be purified.

But everyone has experience that we *do* try to purify ourselves of unwanted habits and it's not so simple to remove them, like if you have some dirt on the floor and you sweep it up and you throw it out and it's gone. But our unwanted habits are not such an easy thing to dispose of. So the question arises in this verse. Let's say I have subdued lust and anger, but what about deceit? It still remains. In other words, we're seemingly unable to get rid of all of these characteristics. Bhaktivinoda Ṭhākura explains there are two alternatives of this particular point. The first is you become a deceitful devotee. That's one natural consequence, which means you don't purify the deceit but you let the disease intermingle with your so-called devotional service. Then while it's creating havoc to your devotional creeper you are called a deceitful devotee, and when the damage is finally done then you will no longer be a devotee.

The second alternative is you purify yourself of this deceit. This deceit is generally being described by Bhaktivinoda Ṭhākura as any desire other than the desire to serve Kṛṣṇa. Which means, practically speaking, it's a carpet and you can sweep any material thing under this label of deceit. Any desire other than the desire to serve Kṛṣṇa, or having a purpose for serving other than pleasing Kṛṣṇa, falls under the category of deceitfulness. Two specific characteristics of deceit are being mentioned here: *kapaṭa* and *kuṭināṭī*. *Kapaṭa* means deviousness and *kuṭināṭī* is hypocrisy. In *Caitanya-caritāmṛta* these things are also described. Hypocrisy manifests in the form of diplomacy, mercilessness, and meeting to gossip with others and criticize – all these forms fall under this realm of hypocrisy. Because hypocrisy means that I pretend that I am doing one thing, or I am one way with people, but I think a completely different way about them. In other words, I behave to their face in one way but behind their back I do something completely different.

Bhaktivinoda Ṭhākura explains that there are different classes of devotees and these elements infect all different grades of devotees unless they are purified. From the very neophyte or the lowest devotee to the most advanced devotee deceit affects and influences everyone. Specifically, Śrīla Bhaktivinoda Ṭhākura uses names which are not usually used elsewhere, but it's not uncommon for *ācāryas* to coin terminology of their own, or to use terminology in their own way. In Rūpa Gosvāmī's *Ujjvala-nīlamaṇi* and other books he also creates some of his own terminology.

Similarly, here Bhaktivinoda Ṭhākura talks about three different types of *sādhakas,* saying that all of these three types of *sādhakas* can become infected by deviousness and hypocrisy. We will examine the three different types of devotees and also see what type of deceit manifests in each of them according to the type of work that they do and what the resulting symptoms will be, as they will vary.

The first type of *sādhaka* is called a *sva-niṣṭha bhakta,* the second is called *pariniṣṭha* and the third is called *nirapekṣa. Sva-niṣṭha* is a householder devotee who is very much devoted to self realization, to Kṛṣṇa consciousness, but has the specific characteristic that he or she does not particularly act in the *varṇāśrama* system. This person's desire is simply to serve and satisfy Lord Hari. Which means, for instance, householder devotees who are residents in the temple, who are really just doing everything that they can. Practically speaking, they are living like *brahmacārīs* and *brahmacārīṇīs,* having an austere and simple lifestyle. These are *sva-niṣṭha bhaktas.*

The *pariniṣṭha bhakta* is another type of householder, who is also a good devotee. Such persons are dedicated to following the rules and regulations. They live at home and organize their life to conform with the rules of devotional service, and make the worship of the Deity the center of the home.

And the third type, a *nirapekṣa bhakta,* is a renunciate, a celibate, a detached *sādhaka.* These are the *brahmacārīs, brahmacārīṇīs, sannyāsīs,* and so on. Now let's see what happens to each of these three different types of individuals.

The *sva-niṣṭhas* become contaminated by deceit when they indulge in sense gratification in the name of satisfying the Lord. Indulging in sense gratification means that for the sake of preaching or performing other activities they use the principle of *yukta-vairāgya* as a means of legalizing sense gratification. The result will be that instead of serving devotees, they end up going out to serve the rich and collect money beyond their needs. The symptom of that collection is that they themselves become the enjoyer of that wealth. They enjoy the association of the wealthy. They take personal benefit from the funds they collect from their wealthy associates, and although the wealthy may actually give the funds to such devotees for the institution, the deceitful *sva-niṣṭhas* use the funds for themselves.

Furthermore, with the excuse of education for the sake of preaching they become attached to speculation and logic as a means of trying to make a livelihood and really give up the principles of purity, simplicity, and faith. The third symptom is that such a person may then put on the dress of a renunciate thinking, "Oh! I will leave my household life," in order to increase prestige amongst the circle to whom he or she is preaching. So, the deceitful *sva-niṣṭhas* become speculators.

The *pariniṣṭha* devotees are deceitful when they make a real show of being a strict adherent and being dedicated to spiritual life. Externally they seem to be an ideal and exemplary person in the *varṇāśrama* system but internally they are attached to all kinds of material objects and sense gratification. This type of person is described in the third chapter of *Bhagavad-gītā* where Kṛṣṇa says:

karmendriyāṇi saṁyamya
ya āste manasā smaran
indriyārthān vimūḍhātmā
mithyācāraḥ sa ucyate

> One who restrains the senses of action but whose mind dwells on sense objects certainly deludes himself and is called a pretender. (*Bhagavad-gītā*. 3.6)

Externally they appear to be exemplary but internally they are indulging, making plans for so many different material objectives. Their symptom is that in due course of time they become argumentative and always quarrel with the general mass of devotees. Ultimately they prefer association with worldly minded people in opposition to devotees.

They think, "Actually, these *karmīs* are not so bad. They have so many good qualities. It's unnecessary to really deride them. Why should we always call them demons and so on. Actually there is so much that we can learn from them." And they think, "We should be spending more time learning from them then deriding them." True, that materialists should not be derided, but on the other hand, too much association with worldly people, as Hiraṇyakaśipu pointed out, will simply increase the severity of such a person's plight and ultimately there will be a falldown. So the deceitful *pariniṣṭha* becomes very argumentative.

The third devotee, the renunciate, when deceitful, thinks, "I am a *sannyāsī*. I have my *daṇḍa*. I am a celibate. I must be a very elevated devotee." Because the nature of deceit is, of course, that you deceive others, but the extraordinary nature and very tricky part of this deceit is that you deceive yourself. Therefore, one begins to be extremely proud of one's position. An example of this deceit being taken to an extreme is that of Pauṇḍraka. He became convinced that he was the Supreme Personality of Godhead. The whole story is told in *Kṛṣṇa* Book. Because Pauṇḍraka was a king, and everything was going well in the kingdom, he had nothing to do, and he was bored. His ministers thought, "How should we make the king happy?" and they decided, "Well, why don't we start glorifying him like he is the Supreme Personality of Godhead, and bowing down to him and behaving with him in that way? Certainly then he will become very happy." Soon they came to him and said, "Oh, you are the Supreme Personality of Godhead, Lord Nārāyaṇa. You have decended into this world!"

At first he thought to himself, "What is going on?" But then he started thinking, "Well, they are my advisors; they are my ministers. Obviously they must know what they are talking about. So, yes, they must be right, and come to think of it, I have some divinity within me."

In due course of time he deceived himself to the extent that he challenged Kṛṣṇa, "You are the imposter. Let's fight!" So, that was the end of him.

Nirapekṣa, going back to the *sannyāsī*. He considers himself a very elevated devotee simply due to the externals of his so-called renunciation, expecting prestige and honor simply for wearing the dress of a renunciate . He sees other devotees as being very inferior, deriding the position of others. He collects objects and wealth beyond his basic requirements and necessities. In addition, as a result of all his association with wealth and worldly-minded people, as well as committing offences to other Vaiṣṇavas, he ultimately starts to associate with women in the name of preaching. "Yes, honestly, in order to preach, half the population or more are female. Therefore I have to also preach to them," he thinks to himself. But he is not simply thinking like that. He is tending to preach more to women because he is attracted to them. His concentration and meditation becomes fixed on them. Therefore, he becomes overly attached to his dress and position of a renunciate. Ultimately he becomes very attached to members of the opposite sex and in the meantime, he neglects his real attachment to Kṛṣṇa. Ultimately he falls down.

So, *are cetaḥ*, "O my mind!" *Prodyat*, means rising or expanding. This *kapaṭa* and *kuṭināṭī*, deviousness and hypocrisy are still there, fully or expanding. Raghunātha Dāsa Gosvāmī says when you indulge in this thing, it's like bathing in the urine of an ass. He's using such graphic language because who in their right mind will want to bathe in such a thing? We get so carried away with all of these externals, with the influence of this deceit and this deviousness, this hypocrisy, that we actually think what we are doing is spiritual life, the real thing. Raghunātha Dāsa Gosvāmī says no, this is not the real thing, this is just an ass. What you are doing is entirely the wrong thing. This deceit is not what you're meant to be indulging in or bathing in because bathing means to be clean. He's using a bathing example for both the positive and the negative, as he says *bhara-khara-kṣaran-mūtre snātvā*, and *sudhāmbhodhau snātvā*. Caitanya Mahāprabhu uses a bathing example when he says, *ceto-darpaṇa-mārjanaṁ*. We want to cleanse our hearts. It's a bathing process, *sarvātma-snapanaṁ*. And it's the same here with *snātvā*. We want to cleanse our heart, cleanse our body. So if we want to cleanse ourselves, if we want to bathe, are we going to use donkey urine to bathe with? No matter how much we bathe with that, we simply get dirtier and stinkier and ultimately no one will come near us.

Rādhā and Kṛṣṇa are not going to come close to someone who

constantly bathes in this type of thing. Such persons are not very clean. They are not very nice to be around. Beyond that obvious point, Raghunātha Dāsa Gosvāmī specifically uses this example because the symptom of an ass is that it's a stupid animal. Who associates with a stupid animal and will bathe in a stupid animal's urine? Only another such stupid animal. Therefore he is trying to wake us up. Why should we put ourselves in this situation? Why be so humiliated? The graphic language here is *kṣaran*. He not only says that it's just urine but he says it's trickling. Trickling means that it is a persistent *drop, drop, drop, drop*. It's a disgusting scene and ultimately only a fool will do such a thing. Raghunātha Dāsa Gosvāmī says that we should not be foolish and bathe ourselves in these things thinking that anything good is going to come out of it.

The last point that Raghunātha Dāsa Gosvāmī makes about the donkey urine is *dahasi katham ātmānam*, we burn ourselves. *Dahasi* means to burn. *Ātma* means the soul, which of course cannot be burnt. The "burning" is that one becomes so disheartened or poisoned by deceit that it more or less destroys any opportunity for one's advancement in spiritual life. It is as if the soul is burning in a fire of deceit and hypocrisy, a very unpalatable and uncomfortable situation, detrimental for spiritual life.

But now he gives the other side, which is very nice:

sadā tvaṁ gāndharvā-giridhara-pada-prema-vilasat-
sudhāmbhodhau snātvā tvam api nitarāṁ māṁ ca sukhaya

The contrast to bathing in an ass's trickling urine is that we should bathe in, "the ocean of love emanating from the lotus feet of Śrī Śrī Gāndharvikā-Giridhārī," *prema āmbhodhau*. So when you hear one and then the other, then certainly the choice is obvious. No one would want to bathe in the urine of a donkey, an ass. No one will want to bathe in urine when there is a beautiful ocean of nectar to be bathed in. What is that particular bathing that we want to do in the ocean of love? In contrast to the deceitful behavior which we just learned in regards to these three types of devotees, there are prayers to Śrīmatī Rādhārāṇī by Rūpa Gosvāmī, from *Stava-mālā*. Śrīla Bhaktivinoda

Ṭhākura quotes these prayers, not to gave us the contrast to the other undesirable and disgusting situation described in this verse but also as a solution of how to become free from a deceitful mentality and hypocritical attitude. He says we should pray. We should pray to Kṛṣṇa in a systematic process of surrendering. While we are praying we are also meditating on the Supreme Lord, which may be done through the process of chanting the holy name. If such praying, surrendering, meditating, and chanting are done with the right mentality, mainly humility, then deceit will be vanquished from the heart and will never be able to re-enter.

Śrīla Rūpa Gosvāmī says, "O Śrī Rādhā, I offer obeisance to you. You have a complexion of pure golden hue." When we read this, we are aware of the comparison to *kṣaran-mūtre snātvā dahasi*. Bhaktivinoda Ṭhākura quotes more prayers from Śrī Rūpa Gosvāmī which we can read in his commentary. These prayers are a meditation to direct our minds from the duplicity of materially contaminated devotional service towards what is really pure devotional service. One then learns how to meditate on Lord Kṛṣṇa and Śrīmatī Rādhārāṇī. In *Kṛṣṇa* Book, *Śrīmad-Bhāgavatam*, and *Caitanya-caritāmṛta*, Prabhupāda has given us so many beautiful pastimes, so many nice prayers and poems. We also have so many nice songs. All these are meant to actually invoke our meditation. These are not just books to be just kept on a shelf and, occasionally for entertainment, gone through, but rather they are can be a constant source of practice. That's what a *sādhaka* is doing – constantly practicing. When people ask what our meditation is, we answer: *smartavyaḥ satataṁ viṣṇur, vismartavyo na jātucit, a*lways remember Kṛṣṇa and never forget him.

The next point is that we should always surrender with great hope for service. Why should Rādhārāṇī give us service? Raghunātha Dāsa Gosvāmī says that he is guilty of being an offender, a rascal, a useless wretch. It's a fact that we are at least these things, and a lot more, but Rādhārāṇī is prayed to here, "You have a butter-soft heart which melts constantly by the warmth of your compassion." So whether qualified or unqualified one can actually make a claim for mercy. That is what mercy means. Mercy means you don't have to be qualified; you just simply have to ask for it. And it may come, or it may not come, but you can always ask. We don't have to wait until we are highly qualified. When will one think, "I am qualified for mercy"? One will never think oneself to be qualified. Therefore, whatever our condition, we may start actually asking and begging for mercy.

Asking for mercy is the mood or the process of chanting the holy names of the Lord. This is what chanting Hare Kṛṣṇa means – that we are begging for the mercy of Rādhā and Kṛṣṇa. We are hearing the holy names, meditating on the pastimes, hoping against hope that all of these impurities within our hearts will become eradicated. And at the same time if we concentrate, and if we absorb ourselves in this activity, then all these impurities will be blocked. Neither will we indulge in them, nor will they be able to penetrate our consciousness or have any particular effect. The summary of this particular verse is that one has to learn how to beg for the mercy of Rādhārāṇī and Kṛṣṇa. The mood of begging is called humility. Caitanya Mahāprabhu has given this instruction:

tṛṇād api sunīcena
taror api sahiṣṇunā
amāninā mānadena
kīrtanīyaḥ sadā hariḥ

This mood is the only way one will be able to constantly chant the holy name or practice devotional service in a systematic and consistent fashion. Without humility doing so is not possible. Rather, our practice will always go up and down. I will go to *maṅgala-ārati* and the morning program, but as soon as I leave then I revert to a different consciousness. Sometimes I am up and sometimes I am down. Therefore humility is extremely important. And humility may be acquired by practicing the symptoms of humility, and specifically by associating with those devotees who are also themselves genuinely humble. By this humility a devotee's life should be saturated with chanting the holy name, *satataṁ kīrtayanto mām*. We should always chant because when we are always chanting in this mood we will not give the opportunity for something else to come in. Otherwise, as soon as we stop, then immediately so many things will start coming through the mind. So an important point which Bhaktivinoda Ṭhākura makes is that the mind must be engaged in thoughts which are essential for advancement in devotional service, such as, "How can I perfect my service?" Thinking about Kṛṣṇa, thinking about spreading Kṛṣṇa consciousness, remembering the Lord's pastimes, and chanting the holy name loudly are all such essential activities. He says as soon as you don't think about essential activities, you will start thinking about non-essential activities. And these non-essential activities will allow all kinds of other things to come back into the mind.

Such consciousness is what yoga is. Yoga means to control the mind and the senses, *yoga indriya-saṁyama*. There are six senses, including the mind. Externally to engage our body and gross senses is one thing, but the other thing is to fix our mind and always be absorbed in thinking about Kṛṣṇa. It is a fact that we may be keeping financial accounts, or like Arjuna fighting in a battle, and we may not be thinking exactly about a pastime, but at least we can have thoughts which are very essential to the execution of the service, which are facilitating the service. And at times when we are not so engaged in service then we can think about Kṛṣṇa directly, Kṛṣṇa's pastimes and activities and so on. We can't wait for such things to just sort of happen at some particular point. It's not just going to happen unless we make it happen. That is what Kṛṣṇa consciousness means – to always practice thinking about Kṛṣṇa.

So, in conclusion Śrīla Bhaktivinoda Ṭhākura says of this verse that the heart must be purified by humility in order to drive deceit out, and the heart must be saturated with humility in order to keep deceit from coming back in. That's the summation. We can see how easily and in how many ways deceit (*kapaṭa*) and other things can come in as soon as we let our guard down. The conclusion of verse six is our hearts must be purified by devotional activities, specifically chanting Hare Kṛṣṇa. Perform them with great humility in order to drive deceit out and keep it out. This is a warning because sometimes we feel that by execution of devotional service we have gotten somewhere and we immediately sit back and relax. We should be very careful.

We should just want to read these particular prayers from Rūpa Gosvāmī, listed in Bhaktivinoda's commentary, again and again because they actually have such a nice mood. And either we should pray like this, or we should read similar traditional prayers, or we can compose our own prayers but the mood of these prayers is so very nice:

"I beg you with sweet words while rolling on the banks of the Yamunā!"

Rolling on the banks of Yamunā means we must be willing to beg on the ground. Rolling on the ground means asking for mercy. We must know how to pray.

"This unhappy soul is not fit to be neglected by you."

This is the nature of the world, that we have hope. Anticipation means I have great faith that Rādhārāṇī is very merciful. Lord Kṛṣṇa is very merciful. Somehow or other if they see how much I want their mercy, sooner or later they will give it to me.

"Although I am unfit, an offender with a crooked mind."

We should realize the more we become a little advanced in Kṛṣṇa consciousness, the more we will feel like this and think like this. Rūpa Gosvāmī doesn't just write those humble words, thinking, "Well yes, this is a nice composition. It will sound good when someone reads it." No. He is writing what he actually feels.

"Please bestow on me a fragment of the gift of service to you, for you have a butter-soft heart which melts constantly by the warmth of your compassion."

COMMENTARY BY BHAKTIVIJNANA GOSWAMI

Let us examine the words of this verse. The Sanskrit word *are* approximately means "Hey, you, fool!" *Are* is a very crude way of address. *Cetaḥ* is the mind, and it is for a good reason that Raghunātha Dāsa Gosvāmī addresses his mind in such an abrupt way, because he has reached the limit at this point in his instructions to his mind. *Prodyat-kapaṭa-kuṭināṭī-bhara-khara kṣaran-mutre snātvā* indicates that he is saying, "Hey, fool, what are you doing? You are bathing in an ass's urine, and not simply any kind of ass but a great ass." *Khara* means ass, and *bhara khara* means a great ass, because only from a great ass will there be enough urine to bathe in. *Kapaṭa* means deception; *kuṭināṭī* means hypocrisy. We will look later at the difference between *kapaṭa* and *kuṭināṭī*. *Mūtre* means urine – you have bathed in that urine.

The ayurveda explains the different properties of various living entities' urine and that of an ass is extremely burning. Raghunātha Dāsa Gosvāmī is having a dialogue between the soul and the mind, where the soul tells the mind, "Mind, whom are you cheating? You yourself feel the fire of remorse for having bathed in that filth. I am burning, you are burning, and we both are burning. Why are you doing this?"

Instead of bathing in the urine of a big ass, we need *sadā tvaṁ gāndharvā-giridhara-pada-prema-vilasat sudhāmbhodhau snātvā* – we need to bathe in *ambhodhau sudha,* the ocean of nectar. *Vilasat* – this nectar is shining. *Gāndharvā-giridhari-pada-prema* – the nectar is *prema* or love for the lotus feet of the divine couple. "If you always bathe in that nectar," he says to the mind, "then both you and I will be happy." Raghunātha Dāsa Gosvāmī presents before us an alternative. He says a person will either somehow or other cheat and as a result burn inside from shame, or if they think of Kṛṣṇa, they and their mind will be joyful.

DECEPTION AND CHEATING

To understand exactly what deception is, we can look in *Caitanya-caritāmṛta, Ādi-līlā* (1.90), where Kṛṣṇadāsa Kavirāja Gosvāmī provides a definition:

> *ajñāna-tamera nāma kahiye 'kaitava'*
> *dharma-artha-kāma-mokṣa-vāñchā ādi saba*

Ignorance in our heart takes the form of deception, *kaitava*. Ignorance is here defined as *vāñchā*, desire, for *dharma, artha, kāma,* and *mokṣa*. This is a highly radical statement because we know that the entire Vedic culture is built on helping a person achieve *dharma, artha, kāma,* and *mokṣa*. But Kṛṣṇadāsa Kavirāja Gosvāmī says that each of them is a deception.

All these life goals, in one way or another, put us in the center. These mundane goals can be pious forms of egocentrism or disgusting, nasty, horrible forms of egocentrism – but they are still egocentrism. Viśvanātha Cakravartī Ṭhākura explains that the living being is by nature a servant of God and therefore the main duty is to serve. When we forget our true nature, focusing on the body and the interests related to the body, this focus is called cheating.

There is cheating in the form of the desire for *dharma,* the desire to be pious; there is cheating in the form of the desire for *mokṣa,* liberation; there is cheating in the form of *kāma* or lust; and there is cheating in the form of the desire for *artha,* wealth. The desire for *mokṣa* is the worst one. The point is that in the first verse of *Śrīmad-Bhāgavatam,* Kṛṣṇa is defined as *satyam param,* which means the Supreme Truth. We can not, preserving our inner propensity to cheat, approach the Supreme Truth. Truth and lies are the exact opposites of each other.

Those who say, "I want to serve Kṛṣṇa," but instead keep on serving themselves are cheating. The opportunity that we have to serve Kṛṣṇa is the most amazing and rare. But it can also lead us to the heaviest offenses because, having taken up the path of serving Kṛṣṇa, we can turn into most terrible cheaters. Under the cover of serving Kṛṣṇa, we serve ourselves – our own interests, our own petty desires, our ambitions.

In this sense cheating is the exact opposite of love. We can only approach Kṛṣṇa if we completely eradicate our habit of hypocrisy. We must very clearly understand how the tendency of hypocrisy is situated in our hearts, how and in what various forms it reigns. There are many sins such as murdering a *brāhmaṇa,* and committing adultery. There are *mahā-patakas,* five or six greatest sins in accordance with the *Manu-saṁhitā,* but in the Eighth Canto of *Śrīmad-Bhāgavatam* it is stated the worst sin is cheating. Bali Mahārāja quotes Mother Earth saying, "I can bear all kinds of sinners, but I cannot bear someone who is cheating."

THE ROLE OF THE MIND IN CHEATING

Hypocrisy inevitably comes to us precisely because we are covered by a mind which is constantly filled with endless desires. Kṛṣṇa himself compares these desires to a fire. He says that no matter how much a person attempts to satiate the senses, these desires are never satisfied. Those who have taken up the spiritual path are also faced by these mental desires. Even if such persons do not give the desires an opportunity to manifest themselves outwardly, they may be tearing the mind apart from within. Here Raghunātha Dāsa Gosvāmī compares this state of internal disgrace to a fire and says, "What is the point? There is no need to bathe in all this burning urine. Instead, choose to bathe in the ocean of love for Rādhā and Kṛṣṇa and feel like you have been born again."

Interestingly enough, in the *Manu-saṁhitā*, in the section "Penalties for various crimes," it is said that in Vedic times if a person committed treachery or deceit, the punishment for *kṣatriyas*, the men of honor, was to bathe them in ass's urine. As a result, all their hair would fall out and they would remain bald-headed to the end of their days; everyone would know of their crime, saying, "Look, that's a rascal; that's a cheater."

In one way or another all the disgrace or deception we have inside will sooner or later surface and become visible to everyone. Here Raghunātha Dāsa Gosvāmī is warning us not to cheat, exposing ourselves to ridicule by trying to secretly fulfill foolish desires that haven't made us happy anyway.

We can consider what happens to those who allow themselves, without even noticing it, to be cheated by their minds. Raghunātha Dāsa Gosvāmī talks about this because on the spiritual path we need to go to the end. Although Kṛṣṇa says that even small progress on this path can save us from the greatest fear, eventually we will still want to go to the end. To do so, we will have to completely destroy the pride within that Raghunātha Dāsa Gosvāmī speaks about in the first verse.

PRETENSE

It is pride that makes us pretend. Because we are constantly putting on guises, we cannot understand or see God. We are unable to see him in the heart of other living beings; we can't see how he manifests himself outwardly; we can't hear his voice within; and we cannot understand how he speaks to us through the mouth of our spiritual master. It is very difficult for us to actually recognize Kṛṣṇa. Although God is everywhere and there is nothing easier than seeing him, we cannot because pride does not allow us to do so.

In the *Rāmāyaṇa* there is a remarkable episode when Sugrīva sends Hanumān to find out who Rāma is. Rāma and Lakṣmaṇa appeared near Mount Ṛṣyamūka where Sugrīva with his retinue were hiding with a handful of monkeys who had remained faithful to him. For fear of his brother, Vāli, he was hiding there. When Sugrīva saw Rāma, he was terribly scared, saying, "Who's that? It must be someone sent by Vāli to kill me!" He said to Hanumān, "Go and find out who it is. You are smart – take on a disguise and pretend to be a *brāhmaṇa*."

Hanumān disguised himself as a *brāhmaṇa*, with *mālā* in hand, and appeared before Rāma and asked, "Who are you? Why are you here?"

Rāma told Lakṣmaṇa, "A good man has come to us, so please explain to him who we are."

Lakṣmaṇa explained to Hanumān, "This is Rāma, the son of King Daśaratha. Due to some misunderstanding he was exiled to the forest, and I am with him because I am his eternal servant."

Hanumān slapped his forehead in consternation, because since early childhood he had been chanting the name of Rāma, "Rāma, Rāma, Hare Rāma, Hare Rāma." He asked Lord Rāmacandra, "Rāma, is it you, my Lord? I've been worshiping you since childhood, always chanting your holy name! You have appeared before me directly, so please tell me why I did not recognize you?"

The Lord replied, "How could you have recognized me? Look at the disguise you have on. *Ye yathā māṁ prapadyante tāṁs tathaiva bhajāmy aham* – you have come to me in a false disguise, pretending to be someone else, so how could you have recognized me?"

That is a very important lesson for all of us – as long as we pretend to be someone else we won't be able to recognize Kṛṣṇa, even if he is standing right in front of us.

Accordingly, Raghunātha Dāsa Gosvāmī is urging us to give up cheating. He says that if you want to cheat Kṛṣṇa, then Kṛṣṇa will necessarily have to cheat you and deprive you of the opportunity to see and recognize him. Giving up cheating is a vital stage in spiritual life, the nature of which we must clearly understand. This stage is called *anartha-nivṛtti.*

Initially in spiritual life we are extremely enthusiastic, feeling that this is exactly what we need, especially if we came to Kṛṣṇa consciousness after having suffered or having been disillusioned in material life. We think that the beginning attraction and ecstasy will last forever. At some point this ecstasy is over and we are faced with our gross and subtle *anarthas,* preventing us from truly seeing or feeling God.

Raghunātha Dāsa Gosvāmī is urging us to watch our motives in order to eliminate our *anarthas.* In a number of lectures, Śrīla Prabhupāda very easy defines *anartha-nivṛtti.* He says you've stopped smoking – that is already one *anartha* less. These cigarettes are definitely an *anartha;* there's nothing of value in them. You've given up meat-eating – another *anartha* less; you've removed the desire for gross sex and you have given up gambling: two more *anarthas* gone. In the beginning, on the gross level we are getting purified. Gradually, as the process of cleansing our mind goes on, new *anarthas* become obvious to us in the form of false motives and deception. The desire for recognition and honor is a most dangerous *anartha* because we begin seeking satisfaction of this *anartha* in the society of devotees. As long as we are respected, we think that we do not care whether we are respected or not. But as soon as someone passes by without greeting us, a storm rises in our mind, "Who is he anyway? He is a junior devotee, why didn't he say 'Hello' to me? Who does he think he is? He's got nothing but *anarthas,* for he has no respect for the devotees." This subtle desire for recognition, in essence, is the same as the most subtle desire for sex. We want to be recognized and respected so that in one way or another we are put in the center.

Another very important point we must understand is that sometimes the *anarthas* come in a very subtle way. That is what deception is about. Sometimes our material attachments disguise themselves so well it is impossible to recognize them. They may come in the form of some noble ideas or in the form of austerities in our service. For example, sometimes when we chant the holy name we get distracted by some great revelation and before we know it this revelation has already distracted us fom Kṛṣṇa.

Therefore, we must understand that all these *anarthas* or material attachments that we face in the process of cleansing the heart will take very perverted forms. Arjuna's attachments came to him in the form of compassion and love for his spiritual master, which Arjuna thought was very noble. However, Kṛṣṇa saw this attachment as an *anartha*. *Anarthas* came to Yudhisthira in the form of attachment to the fact he had never lied.

In the *Purāṇas,* there is this recurring phenomenon that the demigods worry when someone successfully engages in spiritual practice or some kind of austerity and start sending him various obstacles. Indra in his heavenly kingdom sends some Apsarā to distract the practitioner from his austerities. Sometimes *brahmacārīs* think, "Why hasn't Indra sent me an Apsarā yet? Doesn't he see what progress I've made and the austerities I am performing?" But actually Indra does send us Apsarās. You chant the *mahā-mantra* and suddenly an Apsarā appears in your mind and starts dancing – she is sent by Indra because all the demigods are situated in our body and senses.

When we are performing devotional service all the distractions we are subject to are sent by the demigods. But we should think about what an Apsarā is. This is a very important point: sometimes obstacles can take on a very beautiful shape. Caitanya Mahāprabhu himself said *na dhanaṁ na janaṁ na sundarīṁ kavitām* – I do not want *sundarīm* or *kavitām,* I do not want lovely words, lovely ideas and thoughts. When *anarthas* come in a gross form they are not as dangerous as when they come in a subtle form.

As a result of deception, we lose the ability for introspection. Alexander Pushkin used to say, "It is easy to deceive me for I myself am glad to be deceived. There is no need for anyone to cheat me; I will cheat myself." People lose their ability for introspection and for self-analysis, so they start reassuring themselves that everything is fine, when it is not. Sometimes you can see that people are lying to themselves, but the defense is so dense that it is impossible to give them the opportunity to look at themselves from a different angle. That is the problem of deception – it is sometimes so deep a person loses the ability to see their self-deception. This is why it is the duty of the devotee to be constantly introspective and to ask, "How sincere am I? What are my motives? What drives me?"

At first the tendency to deceive is exhibited in a harmless way – a person has been given extra change and he thinks, "A nice way to earn money." Sometimes a person jokes, and for the sake of being witty he slightly exaggerates; sometimes a person argues and in the heat of debate he resorts to lies. Sometimes a person assigns to himself something that does not belong to him or speaks rudely. The *ācāryas* say that all these actions are based on *asat*.

THE PATH OF DECEIT

Narottama Dāsa Ṭhākura calls such actions *asat-kriya*, or actions based on a false concept of life. A person does such trifles and becomes accustomed to behaving in this way. When we begin rendering devotional service, and we start behaving in the above ways out of habit, then small sins or innocent trifles turn into offenses. Narottama Dāsa Ṭhākura says *dehe nā kariha āsthā* – do not trust your body and your mind because you will be cheating out of habit. When you project your bodily concept onto the spiritual realm, you'll start committing offenses. If we have this tendency to deceive, we will end up deceiving not only ourselves but we will deceive our spiritual master and the Vaiṣṇavas and in this way we will be committing offenses.

This sixth verse of the *Manaḥ-śikṣā* is about how dangerous it is to commit offenses on the spiritual path. These offenses burn us from within and deprive us of the opportunity to attain a true spiritual experience. The word *kapaṭa* that Raghunātha Dāsa Gosvāmī uses here has numerous meanings. The words that define *kapaṭa* include deception, cunning, hypocrisy, slyness, fraud, trickery, evasion, self-justification, and eventually godlessness and sin.

Śrīla Jīva Gosvāmī gives a very important definition of deception on the spiritual path. In his *Bhakti-sandarbha* he explains that deception on the spiritual path is that outwardly we bow down before our guru, the sā*dhus*, the Vaiṣṇavas and Śrī Bhagavān, while internally we do not have faith in them. So, Raghunātha Dāsa Gosvāmī says that *kapaṭa*, the absence of faith in the Vaiṣṇavas, in the sā*dhus*, in the spiritual master and ultimately in Kṛṣṇa gives rise to *kuṭināṭī*. *Kuṭināṭī* is hypocritical activities, absorption in extraneous matters, spiteful talk, cruelty, and ultimately violence. This all starts with the fact that inside I do not have complete sincerity or absolute unconditional faith, and I justify myself in every possible way. Such a mood manifests itself in the fact that I start focusing on something extraneous, such as watching TV or movies and start thinking, "I need this for my preaching, so that I can preach in a more efficient way; I'll tell them about this movie in the class." Then we engage in spiteful talk, and then into cruelty, and ultimately into violence.

Śrīla Prabhupāda sometimes translates *kuṭināṭī* as spiteful talk. In fact, it is a very sad chain. The *ācāryas* explain that the first manifestation of deception is that our attitude towards the spiritual master becomes like the one we have towards common people. Deception starts saying, "What's so special about the guru?"

Satsvarūpa Mahārāja tells an amazing story. In the beginning, when Śrīla Prabhupāda had just started spreading Kṛṣṇa consciousness in New York and his first disciples joined him, they arranged a public program for Śrīla Prabhupāda. Among them was Rāyarāma, one of the first disciples of Śrīla Prabhupāda. Rāyarāma printed posters which he stuck all over the East Side in Manhattan, where they had their preaching activities. The poster read, "This man has changed the consciousness of the world."

At that time Śrīla Prabhupāda was away, so when he came back to New York after some time Rāyarāma proudly showed him the poster. Śrīla Prabhupāda made a grimace and said, "It is a very poor poster." At first Satsvarūpa Mahārāja did not understand why Śrīla Prabhupāda did not like it. Then Prabhupāda said, "Guru cannot be called 'a man.'"

First we pull down the guru to a level closer to our own. This is what hypocrisy or deception is about. Then we give our mind the opportunity or the license to focus on extraneous things. As a result of this, people start to speak ill of each other. Sometimes people tell me that when they belonged to other societies, people did not talk so badly about each other. But here devotees are always backbiting. This terrible behavior leads to the beginning of cunning in our life and deception. This is a sad situation, because sometimes when we are careless in our spiritual practice, instead of purifying our heart the spiritual practice starts reinforcing the problems found there. In world history, religious people committed so much evil and cruelty for this same reason: because they were not attentive to themselves and did not catch themselves cheating in time. The sequence of events is very important – we have a slight tendency to deception, it gradually starts growing until it finally turns into a demon. This demon can completely devour us. Therefore the main quality of a devotee is frankness, simplicity, and absence of hypocrisy.

SIMPLICITY AND DETERMINATION

In the *Hitopadeśa* there is a very interesting verse:

> *manasy ekaṁ vacasy ekaṁ karmaṇy ekaṁ mahātmanām*
> *manasy anyat vacasy anyat karmaṇy anyad durātmanām*

Manasi ekam vacasi ekam karmaṇi ekam – one who thinks, speaks, and does the same thing is called *mahātmanām*. *Manasi anyat vacasi anyat karmaṇi anyat* – one who thinks one thing, says another, and does a third thing is called *durātmanām*, a fool, or in Russian, *durak*. That is why it is so important, and the *ācāryas* emphasize this point, that the main quality of a devotee is simplicity.

Bhaktivinoda Ṭhākura explains that there are four essential qualities of a pure devotee. These are simplicity or frankness; being focused on the purpose; determination, or having one goal and determination to attain it; and not depending on the opinions of others. This last quality is very important, because we will be able to preserve all these qualities, especially simplicity, if we do not depend on the opinions of others. We cheat because we always want to appear different from what we really are to impress others.

In another article in *Sajjana-toṣaṇī*, Bhaktivinoda Ṭhākura says that for the dull people of Kali-yuga who find it difficult to remember four things, it is enough to remember just two things: simplicity and determination. To do *bhajana* and to worship Kṛṣṇa, we need these two things. However, if we lack even one of them it will be very difficult for us. If there is no basic simplicity of heart and no determination, we naturally won't be able to do make advancement.

A dependence on other people's opinion creates a situation where we are inconsistent. When alone we are one kind of person, but in society we are different. In some homes in the hallway there is a mirror, because before going out we ask, "How do I look? How will people regard me?" Sometimes, even in the homes of devotees, in the living room everything's nice and clean but in the bedroom there is a bed that hasn't been cleaned for two weeks. Sometimes our mind resembles a two-bedroom apartment consisting of a bedroom, where our filthy nest is, and a livingroom, where everything is in order, neat and tidy to impress others.

Our honesty in desiring to attain Kṛṣṇa also becomes manifest in our respect towards everything that is somehow or other connected with Kṛṣṇa. If we want to achieve success on this path, this respect is a very important quality. Above all, we must feel respect for the devotees. In no case should we offend them or talk ill of them.

Hypocrisy is there within our hearts. If we bring this hypocrisy into our society, it turns into an offense and becomes even stronger. Śrīla Jīva Gosvāmī illustrates this problem by an example from the *Mahābhārata*.

When Kṛṣṇa came to Hastināpura, Duryodhana wanted to serve him. Duryodhana had organized a sumptuous reception for Kṛṣṇa. All along the roadside he built banana arches and had women showering Kṛṣṇa with flower petals as he went by. Dancers were performing to beautiful music and a sumptuous reception was arranged with all the best food prepared by top chefs from all over the kingdom. Duryodhana said to Kṛṣṇa, "Janārdana! Keśava! You are our dear guest, our relative! You are our good friend! Please eat."

Kṛṣṇa refused. Duryodhana complained how unfair it was, that Kṛṣṇa was more favorably disposed to the Pāṇḍavas than to them. "I have prepared this *prasādam* for you with love! You must accept it!"

Kṛṣṇa replied, "I'm not obliged to accept anything!"

Duryodhana said, "But aren't we your relatives?"

But Kṛṣṇa's heart did not budge. He said, "You have been hating the Pāṇḍavas since your childhood, offending them without any reason, and trying to harm them. The Pāṇḍavas are non-different from me. You don't love them, which means that you hate me. One can eat only when the food is offered with love, or if one has nothing to eat. I have enough to eat, and I do not feel any love. So, please do not feed me. I will go to Vidura. I do not want to get contaminated by your nasty food, because there is no love in it; there is only cheating."

Śrīla Jīva Gosvāmī says that sometimes people appear to be serving Kṛṣṇa but if while doing so they do not respect the Vaiṣṇavas, then they are committing an offense and Kṛṣṇa will not accept their so-called service. In the end, the heart may only get farther from Kṛṣṇa than it should have been.

OFFENSES AND CHEATING: THE RELATIONSHIP

Hypocrisy generates offenses. In referring to a verse from the *Viṣṇu-dharmotara-Purāṇa,* Śrīla Jīva Gosvāmī also says that when a person doesn't stop themselves from committing offenses, then one hundred offenses make a person a hypocrite. Offenses and hypocrisy are thus each related as cause and effect of each other.

Therefore, lack of sincerity is the result of having already committed offenses against some Vaiṣṇavas or against the spiritual master. Further on, he says that one thousand offenses deprive a person of the opportunity to perform austerities in the name of *bhakti.* If we do not stop there but go on committing further offenses, we lose our power and can not follow even the basic principles of spiritual life.

First a person offends the Vaiṣṇavas and for a while everything seems all right. They go on offending them and slandering them as much as possible behind their backs. Sooner or later, after a certain point they will have no power to follow the basic principles. Further it is said that 10,000 offenses deprive a person of the opportunity to practice *bhakti.* Of course, all these numerical values should not be taken literally, but the point is that if people do not stop committing offenses, then in the end they will lose the opportunity to even pronounce the holy name. Lord Caitanya Mahāprabhu said of the Māyāvādī *sannyāsīs* in Benares that he came to these great *paṇḍitas,* but despite all of their knowledge their tongue cannot turn to pronounce "Kṛṣṇa". They say "Brahman, Brahman" but their tongue cannot say "Kṛṣṇa".

Here Raghunātha Dāsa Gosvāmī warns us against this cycle of offenses and deceit. He says that everything starts very innocently, with just a slight tendency to small deceptions.

Therefore, the two topmost qualities of the devotee are determination and simplicity in order to realize the supreme ideal of devotional service. Simplicity will protect us against offenses and will help us preserve pure, simple faith without obscuring it. Determination will help us overcome all the obstacles that will inevitably arise on our way. If we have these two qualities, we will attain Kṛṣṇa. If we don't have these two simple qualities we will not be able to understand anything.

Bhakti is our attempt to enter into a relationship with God himself, the Supreme Personality of Godhead. I have already mentioned that in the introduction to *Śrīmad-Bhāgavatam,* Śrīla Vyāsadeva calls Kṛṣṇa *paraṁ satya,* the Absolute Truth. This means that to enter into a relationship with Kṛṣṇa we must acquire the same nature of truth. We cannot have a different nature because then a relationship with Kṛṣṇa would be impossible. Even in the material world, if we consider the science of relations between human beings, astrology recommends selecting those whose nature is as close as possible to our own. Any difference in nature will eventually bring about a conflict. To a much greater degree, this is true in terms of our relationship with the Supreme Personality of Godhead. We must acquire one hundred percent the same nature; that is, we must become absolutely pure, just as we cannot approach the sun unless we have a body of fire like the sun.

When we take up the path of *bhakti,* it is like fire rapidly burning up all our impurities. The holy name can almost immediately cleanse the human heart of all sins. But there is something very significant preventing this, and it is offenses. If we commit them while taking up the path of *bhakti,* these offences deprive *bhakti* of its power. We practice *bhakti,* but instead of purifying us, *bhakti* can sometimes contaminate us. This seems paradoxical, but that situation is exactly what Raghunātha Dāsa

Gosvāmī is writing about here. We are bathing in urine and therefore are not getting cleaner, but dirtier. If we were bathing in the ocean of nectar, there would be no problems; we would get clean very soon. The problem is that we start bathing in the donkey urine of our own deception, which is the urine of the offenses we are committing. That's the reason our hearts grow hard. *Bhakti* is supposed to soften our heart, which the *ācāryas* compare to butter.

Love makes a person very sympathetic; a loving person will never hurt those they love. Therefore Prahlāda says, *yasyāsti bhaktir bhagavati akiñcanā* – when a person attains *bhakti* immediately all the best qualities emerge. *Bhakti* itself is what makes a person marvelous and very attractive. But he also says that if people have no *bhakti,* then their minds are always fixed upon, or attached to, external things. In the Third Canto of *Śrīmad-Bhāgavatam,* there is another very important verse (3.19.36):

taṁ sukhārādhyam ṛjubhir
ananya-śaraṇair nṛbhiḥ
kṛtajñaḥ ko na seveta
durārādhyam asādhubhiḥ

This verse says that it is very easy to worship Kṛṣṇa. *Arādhyam* means to worship and *sukham* means very easily and joyfully. Those who can easily worship him are called *ṛjubhiḥ,* those who have a simple heart. *Ananya-śaraṇair nṛbhiḥ:* they take shelter exclusively of Kṛṣṇa. *Kṛtajñaḥ:* they have a grateful heart. This is a very important word in this verse. A simple heart means a grateful heart. If the heart is grateful we will do anything for the one we love. If we are grateful to Kṛṣṇa, who has given us everything, we'll do anything. But then it is said, *durārādhyam asādhubhiḥ:* but if persons are *asādhu,* and their hearts are defiled above all by deception, *durārādhyam,* it is very difficult for them to worship Kṛṣṇa. Obstacles will naturally arise in the process of worshiping Kṛṣṇa.

Since we have taken up the path of *bhakti,* we have this unfortunate possibility of committing offenses, primarily using *bhakti* for our own purposes. We forget – and this is the very beginning of the mistake people make at first – we forget that *bhakti* is a goal in itself. *Bhakti* is not the means to achieve something else. It is not that we need something else, such as material prosperity or liberation, and that is why we practice *bhakti*. *Bhakti* is the goal. But when we start using *bhakti* as the means for our own prosperity, we are deceiving Kṛṣṇa and thus we are committing an offense. This is the offense that lives in our hearts: we want something for ourselves. At the same time, in pursuit of transient benefit, we lose our eternal benefit.

There are two fundamental principles which help us to keep our *bhakti* pure. Those are respect and gratitude. In the traditional Vedic system, a person is taught very consistently to respect their elders, to respect all living beings and to be grateful. When a person has these two simple qualities, it is easier to practice *bhakti*. Otherwise obstacles will arise.

The mind is programmed to enjoy by feeling its superiority over others. We can say this desire to feel superior over others is the operating system of the mind. When a person takes up the spiritual path this same program continues to function, and we still try to prove our superiority over Vaiṣṇavas, and in due course, over our guru and eventually over Kṛṣṇa. In the mind there is a very clear algorithm for proving its superiority over others. In order to do this, it must see the faults of others. This is how the mind works independently of us; we do not need to force the mind to look for these faults, it will find them itself.

Jīva Gosvāmī explains that as a result of this desire for superiority a person seems to be outwardly worshiping the Vaiṣṇavas, the spiritual master, the *sādhus*, and Kṛṣṇa, while inside disrespect for them is appearing. Such a person starts looking for material qualities in them so they can feel superior. They look at the Vaiṣṇavas and see them as non-Vaiṣṇavas. They do not see the essential quality of the Vaiṣṇava and how rare they are. How many people really strive for God or are ready to give up something for his sake? But all we see are perceived bad qualities.

Śrī Caitanya Mahāprabhu calls the *anarthas* that grow along with *bhakti* "*upāsaka*." *Upa* means secondary and *saka* means branch. In tropical countries, parasitic species grow on the host trees, sucking out the juices of the original tree until it dries out. The same happens to us; if we project the material tendencies that are within us onto the sphere of *bhakti* without trying to hinder them, then eventually these material tendencies grow stronger and completely destroy our *bhakti*.

HOW THE WEEDS OF DECEIT GROW

In his purport to *Caitanya-caritāmṛta, Madhya-līlā* 12.135, Śrīla Prabhupāda explains that these weeds or parasites growing on the body of our *bhakti* begin with *kuṭināṭī* – nitpicking or the desire to find faults in others. We have this innate tendency. When we become devotees this tendency is polished to perfection, because as devotees we can better understand our own psychology. We can then see in a clearer way the smallest faults in others. Previously we did not notice how the cheating mind works and how pride manifests itself. Now our heart rejoices when we see faults in others.

Further on, Prabhupāda says that what follows next is *pratiṣṭhāśā* or the desire for recognition. *Pratiṣṭhā* means recognition, and *āśā* means the desire or hope that we will be recognized. In this regard, he gives an example of a person trying to imitate Śrīla Haridāsa Ṭhākura.

For example, I adorn the Deities or I make them an outfit. But I am hoping for praise for my efforts or my "talent." Persons are decorating the Deity, but it may be their own false ego that is standing on their altar and showing their expertise to everyone. If people do not say, "How wonderful you've made that," we are disappointed and think, "This society of devotees is not like what I was promised!" We demand recognition and the thirst for it grows stronger and stronger. We preach, so someone admires how many followers we have, or we distribute books so we will be praised for it. We fast on Ekadasi, but we make sure we tell everyone what we fast from, the way we fasted, how many rounds we chanted, how we didn't sleep that night. We give a lecture so that someone says afterwards, "Oh, what a lecture!" And if devotees do not say that, we think, "Everyone is in *māyā*! No one has appreciated it!"

First is *kuṭināṭī*, second is *pratiṣṭhāśā*, and the next thing is *jīva-hiṁsā*. *Jīva-hiṁsā* refers to the pain we cause. After deceit and hypocrisy, and the attempt to exalt ourselves, comes Aghāsura, the serpent with foul breath, like that of a dead fish. Bhaktivinoda Ṭhākura explains that this demon is the cruelty in our heart. What did he do with the cowherd boys? He devoured them. Aghāsura represents cruelty. In the society of devotees we also have opportunities for showing cruelty. Again, the same knowledge of psychology allows us to more painfully hurt others when we start pointing out their faults. First, I think ill of others, then I start speaking ill of others, being rude to others, cutting their false ego. One woman was complaining to me about her husband, "He comes and says to me, 'Let me see where your false ego is. Now I'm going to cut it.'" He has children and a wife whom he needs in order to cut their false ego.

Recently I happened to come across an article written by a very respected Vaiṣṇava analyzing an article written by another Vaiṣṇava, finding some trifles there and then publishing his condemnations on the internet in order to hurt. This is something that unfortunately happens under the pretext of fighting for purity. He is exposing other Vaiṣṇavas to a public "flogging". Again, knowledge of psychology of other people allows us to more easily exploit others. Under the pretext of devotional service people sometimes simply exploit each other, saying that we should selflessly serve but at the same time taking advantage of others. This is a manifestation of *jīva-hiṁsā*.

Śrīla Prabhupāda describes the next inevitable step in that purport to the *Guṇḍicā-mārjana-līlā*. This is called *niṣiddhācāra*, when a person loses the ability to follow the principles of *bhakti*. Why does this happen? Previously, they seemed to have overcome all these bad habits and had been following the principles of *bhakti* over a long period of time. However, at a certain point they lose the ability to do this. It is not just because of the *anarthas*. What happens at this point is that due to the offences committed, the mind fully focuses on matter and tears itself away from Kṛṣṇa.

Śrīla Prabhupāda had a disciple who used to take LSD; later on he achieved a very high position but returned to LSD. Due to the tendency to deceitfulness, he started justifying his behavior. He said that LSD was the dust specks from the lotus feet of Śrīmatī Rādhārāṇī! He said that when he took drugs, he became closer to God. He wanted to open a whole training center to teach others how to get closer to Kṛṣṇa using LSD. There was one other *āśrama* I knew about personally where all the discourses consisted in discussing the faults of other Vaiṣṇavas. There are many Vaiṣṇavas and there are many faults, too, so there were many topics of discussion. And they all said, "We are for Prabhupāda! We are for Prabhupāda!" They would still go on with *saṅkīrtana*. However, since the *āśrama* is located in quite a cold zone, before going out on *saṅkīrtana* they drink some vodka to Śrīla Prabhupāda in order to warm up and go out to distribute. Unfortunately all this is true and I am not exaggerating at all in this particular case. This is what Śrīla Prabhupāda says, *niṣiddhācāra,* the next logical step: we lose the ability to follow the principles of pure behavior. And all begins with the fact that in one way or another we focus on the faults of others.

In the next step, *kāma* (lust) becomes completely uncontrollable and devours us whole. A person in this situation naturally and gradually forms material tendencies in their mind. We have come to the path of *bhakti* in order to remove these tendencies, but we may be giving vent to the most subtle tendency of all, which is to relish finding faults in others. Step-by-step it very soon becomes more and more gross. One problem is that a person at this point may not enjoy just ordinary *kāma,* but may do so in a perverted way.

Following *kāma* is the demand to be worshiped. Śrīla Jīva Gosvāmī makes a similar analysis in his *Bhakti-sandarbha,* where he explains the consequences of *aparādhas* or offenses. He says that at first *kauṭilya* or hypocrisy appears in a person, then *aśraddhā* or faithlessness. After *aśraddhā* a quality appears that he calls *bhagavan-niṣṭhā-cyavaka-vastv-antarābhiniveśaḥ,* or a focus on external things that destroy our *niṣṭhā* or faith in Kṛṣṇa. Next is *bhakti-śaithilyam,* where we cannot focus on *bhajana* because the mind is already completely elsewhere. After that, *sva-bhakty-ādi-kṛta-mānitvam,* pridefulness or pride for our own achievements in *bhakti* appear. We start competing with others. What does competition with other Vaiṣṇavas mean? The very spirit of rivalry or jealousy towards others means that I want respect only for myself. The nature of *bhakti* is that it makes us willing to cooperate; *bhakti* is love and love means that I love everyone and I try to do things together with the others.

Śrīla Prabhupāda said that our love for him will be shown by the extent to which we will be able to cooperate with each other. Some may have misheard that to mean, "Your love for me will be shown by the extent to which you will be able to compete with each other." *Sva-bhakti-kritam-manitva* or *pūjā*, the desire of honor or the desire that only I should be respected, is the final stage of *Vaiṣṇava-aparādha* that happens to a person.

Śrīla Prabhupāda concludes this description by writing, "Therefore one's heart is again filled with dirt and becomes harder and harder, thus starting to resemble the heart of a materialist."

Commenting on this sixth verse of *Manaḥ-śikṣā*, Bhaktivinoda Ṭhākura explains that there are three kinds of Vaiṣṇavas: *sva-niṣṭha, pariniṣṭha,* and *nirapekṣa*. He says that a *sva-niṣṭha* Vaiṣṇava is a householder who performs *bhajana* without regard for *varṇāśrama-dharma*. Their material tendencies begin to appear if instead of serving pure Vaiṣṇavas they start serving some rich people. *Pariniṣṭha-bhakta* is a householder who also follows *varṇāśrama-dharma*. When they are deceitful then outwardly they show everyone how firmly they are following everything, while internally being unable to cope with their attachment to material things. The *nirapekṣa* Vaiṣṇava is one who has accepted renunciation, but might start collecting money from everyone as much as possible and associate with materialists all the time.

In this verse Raghunātha Dāsa Gosvāmī asked why we would bathe in this ass urine. We should bathe in pure nectar, but the mind does not want to. The mind has no attachment to Rādhā and Kṛṣṇa. It has no attachment to thinking about them or reading about them. Prahlāda Mahārāja himself explains that despite hearing about Kṛṣṇa from others, despite trying to think about Kṛṣṇa themselves, despite trying to achieve some combination of both, many persons' minds are unable to think of Kṛṣṇa, and *bhakti* does not manifest itself in their hearts.

Bhaktivinoda Ṭhākura explains why a person does not get spiritually attached and instead the uncontrolled senses lead to hell. *Punaḥ punaś carvita-carvaṇānām* – again and again we chew what has already been chewed. Inside we have a certain subtle concept or ego which we have not given up, even having taken up the path of *bhakti*. Bhaktivinoda Ṭhākura said that there is only one solution, humility. If we have taken up the path of *bhakti*, we must surrender with complete humility.

Bhaktivinoda Ṭhākura writes in his purport to this verse of the *Manaḥ-śikṣā*: "As soon as the mind allows trifle thoughts to come in, immediately deception or hypocrisy appears. Hypocrisy starts attacking the soul again. When one's heart has been completely cleansed by humility, it will never again open its doors to deception."

HUMILITY AND OUR RELATIONSHIP WITH GURU

We need one single attribute – complete, absolute humility. In this humility I must fold my palms and say, "Yes, I am fallen. But I don't want to be like this anymore." This attitude constitutes honesty to ourselves. This complete humility begins with my surrendering this most subtle concept, my false ego, to my guru.

Kṛṣṇa explains this in the *Bhagavad-gītā* (4.34):

tad viddhi praṇipātena
paripraśnena sevayā
upadekṣyanti te jñānaṁ
jñāninas tattva-darśinaḥ

In our relationship with guru we must practice humility of body, mind, and speech. Guru will give us *sambandha* or a connection with Kṛṣṇa. Through the connection with the spiritual master, I will become aware of my connection with Kṛṣṇa. When I have a relationship with Kṛṣṇa, I will develop interest in everything related to Kṛṣṇa.

We must actually understand what the guru likes and doesn't like, and act for the guru, not for oneself. The humility that appears in the mind is when a person does not act out of self-interest but rather wants to serve and do what the other person wants us to do. With no actual relationship with the spiritual master this attitude is practically impossible because we will still continue in one way or another to retain our subtle pride. Sooner or later it will grow more and more. The subtle will then become gross. *Bhakti* means to find this problem in ourselves and start dealing with it.

Therefore, *sādhana-bhakti* starts with *guru-pādāśraya tasmāt* — we must go to the spiritual master and take shelter of his lotus feet. We must give up everything else, *guru-padasraya tasmad*. After that comes *kṛṣṇa-dīkṣādi-śikṣaṇam* — we must take *dīkṣā*.

People think they have received *dīkṣā* and now they are free to go. I have been given a name, my beads, and that's it. But after *dīkṣā* we must receive *śikṣā*. *Dīkṣā* was given to young boys who started studying the scriptures. *Dīkṣā* is the first step. *Śikṣā* means I try to do what we are told. We try to serve not ourselves, but what we are told by the spiritual master. As a result humility appears. Humility allows us to attain *sambandha* or a relationship with Kṛṣṇa through our relationship with the spiritual master, because it is the spiritual master alone who gives this connection. Without connection there is nothing.

The meaning of our relationship with guru is not to make yet another cult of personality. Śrīla Prabhupāda warned us against this in a letter to Govinda dāsī. In her letter, Govinda dāsī had written to Śrīla Prabhupāda saying how she loved him.

Śrīla Prabhupāda replied, "I liked very much those beautiful feelings you have described in your letter. However, you should never forget that all our activities are carried out in accordance with the *paramparā* originating from Lord Kṛṣṇa. Therefore, your love must be directed not so much towards the physical manifestation of the guru, but towards the spiritual message he carries. By lovingly serving the teachings of our guru we prove our love for his physical manifestation."

Śrīla Prabhupāda said we must be devoted not to the cult of personality, but devoted to what he teaches and surrender to what he teaches. We must overcome this most subtle obstacle that envelops our soul because if we do not remove it, ultimately it will prevent us from truly hearing about Rādhā and Kṛṣṇa. If we attain this *sambandha*, or humility, if we attain love for Kṛṣṇa, then everything else will come to us.

Raghunātha Dāsa Gosvāmī is teaching us here to very honestly and frankly see the deceit in ourselves. We must take devotional service very seriously. It is never too late to start; Kṛṣṇa is infinitely merciful and can give us complete happiness. Therefore, in our *bhajana* we must show two qualities: honesty or simplicity, frankness; the second is determination to go to the end by any means. If we have these two qualities we will certainly be successful on this wonderful path of *bhakti*.

COMMENTARY BY ŪRMILĀ DEVĪ DĀSĪ

The devotee on the path of spontaneous devotion for Kṛṣṇa in Vṛndāvana has, by verse six, relinquished the gross hypocrisy of secretly engaging in wicked deeds as a slave to lust, envy, and so forth. However, the inclination for deceit and hypocrisy may still remain. In verse five the evil enemies were blatant – robbers along the side of the road with nooses! But here in verse six the problem is harder for the practitioner to discern. Devotees at this stage have received the jewel of Rādhā-Kṛṣṇa's love. To hold such a jewel, to be the setting for such a jewel, one should be clean and polished. Thinking like this, the fortunate devotee seeks to bathe and become clean.

The devotee on the shining path of *bhakti* will see two possible sources for this bath. One is an ocean of pure delight (*sukhaya*) coming from the feet of Gāndharvikā-Giridhārī. (The ending *ikā* indicates affection, and Gāndharvā is a name for Kṛṣṇa's internal energy, meaning a woman who sings with great artistic skill. Giridhārī is a name for Kṛṣṇa who lifted Govardhana Hill.) This first bathing choice for the holder of the jewel of divine love will fully wash away the tendency for deceit and hypocrisy which had attracted lust and so forth.

The second source for this bath is a trickle of liquid that offers only an appearance of cleanliness. Those who have become free from the obvious cheating of wicked deeds may hesitate to become thoroughly honest. If a person's answer to the question, "Am I willing to face the full truth about the state of my heart and motives?" is, "No," then cheating and hypocrisy manifest in that person as activities that appear to be *bhakti* but are not, just as the trickle of liquid appears to clean, but is something else entirely. It burns us. It burns because it comes not from divine lotus feet, but is the urine from a very large donkey. We know we are bathing in donkey urine when others' greatness creates a burning sensation within us. The jewel we received becomes covered in this donkey urine and cannot show its brilliance.

When we read through Bhaktivinoda's lists of the ways three categories of *sādhakas* can be deceitful at this level of progress in *bhakti*, we find a common thread – they are all activities that often appear like *bhakti* while being something else. *Seka-jala pāñā upaśākhā bāḍi' yāya, stabdha hañā mūla-śākhā bāḍite nā pāya* (*Caitanya-caritāmṛta, Madhya-līlā* 19.160). There are weeds that grow near the *bhakti* creeper, and may look like *bhakti* to the undiscerning person, just as donkey urine may appear to be a welcome shower. If we water the weeds instead of the creeper, we simply burn inside and outside rather than being refreshed. How unfortunate!

The jewel on the altar is a garbage heap
Smelling and filthy, symptom of deep
Attachment to *māyā* in grip of her modes
All is just rotten, a large heavy load.
Somehow we used this trash to act for you
But it remains garbage through and through
It's mercy to know it, but please purify;
Can't do it alone, though with strength we do try.
All and everything we offer so sweet
Thinking it's love that we bring to your feet
Oh! We discover with shocking great pain
The pattern on cloth was simply a stain.

One possible consequence of cheating disguised as *bhakti* is that eventually inner hypocrisy may become strong enough to again attract the thieves of lust and his friends. Gradually the person will again take up hearing and talking about material enjoyment and liberation. Spiritual progress then stops. We may get a sense of how this may be so from *Śrīmad-Bhāgavatam* 4.8.2–4:

> Another son of Lord Brahmā was Irreligion, whose wife's name was Falsity. From their combination were born two demons named

> Dambha, or Bluffing, and Māyā, or Cheating. These two demons were taken by a demon named Nirṛti, who had no children. Maitreya told Vidura: O great soul, from Dambha and Māyā were born Greed and Nikṛti, or Cunning. From their combination came children named Krodha (Anger) and Hiṁsā (Envy), and from their combination were born Kali and his sister Durukti (Harsh Speech). O greatest of all good men, by the combination of Kali and Harsh Speech were born children named Mṛtyu (Death) and Bhīti (Fear). From the combination of Mṛtyu and Bhīti came children named Yātanā (Excessive Pain) and Niraya (Hell).

Another consequence is that the practitioner stops feeling the sweetness of devotional service. What used to be blissful has been replaced with burning. Such persons, refusing to face their inner deceit, may blame others for their lack of ecstasy. They then believe their service is fault-finding and criticism. Others lose faith in the process entirely, yet may cynically continue with the externals in exchange for a life where they get some respect and material facility for being a so-called religious person.

How people in this predicament can move out of the donkey urine and into the delightful ocean of love starts again, unsurprisingly, with freedom from pride. It takes great humility to admit that one has been, of one's own free will, bathing in donkey urine in the name of spiritual life. It takes great humility to fall at anyone's feet, even the feet of God himself.

Bhaktivinoda gives us some specific guidance as to what it means to bathe in the delightful ocean of love at the feet of the divine couple. He tells us to mediate on their names, forms, qualities, and eternal pastimes in the eight parts of the day (*aṣṭa-kālīya-līlā*). He warns us that we have to be vigilant at this stage, as the root of hypocrisy still remains and can grow back again. In the next verse, we learn how that root can be eliminated completely and permanently.

VERSE SEVEN

pratiṣṭhāśā dhṛṣṭā śvapaca-ramaṇī me hṛdi naṭet
kathaṁ sādhu-premā spṛśati śucir etan nanu manaḥ
sadā tvaṁ sevasva prabhu-dayita-sāmantam atulaṁ
yathā tāṁ niṣkāśya tvaritam iha taṁ veśayati saḥ

As long as the unchaste, dog-eating woman of desire for prestige dances in my heart, how can the chaste and pure lady of love for Kṛṣṇa touch it? Therefore, O mind, you should always serve the incomparable, beloved devotee commander of Kṛṣṇa's army, who will immediately throw out the unchaste woman and establish the pure lady of love in the heart.

COMMENTARY BY ŚIVARĀMA SWAMI

Pratiṣṭhā means fame and *āśā* means desire. Our desire for fame is like *dhṛṣṭā śvapaca-ramaṇī*, a bold, outcaste woman. And what does this outcaste woman do? She is *śvapaca,* a dog eater. So she is eating dog's flesh in my heart. That is the actual meaning here. And she's dancing at the same time, *hṛdi naṭet,* having a great party. Dancing around in such a frivolous mood and having a great time, and in one hand is a dog's leg she's chewing on as she's dancing in my heart. But she didn't get in there by accident. I invited her in. I opened the door. I said, "Yes, please come in." So Śrīla Bhaktivinoda Ṭhākura explains that this is what happens after repeated attempts to weed out deceit while still hankering for honor and distinction.

Such a graphic picture is being painted here of the problem. And the solution is also given. We have to serve the pure devotees of the Lord. This is the only means to drive this problem out. There is a scientific process of how the transcendental, *viśuddha-sattva* potency in the heart of a pure devotee is able to penetrate our hearts. In other words, we are now dependent on mercy. We couldn't do anything on our own. Now we are very much dependent on mercy from others who will actually illuminate and eradicate this problem from our heart.

Desire for *pratiṣṭhā* – distinction, fame, honor, position – especially in spiritual circles, just hangs in there. It's very tenacious, excruciatingly difficult to get out. It is the last of the enemies that we subdue, and why is it the last? Because it is the greatest obstacle.

We are allowing this shameless personality to come within our heart. The nature of this obstacle is that it very conveniently overlooks its own evil influence. There is a clear example of this – not a nice example, but a clear one – and that is Duryodhana. When he was approached by Kṛṣṇa after the Pāṇḍavas ended their exile, Kṛṣṇa asked him, "Make a truce. Give them five villages and finish the whole thing. You cannot persecute your cousins this way."

Duryodhana's response was, "I am a *kṣatriya*. I am the king of the land. I am the representative of the Supreme Personality of Godhead." He said, "I looked in my heart very deeply for any trace of flaw, imperfection, pride or arrogance, to see if I have actually done anything against the Pāṇḍavas which was adharmic. And I have come to the conclusion that I am completely flawless in this regard. Therefore, don't push me. Don't ask me to give five villages."

Imagine completely overlooking one's own degraded and fallen position. Why? I am now pretending something that I am not. And I am so convinced that I will walk naked on the street. Everyone knows this story of the emperor without any clothes. Ultimately he becomes so convinced of his position, and his followers were so convinced, that even though he is completely naked he thinks, "I have the best clothes. I am wearing the best of all robes, king's robes."

Fame is like a dog's flesh, and if you run after the flesh of a dog it means: I want to be famous as a great devotee. There is a nice example from the life of Mādhavendra Purī. When Kṣīra-chora Gopīnātha specifically stole *khīr* for him and sent it out via his own *pūjārī*, the Lord told the *pūjārī*, "You take this sweet rice out to Mādhavendra Purī."

When Mādhavendra Purī received that sweet rice and ate it he thought, "As soon as everybody hears of this event, they are going to come after me thinking that I am a great devotee." So immediately he ran away. He left town so no one would come and recognize him or try to offer respect and praise him. That is the mentality of a real Vaiṣṇava.

In *Caitanya-caritāmṛta,* Śrīla Kṛṣṇadāsa Kavirāja Gosvāmī says, "I am lower than Jagāi and Mādhāi. I am like a worm in stool. If somebody even chants my name that person becomes fallen." He is thinking like that because that's what it means to be a real Vaiṣṇava. He is not just writing it, but actually thinks and feels it.

This image here in this verse is this shameless prostitute, a dog-flesh eating prostitute dancing in the heart, but she isn't alone. Bhaktivinoda Ṭhākura says in his song commentary, "Who does she dance with? She dances with her lover. And what's her lover's name? *Kāpaṭya tad-upapati:* Deceit is her paramour." After the party they are all in for the evening! And what is the by-product? Naturally they start to beget children, such as *hiṁsā,* violence, ill-will. Violence and ill-will become a by-product of that little party in the heart. Therefore, ultimately this dance of the prostitute and her lover will destroy all the good virtues in the heart, and will fill the heart with cruelty. One will become a cruel-hearted person. One has to be very careful to not allow these things to remain. Therefore, Śrīla Bhaktisiddhānta Sarasvatī Ṭhākura said, "Better that I am in the association of those who are pointing out my faults and helping me maintain a humble attitude, than to be with those who praise me."

Now, we refer once again to these three *sādhakas. Sva-niṣṭha, pariniṣṭhā, nirapekṣa*. What will happen to them if they also continue to harbor this deceit within their hearts and this desire for honor and distinction? This is subsequent to what we read in the previous verse. This *sva-niṣṭha bhakta,* or the householder who is trying to be fully surrendered, who is fully engaged in preaching activities, starts to yearn for honor and manifests the hope for being seen as being a great religious leader, a very generous personality, and sinless. He wants recognition for his position. The *pariniṣṭhā,* or devotees nicely following the rules of *bhakti,* worshiping the Deity in their home, and working in whatever particular way, they want to become recognized also as great devotees, to be seen as very detached and very knowledgeable. And the *nirapekṣas* are the same – everyone should recognize that they have become pure devotees, being completely detached, understanding the purport of all the *śāstras,* and being the masters of all aspects of *bhakti*. For all types of devotees, the problem is mainly always wanting recognition.

An important point is that Bhaktivinoda Ṭhākura says this honor is one of the elements of deceit. He says deceit can be rooted out to the proportion that one is free from this desire for honor. So to the degree we are actually free from this honor, to that degree the deceit will actually leave the heart. And the heart is like a cup. You have a cup of ink, and if you just keep pouring in milk then ultimately all the ink will be out. Therefore, what we want to fill the heart's cup up with is pure devotional service rendered with real humility. Here specifically, what is being stated is that one should serve the pure devotees. So he says, *kathaṁ sādhu-premā spṛśati. Spṛśati* means touch. He says this *sādhu-premā*, love of Godhead, will not even touch us. Not to mention we will not get it, we won't even be able to touch it. We won't touch it, and it will not touch us, as long as our consciousness is contaminated by this desire for honor. What to do? The verse says *sadā tvaṁ sevasva,* always serve *prabhu-dayita-sāmantam,* pure devotees of the Lord who are *atula* (pure). Then, *niṣkāśya tvaritam,* they will very quickly kick out all these impurities and *veśayati,* they will establish *sādhu-premā,* that pure love.

So, *sadā sevasva,* we should always serve the devotees, because serving Vaiṣṇavas induces humility. Even if you don't have humility now, if you serve devotees you will become humble. The serving mood, the mood of humility, is the antithesis of pride and desire for honor. It neutralizes and destroys them. Serve those who are very dear to the Lord. Bhaktivinoda Ṭhākura says that the hearts of pure devotees are saturated with *hlādinī-śakti,* and when we serve them, they become compassionate. The result of that compassion is they bestow their mercy on us.

Bestowing mercy means that they transfer *hlādinī-śakti* from their hearts – a ray of that potency becomes transferred to the hearts of others and the *hlādinī-śakti* purifies all the contaminations present in one's heart. It not only purifies but also generates love (*sādhu-premā*). The verse says this process happens immediately (*tvaritam*). It will happen quickly, but we must do it. So, *niṣkāśya tvaritam iha taṁ veśayati saḥ*, the association of devotees in a proper mood will expel all these unwanted qualities and will simultaneously give us access to love. We can only get love of God from devotees. Maybe we can get it from Kṛṣṇa, but that is very rare.

The conclusion is that one should serve the Vaiṣṇavas. One should serve the dust of their lotus feet, take the remnants of their foodstuff, and take their instructions, because all of these things possess that same *hlādinī-śakti*. Then we will become free of all of these impediments to our spiritual life.

We can also remember to read and study pastimes concerning the particular demons which are representative of these disturbing elements, specifically deceit, which is Bakāsura. Don't forget to call out, "O servants of the killer of Baka," read that story in *Kṛṣṇa* Book, and hear that particular pastime. The other three qualities which we read about happening to the *pariniṣṭhā, nirapekṣa,* and *sva-niṣṭha* devotees – speculation, fault-finding and argumentation – those *anarthas* are represented by Tṛnāvarta, Aghāsura, and Tṛnāvarta again. Also, this quote from the *Padma Purāṇa* which everyone should know:

ārādhanānāṁ sarveṣāṁ
viṣṇor ārādhanaṁ param
tasmāt parataraṁ devi
tadīyānāṁ samarcanam

Of all the different kinds of worship, worship of the Supreme Lord Visnu is the highest. But even greater than this is the worship of his pure devotees.

That *tadīya*, that is even better. Then from *Śrīmad-Bhāgavatam* (3.7.19):

yat-sevayā bhagavataḥ
kūṭa-sthasya madhu-dviṣaḥ
rati-rāso bhavet tīvraḥ
pādayor vyasanārdanaḥ

By serving the feet of the spiritual master, one is enabled to develop transcendental ecstasy in the service of the Personality of Godhead,

> who is the unchangeable enemy of the Madhu demon and whose service vanquishes one's material distresses.

In this connection, Rūpa Gosvāmī makes a very important point in the conclusion of *Bhakti-rasāmṛta-sindhuḥ*, where he says, "All the different aspects of devotional service which are stated in *Nectar of Devotion* all pertain to Kṛṣṇa." In other words, he's explained how to make advancement by one way or another in relationship to the Lord. Then he also says, "All the different aspects of devotional service to the Supreme Lord which have been discussed in *Bhakti-rasāmṛta-sindhuḥ* also relate to serving the Vaiṣṇavas." In other words, whatever is described in *Bhakti-rasāmṛta-sindhuḥ* in relationship to Kṛṣṇa, you can do the exact same thing in relationship to Vaiṣṇavas. He continues, "This is the opinion of the *paṇḍitas*."

To conclude our commentary on this verse, here is the quote from *Bhakti-rasāmṛta-sindhuḥ* 1.2.241, which Bhaktivinoda quotes at the end of his commentary to verse seven, describing a pure devotee:

> Ever since that person whose body was washed by tears flowing from his eyes; whose body was decorated with multitudes of hair standing on end due to ecstasy; faltering as he walked; who was experiencing ecstasy within himself; who exhibited symptoms such as great shivering of the body etc. has entered the path of my vision, I do not know what has happened. My mind simply refuses to take interest anymore in household affairs.

This is the nature of the real Vaiṣṇava.

COMMENTARY BY ŚACĪNANDANA SWAMI

We find it so difficult to renounce the desire for distinction. Never touch this stool-like desire if you want to develop love for Kṛṣṇa. It may seem strange that this desire for name, fame and glory is the root of all problems. We may feel that some self-esteem needs to be there, otherwise we may feel depressed and insecure, and the world will trample on us. But this self-centered desire is a big problem.

From the desire "I must be glorified" – and not Kṛṣṇa – arises envy, an aggressive mentality, and an inclination to criticize. The moment we don't surrender to Kṛṣṇa, having a "my way" style of thought, we will become envious of others, we will be violent, aggressive, and we will criticize. So many *anarthas* come from this.

Raghunātha Dāsa Gosvāmī uses the example of an outcast woman, who lives by selling her body and devours dog meat. This woman is shamelessly dancing in our hearts. The desire for fame supersedes all other desires. People can be manipulated even out of their money if you flatter them for fame! If this desire for fame is allowed to stay in our hearts, she will not stay alone; she will invite envy. The desire for fame will always be united with envy, and they will mate and produce children of aggressiveness and criticism. When they dance in our hearts, they will start a dance of destruction and destroy all our Vaiṣṇava qualities.

We need to be vigilant and alert to quickly recognize this weed of *pratiṣṭhā*. If we allow this to stay on, all our chanting and hearing will not serve our spiritual advancement, but it will only help to grow *pratiṣṭhā* and her family. We do not perform our *bhakti* for the recognition of others. It is not that *we* should be recognized, but that Kṛṣṇa is recognized. *Pratiṣṭhā* is like poison. If we swallow it, it will poison us. If fame comes to us, be aware that it is by the mercy of our guru.

What is the cure for this desire for fame? Raghunātha Dāsa Gosvāmī says, "*sevasva prabhu-dayita-sāmantam*" – serve the leader of those who are dear to the Lord. He compares such a devotee to a powerful general. The desire for fame is strong, so we need some force to remove it, a pure devotee. Military action is required for this! If we want this desire to be removed, we need a special squad – a real devotee whom we should serve. He will bring love into our hearts.

There are two effects when we meet such devotees: 1 love will come into our heart; and 2 material attachments, fear of material existence, and other obstacles are destroyed. Please serve a pure devotee, giving your best and forgetting your own concern. Then we will feel, "I'm so different, so enlivened." By this contact with a pure devotee, something wonderful happens. Find such a devotee, then associate and serve such a person. Dullness, fearfulness, and ignorance will be destroyed. The fire of devotees will dispel darkness in your heart. Great devotees are like a sacrificial fire. Darkness will go, and Kṛṣṇa will appear. But as long as the desire for *pratiṣṭhā* is pre-eminent in the heart, cheating of others and ourselves will not be driven away. We need a transfusion of the Lord's potency, which will come through the pure devotee and empower us. We may say we have heard all about this before, but such exalted association is very rarely attained. What to do if we can't find such an exalted devotee is given in verse eight of the *Manaḥ-śikṣā*.

Why is the association of exalted devotees so powerful? The Lord is finding rest only in the hearts of his devotees, where he can repose and rest in peace. He cannot rest in the hearts of the *karmīs* or *yogīs*, because they have selfish desires, but he can do so in the hearts of the devotees, because they want to satisfy him.

Let us consider the *gopīs'* meditation on Kṛṣṇa, how they see Kṛṣṇa and install him in their hearts. Early in the morning, Kṛṣṇa leaves the village of Vṛndāvana with the cowherd boys. The *gopīs* stay behind. They feel deep, deep longing for Kṛṣṇa. In order to soothe their hearts, they assemble in one place to talk about Kṛṣṇa. As they are just starting to talk about Kṛṣṇa, the sound of Kṛṣṇa's flute carried by his dear servant, the wind, enters into Vṛndāvana. As the *gopīs* hear this sound, their inner eyes open, and through the eyes of the flute, through the *vāṇī* of Kṛṣṇa, they see a scene that is beyond description, rendering them speechless. They sit there, all seeing the same scene, but they cannot talk about it. But Śukadeva Gosvāmī describes it. Kṛṣṇa is wearing a peacock feather ornament on his head, and blue trumpet-shaped *karṇikāra* flowers on his ears. His hips are decorated by a yellow garment as brilliant as gold, and the *vaijayantī* garland is moving on his chest. Kṛṣṇa is in the mood of the greatest of dancers as he enters the forest of Vṛndāvana, and he beautifies it with the marks of his footprints. He fills the holes of his flute with the nectar of his lips, and all the cowherd boys sing his glories.

Kṛṣṇa is dressed as a dancer, decorated with different lotus flowers, mango sprouts, and clusters of flowers and buds. The clay of Vṛndāvana's earth is used to draw designs on his cheeks, in yellow and reddish colors. He is dressed like a dancer, ready to enter the stage. Even in ordinary life, just before entering a stage, a certain *śakti* enters the performer. Similarly, Kṛṣṇa is full of excitement. The moment he enters the forest, with his beautiful dress and mood, Kṛṣṇa starts to dance! The form that makes every living entity dance, also dances! In other *avatāras*, Kṛṣṇa is not so fond of dancing, but as Kṛṣṇa he is, and he makes others dance, too. Peacocks dance, swans dance, *gopas* dance. Even when he kills a demon, at the height of the fight, Kṛṣṇa dances! Even when he does something as serious as lifting Govardhana Hill, he starts to dance, because he is the lord of *rasa* (joy). Seeing him, all the *devatās* start to dance.

Kṛṣṇa is is Naṭavara. In contrast, Śiva is Naṭarāja who performs the dance of destruction. Kṛṣṇa never destroys when he dances – he elegantly inundates the world with waves of bliss. He is the lord of joy and the lord of dance. When Kṛṣṇa goes into the forest he brings it to life with his presence. Once he has entered the forest, the *vrajavāsīs*, with the exception of the cowherd boys and cows, turn back to go to the village. Some of them are carried back because they fainted. The moment Kṛṣṇa is just with the boys; his feet start to dance in such a way that the art of dancing becomes ashamed. Then his ankle bells start to sound. Kṛṣṇa wants to really move when he dances, so he takes his *chaddar* and ties it around his waist. Then the garland dances, and Kṛṣṇa's eyes, more beautiful than a baby deer's, also dance. His eyebrows dance, his *makara* shaped earrings dance, everything dances – even the peacock feather begins to dance. There is not one single part of Kṛṣṇa's body that is not dancing! In such a way he makes the whole world dance.

Kṛṣṇa's *makara* earrings are expert in teaching his eyes how to dance. He pleases all directions with the luster of his golden cloth that sways in the gentle breeze. His luster is emanating in bluish waves. His dance is multi-dimensional, covering the whole forest of Vṛndāvana. The luster of his *dhotī* is like the light-colored Gaṅgā and the luster of his body is like the dark Yamunā. Together it appears as if there is a confluence between the Gaṅgā and the Yamunā.

When Rādhārāṇī hears about Kṛṣṇa's dancing from Kundalatā, she drinks the information as if her ears are cups. She closes her eyes and internally sees Kṛṣṇa dancing with the *gopas*. She faints from the effect of two kinds of nectar — *kathā* and internal meditation. As Rādhā falls down, Kṛṣṇa knows that she has fainted and he tells the wind to awaken her. The wind then carries his fragrance to wake Rādhārāṇī.

In summary, in verse seven we have heard about the main obstacle, from which other obstacles grow. It's the desire for fame. In Buddhism it is called self-indulgence. We are then not absorbed in Kṛṣṇa, but in our own glories, and we thus try to control our environment to get our glorification. It's very subtle, and sometimes difficult to recognize. We need the association of a pure devotee. We will hear in text eight how to find such a devotee. We have discussed the greatest devotees, the *gopīs*, and their vision of Kṛṣṇa, and we have tried to see through their eyes. Hopefully at least for a fraction of a second while reading the description, we could contact Kṛṣṇa's beautiful form, his qualities, and his playfulness. We can do this when we read the *śāstras* — see through the eyes of these great devotees. After some time, we will not be interested anymore in the desires of an unfulfilled heart.

COMMENTARY BY BHAKTIVIJNANA GOSWAMI

INSTRUCTIONS FOR LOVE OF GOD

Raghunātha Dāsa Gosvāmī is the *prayojana-ācārya* (teacher of the ultimate goal) of our *sampradāya*. He teaches the highest goal of all our endeavors and aspirations. Bhaktivinoda Ṭhākura, in his *Jaiva-dharma*, describes how Raghunātha Dāsa Gosvāmī's various works explain what is going on in the spiritual world. It is very difficult to understand such explanations because we have the tendency of projecting our understanding of the material world onto the spiritual world. Everything that is somehow or other related to eternity is very difficult to comprehend with our limited mind, which is programmed to perceiving the temporary world. For example, when we think about eternity we may imagine a static picture. To counter these problems, Raghunātha Dāsa Gosvāmī succeeded in explaining the way in which love is an eternal dynamic state, and that in the spiritual world there is no boredom. Bhaktivinoda Ṭhākura explains that especially in *Manaḥ-śikṣā* Raghunātha Dāsa Gosvāmī is teaching us how a person can enter into this kingdom of love, of spiritual *rasa*.

Bhaktivinoda Ṭhākura makes a unique, surprising and even shocking statement. He says that Rūpa Gosvāmī, having described the *rasa* and the nature of spiritual love, has not fully explained how to enter into it. It is a very strange statement because first of all Rūpa Gosvāmī is our *abhidheya-ācārya* (teacher of the way or the method). Secondly, if we study his *Bhakti-rasāmṛta-sindhuḥ,* and even *Ujjvala-nīlamaṇi,* we will see that there he explains in great detail the practice of *sādhana*. Nevertheless, Bhaktivinoda Ṭhākura makes this statement that Rūpa Gosvāmī has not explained how to enter *rasa,* whereas Raghunātha Dāsa Gosvāmī has done so in his *Manaḥ-śikṣā*.*

In my opinion, the reason for this statement is that in these *sūtras* Raghunātha Dāsa Gosvāmī has explained in a succinct and encrypted form the main obstacles that await us on this path. He explains the realm of spiritual affection, or love, and what is internally preventing us from developing this affection. All those in Kṛṣṇa consciousness want to experience spiritual love. When it is not achieved, sometimes people start going down to some other level, engaging in psychology or yoga or the like, and think those things are going to help them to find love. The uniqueness of the *Manaḥ-śikṣā* is that it explains our own psychology which resists spiritual life, and prevents us from attaining the very spiritual experience that has been promised to us.

INSTRUCTING OUR MIND WITH LOVE

We are trying to understand this book as instructions to the mind. In accordance with the *sāṅkhya* philosophy, the mind is one of the

* "Śrīla Rūpa Gosvāmī has exhaustively elaborated upon the details of *rasa-tattva*. Śrī Caitanya Mahaprabhu personally gave him this service and specially blessed him to fulfil the responsibility. However, the methods by which an aspiring soul may develop such *rasa* in the intimate service of Rādhā-Kṛṣṇa have been compiled by Śrīla Raghunātha Dāsa Gosvāmī from the famous diaries of Śrīla Svarūpa Dāmodara Gosvāmī." (*Jaiva-dharma* 39: Entering the pastimes of the Lord)

sense organs called *antaḥ-karaṇa*. We have five external sense organs that collect information from the outside world. There is one internal sense organ that processes this information. However, this sense organ, *antaḥ-karaṇa*, or *svāntaḥ*, as Raghunātha Dāsa Gosvāmī calls it in the first verse, has one amazing quality: it does not obey us. All the other senses more or less obey us, but the mind will think what it wants to because it has a certain independence. On one hand, this is a "blessing" because the mind is given to us so that it can prove something that even we don't believe in. The mind is constantly proving to us that we are God even though deep down in ourselves we do not believe it. But this same blessing is also a curse for us because we can't easily change that programming.

Kṛṣṇa says that depending on what the program in our mind is, we obtain our next body. At the time of death we cannot tell our mind, "Think about Kṛṣṇa!" Even throughout our life we cannot do it. The mind thinks what it wants to. The meaning of human life and the meaning of *sādhana* are to replace this program in the mind and teach the mind how to think of Kṛṣṇa.

There are basically two ways to do this. One way is to explain to the mind that this is good and it is necessary. The mind will reluctantly do what it has understood to be useful. We can logically convince the mind. Therefore the *śāstras* have their own logic and, generally, people are attracted to logic, various evidences, and philosophy. When someone proves to us in detail that God exists, that Kṛṣṇa is God, we think, "Well, I'll think a bit about that in my spare time." This is one way and it works to a certain extent, but Caitanya Mahāprabhu says that this method is *abalā*. *Abalā* means deprived of power or having no power.

The other way to change the program in our mind is to somehow or other instill it with spiritual desire, with attachment, because the mind thinks of that to which it is attached. We can understand very well what our mind is attached to. You can try an experiment by shutting yourself in a room for a day and say aloud any thought that crosses your mind; record it and then listen to it. Or better yet, sit down and chant and listen to what the mind is thinking about. In Sanskrit, the word *rāga* comes from the root *ranj*, which means to color. The mind is colored in a certain way, and rushes to where its attachment is. Therefore, Śrī Caitanya Mahāprabhu explained a form of spiritual practice of putting spiritual attachment in the mind. The only problem is where to get spiritual attachment from. This attachment can only be obtained from someone who has it very strong in their heart. Therefore, the method of *rāgānuga-sādhana* is not meditation only on Kṛṣṇa, but also meditation on those who have affection for Kṛṣṇa.

When we understand that we need the same love that lives in the heart of the pure associates of Kṛṣṇa and nothing else, we start thinking about them. Thinking about them, we try to serve in the same way they serve. These attempts eventually lead to their bestowing this affection on us out of their mercy. Affection is causeless; it is the result of their mercy, which naturally comes to those who are trying to follow in the footsteps of Kṛṣṇa's great devotees.

The problems in this world arise only from lack of love. Whether it is disease, old age, loneliness, the crimes that are committed, whether it is violence, cruelty, or spite – it is all the result of a single problem: lack of love. The *śāstras,* in particular *Śrīmad-Bhāgavatam,* describe that there is a place in God's creation where there is an abundance of love. This place is called Vraja, Vṛndāvana, part of a place called Vaikuṇṭha which means "a place where there are no problems." There are no prisons and no police. There are no means of coercion and even no managers in the mundane sense. Everything is done out of love and everything is so simple. The people there cooperate with each other and love each other because they all love Kṛṣṇa. This is a society that we are trying to re-create on earth to a certain degree.

All desires other than the desire for love appear in our heart due to this lack of love. Our heart is empty, giving rise to desires that generally do not make anyone happy. People go crazy because of these desires, such as their desire for respect, honor, money, and so on. What do we actually need? Only love. When there is love, we need nothing else. When there is no love, we need everything else. And when we have everything else it is still not enough. Vāmanadeva says that, "Even if one is in possession of the entire world, it will still be not enough! One will start war with another universe and will try to conquer it." Because the greed in the heart is insatiable, when there is a vacuum in the heart due to the absence of God, that vacuum sucks in everything but can't be filled because it is only God who can fill it.

This desire to be near Kṛṣṇa and love Kṛṣṇa the way his devotees love him, without any deception, is the beginning and the foundation of *rāgānuga-sādhana*. Caitanya Mahāprabhu brought us the method to attaining the same love, completely pure and absolutely selfless. This is the potential we can develop. It is not for nothing that the human form is called *sādhana-deha* – it is because *sādhana* means a certain practice through which we can achieve the goal (*sādhya*).

People in this world achieve amazing goals through practice. Some run very quickly, some jump very high, some swim very deep, some fly very high. They can mentally multiply and divide multiple digit numbers if they want to or they can play chess and see twenty moves ahead. Using various methods of practice we can develop incredible skills. The most amazing thing is that I can learn to love Kṛṣṇa the way he is loved in Vṛndāvana. This is the most amazing ability, which is given to us at birth, and the *sādhana* we are practicing is supposed to bring us to the state in which the potential that's built in us fully reveals complete, absolute, pure, and selfless love.

This is what we are looking for. What are people looking for in the material world? They are looking for Kṛṣṇa, because the ideal is sought after all the time. The *śāstras* say that to that end we should hear about Kṛṣṇa with faith and in a certain mood. On the pages of *Śrīmad-Bhāgavatam* we can meet Kṛṣṇa because it is non-different from Kṛṣṇa himself.

That's why in his writings and books Bhaktivinoda Ṭhākura has created a synthesis of these two paths. The first path, *vaidhī-sādhana-bhakti*, is when we have faith in the *śāstras* and are convinced by their logic. Thanks to this logic we constantly make efforts in our spiritual practices, such as hearing *Śrīmad-Bhāgavatam* discourses. At some point, hearing the *śāstras*, we get a spark of attachment for Kṛṣṇa. Bhaktivinoda Ṭhākura speaks about this in a very interesting way in his *Kalyāṇa-kalpataru* – "Kṛṣṇa eventually bestows the jewel of independence unto those persons who are attached to the path of rules and regulations, thereby allowing them entrance into the path of spontaneous loving service. Becoming influenced by such spontaneity, remaining under the shelter of the mellows of unwedded love, the soul finally attains all the symptoms of ecstatic love for Kṛṣṇa." In other words, when we get attached to adherence to the rules of devotional service, beginning first of all with *śravaṇam,* we obtain the jewel of freedom. We do this not because we have to, but because we want to. This precious jewel appears in our hearts and becomes the reason we take to the path of *rāga,* attachment to Kṛṣṇa. As a result, as Bhaktivinoda Ṭhākura says, we attain the desire for this secret love of God.

THE UNCHASTE WOMAN DANCING IN THE HEART

When we have driven deception out of our hearts, all the while there remains one last thing. There is no cheating any more, but still I want a little something and that is the chief subject matter of the seventh verse. *Pratiṣṭhāśā dhṛṣṭā śvapaca-ramaṇī me hṛdi naṭet* – Raghunātha Dāsa Gosvāmī says, "In my heart there is a dancer – *śvapaca-ramaṇī.*" *Ramaṇī* means a woman of easy virtue, a harlot; moreover, she has special dietary preferences, *śvapaca. Śvapaca* means she loves to cook dogs. And *dhṛṣṭā* means she is absolutely shameless. The name of that *dhṛṣṭā śvapaca-ramaṇī* is *pratiṣṭhā-āśā,* the desire for respect, honor, and fame. And then he goes on saying, *kathaṁ sādhu-premā spṛśati śucir etan nanu manaḥ* – "Think for yourself, my dear mind, whether *prema,* which is pure by nature, will touch your heart, if there is this untouchable woman dancing?"

Perhaps the most interesting word here is *dhṛṣṭā* meaning that she's shameless. This actually means that all the *anarthas* have already gone away by virtue of the holy name, but the shameless one (the desire for respect) is staying.

Bhaktivinoda Ṭhākura explains that the very last demon is when we want to be distinguished for our devotional service. A person may say, "Look how well I know the scriptures! I am a great preacher, so now I'm going to save everyone by my preaching!" In other words, when people start deeming themselves to be spiritual master or guru, this *anartha* is the root of all the other *anarthas,* in accordance with the teachings of Sanātana Gosvāmī and the *Hari-bhakti-vilāsa*. If we don't drive this away, everything else will come back. The merry woman that's dancing in the heart will call back all the other *anarthas*, "Come on, come on!"

Raghunātha Dāsa Gosvāmī says, "As long as she is there, *sādhu-premā*, pure *prema*, will never touch the heart. There will be no love in the heart, because it will remain desecrated." Kṛṣṇa provides all opportunities to fulfill this desire to be great. This persisting childish desire for recognition, honor, and to be the center of attention is the last to remain in our hearts, and it desecrates everything else that we are doing.

All other problems come as a result of the envy that appears because of *pratiṣṭhā-āśā*, the desire for *pratiṣṭhā*, the desire to be distinguished, to show off, the desire to show that I am special, I am exclusive, and the best. Therefore, we can see that true spiritual culture always teaches humility. Humility is the password through which, to some extent, a person can feel Kṛṣṇa. If we look at Vedic culture, from the very beginning it explains that God does everything, not us.

There are many achievements in Vedic history which are anonymous; no one puts any signatures to them. Most of the names we don't know, not even the number of holy persons there were, what to speak of their names. History has not preserved them, and they did not want to be noted. For example, we practically know nothing about Gopāla Bhaṭṭa Gosvāmī, one of the greatest *ācāryas* in our *sampradāya* — essentially the next one after Caitanya Mahāprabhu. Practically speaking, Śrī Caitanya Mahāprabhu made Gopāla Bhaṭṭa Gosvāmī his successor. He sent him his *āsana*, *kaupīna*, and *bahiḥ-vāsa*, all of which are still preserved in the temple of Rādhā-Ramaṇa. Even Rādhā-Ramaṇa himself came to him in response to his prayers. But Gopāla Bhaṭṭa Gosvāmī asked Kṛṣṇadāsa Kavirāja, "Please don't say a word about me!"

If someone starts to be aware of himself as a guru, or imagine himself to be a guru, then that's the end of his spiritual life. Love is out of the question, the only thing left in the heart is vanity.

The more Kali-yuga evolves, the more this problem also deepens. The word *guru* in Hindi initially meant a master; now in Hindi it is almost a swear word. Besides everything else, *guru* also means a trickster. This spiritual vanity is a very dangerous thing and it can haunt us up to the very end.

For instance, the famous Kumbha Mela in India is practically the best fair of spiritual vanity. The gurus gather there, seated on jewel-bedecked silver thrones on top of elephants. Recently even the elephants went out of fashion – they put the silver throne on top of a jeep. This behavior is a very sad thing, because actually we must understand that if I'm a true devotee I should not expect honor. Moreover, if I am a true devotee, I will expect to be reproached by others. Mādhavendra Purī wrote a wonderful verse where he says, "Let other people think that I have gone mad; let my friends think I am totally confused; let my relatives say that I am a complete fool; and let those who know the Vedas consider me just some proud fool." If we are a true devotee, we can expect people not to like that we live a life of complete and absolute devotion; they will start reproaching us. This is something important that we must remember.

Raghunātha Dāsa Gosvāmī gives a solution, he says, *pratiṣṭhāśā dhṛṣṭā śvapaca-ramaṇī me hṛdi naṭet*: that *śvapaca-ramaṇī* – this shameless prostitute is dancing, *kathaṁ sādhu-premā spṛśati* – so how can pure *prema* touch my heart? *Śucir etan nanu manaḥ* – think for yourself how the pure can touch the impure. My heart becomes untouchable because this woman there has cast off all restraint. So, he gives a solution to how we can protect ourselves from this problem: *sadā tvaṁ sevasva prabhu-dayita-sāmantam atulam* – constantly serve the servant of the Lord. Not Kṛṣṇa, but the servant of the Lord: *prabhu-dayita-sāmantam* – the best of the servants of the Lord (*sāmanta* means a general). *Yathā tāṁ niṣkāśya tvaritam iha taṁ veśayati saḥ* – then very quickly that woman will be banished from your heart.

In other words, Raghunātha Dāsa Gosvāmī says that to expel that woman from the heart the cure is association with the devotees, association in the process of service with the understanding of their greatness. When internally I am with them, I understand what true devotion is, who I am, and what the scale of my so-called devotion is.

The *Hitopadeśa* starts with a very instructive story about a tiger who represents the bogus *sādhu*. Its hidden meaning is to learn how to distinguish a true *sādhu* from a pretender. He's standing on the banks of a lake where there is an innocent traveler passing by. The tiger says, "Come here, my dear, come, I have a golden bracelet for you. I've repented all my sins; yes, I didn't used to be a vegetarian but now I am!"

The tiger says to the traveler that there are eight kinds of religiosity. These are performance of sacrifices, study of scriptures, distribution of donations, performance of ascetic feats, truthfulness, patience, forgiveness, and lack of greed. So he says, "Look at me – you can imitate the first four: you can perform sacrifices, you can perform penance, you can study the scriptures, you can give a donation – all this you can do with a contaminated heart, but the last four are impossible to imitate. It's impossible to pretend to be truthful!" It is a cheater who is saying that and he is exposing himself. He says that it is impossible to pretend to be patient; it is impossible to pretend to be able to forgive; and it is impossible to pretend to have no greed. Because the tiger speaks like this, the meaning in this fable is that even these can be imitated. Even these qualities do not serve as criteria, actually. If we want to know the true criterion for understanding who is a *sādhu* and who is not a *sādhu*, then it is not enough to just listen to what the person says. We need to examine him and look at the way he associates. The criterion that Raghunātha Dāsa Gosvāmī is giving here is very important, which is that a person should not internally deem himself to be a guru, and this means that he must always seek higher association. He must always consider himself to be a disciple.

There is a story in this regard about Gaurakiśora Dāsa Bābājī. A young man came to him trying to somehow serve him, but then he became bored and left for Purī. After some time, he came back, this time in the robes of a *sannyāsī*. He was accompanied by some *mahānta*, the Prior of some temple. The *mahānta* introduced himself, saying, "*Bābājī*, this disciple of yours has now become an elevated devotee. Please accept him. In Purī he served Haridāsa Ṭhākura and chanted three *lakhs* of the holy names."

Gaurakiśora Dāsa Bābājī looked at him closely and said, "I do not recall having such a disciple." Then he looked again and said, "Actually,

I don't consider anyone to be my disciple in this world, because I myself have failed to become a disciple. So, since I have failed to become a disciple myself, how can I teach someone else?" Because the only thing we can teach someone is how to become a disciple, how can I consider myself to be another's teacher or a preacher or a lecturer, or anything like that unless I have learned to be a humble disciple? He finally said, "Go away! I do not want to see you!"

This humility is actually the essential criterion. In his songbook *Kalyāṇa-kalpataru*, Bhaktivinoda Ṭhākura explains that if I think, "I am a Vaiṣṇava," then I shall look forward to receiving respect from others. And if the desire for fame and reputation pollute my heart, then certainly I shall descend towards life in hell. He says that if a person considers himself a Vaiṣṇava, that person will never become humble. Sometimes we also have this pride inside – we are proud that we don't eat meat or take intoxications, nor even do we eat garlic. There are many other reasons to be proud. Therefore, Bhaktivinoda Ṭhākura instructs us to have the mood of always remaining a *śiṣya* (a disciple). Let us never want any *pūjā*, respect or honor.

Śrīla Prabhupāda is a very good example for all of us. Śrīla Prabhupāda, although he was a spiritual master and the founder-*ācārya* of ISKCON, he constantly taught by his example that we should not strive for position; we should strive to be a disciple. He taught us to think that we are always, by nature, a follower and a servant, never a master. There is an amazing letter Śrīla Prabhupāda wrote that touched me very deeply. It is a letter he wrote to his spiritual brother Bhagavat Mahārāja in August 1969, when he already had a couple of dozen temples around the world, from America to Japan. There were not many of them, but they were around the globe. This letter was written after he read the statutes of the organization of this Bhagavat Mahārāja. He writes, "I have also read specifically your articles on the matter of *ācāryas*, wherein on the 14th paragraph I see the *ācārya* shall be entitled to nominate in writing his successive *ācārya*." He writes as if casually, but he says, "But we do not find any record where our Śrīla Prabhupāda nominated any *ācāryas* after him. Different persons have interpreted on this point, and every one of our godbrothers are acting as *ācārya*, so this is a controversial point which I do not wish to enter into while we are proposing for cooperation."

Further on Śrīla Prabhupāda writes that Bhaktisiddhānta Sarasvatī Ṭhākura Prabhupāda wanted his disciples to cooperate with each other. Therefore, at the very end of that letter Śrīla Prabhupāda essentially says that he wants to work together: I have temples. Send your preachers. You will be preaching in my temples, that doesn't matter. We'll send you visas, whatever. That's what Bhaktisiddhānta Sarasvatī Ṭhākura Prabhupāda wanted. He did not want us to become *ācāryas*; he wanted us to remain servants and serve the mission. Finally, he writes, "Also please let me know if personally I can become a member of your society under Clause 3 on page 19 of the Memorandum." An ordinary member of your society is what Śrīla Prabhupāda writes. Once again, he has temples all over the world, he is an *ācārya*, with many disciples from the West, which is a great triumph, but he asks if he can become a member of his godbrother's society.

Although pride is the last thing, we can see how it works even on some earlier stages of our service, preventing us from appreciating other people and cooperating. This idea that I am a preacher, that I can do something, and that I can teach someone, actually destroys our society. We'll never be able to achieve anything in devotional service as long as we do not banish this from our hearts through devotional service to the other devotees, as long as we don't take this service to other devotees and turn it into our daily nourishment on which we subsist. This is the last and most important obstacle on our spiritual path that we must constantly be aware of.

PROGRESS TO PURITY

Raghunātha Dāsa Gosvāmī appeals to the minds of those who practice *bhakti*, "Oh, mind, judge for yourself. If your heart is desecrated by the shameless whore dancing there, this expectation of honor and glory, who has cast away all shame, how will pure *prema* touch it?" *Sādhu-premā* means pure love or beautiful love. It will be repelled from having something to do with such a heart. But Raghunātha Dāsa Gosvāmī gives a way out of this: *sadā tvaṁ sevasva* — always serve. *Prabhu-dayita-*

sāmantam atulam – serve whom? The generals among the Lord's servants. Which ones? *Atulam* – the matchless, unparalleled ones. What will happen then? *Yathā tāṁ niṣkāśya tvaritam iha taṁ veśayati saḥ* – this prostitute will be driven out of your heart. There will be nothing left of her, because you will be seeing how the Lord's servants behave, how their every movement, every glance, every word is permeated with humility. And although they are *atulam*, unparalleled, they consider themselves to be lower than a blade of grass lying on the street, ready to patiently accept everything that Kṛṣṇa sends to them. They will drive that prostitute out of our hearts. Then *iha taṁ veśayati saḥ* – *kṛṣṇa-prema* will rise in our hearts, taking her place.

It is a very important verse for each of us, especially for those who have been practicing Kṛṣṇa consciousness for a long time and who feel we have something to be proud of. In reality, none of us have anything to be proud of. If we look, there is no merit of ours in anything, but it is the nature of the mind that it expects honor. What is most disgusting is that it expects honor even for our spiritual activity and practice. As I have previously mentioned, this is the last obstacle that can remain in a person even at the level of *bhāva*. As a result of carelessness, if we do not drive this out through any available method with the help of association, service, and humility, if we are taking service from others for granted and expecting respect, fame, and honor as something well-deserved, then the consequences can be very unfortunate.

Rāgātmikā, the state of attachment or love for Kṛṣṇa that initially attracts a person to the path of *bhakti-sādhana,* is defined by Śrīla Rūpa Gosvāmī as *iṣṭe svārasikī rāgaḥ paramāviṣṭatā bhavet.* When attachment to Kṛṣṇa, to the object of my desire, becomes absolutely natural and there is the highest degree of absorption in the object of my love or the one I want to attain, such a state or such devotees are called *rāgātmikā.* This state is achievable, but as long as *anarthas* remain, we cannot surrender our entire mind. Rūpa Gosvāmī tells us that the ideal is when the mind is completely absorbed in Kṛṣṇa and thinks of nothing else.

Śrīla Bhaktivinoda very interestingly describes the gradual stages of purification of the mind. He says that we must start our journey by chanting the holy name, and not simply chanting, but chanting with the understanding of who we are. *Sambandha-jñāna* – I understand that I am part and parcel of Kṛṣṇa, his servant. If our chanting of the holy name is permeated by this understanding and awareness of my subordinate position and eternal connection with Kṛṣṇa, then gradually the holy name will be purifying. If I chant the holy name and I do not have this understanding, if I chant simply as a mechanical ritual, or because I am supposed to, or because everyone else does it, or because I'll not be fed *prasādam* if I don't, or because my husband gets angry and rails at me if I don't, then the holy name's purifying effect will take a long time. If we have this understanding that we are 1/10,000 part of the tip of a hair when chanting the holy name, the holy name will gradually start to have an effect, reveal its cleansing power, and drive *anarthas* out of our heart.

As a result of this purification, the next stage, as explained by Bhaktivinoda Ṭhākura, is called *nairantarya* – when our mind begins to love the holy name and everything that is connected with Kṛṣṇa. At this stage, we like hearing about Kṛṣṇa and chanting the holy name incessantly. Although at this point, the chanting process may still somewhat bear traces of being mechanical or unaware, at least we do not want to interrupt it. We want to hear *kīrtana* and hear about Kṛṣṇa. We always want to do something for Kṛṣṇa. If we go further into devotion, everything happens by itself. But it is very hard to reach this level because there is a force that constantly throws us back. Bhaktivinoda Ṭhākura says about this level – *svecchā-pūrvikā* – which means that at my own will, I can at any time sit down and remember Kṛṣṇa. I will remember not just Kṛṣṇa, but an amazingly beautiful picture of Vṛndāvana will appear before my mind's eye, and I will see how the devotees serve Kṛṣṇa, and how Kṛṣṇa serves his devotees. Whenever I want to, I can meditate on the Lord's *līlās*. This stage is *āsakti,* or attachment. The mind becomes so clear and so well-trained that as soon as we wish, our mind itself starts serving Kṛṣṇa, and I find myself there with Kṛṣṇa in my meditation.

The next stage is *svārasikī* which means that never mind whether I plan to or not, I think of Kṛṣṇa all the same, even when I don't try. We will think of him all the time, because the *līlās* enter into us by themselves. We are there all the time, together with Kṛṣṇa. On their own volition these *līlās* are revealed in our heart. At this stage, we have already tuned the receiver of our heart to the wave of the spiritual world. Thus it always picks up the transmissions from there. It is at the level of *bhāva* that a person reaches this *svārasikī* stage. At the level of *prema,* a person enters these pastimes. Sometimes Kṛṣṇa comes to such a person and they don't know whether they are here or there. However, at the initial stages the *anarthas* interrupt our meditation, constantly focusing us back on ourselves, our problems, and on our useless desires, and on the image of ourselves that we have invented. This is what ego is. The trick of the false ego is that a person invents an image of how they are and then serves it. This called idolatry, and we worship the idol that we ourselves have created.

Bhaktivinoda Ṭhākura makes a very interesting point in his book *Śrī Tattva-sūtra*. He says that as long as attachment to Kṛṣṇa is not developed to the proper degree of intensity, and as long as we still have *anarthas,* there are three things that will help us preserve spiritual attachment and that will give us a taste for it. These are *kīrtana,* association with *bhāgavatas,* and discussion of *bhagavad-kathā,* or philosophy of the *Bhāgavatam*.

We sing *kīrtana* and we think, "What nice music! A new tune..." and we sing unwittingly: Hare Kṛṣṇa, Hare Kṛṣṇa, Kṛṣṇa Kṛṣṇa, Hare Hare/ Hare Rāma, Hare Rāma, Rāma Rāma, Hare Hare. Thus I come in direct contact with Kṛṣṇa himself through the sound of his holy name, and the taste, despite the *anarthas,* can be felt.

Secondly, although our tongue is covered and we can't feel the taste, nevertheless, if we associate with *bhāgavatas,* those devotees who have fully surrendered their hearts to Kṛṣṇa, we feel easy and free, and we see everything in a completely different perspective.

And the third is discussion of the *Bhāgavatam* philosophy. When we read *Śrīmad-Bhāgavatam* or hear *bhagavad-kathā,* it also gives us a special taste. If, despite of the lack of taste we come into contact with these three sources of taste, we can survive this difficult period. But if I interrupt my association with these carriers of taste, eventually my interest will all go away.

HUMILITY

Even at the level of *bhāva*, the desire for fame may remain. This is the very last obstacle that we have to overcome. Śrīla Prabhupāda taught exactly this, that we must be humble. There is a wonderful story about Śrīla Prabhupāda that Tamal Kṛṣṇa Mahārāja loved to tell. At the time he was the temple commander in the Los Angeles temple on La Cienega Boulevard.

Once he brought to Śrīla Prabhupāda's room a large painting by Murlīdhara depicting the spiritual world. This painting is reproduced on the cover of the First Canto of *Śrīmad-Bhāgavatam*. It shows the Vaikuṇṭhas and the material world where Mahā-Viṣṇu is lying. When Tamal Kṛṣṇa brought it in, Śrīla Prabhupāda started telling him, "Each universe is filled up with unlimited numbers of living entities who inhabit all of the planets and stars. One of these planets is our earth, and on this planet are many continents. On one continent there is America, and in America there are so many big cities. Here is Los Angeles, and in Los Angeles there is a street, La Cienega Boulevard. On this boulevard, among all of the buildings, is a temple of Lord Kṛṣṇa. And in this temple there is one Tamal Kṛṣṇa. He is there, and is thinking that he is very important."

This is how Śrīla Prabhupāda taught us that this idea of self-importance is a complete, absolute illusion. The most disgusting is when we try to strengthen this idea in ourselves through spiritual practice. In essence, what we do is we come to Kṛṣṇa in the robes of a *sādhu* and try to enjoy his spiritual energy. When we enjoy the material energy, that is half the problem, but the most terrible offense we can commit is when we try to enjoy by means of our spiritual activity.

Rāvaṇa came to steal Sītā wearing the robes of a *sannyāsī*. When Sītā invited him to take some refreshment, he said, "No, no, I'm very renounced, I cannot come in. You must come here." He had already tried to enter but was prevented, so he made the excuse that he was too renounced. Similarly, we come to Kṛṣṇa, changing our apparel, wearing *tilaka* and so on. We think, "I am disguised perfectly. Now I am going to steal Kṛṣṇa's internal energy and enjoy it for myself." This is what is called weakness of the heart.

Bhaktivinoda Ṭhākura says in his *Śrī Bhajana-rahasya* that there are four manifestations of *hṛdaya daurbalyam*, or the weak heart that is imprisoned here by the material energy. These are 1 *tucchāsaktiḥ śakti* – attachment to things that are not related to Kṛṣṇa; 2 *kuṭināṭī* or duplicity, hypocrisy; 3 *mātsaryam* – envy of others' progress which leads to slander, when we talk badly of others, humiliate them, or offend them; and 4 *pratiṣṭhāśā* – the desire for fame.

These four things give rise to the six enemies and the six waves that carry us throughout the material world. The six enemies are *kāma, krodha, lobha, moha, mada* and *mātsarya*: lust, anger, greed, envy, illusion, and pride. All other bad qualities arise from there. Bhaktivinoda Ṭhākura then explains that the six waves are hunger, thirst, old age, death, grief, and illusion. As long as we retain attachment to material things and *pratiṣṭhā*, the desire for fame, we will never find peace.

Sanātana Gosvāmī goes even further. He says that of everything else, this *pratiṣṭhā* is the root of all other *anarthas*. In one of the last verses of the *Hari-bhakti-vilāsa* it is said – *sarva tyāge 'py aheyāyāḥ* – even if a person has renounced everything else all *anarthas* can return to him – *sarvānartha bhuvaś ca te kuryuḥ pratiṣṭhāviṣṭhāyā* – why? Because in our mind we come in contact with *pratiṣṭhā*.

Sanātana Gosvāmī says that if you don't drive away the desire for fame, you will never be clean because it is like excrement. Even if we purify ourselves by *ācamana* and all the *mudrās*, if inside there is excrement, we will never be clean. Bhaktisiddhānta Sarasvatī Ṭhākura Prabhupāda calls this *pratiṣṭhā* not just ordinary excrement, but pig's excrement. A pig eats other excrements because they are tasty, but their own excrements even the pigs do not eat. This is what *pratiṣṭhā* is – it is *śukarera viṣṭhā* – pig's excrement.

As mentioned earlier, a very important principle is that if there is this one *anartha* left, then all the others will return. This *anartha*, the desire for fame, may be seemingly harmless. It makes us study the scriptures, become very renounced, preach, and perform extraordinary feats in our devotional service. Yet, Kavi-karṇapūra cites this problem in the *Caitanya-candrodaya-nāṭaka* where he says, "If one thing has remained, all the rest will come back." The Sanskrit is: *eka-yoga-nirdiṣṭānāṁ saha vā pravṛttiḥ, saha vā nivṛttiḥ* – if one thing out of a group of things remains, it will attract all the rest. In other words, if one *anartha* remains, then everything else will come back.

We may be following all the regulative principles, but if we still want glory it invites everything else back again. The principle is simple. If something contaminates us, our consciousness, our aura, then a channel appears through which all the other contamination can enter there. If someone is immaculately pure then naturally no contamination will stick to him. Therefore, people do not attach importance to this desire for fame, but as Śrīla Prabhupāda explains in the *Guṇḍicā-mārjana-līlā*, if a person's desire for fame remains, one may go into seclusion and be chanting the holy name – but 128 rounds, or 164, or 192 rounds or five *lakhs*, ten *lakhs* will not help. Śrīla Prabhupāda says that the heart of such a person becomes harder and harder because *pratiṣṭhā* gives rise to *jīva-hiṁsā* (violence towards others).

People who have *pratiṣṭhā* will be offending the Vaiṣṇavas. They will in one way or another find all possible faults and rejoice. Therefore, the essence of Vaiṣṇava ethics is humility, and by no means should we let that *pratiṣṭhā*, the desire for fame, which is somewhere there in each of us, become manifest. It can remain until the very end. Sanātana Gosvāmī says, "Just don't touch it. It will go away, just go on serving humbly." If this humility is there then the mercy of Kṛṣṇa and the devotees will come to you. When there is humility, mercy comes in a natural way. We will then be safe and the holy name will be with us all the time, the Vaiṣṇavas will be with us, and our spiritual experience, the experience of love, will grow deeper and deeper.

If we read the *Caitanya-bhāgavata*, Vṛndāvana Dāsa Ṭhākura says again and again "If you see a Vaiṣṇava, bow down to him! If you can't bow down, then at least bow down to him in your mind. If you see a Vaiṣṇava, be glad to see him." He says that a person should have this one quality: not to distinguish between Vaiṣṇavas, not judging them and not saying, "This Vaiṣṇava is at that level of advancement, that one is there, and I'm here." If we consider all Vaiṣṇavas to be above ourselves, we will go directly to Kṛṣṇa.

Further on he says, "If a person doesn't bow his head before the Vaiṣṇavas, then that head will bring him to hell." Behind all the possible offenses there is one single thing that eventually destroys our consciousness and prevents us from chanting the holy name. It is very important in our dealings with the Vaiṣṇavas to first consider each Vaiṣṇava above ourselves. We can think, "He is my guru; Kṛṣṇa has sent him to teach me something. If I consider him my guru, my teacher, I can learn something very important from him."

If someone comes up to you and starts criticizing another Vaiṣṇava, tell that person, "I have to do something very urgent. I have to run." Run far away, beause when we hear offenses against others, our respect for the Vaiṣṇavas diminish whether we want it to or not. Therefore, we must not commit offenses ourselves but we also must not hear offenses against a Vaiṣṇava. If we see a fault in a person, I should think, "Why do I see this fault? It is because I also have the same fault." Then *pratiṣṭhā* will go away.

COMMENTARY BY ŪRMILĀ DEVĪ DĀSĪ

By verse seven, the practitioner on the path of spontaneous devotion has stopped trying to enjoy money, mundane knowledge, possessions, and gross or subtle sex on the plea of *bhakti*. With great care, such a person swims in the ocean of divine love, holding the jewel of love. But the root of all pride and deceit remains in the heart. The ocean of love, after all, is all around the practitioner, but not within. Bhaktivinoda again lists ways in which this root manifests at this deepest level. What each item on his lists has in common is this yearning: "I want others to see how great I am! I am pure, learned, and detached! I want others to appreciate how I am swimming in the ocean of spiritual love! I am a great saintly person! Honor me! Glorify me!"

Unlike the sensations of having a prostitute stealing one's wealth, a tigress eating one's heart, robbers pulling one around with a strong rope around the neck, or burning stinky urine all over oneself, at this point a person may feel that a party is going on in the heart. There is food, singing, and dancing! "This must be spiritual," a person could think. Raghunātha Dāsa Gosvāmī tells us to take a closer look in our heart — to smell the food, and listen to the songs going on there. The dancing in the heart may not be that of the pure ladies of spiritual love (*sādhu-premā* — note the feminine form with the final *ā*), but someone else entirely. It's a woman, yes, but the wrong kind. Instead of chaste love, this woman is filled with impure lust. Her boyfriend Deceit dances with her, and they are eating a dead dog!

With the dog-eating dance of desires for distinction going on in our heart, the ladies of love go elsewhere. We may think we want their presence, but they will not stay in such a place. Fame is like dog meat because it seems like nourishment but only brings pain and disease. Because fame is so flickering, and can turn to nothing or infamy in a moment, those who seek it are filled with fear. People seeking fame must always adjust themselves to appear pleasing to others. Anxiety thus pervades such people's lives as they attempt to constantly modify everything about themselves to ensure a good reputation. The desire for such dog meat is like a dancing promiscuous woman. She's promiscuous because the desire for fame is about going to wherever accolades and glorification can be found, rather than loyalty and service. In the same way a prostitute destroys her health and body for others' pleasure, the desire for fame destroys our peace and devotion in order to pretend to be what others want us to be. Thus we invite her boyfriend of Deceit and Pretentiousness. We wear a variety of masks so everyone will praise what they think we are. Truth, what to speak of the Absolute Truth, cannot blossom in such a heart.

The problem is that this wanton woman has been dancing in our heart for a very long time. It's difficult for us to recognize how much she's hurting us, and almost impossible to drive her out by our own strength. In the fifth verse, we were advised to call for help from the devotees of the killer of Baka, personified hypocrisy. Here, we are advised help must come from *prabhu-dayita-sāmantam*. In other words, now we need not just any devotee of Kṛṣṇa, but generals in his army. We may ask why top commanders are necessary. Because the dancing dog-eater is the desire for our own honor, her presence makes us envy those who are worthiest of honor. Therefore, to evict her, we take a servant's position to those whom we would otherwise envy. We engage always in the service of such persons, *sadā tvaṁ sevasva*. Honoring devotee commanders in a practical way through serving them, gets us free from the desire to receive honor ourselves. We then feel satisfied to be in our honest position. When the unchaste dancer is thus gone, and the pure ladies of divine love then take up residence in our heart, we can go through the doorway into fully realized spiritual service in our eternal form, starting with verse eight.

VERSE EIGHT

yathā duṣṭatvaṁ me davayati śaṭhasyāpi kṛpayā
yathā mahyaṁ premāmṛtam api dadāty ujjvalam asau
yathā śrī-gāndharvā-bhajana-vidhaye prerayati māṁ
tathā goṣṭhe kākvā giridharam iha tvaṁ bhaja manaḥ

Even though I am a cheater, the Lord's mercy can drive away my inherent wicked nature, give me the glowing nectar of divine love, and inspire my heart with the process to worship Śrī Gāndharvikā. Therefore, O mind, with pleading words, you should worship Śrī Giridhārī here in Vṛndāvana.

COMMENTARY BY ŚACĪNANDANA SWAMI

This verse happens to be my favorite verse of *Manaḥ-śikṣā*. Raghunātha Dāsa Gosvāmī looks back at what he discussed in verses 4–7 – innumerable obstacles. He says that his heart is full of lust. His mind is bathing in duplicity, which is like acidic donkey's urine. He has so much desire for recognition, and needs the good association of a devotee who can remove it all.

All the obstacles can be summarized with one word, *duṣṭatvaṁ* or wickedness – this is meanness or pollution of the consciousness, according to the *ācāryas*. The original spiritual consciousness or Kṛṣṇa consciousness is pure, but when this spiritual consciousness is covered over, it becomes polluted.

Śrī Raghunātha Dāsa Gosvāmī has already discussed in previous verses two solutions for the wickedness of the heart: 1 utter humility; 2 the *bhakti* general.

Why is humility important? A fruit needs a protective skin. Without it, very quickly the flies come and infect it with germs. If devotees do not have a protective peel of humility and want to show off, immediately their so-called devotion becomes corrupted. Without protection, a good fruit is in danger of being contaminated.

After going through the obstacles honestly and realistically Raghunātha Dāsa Gosvāmī discusses the solution of the shelter of the *bhakti* general. We may wonder where we can find this association. So here in verse 8, he offers the answer that we can just worship Śrī Girirāja Govardhana in such a way that he becomes pleased. Girirāja Giridhārī is the greatest of all devotees and is Kṛṣṇa himself. Let us turn to Girirāja Govardhana. If we have any spiritual desire, Girirāja will fulfill it. When we circumambulate Govardhana Hill, it is said that he follows us to see what we want, and he fulfills it. Raghunātha Dāsa Gosvāmī himself turned for shelter to the Girirāja *śilā* he received from Śrī Caitanya Mahāprabhu. Govardhana worship is how we can enter the camp of Śrī Rādhā.

So, Raghunātha Dāsa Gosvāmī writes from his experience. He turned to Giridhārī Kṛṣṇa, but I encourage you to turn to Raghunātha Dāsa Gosvāmī himself, in the same way that Śrīla Prabhupāda told us we can always contact him in his *vāṇī*, instructions.

I found an old manuscript describing the mode of conduct of a renunciate in Vraja. There it says that of all manifestations of wickedness, the worst of all is fault-finding. So it gives seven prescriptions:

1. Be always absorbed in your *bhajana* and *sādhana*.
2. Speak only about *sādhana* and the Lord.
3. Speak only about beneficial things.
4. Walk on the road with your head lowered, palms joined and show respect to everyone.
5. Never criticize others.
6. Know that everyone is superior to you.
7. If someone comes to you and criticizes someone else, say, "Oh, I have something urgent to do," and leave the place immediately. We know that other defects are somewhat correctible, but finding fault or Vaiṣṇava *nindā* erases everything. It uproots our *bhakti-latā*.

Raghunātha Dāsa Gosvāmī must have had specific thoughts when he spoke of Śrī Govardhana. He said, "Śrī Caitanya Mahāprabhu, by offering me the *govardhana-śilā* offered me shelter at the Govardhana Hill, and by offering me the *guñjā mālā* necklace, he offered me the shelter at the lotus feet of Śrīmatī Rādhārāṇī."

My dear devotees, we all have direct access to Girirāja, and we can pray to him to remove all wickedness from our hearts. He will then do something that will make our hair stand on end.

Another important point in this verse is that if we want to experience Kṛṣṇa with all his qualities, we can only do so by worshiping him through Śrīmatī Rādhārāṇī. Just like we cannot get the nectar-honey directly from a flower, but only from the bees, so we cannot get the highest *ujjvala-rasa* without entering the camp of Rādhā.

Turn to Girirāja and Girirāja will turn us to Rādhārāṇī. In Rādhā's camp we will find our good fortune and the honey of what Kṛṣṇa consciousness is. She is the bee-like, topmost devotee of Kṛṣṇa, who draws all of Kṛṣṇa's honey, as well as his divine qualities that will flood our hearts when we become her servant.

So what is the process of becoming a servant of Śrīmatī Rādhārāṇī?

This is so sublime that it is a well-kept secret of our *sampradāya*. It has to be kept confidential because we can make so many mistakes. In my personal practice, I find we can go through Śrī Gaurāṅga Mahāprabhu who is the combined form of Śrī Rādhā and Kṛṣṇa. The first step is forgetting all self-identification as "an enjoyer." Be humble, be realistic, but know what anyone can become, and yearn.

After more than 40 years of practice, what works for me is changing the heart by association – with a person, food, object, environment, and literature. Associate with high things and your consciousness will become higher.

In the *Nectar of Instruction*, verse 4, purport, Śrīla Prabhupāda says, "In *Bhagavad-gītā* (2.62) it is stated, *saṅgāt sañjāyate kāmaḥ*: one's desires and ambitions develop according to the company one keeps. It is often said that a man is known by his company, and if an ordinary man associates with devotees, he will certainly develop his dormant Kṛṣṇa consciousness."

Yes, dear devotees, you can change! Raghunātha Dāsa Gosvāmī says that he is wicked, and dishonest, but can change with the association of Giridhārī. Associate with affection not with the computer, which I call a modern mind without a conscience, but associate with affection with the proper things and they will transform you.

COMMENTARY BY BHAKTIVIJNANA GOSWAMI

Yathā duṣṭatvaṁ me davayati śaṭhasyāpi kṛpayā. Raghunātha Dāsa Gosvāmī explains how we can eradicate *duṣṭatvam* (wickedness). He says that mercy will deliver me from my wicked nature.

It sometimes happens that when we are performing *sādhana,* it feels like we are just marking time, and there never seems an end to our *anarthas.* Some things may seem to have already gone, yet here they are again. This is because our perverted nature has actually always been here, due to our material body and mind which are influenced by the *guṇas* of material nature. Raghunātha Dāsa Gosvāmī calls this perverted nature *duṣṭatvam.* Another word he uses is *śaṭhasyāpi,* meaning I am a cheater and hypocrite.

Naturally, in one sense, this mood of a struggling devotee is the reflection of the nature of *bhakti* because even when devotees develop *prema,* they say, "I am still a hypocrite." Śrī Caitanya Mahāprabhu authors an amazing verse in *Caitanya-caritāmṛta, Madhya-līlā* (2.45):

na prema-gandho 'sti darāpi me harau
krandāmi saubhāgya-bharaṁ prakāśitum
vaṁśī-vilāsy-ānana-lokanaṁ vinā
bibharmi yat prāṇa-pataṅgakān vṛthā

> Śrī Caitanya Mahāprabhu continued, "My dear friends, I have not the slightest tinge of love of Godhead within my heart. When you see me crying in separation, I am just falsely exhibiting a demonstration of my great fortune. Indeed, not seeing the beautiful face of Kṛṣṇa playing his flute, I continue to live my life like an insect, without purpose."

In one sense this is the nature of *prema* – *prema* never knows it is within someone's heart. If people say, "I have *prema,*" flee from them because not only do they not have *prema,* they have no conscience. Caitanya Mahāprabhu says, "I have not the slightest tinge. I am a cheater." Even on the highest levels of devotional service such a person feels like a cheater.

One devotee, trembling and crying, asked Gaura Govinda Mahārāja if she would ever develop *prema.* He looked at her and said, "You will, but you'll never know that you have." This is the nature of love. I've already mentioned that when wandering in the material world we cannot feel satisfied with anything material, so we look for spiritual love. But when we develop this love, we will be satisfied but not satiated. We will continue to feel spiritual thirst or spiritual insatiability.

In one sense, these words by Raghunātha Dāsa Gosvāmī describe both the highest platform and the state of mind of a devotee still on the path. It sometimes seems impossible to eradicate our perverted nature. It is true that as long as we have this material body and mind, our vices will emerge seemingly from nowhere. Then we catch ourselves desiring to enjoy the material world again. Cheaters want to enjoy like Kṛṣṇa, deeply within convinced that they are meant to enjoy. This lust or desire to enjoy pervades everything. So, Lord Caitanya says, "I am *śaṭha*. And, even though I am a cheater, despite my complex nature, I'm hoping for your mercy."

This famous verse from *Caitanya-caritāmṛta* describes a devotee as the one who in spite of everything hopes for Kṛṣṇa's mercy, because he knows he is absolutely hopeless. Sometimes we may feel desperate, thinking there is no hope for us. But at this point we remember, "Kṛṣṇa is merciful and his mercy is more than my hopelessness. Despite all of my hopelessness, his mercy excels." Therefore *kṛṣṇa kṛpā karibena – dṛḍha kari' jāne,* there is this confidence that Kṛṣṇa's mercy will come.

Raghunātha Dāsa Gosvāmī makes a very important point here in verse eight: *yathā duṣṭatvaṁ me davayati śaṭhasyāpi kṛpayā*: "Even if I am *śaṭha,* I will be able to be rid of it by your mercy." Moreover, he says, *yathā mahyaṁ premāmṛtam api dadāty ujjvalam asau*: "You'll even give me *premāmṛtam,* the nectar of *prema,* and not just *prema* but *ujjvala-prema,* which means the most elevated love for Kṛṣṇa. *Dadāty-api* – you will give it to me. There is no getting away from it." He says, *yathā śrī-gāndharvā-bhajana-vidhaye prerayati mām*: "There's a third thing you will give to me, and that is the opportunity to serve Śrīmatī Rādhārāṇī." He addresses Kṛṣṇa directly, saying, "You will give me these things: you'll smash all of my wickedness, make my heart absolutely pure, and give me *premāmṛta* – *ujjvala-premāmṛta* – nectar or immortality, which can give love for Kṛṣṇa. And you will give me the opportunity to serve Śrīmatī Rādhārāṇī." *Yathā śrī-gāndharvā-bhajana-vidhaye prerayati mām.*

In the fourth line he clarifies when this will happen: *tathā goṣṭhe kākvā giridharam iha tvaṁ bhaja manaḥ*. Literally, these words mean: *tathā goṣṭhe*: "It will happen if I am in Vṛndāvana" (*goṣṭha* means Vraja), *kākvā giridharam iha*: "if I am here." I will get those mercies if you, my mind, worship Giridhārī, the Lord who lifted Govardhana Hill here in Vṛndāvana. And how will you worship? *Kākvā* means with one's heart burning, with deep emotion within one's heart.

Raghunātha Dāsa Gosvāmī mentions the devotees he associated with: Rūpa Gosvāmī, Sanātana Gosvāmī, Svarūpa Dāmodara Gosvāmī, Śrī Caitanya Mahāprabhu – all of them had just left the planet. In the previous verse, he said that all the problems will be solved if I serve these advanced devotees: *prabhu-dayita-sāmantam atulam*, the generals of the army of devotees. But he is no longer able to associate with them, because they are no longer here.

In verse 8, Raghunātha Dāsa Gosvāmī tells us what we are supposed to do even if there is no chance of physically associating with an advanced devotee. He recalls the gift Caitanya Mahāprabhu gave to him – the *Govardhana-śilā*. This tiny *Govardhana-śilā* is still in the Rādhā-Gokulānanda temple in Vṛndāvana. Śrī Caitanya Mahāprabhu himself washed this *śilā* with his tears, leaving his thumbprint on it. That *śilā*, along with a *guñjā-mālā*, a garland of small red and black berries, was brought from Vṛndāvana to Purī and given to Śrī Caitanya Mahāprabhu. He later gave that *śilā* to Raghunātha Dāsa Gosvāmī.

Śrī Caitanya-caritāmṛta describes how Raghunātha Dāsa Gosvāmī worshiped the *śilā* as Kṛṣṇa himself. He realized that the *śilā* would be his inspiration now that these great associates had departed. Raghunātha Dāsa Gosvāmī uses the word Giridhārī, and it is not without reason that he uses this name of Kṛṣṇa in the verse.

DEITY WORSHIP

It is important for us to understand that we always have a chance to receive Kṛṣṇa's mercy. Our spiritual master gives us permission to worship Deities, which is supposed to be done in a special mood. We should realize that Deities are non-different from Kṛṣṇa himself and then we'll have *kākvā* within our hearts.

Śrī Caitanya Mahāprabhu relished the story of Sākṣī Gopāla. When a young *brāhmaṇa* came and addressed Sākṣī Gopāla, who was then just called Gopāla, "Gopāla, Gopāla! You should come with me and bear witness! The old *brāhmaṇa* made the promise before you that he would marry me to his daughter. He is your devotee; you should uphold his promise. I don't care about marrying his daughter but you must come and bear witness to protect this old *brāhmaṇa*."

Gopāla replied, "Have you ever seen a statue walking? They don't. I am a *mūrti*. I can't walk. What do you want from me?"

The young *brāhmaṇa* looked at him and said, "If you can talk, why can't you walk?" He continued, *Pratimā naha tumi – sākṣāt vrajendra-nandana*. "You are not a statue." *Pratimā* means a statue or a picture. "You are the son of Mahārāja Nanda himself, and can walk and talk. You can also run!"

This is a most important thing we have to understand: *arcye viṣṇau śilā-dhīḥ*. There is a verse in the *Padma Purāṇa* quoted in *Padyāvalī* by Rūpa Gosvāmī, which says that if one thinks that the *arcā-vigraha* on the altar is a stone, marble or bronze, or iron, then where does one live? If one hasn't understood the real nature of the Deity, one lives in hell and will continue to live there. This verse says that we need to understand that hellish consciousness means material consciousness, which deprives us of the opportunity to truly worship Kṛṣṇa or approach him.

Śrīla Jīva Gosvāmī makes a very important point in the *Bhakti-sandarbha*. He says that people who truly worship Kṛṣṇa, who know what it is to worship Kṛṣṇa, do not see the difference between *arcā* and Kṛṣṇa himself. This is where the difference between our philosophy and practically all the other spiritual philosophies lies. Worshipping Deities is so valuable. Wherever you go, you'll hear people decrying worshiping idols. They think that Deity worship is idolatry. But the common person does not understand that God is almighty and is capable of associating with us through any form. What to speak of other people, even we do not understand that God and his energy are almighty, and that he will personally associate with us through his Deity form if we are in the right state of consciousness.

This is a very important point in our philosophy because, after all, all the other philosophies are more or less contaminated by Māyāvāda. There is no difference between Kṛṣṇa and a Deity installed according to *pañcarātra* principles. Jīva Gosvāmī himself says that the very moment a Deity is installed according to all the principles, Kṛṣṇa comes there in person.

Kṛṣṇadāsa Kavirāja Gosvāmī makes a similar point in *Caitanya-caritāmṛta, Madhya-līlā* (17.131):

'nāma', 'vigraha', 'svarūpa' – tina eka-rūpa
tine 'bheda' nāhi, – tina 'cid-ānanda-rūpa'

Tina means three, *nāma* means name, and *vigraha* means form. *Svarūpa* means Kṛṣṇa himself. They are the same. There is no difference. *Eka-rūpa* means the same. The name is Kṛṣṇa himself. *Vigraha* is Kṛṣṇa himself. He further says: *tine 'bheda' nāhi, – 'cid-ānanda-rūpa'*; there is no difference at all because all these three are *cid-ānanda-rūpa* – they consist of eternity, knowledge and bliss.

Raghunātha Dāsa Gosvāmī is implying that sometimes we have no chance to associate with advanced devotees, but we always have a chance to associate with Deities. We should just understand who this is on our altar.

Śrīla Jīva Gosvāmī confirms this fact. He states that worshiping a Deity is the way to get rid of all of our problems. Sometimes we look for other ways to solve our problems. He says we have two problems (*Bhakti-sandarbha*, 284): *kadarya-śīlānām* and *vikṣipta-cittānām.*

Kadarya-śīlānām means bad character developed in previous lives. In the material world we developed inevitable bad habits, because such is the nature of material life and the nature of material relations in this world. We wonder what others will do to us if we don't have the ability to become angry, for example, and protect ourselves. Therefore, Jīva Gosvāmī says: *kadarya-śīlānām* – we don't need anger to associate with Kṛṣṇa, because anger destroys this association.

Vikṣipta-cittānām is the flickering mind which cannot concentrate, cannot meditate or think long about anything. It is a mind that always desires something. Today it wants one thing, tomorrow another. After fifteen minutes, it wants something else. *Vikṣipta-cittānāṁ* means that we always want to do something other than what we are doing. If I am sitting, I want to walk. If I am walking, I want to lie down.

Śrīla Jīva Gosvāmī says in *Bhakti-sandarbha* that worshiping a Deity delivers people from those two things if they worship properly. Worshipping a Deity keeps us within limits if we really understand that this is Kṛṣṇa himself. And this *if* is of great importance here, because if one thinks the Deity is a statue, it is clear that nothing will come out of the worship. We invite Deities to our home and connect with Deities to remove our problems and vices as soon as possible. It is said that if we worship a Deity, placing all of our thoughts towards his lotus feet, this Deity will come to us at the moment of death. Not just some abstract Kṛṣṇa, but Kṛṣṇa in this same form. He'll save us. If we have realized that we are part of our Deity's entourage – we will remain in this retinue. Everything will come to us due to correctly worshiping the Deity in the proper consciousness.

This topic surfaces again and again. At the beginning of *Caitanya-caritāmṛta*, Kṛṣṇadāsa Kavirāja Gosvāmī enumerates the three Deities he had visited before writing the book. He categorically states that Madana-mohana is Kṛṣṇa himself.

DEITY STORIES

The following are stories illustrating that Deities of Kṛṣṇa are non-different from Kṛṣṇa himself. First is a story of Sākṣī Gopāla. Before Sākṣī Gopāla had come to Vijayanagar in Andhra Pradesh in the south of India, there was also an interesting story of him getting to Cuttack.

One of the ancestors of Mahārāja Pratāparudra, the king of Orissa (modern day Odisha) had heard of this Deity who had walked all the way from Vṛndāvana to Vijayanagar to bear witness for the young *brāhmaṇa*. This ancestor thought, "I have the best Deities in my kingdom, Lord Jagannātha, but I want to have this Gopāla in my kingdom as well." With a small army he came to the king of Andhra Pradesh and said, "I have only one request – give me Gopāla."

The king of Andhra Pradesh refused, preferring battle rather than giving him the Gopāla Deity, but he lost. His opponent said, "Again, I make the same request of you. I have defeated you. I don't need your kingdom. Just give me Gopāla."

The king of Andhra Pradesh replied, "I am sorry, I can give you my kingdom but I won't be able to give you Gopāla because he doesn't belong to me, I belong to him. You should sort it out with Gopāla. If he wants to go with you – you are welcome."

The king came to Gopāla and said, "Gopāla, I want you to be in Orissa." Gopāla decided to speak from the sky.

"You want me?"

"I want you to come with me and I will serve you. I will build a temple for you and take care of you."

"Okay. I am used to walking, I love it. But you should meet the same requirements. That young *brāhmaṇa*, when he was walking along every day, begged rice and cooked a hill of it for me. I still remember how delicious it was. So, you will have to do the same thing. You should ask for rice in every village and cook a hill of it for me."

"As you say; I am your servant."

The king took off his crown, his royal armor and his weaponry. He clad his body in simple clothes and went to beg alms. Gopāla watched him to make sure that he wasn't cheating. All the way to Orissa he begged alms until at last they reached Cuttack. When he arrived in Cuttack, his wife, who had a valuable pearl that had been handed down from generation to generation, knew that Gopāla was coming. She thought, "What shall I give to Gopāla? I should give him everything, right? If I belong to him, I should give everything to him."

So she prepared this valuable pearl nosering to give to him. She called the *pūjārī* and said, "Dear *pūjārī*, please decorate Gopāla with this pearl."

The *pūjārī* approached the Deity and started looking for a hole in the nose. "There's no hole in Gopāla's nose," he said.

She became upset and said, "Okay then, keep this pearl somewhere, but I want to see Gopāla with this pearl in his nose."

Gopāla came to her in a dream that night and said, "This *pūjārī* doesn't know anything. Yaśodā pierced a hole for me – the *pūjārī* just couldn't find it. Tell him to look carefully. I remember having Yaśodā pierce the hole!"

The queen woke up, happy, and ran to the *pūjārī* first thing to say, "Look for the hole! It's there!" The *pūjārī* went and found the hole, although it wasn't there the day before. So, he had this valuable pearl put on the Lord, thus responding to the queen's devotion and *bhakti*.

Another story is about a village in Rajasthan called Karoli, where the Deity of Madana-mohana is now living. This is the Deity that Advaita Ācārya originally found, and later Sanātana Gosvāmī worshiped him in Vṛndāvana. Even later, when the Deity had left Vṛndāvana in fear of Aurangzeb's invasion, he was moved to Jaipur where he resided for some time, worshiped by the kings's daughter. Her father, as is the custom in traditional Indian families, had arranged for his daughter to marry a prince of a small kingdom in Karoli. When he announced this to his daughter, she fainted. She said, "I've already given my heart to Madana-mohana. How can I go somewhere and part with him? For the sake of propriety I can get married, but I am not leaving here."

Her father replied, "I am sorry, but everything has already been arranged."

His daughter said, "Then you should give me Madana-mohana because I am not going without him."

The king himself was very attached to Madana-mohana and said, "Okay. You'll be taken into the room with lots of Deities. If, blindfolded, you guess which one is Madana-mohana, you may take him with you."

She went to her quarters and started to cry and say, "Madana-mohana, how will I find you?"

Madana-mohana replied, "When you touch me, my skin will be warm and soft, so you'll know at once. Also, I am going to break my flute. I will put my arm down a little and the flute will break. These are the two signs that are going to help you find me." So the blindfolded princess was quick to find Madana-mohana. In this way he moved to Karoli. In Karoli each morning the entire village attends *maṅgala-ārati*. Some people even make *daṇḍavat* all the way from home to the temple. Everyone goes – the sick, the old and the young – everyone.

They sometimes call Madana-mohana, "the one who stole a tray for a Muslim." So, this is the story.

Once there lived a pious Muslim in Karoli. Every day he read the Quran, praying and meditating on Allah. He wouldn't look at Deities because from the point of view of Islam this is the most serious crime ever to consider that God could manifest himself in some tangible form. To prevent people from committing offences all of these warnings are incorporated in Christianity, Islam, and Judaism.

He was a devout Muslim respected by all the Muslims and revered as a saint. Hindus also revered him as a very pious person. Externally, he was an ordinary man who worked in court delivering letters. Once he was sent with some errand to Madana-mohana's temple where a Gosvāmījī was in charge. While passing by, he accidentally looked into the window and saw Madana-mohana. He couldn't believe what he had seen. He fell in love with him at first sight. He delivered the letter to the Gosvāmījī, stopped, and started to look through the bars. Then he thought, "What am I doing? I am a faithful Muslim!" He ran to the mosque and started to pray, "Deliver me from this obsession!" But when he closed his eyes all he saw was Madana-mohana. When he opened his eyes, he only saw Madana-mohana. Wherever he went he saw Madana-mohana. And finally he understood it was hopeless.

Madana-mohana means "the one who attracts and draws us." And at his whim Madana-mohana completely revealed himself to this Muslim. He forgot everything – stopped going to the mosque and reading the Quran, and instead composing songs about Madana-mohana.

All of his Muslim brothers thought, "He's an infidel!" The most terrible thing that could happen to him was to be excommunicated from his religion – and he was. He then went to the temple, but when they learned he was a Muslim, the doorkeepers forced him away, pushing him down the steps and making him fall. Before this, both Hindus and Muslims respected him.

He went back to his home and started to cry, saying, "No one needs me anymore. I've given my heart to God – there's nothing else in my heart. Some way or other God revealed himself to me and entered into my heart, but everyone expelled me."

He decided to keep fasting until death. He had been fasting for just three days, when Madana-mohana couldn't wait any longer.

Usually in the evening the *pūjārīs* would place an expensive silver tray of sweets for Madana-mohana in case he would wake up and feel like something sweet to eat. The *pūjārī* left, closing the altar doors and locking up the temple. Later the Muslim heard a knock on the door. He answered it and saw a youth he had never seen before.

The youth said, "Gosvāmījī from the temple has sent me to you with *mahā-prasādam*. Here it is. Have some, please, but you should bring the tray back tomorrow for *mangala-ārati*."

He replied, "But I was kicked out!"

The youth said, "Tomorrow you won't be. Come for *ārati* early morning tomorrow, bring the tray, and everything will be all right."

What was the Muslim supposed to do? He ate everything on the tray as he had been fasting for three days. But during the night Madana-mohana came to the Gosvāmījī and said, "You shouldn't have kicked out the man. I haven't seen him for three days. He's coming tomorrow morning but you should let him in. You will recognize him because he'll be carrying a silver tray."

Early in the morning, one of the *pūjārīs* woke up, went on the altar and saw no trace of the costly tray. He clutched his head in his hands, ran to the Gosvāmījī and said, "The tray has been stolen! It's been stolen! Honestly, I had nothing to do with that!" The Gosvāmījī smiled and said, "The one who stole it has already admitted it. Don't worry!"

The Gosvāmījī went to the Mahārāja of Karoli and told the whole story. Mahārāja couldn't believe that a Muslim could develop such strong love for Kṛṣṇa. So they were both standing and waiting for him at the temple gate. The Muslim was walking, carrying the tray in his hand with a strange feeling in his heart thinking, "This is a very strange story. First, I've never seen that person in the temple. Second, he gave me this tray. He may have stolen it and then got scared and given it to me. Or perhaps the Muslims may have set me up." When he approached the temple, he saw the Mahārāja himself and the Gosvāmījī standing in front of the gate. So, he thought, "Well, I am dead." He was in no doubt that he was going to be put in jail.

But when he approached, Gosvāmījī said, "I've been waiting long for you. You are so fortunate!"

"Why?" asked the Muslim.

And then both the king and the Gosvāmījī started to talk all at once, "You are incredibly lucky!" He was at a loss. What had happened? Nobody told him anything.

He started to think, "Why has everyone changed their attitude to me so dramatically?" Only a few days ago they kicked me out, not wanting to see me and now they are welcoming me with open arms. A suspicion crept in and he asked, "Where is the servant that brought me the tray? I've never seen him before."

They told the Muslim, "The servant is there waiting for you on the *siṁhāsana*. But he's not a servant any more!"

Suddenly it occurred to him what had happened. Everybody rejoiced. All in all, it ended well except that he couldn't live in the village anymore because of all the fuss people were making over him. There are still songs in that place glorifying this story. The tray that Madana-mohana had taken to the Muslim devotee is still there in the temple.

The moral of this story is what Raghunātha Dāsa Gosvāmī is speaking about, "Even if there's no hope, there is always hope." What hope? This hope comes from understanding that Kṛṣṇa's mercy is more than my hopelessness and that he himself may do everything possible for us if we serve him. This process is the most practical thing ever. People attend seminars learning how to manage their time. But why manage time? Everything is already managed. One should have the following routine: get up when the Deity does; go to bed when the Deity does; eat *prasādam* from the Deities, and then the things will appear as this verse describes. All the *duṣṭatva,* all the impurity, will leave our heart. *Premāmṛta,* love for Kṛṣṇa, will enter into our heart, as well as the opportunity to serve the Queen of Vraja.

COMMENTARY BY ŪRMILĀ DEVĪ DĀSĪ

In this verse the devotee of Kṛṣṇa has crossed beyond practice. Pride is gone completely. Authentic humility saturates the heart with gratitude and acknowledgment that only divine mercy has eradicated one's deep cheating nature. The devotee can now say with full conviction, "I am wretched yet blessed!" The devotee now never wants any trace of cheating or pride to remain. Such devotees, thoroughly honest, open their hearts for full cleansing with nothing held back.

Now one's eternal identity becomes not just hinted at in sometimes hazy glimpses and impressions, but is gradually fully revealed by the grace of Kṛṣṇa's internal potency, Gāndharvā, she of artistic singing. The supplicant therefore begs Kṛṣṇa, as Govardhana and as the lifter of Govardhana, for Gāndharvā's shelter and service. Beyond shelter and service, one needs to make a plea for *mahyaṁ premāmṛtam api dadāty ujjvalam*, receiving the full and glowing nectar of spiritual love. In previous verses Raghnunatha Dāsa Gosvāmī wrote of receiving the jewel of this love, and then bathing in the ocean of this love. Here we beg for that love to be not just external and localized as a jewel in hand, and not just external and pervasive as a bath surrounding us, but internal and pervasive as a drink. As we drink that divine love, its effulgence lights up our very self.

Bhaktivinoda writes in his commentary on verse eight about the five elements of *rasa* – our eternal relationship (*sthāyī-bhāva*) namely: service, friendship, parental, or amorous; our lovable object and shelter (*ālambana*) and stimulus (*uddīpana*) for our eternal relationship; how we display our eternal relationship (*anubhāva*); the symptoms of our eternal relationship (*sāttvika*); and the changing waves of emotions within the context of our eternal relationship (*sañcārī*). It is important to note that all designations of this body and this world must be cast aside at this point to accept our real identity and experience the mixing of these five parts to make *rasa*.

Bhaktivinoda writes in his commentary here about a gradual and progressive training in eternal service, with the example of those who are *gopīs* in Rādhā's group. Those who are in a different relationship will have a similar training, though the details will vary. In all cases, the pleasure potency of Kṛṣṇa now enters our heart and attracts Kṛṣṇa.

VERSE NINE

mad-īśā-nāthatve vraja-vipina-candraṁ vraja-vane-
śvarīṁ tan-nāthatve tad-atula-sakhītve tu lalitām
viśākhāṁ śikṣālī-vitaraṇa-gurutve priyasaro-
girīndrau tat-prekṣā-lalita-ratidatve smara manaḥ

O mind, meditate on Kṛṣṇa, the moon of the Vṛndāvana forest, as the lord of my leader, Śrī Rādhikā. Meditate on Śrī Rādhikā as his most dear object of love. Meditate on Śrī Lalitā as her incomparable friend. Meditate on Śrī Viśākhā as the foremost guru distributing the teachings of love. And meditate on Rādhā-kuṇḍa and Govardhana as givers of the sight and love of Śrī Śrī Rādhā-Kṛṣṇa.

COMMENTARY BY ŚIVARĀMA SWAMI

One may have questions about details of how to go further in this process of *bhajana*. Here the answer is given when Raghunātha Dāsa Gosvāmī says *smaraṇam,* just meditate. This meditation is a great science. Specifically Jīva Gosvāmī describes five specific stages of meditation which we ultimately cultivate as we develop in Kṛṣṇa consciousness. Just like *japa* has its stages and devotional service has its stages, everything has a developmental process. This is called *krama.*

So it is with *smaraṇam.* In the first stage, also called *smaraṇam,* one searches with one's mind for the name, the form, and the qualities of the Lord. We are searching, trying to find. There is no real spontaneous attraction yet. It's an external effort by the mind, to reach out and try to contact. *Smaraṇam* means we are trying to hear, and next thing we know we are thinking about something else. *Smaraṇam* means we are trying to think about Kṛṣṇa's qualities and next thing we are thinking about when it is *prasādam* time. So we try and we make an effort but there is a lack of consistency.

Dhāraṇā, the second stage, is when one can withdraw one's mind from external stimulus and actually maintain a slight contact with the different features, names, pastimes, and paraphernalia of the Lord. We have all experienced it at some point. For example, sometimes we start reading some pastime and get so absorbed we forget where we are. We even forget we are in this material world, and perhaps even forget *who* we are. So that is called *dhāraṇā*.

And the stage of *dhyāna* is when the mind becomes fixed. *Dhāraṇā* is general, but *dhyāna* is very specific, when one is actually able to fix one's mind on specific pastimes and forms of the Lord with great detail, and having heard, one is able to visualize all the different topics which one has read in transcendental literatures.

The fourth stage is called *dhruva,* or *anusmṛti,* that is when *dhyāna* matures to the stage when the meditation is uninterrupted and very deep, with the result that one feels great pleasure, transcendental bliss. It is no longer an effort. In the beginning, reaching out means it's like we are groping. *Dhāraṇā* means that we think of our objects of meditation but we don't really have to struggle to keep out the distractions of the material world. And *anusmṛti* is when one receives that taste where there is no difficulty in being absorbed in meditating, but the difficulty is getting out of this state of meditation and relating to the material world.

The final stage is *samādhi*: Jīva Gosvāmī says this is when the only object of meditation is spontaneously manifested in the totality of the mind – in other words without any effort. This stage of meditation happens of its own accord. In other words, by the mercy of the Lord, coming down from the platform of the transcendental realm, the spiritual world comes into the mind and then takes over the entire mind – not some of the mind but all of it. One becomes completely absorbed in a particular remembrance of the Lord.

So these are different stages of meditation. And we begin by practicing the first one, then later the others. Therefore Śrīla Prabhupāda emphasized the first one, *smaraṇam*: we should learn how to hear and fix our mind on the sound vibration. When we learn how to do that, then gradually that sound vibration will pull us along into deeper and deepest states of meditation.

The question arises, what should we meditate on? Raghunātha Dāsa Gosvāmī gives us so many nice objects for our mediation. He writes *mad-īśā-nāthatve,* the lord of my mistress, namely Kṛṣṇa. And we are meditating on, *vraja-vane-śvarīm,* the queen of the forest of Vṛndāvana, Śrīmatī Rādhārāṇī. Then we meditate on the associates of Śrīmatī Rādhārāṇī and Lord Kṛṣṇa like *atula-sakhītve tu lalitām,* Lalitā-sakhī.

Viśākhām, we meditate on Viśākhā who is guru, who teaches, as in the relationship between Caitanya Mahāprabhu and Rāmānanda Rāya. Rāmānanda Rāya is Viśākhā. In that relationship, Rāmānanda Rāya is teaching Caitanya Mahāprabhu, Lord Kṛṣṇa, how to be in the mood of Śrīmatī Rādhārāṇī, and so many things. Such is the development of Caitanya Mahāprabhu's manifestation of *bhāva.* Up until the meeting with Rāmānanda Rāya, Caitanya Mahāprabhu was not able to enter into full *rādhā-bhāva* because he can't get it unless he gets it from Rādhārāṇī's associates. Just like sometimes people ask, "Do I have to go through guru to get to Kṛṣṇa?" Yes, just like Kṛṣṇa has to go through guru in order to get to Rādhārāṇī. So, even Kṛṣṇa has to learn that process from Rāmānanda Rāya. This is why it is called *śikṣā.* Viśākhā gives the divine couple so many instructions. So Lalitā and Viśākhā are two of the foremost *gopīs.*

We also meditate on *priya-saro. Saraḥ* means lake and *priya-saraḥ* means very dear lake. This phrase in this verse refers to Rādhā-kuṇḍa, which is the very form of pure love of Godhead. Also meditate on *girindrau,* Govardhan Hill. When we go to Vṛndāvana then we go to these places. we go to the birthplace of Lalitā-sakhī. Just behind there is Varṣāṇā. We go to Kṛṣṇa's birthplace, and places of all different pastimes. Why? So that we can meditate, and accumulate memories and thoughts, and appreciate the moods of all these particular places. Everything is intimately connected. Going to the holy places is not just a trip to India. It is not just getting away from the headaches of the West or to get a break from *saṅkīrtana.* Visitng holy places is all part of a systematically planned process to make us Kṛṣṇa conscious. Just like a jigsaw puzzle, every single lesson that we hear, every book, every instruction, everything that Prabhupāda planned and gave us, all fits together – we just have to know which part fits with the other. The picture is already there. We just have to put it all together.

Bhaktivinoda Ṭhākura gives us many prayers in his commentary to this verse about meditation, because prayer is synonymous with *smaraṇam*, or internal absorption or remembrance. Prayer is the essence of spontaneous devotional service. One should learn how to pray. Prayer should not be simply an external thing, but should be a heartfelt call, a personal expression, somehow or other to just get mercy.

When we hear Śrīla Rūpa Gosvāmī verses from *Stava-mālā* like the ones quoted in Bhaktivinoda's commentary on this verse, with much detail and descriptions, we should realize that they are non-different from what is being described, and if we know how to hear nicely then we will be able to see the very same thing. In the same way we can enter into meditation with Raghunātha Dāsa Gosvāmī prayers to Śrīmatī Rādhārāṇī, as well as the *Lalitāṣṭakam*, and the *Yamunāṣṭakam*, which is given because Viśākhā-devī is non-different from Yamunā. Glorifying Yamunā is just like glorifying Viśākhā. Bhaktivinoda also quotes prayers to Rādhā-kuṇḍa and Govardhan Hill.

COMMENTARY BY ŚACĪNANDANA SWAMI

In this verse, Raghunātha Dāsa Gosvāmī goes deep into his heart and gives us the full picture of Vṛndāvana. While he's writing this verse, he's sitting in Vṛndāvana, an elderly, very thin figure. He cannot tolerate the separation from Rādhā and Kṛṣṇa, and he wants to give us instruction how to attain success.

Verse nine is a fantastic guide for meditation. Raghunātha Dāsa Gosvāmī starts with a wonderful picture. He calls Kṛṣṇa, *vraja-vipina-candram*. *Candra* means the moon. Imagine the scene. There is moon-like Kṛṣṇa in the Vṛndāvana forest. Next to him is *vraja-vaneśvarīm*, Rādhikā. Imagine the moonlight nights, where the sand of the Yamunā is illuminated by the rays of the moon. The Vrajavāsīs and *sādhakas* are like *cakora* birds, mystical little birds who live from drinking the moon rays. There are birds who are like those *prāṇa* people who live on air alone. They look at the rays, and they can fly to wherever they like.

The normal devotees are *cakora* birds who drink the rays of Kṛṣṇa.

But the servants of Rādhārāṇī prefer it when Rādhā is the queen of the forest next to Kṛṣṇa. When Rādhā and Kṛṣṇa are together, the experience of taste is much higher. Raghunātha Dāsa Gosvāmī sees himself as the servant of Rādhā, knowing how to relish the highest love in the billowing waves of their loving exchange. This is also the vision of our *sampradāya.*

If we are connected with Rādhā, we are like leaves on the creeper curling around Kṛṣṇa, and whatever Rādhārāṇī experiences, we will also experience. I have heard that in Kolkata, 1930, Bhaktisiddhānta Sarasvatī Ṭhākura went into a state of ecstasy, saying, "O friend, Rūpa Mañjarī, it is well known that you do not look in the face of any other man than that of your husband, and yet there is a mark on your lips, as if someone has bitten them. This means that you are a servant of Rādhā, and she is with Kṛṣṇa." So whatever happens in their loving *rasa* we also experience. If we want something in relation to Kṛṣṇa very much, we have to learn from Rādhā and Kṛṣṇa's servants. If we want *mahā prasādam,* we first make contact with the servant in order to receive it. In transcendental logic, then we also go to the best servants, headed by Lalitā. She is the intimate friend of Rādhā. She carries a piece of cloth to wipe off the droplets of perspiration from Rādhā and Kṛṣṇa. When Lalitā finds someone in Vṛndāvana who has some inclinations towards Rādhā, she will immediately come to that person and arrange a meeting with Rādhārāṇī. We enter the divine couple's association only by recommendation.

Rādhārāṇī is the life-treasure of Kṛṣṇa, and he is the beloved of Rādhā. Rādhā loves Kṛṣṇa, and Kṛṣṇa loves Rādhā the most. This is the divine couple, and to reach them we need intermediaries. First comes Lalitā, and we will find this point in all the Gosvāmīs' literature. She is so dear to them that she controls them. Do you have people whom you love? If you love them, you trust them. Whatever they say, you do. On a Govardhana *parikramā,* BB Govinda Svāmī was there, and he said, "Let's do the *parikramā* every day without rest." Because I love him, I agreed. That is the nature of love – you give your heart. Śrī Lalitā is controlling Rādhā and Kṛṣṇa. Rādhā and Kṛṣṇa have surrendered to her. No one ever says, "No," to Lalitā, not even the divine couple. I pray to Lalitā to recommend me to Rādhā and Kṛṣṇa.

The *sādhaka* sits in the forest of Vṛndāvana and chants and prays as demonstrated by Narottama Dāsa Ṭhākura. One of the assistants, such as Rūpa Mañjarī, will see the *sādhaka*, and she will bring that *sādhaka* to Lalitā. Rādhā will see that devotee and will make enquiries about the person. Rūpa Mañjarī will then suggest that the devotee render some service. In this way, Lalitā recommends.

In devotional service we always go through a hierarchy. First we are *bhaktas*. Initially I was forbidden to live in the temple, because I was always singing Rolling Stones songs. I was very young. Then I decided that school was too boring. I needed a recommendation to stay with the devotees, so I cleaned the temple toilets. One devotee who had previously been the saxophone player with Little Richard, Narendra Dāsa, recommended me to the temple president, saying that I was a good boy and knew how to clean the toilets. Later on I was recommended for initiation. There are different levels of recommendations. When we are in *vṛndāvana-dhāma* we need to behave properly so that Rūpa Mañjarī and Lalitā can give us a recommendation!

The next person to remember is Viśākhā, the *śikṣā guru* who teaches all the arts required. Viśākhā is addressed as a *śikṣā guru* in this verse, as her voice is sweeter than that of a cuckoo in springtime when it eats the new mango. Viśākhā teaches the devotees how they can sing, and she also knows the art of joking. Therefore, the devotees take shelter of Lalitā and Viśākhā. We can take their shelter by reading Śrī Rūpa Gosvāmī's *Lalitāṣṭakam* and *Yamunāṣṭakam*, a prayer about Viśākhā in her form as the Yamunā.

And finally, we should remember Rādhā-kuṇḍa and Govardhana, day and night. If we just see them, even in our mind's eye, they will give us love for Rādhā and Kṛṣṇa, absolutely guaranteed. It is a very important point from this verse of *Manaḥ-śikṣā* not to neglect the holy *dhāma*. The holy *dhāma* is special because everywhere Kṛṣṇa has placed his lotus feet. On Kṛṣṇa's lotus feet there is *rati* or love. His feet are soft, fragrant, and full of the honey of love. If we just stay in that sacred land, we will also get some love for Kṛṣṇa. But we need to come again and again because we are so dull and covered with so many desires. Therefore, repeated treatment is good for us.

Raghunātha Dāsa Gosvāmī wrote that those who bathe in Rādhā-kuṇḍa will find how the creeper of love for Rādhā will grow in their heart. He explained how Rādhā-kuṇḍa reveals *darśana* of the divine couple. One day Raghunātha Dāsa Gosvāmī sat before Rādhā-kuṇḍa and witnessed a wonderful scene. Rādhā and Kṛṣṇa were splashing each other with water, and then Kṛṣṇa splashed water right into Rādhā-rāṇī's eyes. Everyone chastised Kṛṣṇa, saying it wasn't fair. Rādhārāṇī fled and hid herself among the golden lotus flowers so that Kṛṣṇa could not see her.

Kṛṣṇa, when diving into the lotus flowers, saw gold everywhere. He had so much love in his heart that he thought he saw Rādhā everywhere. But he could not find her. Kṛṣṇa looked up and saw a group of bees. "My Rādhā has breath as sweet as honey," thought Kṛṣṇa, so he was able to find her from where the bees were. Then there was a loving exchange. At the conclusion Rādhā put her arms around Kṛṣṇa, and Kṛṣṇa swam in Rādhā-kuṇḍa. (This story is based on the *Rādhā-kuṇḍa-aṣṭakam* of Śrīla Raghunātha Dāsa Gosvāmī's book *Śrī Stavāvalī*)

Raghunātha Dāsa Gosvāmī felt ecstasy, which is there for every pilgrim. The *dhāma* will reveal Rādhā and Kṛṣṇa to us. Just by the vision of Girirāja and Rādhā-kuṇḍa, *rati* will arise. If we are chanting, and are aware of the pastimes, we might catch a glimpse of Rādhā and Kṛṣṇa, the perfect picture for meditation.

Kṛṣṇa *bhaktas* always meditate on the ideal surroundings for service to the Lord. We meditate on the *dhāma*, Girirāja, trees, a soothing atmosphere, bees, birds, Yamunājī, Rādhā-kuṇḍa, and on the associates who will then invite Rādhā-Kṛṣṇa.

Kṛṣṇa's devotees know that Rādhā and Kṛṣṇa will never leave a heart that has become Vṛndāvana, so we make our hearts Vṛndāvana. Vṛndāvanacandra and Vṛndāvaneśvarī come together, and the *cakora* birds are drinking their waves of beauty. This is also the vision of our *sampradāya*, the Hare Krsnas.

Once there was a minister from Bharatpura who was performing a *daṇḍavat-parikramā* around Rādhā-kuṇḍa. One disciple praised him to Bhaktisiddhānta Sarasvatī Ṭhākura. Bhaktisiddhānta made the point that the minister worshiped Rādhārāṇī because she is dear to Kṛṣṇa, but we worship Kṛṣṇa because he is dear to Rādhārāṇī. (from *Śrī Bhaktisiddhānta Vaibhava* by Bhakti Vikāṣa Mahārāja) This is how to think of Rādhā-Kṛṣṇa.

Śrī Raghunātha Dāsa Gosvāmī prays in *Vilāpa-kusumāñjali* 102: "O Varoru (Rādhā), I somehow spend my time here aspiring after oceans of nectar. But if you are not merciful to me then of what use are Kṛṣṇa, living in Vraja, and even life itself?"

Śrīla Prabhupāda writes in *Kṛṣṇa* Book, chapter 21: "Persons who are constantly engaged in the transcendental meditation of seeing Kṛṣṇa, internally and externally, by thinking of him playing the flute and entering the Vṛndāvana forest, have really attained the perfection of *samādhi*. *Samādhi* (trance) means absorption of all the activities of the senses on a particular object, and the *gopīs* indicate that the pastimes of Kṛṣṇa are the perfection of all meditation and *samādhi*. It is also confirmed in the *Bhagavad-gītā* that anyone who is always absorbed in the thought of Kṛṣṇa is the topmost of all *yogīs*."

Here are the perfect meditator *yogīs*, the birds of Vṛndāvana:

prāyo batāmba vihagā munayo vane 'smin
kṛṣṇekṣitaṁ tad-uditaṁ kala-veṇu-gītam
āruhya ye druma-bhujān rucira-pravālān
śṛṇvanti mīlita-dṛśo vigatānya-vācaḥ

> O mother, in this forest all the birds have arisen onto the beautiful branches of the trees to see Kṛṣṇa. With closed eyes they are simply listening in silence to the sweet vibrations of his flute, and they are not attracted by any other sound. Surely these birds are on the same level as great sages. (*Śrīmad-Bhāgavatam* 10.21.14)

There are *cakora* birds, the unusual birds living on the moonlight. Also we find the *cakravāka* birds, the round ducks who fly together in the day but must spend the night separately. There are also *cātaka* birds, who drink only water falling from the clouds. Then we will find the swans of Vṛndāvana and the *khañjana* birds, who move restlessly. Then there are cuckoos and the *papihan* birds, who call "*pi kahan*?" which means, "Where is my beloved?"

The *gopīs* call these birds great saints. The birds sit silently and listen to the flutes. We could say they are ordinary birds, but Pūrṇamāsi says they first take *āsana,* then do *dhyāna,* and then have *darśana,* so they must be *yogīs.* When Kṛṣṇa sees such appreciative birds, he puts his flute aside for a moment. But the spiritually conscious *veṇu* then plays out of its own initiative to please the birds. Kṛṣṇa lifts the flute, blowing special *rāgas* without his breath, and looks at it with amazement. Kṛṣṇa is so much inspired by this scene that his heart opens and he plays inconceivably beautiful music.

The bird *yogīs* then see the vision of Śyāmasundara in their hearts, and then, as Kṛṣṇa continues playing his flute, they start singing their *kīrtana*: "O Kṛṣṇa! O Kṛṣṇa! O Kṛṣṇa!"

This is a perfect meditation under the guidance of the authoritative *Manaḥ-śikṣā.* It is a perfect picture of Rādhā-Kṛṣṇa with their associates, Lalitā and Viśākhā, in Vṛndāvana, with Govardhana Hill and Rādhā-kuṇḍa.

COMMENTARY BY ŪRMILĀ DEVĪ DĀSĪ

Bhaktivinoda shows us a practical way to follow Raghunātha Dāsa Gosvāmī's instruction to meditate. For each person and place listed in verse nine of *Manaḥ-śikṣā* as an object of meditation, Bhaktivinoda gives us prayers and *śāstric ślokas* full of detail. We can regularly recite these *ślokas* or other similar ones. Although anyone at any stage of *bhakti* can learn and feelingly sing prayers such as the ones in Bhaktivinoda's commentary, verse nine has special significance for devotees whose realization corresponds to this point in this instruction manual (*paddhati*).

Rāgānuga bhakti means to emulate the mood and service of particular devotees who exemplify one's desires. In order to do so, one must deeply mediate on those devotees to gain an understanding of their inner and outer disposition and actions. In verse eight, the perfected soul, by the grace of Giridhārī, the lifter of Govardhana Hill, was given to the service of Gāndharvā. Now that *jīva* needs to complete the apprenticeship and perfect the service. Because the orientation of this *paddhati* is towards assistant *gopīs* in Rādhā's group, the *jīva* is here instructed to meditate on the chief personalities and places for that orientation. Others can use verse nine as a general template for their personal situation.

As there is unlimited individual variety in the spiritual world, each *jīva* has a unique relationship with Kṛṣṇa. Therefore, even within the main five groups of relationship, there is still infinite diversity. For example, some devotees in a parental mood will meditate on Rohiṇī more than Yaśodā, and some may be followers mostly of Mukara; or on Upananda rather than Nanda. Some in fraternal moods will meditate on Balarāma more than on Kṛṣṇa, or be particularly attached to cowherd boys such as Maṇḍalībhadra rather than Subala or Ujjvala. In the amorous mood, some of Rādhā's *sakhīs* will particularly meditate on Citrā or Tuṅgavidyā rather than Lalitā. Some persons in the amorous mood may not even be in Rādhā's group, but may be followers of other group leaders, such as Śyāmala, Bhadrā, Palī, and so on. As Viśvanātha Cakravartī Ṭhākura writes in his commentary to *Bhakti-rasāmṛta-sindhuḥ* 1.2.295, "By the word *vraja-loka*, one should understand persons situated in Vraja – Rādhā, Candrāvalī, and others. Following after them, one should perform service using one's physical body also." Some within Candrāvalī's group, for example, may follow Cārucandra, and some may be more a follower of Śaibyā. There are also *jīvas* in the amorous mood who are Balarāma's *gopīs*, who serve him and Pūrṇānandā, whom Śrīla Prabhupāda refers to in a *Caitanya-caritāmṛta* puport (*Ādi-līlā* 10.53) as "the foremost of Lord Balarāma's very dear girlfriends." In conclusion, each devotee on the *rāga-mārga* meditates on a suitable form of the Personality of Godhead with his associates who are in a similar mood to oneself, along with their specific places of pastimes. Certainly, everyone regardless of mood meditates to some extent on Rādhā, Kṛṣṇa, Lalitā, Viśākhā, Rādhā-kuṇḍa and Govardhana. At the same time, those who are, for example, in the mood of friendship, will probably meditate mostly on Kṛṣṇa, Balarāma,

Subala, and Ujjvala and their pastime places, rather than the list given in *Manaḥ-śikṣā* verse nine.

Also, some *jīvas* have plural, simultaneous identities as Bhaktisiddhānta Sarasvatī explains in his commentary to *Brahma-saṁhitā* 5.5:

> The pure devotees following the devotees of Vraja and those following the pure devotees of Navadvīpa are located in the realm of Kṛṣṇa and Gaura respectively. The identical devotees of Vraja and Navadvīpa simultaneously attain to the pleasures of service in the realm of Kṛṣṇa and Gaura.

Śrīla Prabhupāda describes one *jīva* who has three simultaneous identities in his purport to *Caitanya-caritāmṛta, Ādi-līlā* 15.30:

> Vanamālī Ghaṭaka, a resident of Navadvīpa and a *brāhmaṇa* by caste, arranged the marriage of the Lord [Caitanya] to Lakṣmīdevī. He was formerly Viśvāmitra, who negotiated the marriage of Lord Rāmacandra, and later he was the *brāhmaṇa* who negotiated the marriage of Lord Kṛṣṇa with Rukmiṇī. That same *brāhmaṇa* acted as the marriage-maker of the Lord in *caitanya-līlā*.

We may note that Govardhana Hill, very prominent throughout *Manaḥ-śikṣā*, is a pastime place for all the residents of Vṛndāvana, in every mood. Every resident of Vraja, including both the forest and village animals, love Kṛṣṇa in his Giridhārī mood. Govardhana serves all the varieties of devotees, fulfilling all their desires. At Govardhana everyone meets to celebrate festivals and to seek shelter.

VERSE TEN

ratiṁ gaurī-līle api tapati saundarya-kiraṇaiḥ
śacī-lakṣmī-satyāḥ paribhavati saubhāgya-valanaiḥ
vaśīkāraiś candrāvali-mukha-navīna-vraja-satīḥ
kṣipaty ārād yā tāṁ hari-dayita-rādhāṁ bhaja manaḥ

O mind, offer your worship unto Śrī Rādhikā, the beloved of Lord Hari. She outshines Rati [the wife of Kāmadeva], Gaurī [the wife of Lord Śiva], and Līlā [the potency of Lord Viṣṇu] by the effulgence of her beauty. She defeats Śacī [the wife of Indra], Lakṣmī, and Satyā [Kṛṣṇa's wife] by the waves of her good fortune. She defeats the pride of the newly married *gopīs* of Vraja, headed by Candrāvalī, through her power to control Kṛṣṇa.

COMMENTARY BY ŚIVARĀMA SWAMI

The purport of this verse is one cannot attain the mercy of Kṛṣṇa without approaching Śrīmatī Rādhārāṇī. Rādhārāṇī is stated here to be more beautiful than Rati, who is the wife of cupid; than Gaurī, the wife of Lord Śiva; and Līlā, meaning the pleasure potency of the Lord; more resplendent than Indrāṇī, Indra's wife, or Lakṣmī, Lord Nārāyaṇa's wife, and Satyabhāmā in Dvārakā. Rādhā is more expert in controlling Kṛṣṇa than anyone else.

How does she control Kṛṣṇa? We always hear Rādhā is very beautiful. In the material world beauty generally tends to be a material thing, but in the spiritual realm beauty is an indication of love. The more one has love for Kṛṣṇa, the more beautiful one is. Because Rādhārāṇī has the greatest love for Kṛṣṇa, she is the most beautiful. We glorify Rādhārāṇī's beautiful features, or hear how Kṛṣṇa is attracted to Rādhārāṇī, not because she is a nice-looking girl but because her beauty is reflecting her love for him. That love not only attracts Kṛṣṇa but is so intense it makes him subordinate to Rādhārāṇī. This is a concept which no one understands outside of the glory of the Vaiṣṇava *sampradāya*. Even great *ācāryas* have difficulty understanding this.

There is one particular story of when Jayadeva Gosvāmī was writing his Gītā Govinda. As he was writing he was seeing within his heart what he wrote, and in one particular pastime, Rādhārāṇī was very angry and wouldn't have anything to do with Kṛṣṇa. As Jayadeva was writing, he was seeing that Kṛṣṇa is bowing down, pleading with Rādhārāṇī, and finally putting his head on Rādhārāṇī's lotus feet. Jayadeva just couldn't write this meditation down. Kṛṣṇa is the Supreme Personality of Godhead. How can he put his head on the feet of this cowherd girl? With his mind in turmoil over this duality, Jayadeva left his writing and went away. Then his wife saw that he returned very quickly and went back to his writing, and after some time he again went away. And then sometime later he returned.

When Jayadeva came back the second time, his wife, Padmāvatī, asked him, "Why did you come back before?"

He said "Come back? When did I come back? I have been down at Gaṅgā chanting Gāyatrī."

She said, "You went down to the Gaṅgā, then I saw you come back." She paused, her brow furrowing, and said to Jayadeva, "Something is wrong here. Something is wrong with you or something is going on..."

So Jayadeva asked, "What did I do when I came back?"

She said, "You came back and went to your desk. I saw you going to your writing." Jayadeva went in to where he was writing. And then he saw, written in handwriting that he couldn't have written:

smara-garala-khaṇḍanaṁ mama śirasi maṇḍanaṁ
dehi pada-pallavam udāram
jvalati mayi dāruṇo madana-kadanāruṇo
haratu tad-upāhita-vikāram

> Put the buds of your beautiful feet, which destroy the snake-poison of Kāmadeva [the god of love], on my head, making them my decoration. The sun's pain, caused by Kāmadeva and intolerable to me, gives me pain. May your feet remove those effects!

Jayadeva could then understand from this handwriting that it was Kṛṣṇa who had come and personally written in his pages. These dealings are very, very confidential. Even most Vaiṣṇavas can't understand them. Most Vaiṣṇavas would be upset, thinking, "How is that possible?" The answer is Kṛṣṇa is giving his lotus feet to everybody, yet he wants the lotus feet of Rādhārāṇī because she is actually Kṛṣṇa's *hlādinī-śakti*. She is the manifestation of Kṛṣṇa's pleasure potency, and he is incapable of enjoying without her.

Bhaktivinoda gives a nice description of Śrīmatī Rādhārāṇī, and some prayers. Rūpa and Sanātana Gosvāmīs had an argument over one verse of the prayers quoted here. Rūpa Gosvāmī wrote, "Your braids that are decorated with jewels and flowers give the appearance of a serpent's hood."

When Sanātana Gosvāmī read this, he said to Rūpa, "You are comparing Rādhārāṇī's hair to the black hood of the cobra. This is not such a good thing."

Rūpa Gosvāmī replied, "Then how shall I compare it?"

Sanātana said, "I don't know but this is not a good thing."

Rūpa concluded, "Anyway, you are my spiritual master so you should tell me."

So, Sanātana Gosvāmī goes walking, meditating on what Rūpa had written, thinking of a more appropriate comparison. He walked for a long time and finally came to a lake, where he saw young girls playing, and then from behind one of the girls he saw a big snake coming, so he called out, "Watch out, watch out, look out for snake!" They all just laughed, and he still saw this big snake behind the girls, but all of a sudden it just disappeared. Sanātana Gosvāmī could understand that he saw Rādhārāṇī with her girlfriends, and realized that Rūpa's description wasn't at all inappropriate. In that condition her hair did look like the black hood of the cobra. So he went back and apologized to Rūpa Gosvāmī, "No, it's all right. You can write it down like that."

Bhaktivinoda's descriptions of Śrīmatī Rādhārāṇī go on and on. Rūpa Gosvāmī's poetry is voluminous.

COMMENTARY BY ŚACĪNANDANA SWAMI

After the ninth verse, Raghunātha Dāsa Gosvāmī explains the single object of worship out of everything he has said.

Without first approaching the *svarūpa-śakti*, the Lord's internal potency, we can never attain the full aspect of Lord Śrī Kṛṣṇa, just like when we approach a fire; we first approach the light of that fire. If we don't go to the moon rays first, how will we see the moon? The moon is there for us through the moon's rays. So, Kṛṣṇa's own energy is Śrīmatī Rādhārāṇī, and we need to make contact with her first. Therefore, she is our single object of worship.

In the *Bṛhad-bhāgavatāmṛta* there is a very interesting illustration on how we must approach Rādhārāṇī first. Early one morning, Gopa-kumāra goes to visit Kṛṣṇa. On that morning, Śrī Rādhikā-devī herself stops him. Gopa-kumāra remembers that morning he met with Rādhārāṇī and received her order. He thinks, "Rādhikā ordered me, 'There is a *brāhmaṇa* in Mathura, and he is coming to my grove in Vṛndāvana on earth. This *brāhmaṇa* doesn't know what he should know to reach me. Enlighten him with good instructions and console him. Help him quickly attain Kṛṣṇa's grace.' I swiftly changed course and came to Vṛndāvana on earth, overjoyed. I didn't even think I would miss Kṛṣṇa's company that morning."

Sanātana Gosvāmī explains this difficult subject. Gopa-kumāra is there to meet Kṛṣṇa, and then he is stopped on the way, told to go on a preaching assignment. Gopa-kumāra knew that obeying Rādhā would endear him to Kṛṣṇa.

Verse ten of *Manaḥ-śikṣā* mentions three qualities that make Rādhā so special. One is her extraordinary beauty. She is more beautiful than even the wife of the god of love. Second is her ability to control Kṛṣṇa. The third is her extreme good fortune.

In the spiritual world the index by which beauty is measured is by the amount of love. Rādhārāṇī is most dear to Kṛṣṇa and she has the greatest amount of love for him. The smallest love is that of ordinary devotees who have an atomic particle of love for God. The second degree of love is represented by devotees such as Nārada Muni. The first degree of love is held by devotees such as the Vrajavāsīs (*mahān*) and the topmost person with the greatest love for Kṛṣṇa is Rādhārāṇī (*parama-mahān*).

We have a lake in our hearts, and we might have things swimming in there we do not want, like plastic bottles! Kṛṣṇa's heart is like a vast Mānasa-sarovara lake, the highest beautiful lake at the foot of Mount Kailāsa, and in the lake there is a swan named Rādhārāṇī who is swimming. Kṛṣṇa loves Rādhā so much because she has a unique type of love.

Her second quality is the ability to control Kṛṣṇa. By using the mystic power of her intense love for Kṛṣṇa, she has brought him completely under control. Kṛṣṇa says, "Listen, O Rādhā, I am fully under your control. I am unable to think of anyone but you. When I repeat your name, Rādhe, and meditate on your form, I just cannot remain patient. When from anywhere I hear the name 'Śrī Rādhe,' my mind runs in the direction of these words. Crying and crying, I lift my face and cry loudly for Rādhā. Only then my life is saved. You know, I wait for you. I do not like Vṛndāvana if it is without you. I like Vṛndāvana only because of you."

Another quality of Rādhārāṇī is her good fortune, the good fortune to have Kṛṣṇa's feet in her heart.

So my dear devotees, this is Rādhārāṇī. She is the most fortunate, she has Kṛṣṇa fully under her control, and she is the most beautiful. All three are there because of her love for Kṛṣṇa, this singular *mahā-bhāva*.

How do we attain Śrīmatī Rādhārāṇī's mercy? My dear devotees, in the path of Kṛṣṇa consciousness, there are two strands. One is the strand of cultivation, and the other strand is to plead for mercy. Rūpa Gosvāmī tells us of praying for mercy, and it is this path that has also been instructed by Ragunātha Dāsa Gosvāmī in his eighth verse. On this path of pleading for mercy, according to Bhaktivinoda Ṭhākura, we need three qualities to be successful. These are: 1 unpretentious humility (someone is unpretentiously humble when other's mistakes and insults are tolerated); 2 ardor (passionate devotion); 3 one-pointedness.

Rūpa Gosvāmī has written a prayer that starts with a glorification of Rādhikā in the first four verses, and then describes, "Having offered obeisances in these ways, I, a distressed soul belonging to you, beg you with sweet words while rolling on the banks of the Yamunā! Although I am unfit, an offender with a crooked mind, please bestow on me a fragment of the gift of service to you. This unhappy soul is not fit to be neglected by you, for you have a butter-soft heart that melts constantly by the warmth of your compassion." (*Prārthanā-paddhati,* stanza 5)

In the same way, all our *ācāryas* actually plead, "Aren't you the emblem of compassion? Isn't it known throughout the scriptures that you are compassionate? Isn't compassion the movement of the heart? I am most inferior, so shouldn't your compassion extend to me?"

Everyone can say, "I am very humble and very fallen." It is very easy to learn the "humble vocabulary." But it is so difficult to be tolerant if someone steps on our toes. Then we can see the truly tolerant devotees, who even if they are wronged, go on without protest.

Some of us are so cold in our hearts. We have to put some heat in our practice so that there is an intense hankering. And we must have a one-pointed goal. Humility, intense hankering, and a one-pointed goal – this will get us the mercy of Rādhārāṇī.

COMMENTARY BY ŪRMILĀ DEVĪ DĀSĪ

Raghunātha Dāsa Gosvāmī's verse ten is similar to what Rūpa Gosvāmī has written in *Ujjvala-nīlamaṇiḥ* (178):

premoru-sampadvatī-vṛndātiśayitvaṁ, yathā –
advaitād girijāṁ harārdha-vapuṣaṁ sakhyāt priyoraḥ-sthitāṁ
lakṣmīm acyuta-citta-bhṛṅga-nalinīṁ satyāṁ ca saubhāgyataḥ
mādhuryān madhureśa-jīvita-sakhīṁ candrāvalīṁ ca kṣipan
paśyāruddha hariṁ prasārya laharīṁ rādhānurāgāmbudhiḥ

Surpassing the wealth of great *prema* of other women: Look! Rādhā, spreading waves from her ocean of *anurāga,* has stopped Durgā, half of Śiva's body because she is equal to him. She has obstructed Lakṣmī situated on Viṣṇu's chest because of her affection. She has surpassed Satyabhāmā, a lotus for the bee of Kṛṣṇa's mind, because of her good fortune. Because of her sweetness, Rādhārāṇī is excelling Candrāvalī, the friend who has enlivened the lord of sweetness [Kṛṣṇa].*

* The last part can be translated in two other possible ways: 1 Candrāvalī, the friend who by sweetness has enlivened the Lord, or 2 Candrāvalī, the friend who is enlivened by the lord of sweetness.

Bhaktivinoda, in his commentary to verse ten, reiterates the point he made in reference to verse nine about being trained in one's individual attitude and service. The residents of Vraja we apprentice under in *rāgānuga-bhakti* guide us to take our place in the eternal pastimes. The ultimate perfection for a living being is to humbly be under the shelter of the form of Kṛṣṇa's personal energy (*svarūpa-śakti*), assisting in loving service for his pleasure. Verse ten expresses Raghunātha Dāsa Gosvāmī's love for Rādhārāṇī (*svarūpa-śakti*) and encourages development of the readers' affection, appreciation, and devotion for her.

VERSE ELEVEN

samaṁ śrī-rūpeṇa smara-vivaśa-rādhā-giri-bhṛtor
vraje sākṣāt-sevā-labhana-vidhaye tad-gaṇa-yujoḥ
tad-ijyākhyā-dhyāna-śravaṇa-nati-pañcāmṛtam idaṁ
dhayan nītyā govardhanam anudinaṁ tvaṁ bhaja manaḥ

O mind, you should every day drink the five nectars — worship, glories, meditation, listening to divine pastimes, and offering obeisances — and worship Govardhana according to the rules. In this way, follow the instructions of Śrī Rūpa and obtain the direct service of Śrī Śrī Rādhā-Giridhārī, who are captivated by the god of amourous love, in the company of their associates in Vraja.

COMMENTARY BY ŚIVARĀMA SWAMI

Five different activities are being recommended here. In other words, every day we must drink these nectars with Śrīla Rūpa Gosvāmī. One must do everything in the line of Rūpa Gosvāmī as we are all *rūpānugas*. By these five nectars we should be worshiping Rādhā and Kṛṣṇa and all their friends. We should worship them by worshiping the Deity form, and chanting their names in *kīrtana* and *japa*. We should meditate on them by hearing their pastimes and activities, for example from *Kṛṣṇa* Book and *Caitanya-caritāmṛta*, and we should bow down before them, internally within our hearts and externally praying for their mercy and guidance. Every day one must worship Govardhana Hill, to daily offer prayers to Govardhana Hill. Govardhana is very merciful, and by the mercy of Govardhana one can gain residence in the area of Govardhana. So this is the meditation.

COMMENTARY BY ŚACĪNANDANA SWAMI

Verse eleven binds the preceding verses together and brings them into context. There is still a question in the air for the readers of *Manaḥ-śikṣā*. What exactly is the method for deeply performing our devotional service? Yes, we have heard about different concepts that can be almost the *sambandha-tattva* of this verse, but how do we exactly do it?

This question is answered in the eleventh verse, the crystal of sugar that gives success to the whole year of growing the sugarcane: tilling the field, protecting it from the thieves, harvesting, boiling the sugarcane in huge pots down to molasses – and then one piece of rock sugar is placed into it, and it all crystallizes. This verse crystallizes all the teachings because it will now tell us what we should do.

In simple language, if we want to have direct service to Rādhā and Kṛṣṇa, then this is the verse for us. We need to think on how to perform these processes, and what absolutely not to do, such as how should we worship the Deity (*ijyā*), and what is the most important thing we should avoid when worshiping the Deity. I have seen in my personal attempts to worship Deities that the greatest enemy is a mechanical consciousness. Jīva Gosvāmī says that Kṛṣṇa is not hungry. Kṛṣṇa doesn't need our service. It is not like this. But, just like a thirsty person becomes satisfied by water alone, similarly Kṛṣṇa becomes like a thirsty person when a devotee offers him water in love.

I can drink very easily if I pour water into a glass. It is a purely mechanical activity. But Kṛṣṇa is not like that. He will only drink if we offer water plus love or if we offer a flower plus love or if we offer incense plus love. Kṛṣṇa didn't go to Duryodhana's house, but he went to Vidura's. Vidura and his wife were so nervous that she threw away the fruit and offered the peel. Kṛṣṇa ate the peel! He missed the meal by Duryodhana, which was prepared by the best cooks in the country. In the morning, Duryodhana said, "You didn't come to my house to eat. Why?"

Kṛṣṇa said, "You don't love me. I only eat love." This is the single ingredient in Deity worship. We should consider this point before we begin Deity worship.

The next point is *ākhyā*. *Ākhyā* means *nāma-saṅkīrtana* but also means glorification in general. *Kīrtana* means to sing or discuss the pastimes of the Supreme Lord. But, again, merely singing the names is not enough. We must sing, plus we must do something else. If we forget the *plus,* we won't obtain devotional ecstasy. Caitanya Mahāprabhu asks what that *plus* is and tells us how we should chant the holy name.

He teaches that we should consider ourselves lower than the blade of grass. This means that grass has some use – to feed cows, or to cover the roof of a house. I am lower than that grass, and have not been of any use for service. We might say, "I don't want to think like this!" Many think, instead, that it would be so nice if I could get into a lift, press a button, and go *zwip* to pure devotion without such humility. Automatic. However, if we are not in the school of humility, we will be left with false ego and be forced to do offenses. If we chant minus *tṛṇād api,* it is dangerous! The chanting is a very potent medicine. When these powerful processes of devotional service are not used properly, they can cut us. If we swing a sword forward it cuts the enemy. If we swing it backwards, it cuts us. An overload of offenses can really make us materially attached. Be aware and avoid *aparādha,* and chant the holy name in humility. Very soon, we will attain the ecstatic, soft lotus feet of Kṛṣṇa.

Dhyāna is the next point. In our meditations, we should avoid speculation and imagining something or other. The safest way to meditate is to read from the *śāstras* and from the prayers of devotees, what they have written are not imaginations. They are revelations. Our meditation is done through hearing. This is so absolutely important. This experience will give us *śraddhā* (firm faith).

It is important when we read *Śrīmad-Bhāgavatam,* especially those parts directly relating to Kṛṣṇa, that we stop and think about what we have read. First *śravaṇam,* then *mānānāṁ* – reflect on what has been read. Then if this practice is done long enough, as we chant, these things that we have thought about will come up during chanting, by the mercy of the holy name, and we will see things that are so wonderful.

So read, and afterwards, reflect on what has been read. If we want to benefit from scriptural study, we need to apply three techniques from the *Upaniṣads.* We have to hear, then we have to reflect on what we hear, and then we need to meditate on the text and apply it. Reflecting is like chewing our food. If we want to go even deeper, and I believe most of us want to do that, then we should also pray to get full realization. Pray to the author; pray to the text.

In the *Bhakti-sandarbha*, Jīva Gosvāmī mentions that if we want to meditate about Kṛṣṇa, we first have to mediate about the holy *dhāma*, because Kṛṣṇa can only be found in Vṛndāvana. We can read about Vṛndāvana and remember the places in the *dhāma*. We will then be able to have a good meditation about Kṛṣṇa. We should make an effort to chant lovingly, filling our minds with Kṛṣṇa. (*Anuccheda* 286: *atha mukhyaṁ dhyānaṁ śrī-bhagavad-dhāma-gatam ev/ hṛdaya-kamala-gataṁ tu yogi-matam/ smared vṛndāvane ramye ity ādy-uktatvāt*).

We should hear with directed attention. So many people communicate, but so few people connect. So few, and this lack of connection is called *anāsaṅga-bhajana*. They are still in their mental worlds, repeating the same old external thoughts. So we should fill our minds with the sweetness of Bhagavān. I request, dear readers, that you make a study of these points in your life.

In summary, when we want to do *arcanaṁ*, we do so with love and not mechanically. The second is *kīrtanaṁ* plus humility, because if we are not humble, then there will be the ego and then we will commit offenses. The ego doesn't like Kṛṣṇa to take its place in the heart. There is one throne in the heart, and at the moment the ego sits on it. Therefore, *tṛṇād api sunīcena*. The next point is *dhyāna*. What should we avoid? Imagination. Meditation doesn't happen from imagination but from hearing bona-fide sources. *Sat-saṅga* means connection, and *anāsaṅga* means disconnected. Please take this hope, *sat-saṅga-bhajana*.

COMMENTARY BY ŪRMILĀ DEVĪ DĀSĪ

Here at the end of *Manaḥ-śikṣā*, Raghunātha Dāsa Gosvāmī describes the ultimate goal of intimate service to the divine couple. While every *jīva* has an individual eternal service, these five categories are general direction for everyone. Bhaktivinoda, in his commentary to this verse, also explains the application of these five life-giving services in terms of external devotional activities we do while in this world.

As he does throughout *Manaḥ-śikṣā*, Dāsa Gosvāmī uses an analogy here. He tells us to drink these five services, as if they were a medicinal nectar to free us from death. The service is thus internalized, filling us completely. Comparing devotional service to a life-giving nectar, and comparing the doing of such service to drinking that nectar, is an often-used metaphor in Vaiṣṇava literature, as in this *Bhāgavatam* verse (2.2.37):

pibanti ye bhagavata ātmanaḥ satāṁ
kathāmṛtaṁ śravaṇa-puṭeṣu sambhṛtam
punanti te viṣaya-vidūṣitāśayaṁ
vrajanti tac-caraṇa-saroruhāntikam

> Those who drink through aural reception, fully filled with the nectarean message of Lord Kṛṣṇa, the beloved of the devotees, purify the polluted aim of life known as material enjoyment and thus go back to Godhead, to the lotus feet of him [the Personality of Godhead].

The section of Bhaktivinoda's commentary to verse eleven wherein he discusses Jīva Gosvāmī's stages of meditation is important for *bhakti-yogīs* at all stages of progress. The essence of *bhakti* is to change one's consciousness. We are to fill our mind, heart, intelligence, and ultimately our very self with awareness of Kṛṣṇa. Those who aim for perfection in *dhyāna-yoga* try to reach *samādhi* mostly through a mechanical process of posture, breathing, and so forth. The *samādhi* of the *bhakti-yogīs*, however, is different. In *bhakti*, one achieves full absorption of consciousness in Kṛṣṇa through love.

Materially speaking, all of us have experienced situations where our consciousness becomes absorbed in someone or something because of strong emotional attachment. We can become so saturated with meditation, we lose awareness of all else. Similarly, in *bhakti* we seek to channel all our emotions, all our attachments, all our desires, to Kṛṣṇa, his devotees, and their service. By doing so, we naturally and easily enter into transcendent awareness, awake to reality and asleep to illusion.

VERSE TWELVE

manaḥ-śikṣādaikādaśaka-varam etan madhurayā
girā gāyaty uccaiḥ samadhigata-sarvārtha-tati yaḥ
sa-yūthaḥ śrī-rūpānuga iha bhavan gokula-vane
jano rādhā-kṛṣṇātula-bhajana-ratnaṁ sa labhate

Becoming a follower of Śrī Rūpa and his companions, one who with a sweet voice loudly recites these eleven supreme verses, which give instructions to the mind, and strives to understand all of their meanings completely, obtains the incomparable jewel of worshiping Śrī Śrī Rādhā-Kṛṣṇa in the forests of Gokula.

COMMENTARY BY ŚIVARĀMA SWAMI

This verse tells the summary or the result of reading the eleven verses of *Śrī Manaḥ-śikṣā*. It indicates that one should be a *rūpānuga*, following the footsteps of Rūpa Gosvāmī, regardless of how advanced one is, or who one is. Everyone must follow in the footsteps of Rūpa Gosvāmī.

We should associate with those who share our taste or mood of devotional service. That practice is called *sajātīyāśaya-snigdha sādhu-saṅga* (See *Caitanya-caritāmṛta, Antya-līlā* 5.107 purport). We should be more compassionate to those who are less advanced; and we should bestow mercy on others to give them Kṛṣṇa consciousness.

We are concluding *Manaḥ-śikṣā*, which is specifically meant for those devotees who are very serious about perfecting their human form of life and going back home, back to Godhead. These verses are the essence of Rūpa Gosvāmī's teachings and are especially valuable because they are coming down from Śrī Caitanya Mahāprabhu. If we have these verses we should study them and meditate upon them and specifically practice all of these things. It's not enough that we simply hear and read. What we hear and read, we have to put it to practice. We have to practically understand points of scriptures, points of philosophy, points of *rasa*. One by one we should try to put these points in practice in our day to day life, in our meditations, in our prayers, in our chanting, in our hearing, in our relationships, and in our cultivation of devotional service.

COMMENTARY BY ŚACĪNANDANA SWAMI

Let us make it simple. We should become a follower of Rūpa Gosvāmī and read his *Upadeśāmṛta*. This will prepare us. It says we should reside in the forest of Gokula. Let us come to a secluded place within Vraja, and have a clear understanding of the hidden meanings there.

We might ask if *bhakti* is that simple. It is. Narottama Dāsa Ṭhākura tells us that when we perform *sat-saṅga-bhajana*, Kṛṣṇa consciousness will work for us. Be "a mango," now. We can only be a green mango, unripe, but we can join the mango club! Get the concepts right and the understanding right. Practice on our level of *adhikāra* (ability) and we will then mature into beautiful and fragrant mangoes that will please the senses of Kṛṣṇa.

COMMENTARY BY ŪRMILĀ DEVĪ DĀSĪ

Raghunātha Dāsa Gosvāmī follows the tradition of ending his work with a benediction. And what a benediction it is! Just by singing these verses daily, with understanding and affectionate emotion, the singer can attain the jewel of loving service to the divine couple in Vṛndāvana. Lest the reader imagine that mechanical, ritualized daily singing will lead to such a result, the emphasis is on emotion and understanding. It is only through application of these verses to one's own inner life that such emotion and understanding is truly possible.

If we want to appreciate what it means to sing in a sweet voice (*madhurayā girā*), this explanation of what is not sweet singing, from Prabhodhānanda Sarasvatī's commentary to *Gīta Govinda* 2.25, should be helpful. The faults of songs are mentioned by Bharata:

śaṅkitaṁ bhītam udghṛṣṭam
avyaktam anunāsikam
kāka-svaraṁ śiraḥ-kampaṁ
tathā sthāna-vivarjitam

visvaraṁ virasaṁ caiva
viśliṣṭaṁ viṣamāhatam
vyākulaṁ tāla-hīnaṁ ca
gīta-doṣān vidur budhāḥ

The wise know a song is faulty when it is sung with uncertainty, fear, or unclear intonation, inaudibly, nasalized, with the voice of a crow, while shaking the head, without proper pitch, in a disjointed manner, with dissonance, unpleasantness, unevenness, confusion, and without *tāla*.

To fully realize the twelfth verse's benediction, the singer of these verses should associate with like-minded persons and live in Vṛndāvana. Ideally, like Dāsa Gosvāmī himself did for most of his life, one can physically live in Vṛndāvana with people who have similar goals, engaging in *bhakti-yoga* together. However, if our service to Kṛṣṇa or our life circumstances make such an arrangement impossible, we can infuse our consciousness with Vṛndāvana and create a network of like-minded people, even virtually.

PART FOUR

Appendices

ACKNOWLEDGEMENTS

Our deepest thanks are to His Divine Grace A.C. Bhaktivedanta Swami Prabhupāda, Founder-*ācārya* of the International Society for Krishna Consciousness, and my spiritual master. Without him, we would know nothing about *Manaḥ-śikṣā* or the path of loving devotion to Kṛṣṇa.

The initial inspiration for this book came from Śacīnandana Swami's *Manaḥ-śikṣā* seminar at a Govardhana retreat. At that time, he asked me to compile a new translation with commentary of this book. Some years later Śrīmatī Devī Dāsī of Vṛndāvana also asked me to get this book translated, although she was unaware of Śacīnandana Swami's former request. Devāmṛta Swami gave encouragement to see this book to completion. The family of Pāvana Nimāi Dāsa and his wife Kānāi-priya Devī Dāsī, along with their daughters Pṛthā and Viśākhā, gave the first donation towards production, specifically for illustrations. Mahālakṣmī Devī Dāsī donated for production costs from her kind and generous heart, as did numerous others who desired this book to be published. Our gratitude extends to all of them.

Hari Pārṣada Dāsa translated the twelve original verses of Raghunātha Dāsa Gosvāmī as well as most of the Sanskrit verses quoted within Bhaktivinoda's Bengali commentary. Prāṇa Govinda Dāsa did the initial Bengali translations of Bhaktivinoda's prose commentary, and a resident of Vṛndāvana who wishes to remain anonymous did the initial Bengali translation of Bhaktivinoda's song commentary. Kṛṣṇa-abhiṣeka Dāsa checked and corrected all the Bengali and consulted with Hari Pārṣada Dāsa on the Sanskrit. Hari Pārṣada Dāsa also helped in several edits and checks of the Sanskrit, and his service was invaluable.

We also wish to thank the commentators, Jayādvaita Swami, Śivarāma Swami, Śacīnandana Swami, and Bhaktivijnana Goswami, for allowing us to transcribe their spoken seminars on *Manaḥ-śikṣā* and edit them into their current format. Oksana Marchenko, Jānakī-rāṇī Devī Dāsī, and Kṛṣṇāmṛta Devī Dāsī translated and transcribed Bhaktivijnana Goswami's seminars from Russian to English. Kṛṣṇa-Rūpa Devī Dāsī did an initial editing of Śacīnandana Swami and Bhaktivijnana Goswami's commentaries and I did the final editing. Tulasī Priyā Devī Dāsī edited Jayādvaita Swami's commentary, and Radheya both transcribed Jayādvaita Swami's seminar and worked directly with him to polish the final editing. Kāñcana-vali transcribed Śivarāma Swami's seminars and Braja Sevakī Devī Dāsī edited them. Jahnu Dāsa transcribed Śacīnandana Swami's seminars. Chandra Devī Dāsī did line editing and proofreading of Bhaktivijnana Swami's commentary. Mahārāṇī Devī Dāsī did line editing and proofreading of Jayādvaita Swami, Śivarāma Swami, and Śacīnandana Swami's commentary. B.A. Asrama Swami did line editing and proofreading of my commentary and the chapter on Bhaktisiddhānta. Murāri Dāsa did the final, in-depth and exhaustive checking and editing of the original verses and Bhaktivinoda's commentary. He also is responsible for the book design, layout, and all final proofreading and polishing. The staff of In-word assisted with getting the book in the proper form for e-books. Thanks to Prāṇada Devī Dāsī who strongly encouraged me to write a commentary for each verse.

We wish to express our gratitude to Devāmṛta Swami who insisted that I write the chapter showing the relationship between Bhaktisiddhānta and *Manaḥ-śikṣā*. He wanted me to write it in terms of the historical controversy regarding whether and how Bhaktisiddhānta practiced and taught the path of spontaneous devotion. To do so, I studied the following books: *Modern Hindu Personalism: The History, Life, and Thought of Bhaktisiddhānta Sarasvatī*, by Ferdinando Sardella, Oxford University Press, 2013; *The Authorized Sri Caitanya-Saraswata Parampara*, by Swami B.G. Narasingha, Gosai Publishers, 1998; and *Śrī Bhaktisiddhānta Vaibhava*, by Bhakti Vikāsa Swami, Bhakti Vikas Trust, 2009. Also, on the advice of Bhakti Vikāsa Swami, I read the essay entitled *Śrī Guru-Parampara: Bhaktisiddhānta Sarasvatī Ṭhākura, Heir to the Esoteric Life of Kedarnātha Bhaktivinoda*, by Swāmī B.V. Tripurāri. I also interviewed Praṇava Dāsa. Bhakti Vikāśa Swami and Praṇava Dāsa each reviewed the chapter for historical and philosophical accuracy.

Our artists have brought this work to life. The gorgeous black-and-white illustrations to accompany Raghunātha Dāsa Gosvāmī's verses, along with Bhaktivinoda's prose and song commentary, were created by the following artists: Śyāmapriyā Devī Dāsī (verse 9), Śyāmavallabha Devī Dāsī (verse 12), Padma-gopī Devī Dāsī (verse 4), Rādhe Devī Dāsī (verse 8), Aṣṭasakhī-līlā Devī Dāsī (verses 2, 10, and 11), and the sisters Elvira Lukman [Yamunā Devī Dāsī] and Dinara Lukman [Devakī Devī Dāsī] (verses 1, 3, 5, 6, and 7). Padma-gopī Devī Dāsī also did detail work for many days on the Gauḍīya Maṭha logo to make it readable for modern printing, putting the text in Roman characters. Master Italian artist Jñānāñjana Dāsa created twelve stunning oil paintings over a span of two years to highlight the essence of each verse.

Ūrmilā Devī Dāsī

BIOGRAPHIES

RAGHUNĀTHA DĀSA GOSVĀMĪ*

Amongst the Six Gosvāmīs, Rūpa Gosvāmī is the foremost and the others are known as *rūpānugas,* followers of Rūpa Gosvāmī. We are also called *rūpānugas.* In addition to being followers of Rūpa Gosvāmī, Śrīla Bhaktisiddhānta Sarasvatī Ṭhākura, in his parting words, gave the instruction to his disciples that their mission is to follow in the footprints of both Rūpa Gosvāmī and Raghunātha Dāsa Gosvāmī. Also, in *Caitanya-caritāmṛta,* Śrīla Kṛṣṇadāsa Kavirāja Gosvāmī ends each particular chapter by offering his obeisances – *rūpa-raghunātha-pade yāra āśa* – to Rūpa Gosvāmī and Raghunātha Dāsa Gosvāmī. So, Raghunātha Dāsa Gosvāmī, the author of *Śrī Manaḥ-śikṣā,* is also particularly important among the Six Gosvāmīs.

Raghunātha Dāsa Gosvāmī was born in a family of very wealthy landowners, the son of Govardhana Majumadāra. Raghunātha Dāsa's father, and his uncle, Hiraṇya, were extremely rich, and hence much hope rested on Raghunātha Dāsa Gosvāmī as the only son to take over the family business. Such aspirations for the eldest son were very important in that society.

Haridāsa Ṭhākura came to live in the same village as Raghunātha Dāsa Gosvāmī and his father. At that time, Haridāsa Ṭhākura stayed at the house of Balarāma Ācārya, who was the family priest of Govardhana Majumadāra, Raghunātha Dāsa's father. By this connection, Raghunātha Dāsa Gosvāmī had the association of Haridāsa Ṭhākura. As a very young boy, from Haridāsa Ṭhākura he heard the constant chanting of the holy names, and the pastimes of Caitanya Mahāprabhu and Lord Nityānanda. As a result, Raghunātha Dāsa developed a deeply intense attachment to Caitanya Mahāprabhu. He had no other real desire in life other than to just be a servant of Lord Caitanya.

When Raghunātha Dāsa Gosvāmī was 17 years old, he ran away from home and went to meet Caitanya Mahāprabhu in Purī. However,

* Written by Śivarāma Swami

Caitanya Mahāprabhu sent him back, advising him that leaving home at that time was not actually a good plan and that he should not be so fanatical. He advised Raghunātha Dāsa to externally follow in the footsteps of his father and uncle and behave like an ordinary materialist, but internally always meditate on Rādhā and Kṛṣṇa. Caitanya Mahāprabhu told him to pray to the Lord, and by Kṛṣṇa's mercy he would get the opportunity to become free from the shackles of material existence.

Raghunātha Dāsa Gosvāmī did this for about a year, but then his mind became somewhat unhinged, and it was very difficult for him to continue in this vein. Raghunātha Dāsa was constantly trying to run away, but his parents would just bring him back. They even had three or four guards watching him day and night. Finally his mother said to the father, "Why don't you chain him down?"

He said, "You cannot chain somebody down who has already been stolen by Caitanya Mahāprabhu." However, they did try and chain him in another way by marrying him to an extremely beautiful girl, so lovely that she was like a heavenly damsel. Raghunātha Dāsa had everything: a beautiful wife, unlimited wealth, with unlimited facility for sense gratification. But he was not interested in any of it.

At that time, he was only 19 years old, but would not even sleep in the same house as his wife or family. He would sleep outside, while the guards would watch him. One night, just before sunrise, the guards fell asleep. Raghunātha Dāsa thought, "I will try to escape again." And at that time his spiritual master, Yadunandana Ācārya, came and told him that the *pūjārī* for his Deities had left. He requested Raghunātha Dāsa to search for the *pūjārī* and convince him to come back and resume his service.

However, instead of going to find the *pūjārī*, Raghunātha Dāsa took advantage of the opportunity and escaped, following a small path leading to Purī , making sure he avoided the main road. He travelled for around 14 days, and out of those 14 days he only ate three times. He would go to the house of a milkman and beg for some milk. That was all he consumed. Finally he reached Jagannātha Purī.

In Purī, Raghunātha Dāsa was able to fully take shelter of Lord

Caitanya. Caitanya Mahāprabhu at that time handed him over to the care of Svarūpa Dāmodara Gosvāmī , who took on Raghunātha Dāsa Gosvāmī as his secretary or assistant. Raghunātha Dāsa Gosvāmī's father knew that his son had gone to Caitanya Mahāprabhu, but he realized that he could no longer try and bring him back to the family, so he sent some servants and a regular income of money, although this arrangement did not last.

Among the Six Gosvāmīs, Raghunātha Dāsa Gosvāmī was the only one who personally witnessed Caitanya Mahāprabhu's pastimes over an extended period of time. Sanātana Gosvāmī and Rūpa Gosvāmī would visit but again leave. They never lived with Lord Caitanya. Caitanya Mahāprabhu was always with Svarūpa Dāmodara, and Svarūpa Dāmodara was always with Lord Caitanya. So they were constantly together, always associating. Raghunātha Dāsa Gosvāmī, as Svarūpa Dāmodara's assistant, therefore, had personal experience and direct instruction from Lord Caitanya.

It was from that experience and witnessing by Raghunātha Dāsa Gosvāmī that the main framework of *Caitanya-caritāmṛta* was developed, because Śrīla Kṛṣṇadāsa Kavirāja Gosvāmī and Raghunātha Dāsa Gosvāmī were very intimate. After Lord Caitanya wound up his pastimes, Raghunātha Dāsa Gosvāmī resided just between Śyāma-kuṇḍa and Rādhā-kuṇḍa, and Kṛṣṇadāsa Kavirāja Gosvāmī's place of *bhajana* was not far apart from his.

There are many nice stories about Raghunātha Dāsa Gosvāmī's life in *Caitanya-caritāmṛta*; it is also described in *Bhakti-ratnākara*.

Raghunātha Dāsa Gosvāmī is the personification of austerity. In Jagannātha Purī, after a while he felt that his dependence on the gold coins from his father was inappropriate because he had accepted the renounced order of life. Despite the fact that he was using the money only to invite Lord Caitanya and his associates for feasts, still he sent the money back to his father along with the servants.

He then started to beg outside the Siṁha-dvāra gate at Jagannātha temple. People would donate some foodstuffs and Raghunātha Dāsa Gosvāmī would collect two handfuls. But then he started to think, "What is this? I'm standing at this gate and thinking will this person give me something, will that person give me something—just like a prostitute. This is not good."

So he then would go around the shops and ask for a little something. In due course of time, he also stopped that. He would go to the back of the temple where the cooks discarded the charred or hard, inedible portions of rice. The cows would munch on these remnants and what the cows did not eat, Ragunātha Dāsa Gosvāmī would soak and boil with water and eat with some salt. And that was his *prasādam*.

Caitanya Mahāprabhu presented Raghunātha Dāsa Gosvāmī with a *govardhana-śīla* that had been given to him. Lord Caitanya would touch that *govardhana-śīla* to his face, embracing it, thinking that it was nondifferent from Lord Kṛṣṇa. He gave that *śīla* to Raghunātha Dāsa Gosvāmī as well as a *gunja-mālā*, which is a necklace made of little red, black, and white berries found in Vṛndāvana and Māyāpura, along with specific instructions how to worship the *śīla*.

Lord Caitanya was indicating to Raghunātha Dāsa Gosvāmī that by giving him the *govardhana-śīla* he gave him a place to reside near Govardhana, specifically Rādhā-kuṇḍa. The *gunja-mālā* indicated that he would be the recipient of Śrīmatī Rādhārāṇī's mercy.

While Caitanya Mahāprabhu remained on this planet, Raghunātha Dāsa Gosvāmī lived in Purī. That was up until perhaps he was 25 or 27 years old. When Caitanya Mahāprabhu left, all the Vaiṣṇavas were feeling intense separation from him. Raghunātha Dāsa Gosvāmī then resided with Svarūpa Dāmodara Gosvāmī, but within a few months Svarūpa Dāmodara Gosvāmī also passed from this world. Then Raghunātha Dāsa Gosvāmī stayed with Gadādhara Paṇḍita, but then Gadādhara Paṇḍita could not stand the separation so he also departed the planet after a few months. All the devotee associates of Lord Caitanya were leaving the world. Raghunātha Dāsa Gosvāmī decided to go to Vṛndāvana and commit suicide by jumping off Govardhana Hill.

Sanātana Gosvāmī and Rūpa Gosvāmī were living in Vṛndāvana at that time, and they received instructions in a dream from Caitanya Mahāprabhu that Raghunātha Dāsa was coming and they should take care of him like a younger brother, as they were almost another generation older. Lord Caitanya warned them that Raghunātha was planning on committing suicide and they should prevent him from doing so. When Raghunātha arrived in Vrndavana, Rūpa and Sanātana told him about Lord Caitanya's wishes. They instructed him to reside at Rādhā-kuṇḍa, which Caitanya Mahāprabhu personally had rediscovered. Raghunātha Dāsa Gosvāmī was very instrumental in excavating Rādhā-kuṇḍa, finding the different places of Lord Kṛṣṇa's pastimes in the area and restoring them. He lived there at Rādhā-kuṇḍa for 50 years, until he was 75-80 years old.

His specific contribution was writing and compiling many books, such as *Stavāvalī*, *Śrī Vilāpa-kusumāñjali*, *Dāna-keli-cintāmaṇi*, *Muktā-carita*, and *Manaḥ-śikṣā*. These books are very important for followers of Rūpa Gosvāmī. In them Raghunātha Dāsa Gosvāmī explains the science of pure devotional service as it is coming down from Caitanya Mahāprabhu, and which is very rarely understood even by elevated devotees of Lord Kṛṣṇa. Unless one has the mercy of the Gosvāmīs one cannot really understand Caitanya Mahāprabhu's teachings.

Raghunātha Dāsa Gosvāmī, more than any of the other Gosvāmīs, showed how a *sādhaka* (a practising devotee) should follow and execute Rūpa Gosvāmī's instructions, and how to practice devotional service. Rūpa Gosvāmī's contribution was giving the instructions, and Raghunātha Dāsa Gosvāmī showed us how to put into practice what Rūpa Gosvāmī had given.

There are three points that are characteristic of Raghunātha Dāsa Gosvāmī. One is that he showed us by his concrete example how to practice the teachings of Rūpa Gosvāmī to the highest limit. The second is that he showed us by his personal example how to experience the mood of separation from Rādhā and Kṛṣṇa. It is by that mood of separation one actually learns how to cultivate Kṛṣṇa consciousness. That separation is a very important thing to know. It may start even in our present state. For instance, if we are serious about becoming Kṛṣṇa conscious, and we know our position in the material world as being very fallen living entities, then we will feel some separation, "Oh, I want Kṛṣṇa consciousness. I would like to get Kṛṣṇa." That is the particular mood by which we chant Hare Kṛṣṇa. The important thing is this internal mood.

The third point is exclusive dependence on Śrīmatī Rādhārāṇī. In the seed verses of *Caitanya-caritāmṛta* the word *śriyam* means this point is a great treasure and a great secret Caitanya Mahāprabhu has revealed (*Ādi-līlā* 1.4).

Very simply, we hear how Caitanya Mahāprabhu is *rādhā-bhāva-dyuti*. That he is Lord Kṛṣṇa in the mood of Śrīmatī Rādhārāṇī, coming specifically to taste the mood of Śrīmatī Rādhārāṇī. Some persons also make the error that Caitanya Mahāprabhu came to distribute the mood of Rādhārāṇī. But that's false because no one is capable of relishing the mellows of service like Rādhārāṇī does. That is only for Lord Kṛṣṇa as Caitanya Mahāprabhu in that mood. Caitanya Mahāprabhu not only experienced the mood of Rādhārāṇī, but of all *rasas* – sometimes he was in the mood of a cowherd boy, or he was in the mood of *gopī*, or he was in the mood of Rādhārāṇī, or in the mood of Kṛṣṇa. In Navadvīpa he was in the mood of Nārāyaṇa or Viṣṇu.

And specifically he was also often in the mood of *dāsī*, or servant of the *gopīs*. And specifically that is the real treasure, the real esoteric teaching, of Caitanya Mahāprabhu. That mood is the highest gift made available by Caitanya Mahāprabhu to the conditioned living entities through the Gosvāmīs. That is the particular mood of the followers of Caitanya Mahāprabhu like Raghunātha Dāsa Gosvāmī – exclusive dependence on Rādhārāṇī as Rādhārāṇī's servant, or *dāsī*.

We use this term *exclusive dependence* on Rādhārāṇī because in our Gauḍīya *sampradāya* we first worship Rādhārāṇī, and then we worship Kṛṣṇa. We prefer, and we're focused first, on the Lord's pleasure potency, *hlādinī-śakti, svarūpa-śakti,* and then on Lord Kṛṣṇa.

So, these are the three main points which highlight Raghunātha Dāsa Gosvāmī's teachings – how to practice the teachings of Rūpa Gosvāmī, how to always be in the mood of separation, and exclusive dependence on Rādhārāṇī.

We should also note something of Raghunātha Dāsa Gosvāmī's ontological identity. Eternally liberated souls have two particular identities: one is their *sādhaka svarūpa,* or the form as a practicing devotee. The other is called their *siddha svarūpa,* or their relationship in connection with Kṛṣṇa. Raghunātha Dāsa Gosvāmī appears in this world as a *sādhaka*, a practising devotee associate of Caitanya Mahāprabhu. But simultaneously, as Caitanya Mahāprabhu is simultaneously Lord Kṛṣṇa, so Raghunātha Dāsa Gosvāmī also has his identity in Kṛṣṇa's pastimes. In the spiritual world, he is known as Rati Mañjarī or sometimes Tulasī Mañjarī.

We do not consider this *Manaḥ-śikṣā* to be less *śāstra*, or any less Veda, than *Vedānta* and *Śrīmad-Bhāgavatam*. In fact, generally Gauḍīya Vaiṣṇavas' consider the Gosvāmīs' books to be more because they write what Śukadeva Gosvāmī did not speak, and what Śrīla Vyāsadeva did not write. The Gosvāmīs are expanding upon those teachings. And in this book, Raghunātha Dāsa Gosvāmī is expanding the teachings in connection with understanding how to instruct our minds, starting with purifying it from *anarthas* and ultimately directing it to the lotus feet of Rādhā and Kṛṣṇa.

Śrīla Bhaktisiddhānta Sarasvatī Ṭhākura instructed his followers to read this *Manaḥ-śikṣā* on a daily basis as part of their *sādhana*. Raghunātha Dāsa Gosvāmī also gives a *phala-stuti*, a benediction, that by chanting these *Manaḥ-śikṣā* verses every day and understanding them, we can receive the supreme benediction.

BHAKTIVINODA ṬHĀKURA

Śrī Bhaktivinoda Ṭhākura (1838-1914) was named Kedāranātha Datta in his youth. He grew up in Bīrnagar, India and moved to Kolkata at the age of thirteen, after his father died. He first worked as an educator, and was the first to introduce English education to the state of Orissa. Later, he entered government service as a magistrate during the time when the British ruled India. When he lived in Jagannātha Purī with his wife and children, he supervised the temple on the government's request. Bhaktivinoda had fourteen children, all of whom were advanced Vaiṣṇavas. One of his sons, Śrīla Bhaktisiddhānta Sarasvatī, founded the Gauḍīya Maṭha and was the spiritual master of Śrīla A.C. Bhaktivedanta Swami Prabhupāda. Bhaktivinoda took *dīkṣā* (initiation into Vaiṣṇavism) from Vipina-vihārī Gosvāmī and traced his lineage through initiation to Śrīmatī Jāhnavā-mātā, the wife of Nityānanda.

While staying in Jagannātha Purī, he carefully studied the various works of the Gauḍīya Vaiṣṇavas, such as the *Ṣaṭ-sandarbhas* of Śrīla Jīva Gosvāmī, the *Govinda-bhāṣya* and *Prameya-ratnāvalī* of Śrīla Baladeva Vidyābhūṣaṇa, the *Bhakti-rasāmṛta-sindhuḥ* of Śrīla Rūpa Gosvāmī and various other literature written by the close associates of Śrī Caitanya. Śrī Bhaktivinoda also accepted Śrī Jagannātha Dāsa Bābājī as his principal *śikṣā* (instructing) guru.

Among Bhaktivinoda's many accomplishments were the writing of many books, including the prose and song commentary to *Manaḥ-śikṣā*, as is translated here. He also wrote commentaries on several other scriptures and works of the *ācāryas*. He authored several novels and books of philosophy. His many songs continue to be a mainstay of contemporary Gauḍīya Vaiṣṇavas' daily prayers. He also wrote a book in English about Lord Caitanya which he sent to several universities in the West. In addition to being a prodigious writer, Śrī Bhaktivinoda discovered Lord Caitanya's actual birthplace and started many *nāma-haṭṭa* programs of chanting parties that traveled village to village. He wrote and spoke strongly against groups and teachers who philosophically twisted Vaiṣṇava teachings. Overall, Śrī Bhaktivinoda re-established Gauḍīya Vaiṣṇavism as a philosophically sound, ethical, mystical, dynamic, and accessible spiritual practice.

He published the following major books over a period of twenty-five years:

- *Kṛṣṇa-saṁhitā* (1880)
- *Kalyāṇa-kalpataru* (1881)
- Bengali translation of *Bhagavad-gītā* commentaries of Śrīla Viśvanātha Cakravartī and Śrīla Baladeva Vidyābhūṣaṇa (1886)
- *Caitanya-śikṣāmṛta* (1886)
- *Śrī Navadvīpa-dhāma-māhātmya* (1890)
- *Lord Caitanya and His Teachings* (1892)
- *Śaraṇāgatī* (1893)
- *Īśopaniṣad* with Bengali commentary (1894)
- *Caitanya-caritāmṛta* with *Amṛta-pravāha-bhāṣya* (1895)
- *Brahma-saṁhitā* with Bengali translation (1897)

- *Śrī Kṛṣṇa-karṇāmṛta* with Bengali translation (1898)
- *Upadeśāmṛta* with a Bengali commentary (1898)
- *Śrī Bṛhad-bhāgavatāmṛta* (with Sanskrit commentary of Śrīla Sanātana Gosvāmī and Bengali translation) (1898)
- *Jaiva-dharma* (1900)
- *Śrī Harināma-cintāmaṇi* (1900)
- *Bhajana-rahasya* (1902)

Besides these books, he also published the monthly Bengali magazine *Sajjana-toṣaṇī* from 1879 and continued to be its editor for 17 years, after which the magazine was continued by his son Śrīla Bhaktisiddhānta Sarasvatī Ṭhākura.

After retiring from his government service, Bhaktivinoda Ṭhākura adopted the life of a *vānaprastha* and intensified his spiritual practices. At that time, he established an *āśrama* at Surabhi-kuñja in Godrumadvīpa, one of the nine districts of Navadvīpa in Māyāpura, India. He remained there and performed *bhajana* (spiritual practice) for a considerable time. Later he accepted the life of an ascetic, and stayed at Svānanda-sukhada-kuñja nearby.

His literary contributions along with his revolutionary discovery of the actual birth-site of Śrī Caitanya Mahāprabhu earned him the fame of being renowned as the "Seventh Gosvāmī", after the original Six Gosvāmīs of Vṛndāvana. In his final days, he cut off contact with the external world and absorbed himself intensely in his *bhajana* in a mood of self-imposed silence. In such a state, he wrote his final composition named *Sva-niyama-daśakam* – a set of ten resolutions to be adopted by a person who wishes to regulate and perfect his spiritual endeavors.

After he left this world on June 23, 1914, his son Bhaktisiddhānta Sarasvatī Ṭhākura performed the task of carrying forward his message by publishing books and magazines in various languages, and by establishing the Gauḍīya Maṭha. After a few years, A.C. Bhaktivedānta Swāmī Prabhupāda joined the Gauḍīya Maṭha and received the instructions and inspiration to carry forward this message to the English-speaking world. His work has spread the culture and practices of *kṛṣṇa-*

bhakti as envisioned by Śrī Caitanya and Śrīla Bhaktivinoda became accessible to the entire world.

HARI PĀRṢADA DĀSA, SANSKRIT TRANSLATOR

Hari Pārṣada Dāsa is a disciple of H.H. Radha Govinda Dāsa Goswami Mahārāja, who is a disciple of His Divine Grace A.C. Bhaktivedanta Swami Prabhupāda. He was born in a *gauḍa-sārasvatā-brāhmaṇa* family in Mumbai, Maharashtra, India. His father and grandfather are both devotees of Śrī Śrī Rukmiṇī Viṭṭhala of Pandharpur. Hari Pārṣada Dāsa learned Sanskrit grammar in the traditional way in his childhood and was taught the *Laghu-siddhānta-kaumudī* of Paṇḍita Varadarāja. Coming in contact with ISKCON in 2002, he dedicated himself to preaching to the youth in Mumbai. After rendering this service for five years, he started furthering his Sanskrit studies and studied the *Aṣṭādhyāyī*, the complete four thousand *sūtras* by Pāṇini. Because of his scholarly knowledge and Sanskrit translation skills, he was appointed as an assistant editor at Gopal Jiu Publications.

KṚṢṆA-ABHIṢEKA DĀSA, BENGALI TRANSLATOR

Kṛṣṇa-abhiṣeka Dāsa was born and raised in a Vaiṣṇava family in Bengal, India, descended from Bhaktivinoda Ṭhākura. He is a disciple of Tamal Kṛṣṇa Goswami, who is a disciple of His Divine Grace A.C. Bhaktivedanta Swami Prabhupāda. He became a committed Vaiṣṇava in 1992 and earned his MSt and PhD from Oxford University and the University of Chicago respectively. The main focus of his studies and research has been the history of Gauḍīya Vaiṣṇavism, with his doctoral thesis focused on the works of Bhaktivinoda Ṭhākura. He has worked with the Vaiṣṇava traditions of Bengal, Orissa and Vṛndāvana since 2002, and was one of the founding directors of the Bhaktivedanta Research Center in Kolkata. He is a professor of Religious Studies at Grand Valley State University in Michigan, USA.

PRĀṆA GOVINDA DĀSA, BENGALI TRANSLATOR

Prāṇa Govinda Dāsa was born in Bengal, India. Many of his family have been practicing Vaiṣṇavas, including his mother, grandfather, who heard from Bhaktisiddhānta Sarasvatī in Tripura, and great-great grandfather; and Bhakti Caru Swami is his second cousin. In 1981 he was initiated with the name Paraṁ Brahma Dāsa by Bhavānanda Swami, a disciple of His Divine Grace A.C. Bhaktivedanta Swami Prabhupāda. However, in 1986 his guru fell from grace. Shortly thereafter Bhakti Prappana Dāmodara Svāmī, a god-brother of Śrīla Prabhupāda, uttered the Gāyatrī mantra to him to encourage him to continue chanting, and in 1989 gave him the name Prāṇa Govinda Dāsa. In 2003 Dāmodara Svāmī passed away, and his last instruction to Prāṇa Govinda was to always do devotional service under the guidance of Śrīla Prabhupāda. By 2010 he began serving exclusively in ISKCON and took refuge in the guidance of Rādhānātha Swami. He regularly gives classes at ISKCON Alachua, USA, and at devotees' homes.

JAYĀDVAITA SWAMI, COMMENTATOR

Jayādvaita Swami was born in America, and is a disciple of His Divine Grace A.C. Bhaktivedanta Swami Prabhupāda. He served as an editor or assistant editor for nearly all the books of Śrīla Prabhupāda published during Śrīla Prabhupāda's lifetime. He received initiation from Śrīla Prabhupāda in 1968, at the age of nineteen. He has lectured extensively at colleges and universities, especially in the United States. In 1978 he accepted the order of renounced life, *sannyāsa*. He served as the senior editor of a three-volume translation and commentary for *Śrī Bṛhad-bhāgavatāmṛta* (2005), a sixteenth-century Sanskrit philosophical and devotional work by Śrīla Sanātana Gosvāmī, and, by the same author, *Śrī Kṛṣṇa-līlā-stava* (2008). He has also served as the senior editor for Śrīla Jīva Gosvāmī's *Tattva-sandarbha* (2013). He is the author of *Vanity Karma: Ecclesiastes, the Bhagavad-gītā, and the meaning of life*; and numerous articles.

ŚIVARĀMA SWAMI, COMMENTATOR

Śivarāma Swami was born in Budapest, Hungary. His family emigrated to Canada during the failed 1956 Hungarian revolution. In 1970 he came in contact with Śrīla Prabhupāda via his transcendental books. He became an initiated disciple of His Divine Grace A.C. Bhaktivedanta Swami Prabhupāda in 1973 and accepted the renounced order of life in 1979. After serving ISKCON in both Canada and the USA – where he opened and managed temples – Śivarāma Swami moved to the UK, where he served as the temple president at Caitanya College and the UK national *saṅkīrtana* leader. He was requested to accept the responsibility of GBC member in 1986 while serving in the UK. He later became GBC for Hungary. In ISKCON, Śivarāma Swami is well known for his scholarship. He has taught many courses in Gauḍīya Vaiṣṇavism in various parts of the world. He has written many books on Gauḍīya Vaiṣṇava theology and philosophy, including *The Awakening of Spontaneous Devotional Service, Veṇu-gīta, Na Pāraye 'haṁ, Kṛṣṇa-saṅgati, Śuddha-bhakti-cintāmaṇi, The śikṣā-guru,* and the nine volume *Nava Vraja Mahimā.*

ŚACĪNANDANA SWAMI, COMMENTATOR

Of German origin, Śacīnandana Swami joined ISKCON in 1970, and was initiated by His Divine Grace A.C. Bhaktivedanta Swami Prabhupāda in 1971. He teaches and writes prolifically on Vaiṣṇavism and the Hare Krishna movement and has translated the *Bhagavad-gītā* into German. His publications include *The Nectarean Ocean of the Holy Name, The Gāyatrī Book, The Way of the Great Departure, The Art of Transformation,* and *Spiritual Tonic.*

BHAKTIVIJNANA GOSWAMI, COMMENTATOR

Bhaktivijnana Goswami was born in Tashkent, in the former Soviet Union. He took to spiritual life in 1980, during a difficult time of the communist era, when the National Security forces were harassing any type of spiritual practitioner. Despite these obstacles, Bhaktivijnana Goswami – a scientist, a Moscow State University graduate and post-graduate student at Institute of Molecular Biology – decided to experiment with the Hare Kṛṣṇa mantra. To his great happiness, it moved him profoundly. He is a disciple of Rādhānātha Swami, who is a disciple of His Divine Grace A.C. Bhaktivedanta Swami Prabhupāda, and is well known for his Sanskrit and *śāstric* scholarship.

ŪRMILĀ DEVĪ DĀSĪ, COMMENTATOR AND EDITOR

Ūrmilā Devī Dāsī, born in America, has served ISKCON continuously since her initiation by His Divine Grace A.C. Bhaktivedanta Swami Prabhupāda in 1973. She and her husband are in the *vānaprastha* order. She has a PhD in education. Ūrmilā is the chair of the Sastric Advisory Council to the GBC, an associate editor of *Back to Godhead*, and a professor of Sociology of Religion at Bhaktivedanta College in Belgium. She travels worldwide teaching Kṛṣṇa consciousness. She is the author of *Vaikuṇṭha Children, Dr. Best Learn to Read* (an 83-book literacy program), *The Great Mantra for Mystic Meditation*, and numerous articles.

Printed in Great Britain
by Amazon

41212670R00297